INSTRUCTOR'S MANUAL

LITERATURE
An Introduction to Reading and Writing

INSTRUCTOR'S MANUAL

LITERATURE
An Introduction
to Reading and Writing

EDGAR V. ROBERTS

Lehman College,
The City University of New York

HENRY E. JACOBS

University of Alabama

PRENTICE-HALL, INC., ENGLEWOOD CLIFFS, NEW JERSEY 07632

ISBN: 0-13-537580-0

Printed in the United States of America

CONTENTS

LITERATURE

An Introduction
to Reading and Writing

HOW TO USE THIS MANUAL

WHAT WE INCLUDE. For stories, poems, and plays within the chapters we include introductory remarks, interpretive comments, answers to the study questions, teaching suggestions, supplementary information, and suggested topics for writing. For stories and poems in the sections for further reading, we include a brief general and thematic introduction and a discussion of the work that provides some guidance for teaching.

PAGINATION. To make quick reference to the teaching manual easier, we have used the page numbers from Literature: An Introduction to Reading and Writing as a running head along the top of each page. The page numbers of the manual itself are located at the bottom of each page.

FEATURES OF THE TEXT

ORGANIZATION. The text is divided into four major units: (1) An Introduction to Reading and Writing about Literature; (2) Fiction; (3)Poetry; (4) Drama. The introduction discusses general approaches to all three genres, the value of literature, and important strategies and guidelines for writing about literature. Instructors may choose to omit the literary aspects and the literature in this introduction from classwork, but we strongly suggest that you have your students read the section on writing about literature and that you discuss it in class in conjunction with your first or second writing assignment. It provides guidelines and suggestions that we refer to throughout the text.

The sections on FICTION and POETRY follow the same principles of organization. Each begins with an introductory chapter that offers an overview of the genre and most of the important elements. Subsequent chapters take up each important element—such as plot, character, setting, language—in detail. At the end of each of these sections, there are chapters that pull most of the elements back together in a consideration of theme and meaning and, in poetry, the work of three poets. The drama section features a somewhat different organization. Here, all the basic elements of drama are introduced in Chapter 27. This is followed by separate chapters on tragedy, comedy, and realistic and nonrealistic drama. Every chapter of the text includes a section on writing, a sample essay, and commentary on the essay.

CLASSROOM USE OF THE TEXT. Although the text has an overall plan, we do not expect an instructor to use every work in a chapter or even every chapter. A multiplicity of works are included in each chapter (and in the sections of additional readings) to provide options and flexibility. Nor do we expect that the chapters will always be used in the sequence in which they appear in the text. On the contrary, the text is designed to facilitate a great deal of individual adaptation. Chapters in the fiction section may be taught using only one of the stories we include, or even substituting a story from another chapter or from additional stories. Similarly, poetry chapters may be used in class with reference to very few poems from the chapter, or even an entirely new set of poems drawn from other chapters or from the selection of additional poems. Instructors will no doubt choose to skip entire chapters in a given course. With these sorts of adaptations and limitations (of time) in mind, we have tried to make very few assumptions about previous study or reading in each chapter. Where such assumptions are absolutely necessary, we have provided cross references to the pages most immediately relevant. These considerations also account for a certain amount of repetition from chapter to chapter. In the sections called "writing about," for example, our discussions of prewriting, organization, composition, and revision follow the same general pattern throughout. Although each of these discussions is keyed to the literature and the topics or element under discussion in the chapter, we often repeat significant guidelines or warnings on the assumption that the chapters are not being used in sequence. However you choose to use this book, we are confident that the text will help your students read with greater understanding and write about literature with greater competence and conviction.

LINEATION IN THE TEXT. We have tried to provide easy ways to refer to specific places or passages in the works in the text through marginal numbers. All short stories are numbered by paragraph; the numbers are found on the right margin. Similarly, all poetry (and all poetic drama) is numbered by line; here also line numbers are found in the right margin. In drama written in verse, lines devoted to stage directions are not included in the line count. The text of plays written in prose is not numbered; we will use page numbers for reference here, and we suggest that you do the same in class.

A NOTE ON WRITING ASSIGNMENTS AND WORKSHOPS

One of the central goals of the text is to help students learn to write about literature effectively. To this end, we discuss writing processes and strategies in every chapter. We encourage you to have your students read the relevant section(s) of the text before they undertake any writing assignments.

Students often begin an introduction to literature with either the fear that they cannot write about literary works or the conviction that they already know all that there is to know. Both misconceptions have to be overcome in the classroom. One way to do this is to use a number of short writing assignments and to move gradually toward greater complexity. Discussions of prewriting and writing in the text presuppose in-class or out-of-class assignments that will generate fully developed essays (3 to 5 pages or longer). These discussions focus on the movement from the formation of ideas to the finished essay. In the classroom, this process can be taken apart and examined in stages.

SHORT DEVELOPMENTAL ASSIGNMENTS. Writing in a course based on this text can be required for virtually every class meeting without overburdening yourself with grading responsibilities. A small piece of writing, graded pass-fail, can be required for every class. The text introduces three types of shorter assignments--summary, paraphrase, and paragraph. The paragraph assignment is especially useful; you can ask students to write paragraphs on virtually any aspect or element of literature. Such short assignments provide the advantages of constant writing and an ongoing monitor of your students' skills. They can also force students to think about the material they are reading before class discussion, thus leading to more productive and fruitful classes. Paragraph assignments can also serve as the building blocks to full-scale essays.

MAKING WRITING ASSIGNMENTS. Ideally, all assignments should be made in writing. This holds true for short paragraph assignments as well as full-scale essays. In the former instance, a simple statement will suffice: "write a paragraph about the character of Elisa Allen in Steinbeck's 'The Chrysanthemums.'" This same formulation may be employed with reference to any topic or element. These sorts of assignments might even be listed in the class syllabus. In full-scale essay assignments, however, you will usually want to explain the task in more detail (both in writing and in class).

SEQUENCING ASSIGNMENTS. In many instances, this text will be used in courses where the students have had little experience in writing about literature. Under such circumstances, you might want to organize the writing assignments so that they begin with a rather easy (and obvious) goal and become progressively more difficult. Most essays, at any point during the course, will ask the students to support a central idea about the literature under consideration in a logical and convincing way with sufficient supporting details from the text. In initial assignments, you might opt to provide the students with a fully developed thesis of your own devising, and ask the students to produce an essay based on your thesis. Such a procedure cuts the prewriting process short and allows students to focus on the mechanics of organizing, writing, and revising an essay. As the course progresses, you can provide progressively less direction for your students. Ultimately, you might give them complete control of their own writing, including the freedom to choose the work, develop the thesis, and produce the essay.

IN-CLASS WRITING WORKSHOPS. If time permits, in-class writing workshops should be incorporated into your courses. These can be very useful in improving students' writing. Three types of workshops are especially helpful: outlining, rough-draft workshops, and post mortems.

OUTLINING. In this type of workshop, you can establish a sample thesis based on a work that the class has just discussed and ask your students to outline a possible essay, paragraph by paragraph. The resultant discussion can be particularly effective in teaching organization and the selection of supporting details.

ROUGH-DRAFT WORKSHOPS. Time permitting, all out-of-class essays might be submitted in 2 stages: rough draft and final form. You can go over rough drafts quickly and advise students about serious problems. Occasionally, a rough draft workshop can be effective. The idea of a rough draft workshop is to get the students to serve as editors and critics of their peers' papers. The essays—in rough draft— should be very close to finished form. Students should be encouraged to treat the task seriously since a competent job will obviously affect the grade on the paper.

MECHANICS. Students should be paired off and exchange papers. Using a checklist like the sample below, students should go through the paper carefully. Each student of the pair should then explain whatever problems he or she found in the other's paper.

SAMPLE GUIDELINES FOR STUDENT EDITORS IN ROUGH DRAFT WORKSHOPS

Before you begin to work on your partner's paper, you should study the questions on this guide. Then read through the paper carefully, as if you were reading it out loud. When you have trouble reading, understanding, or following the meaning or the logic, or when you think something from the questions below might apply, make a mark in the margin so that you can find the problem again, and continue reading. Then, in conference with the writer, go over the trouble spots in connection with the questions listed below. If the answer to the question is no, discuss the problem with the writer, and try to correct the problem area together.

1. Is the central idea clearly stated in the 1st paragraph?
2. Is the central idea followed out and supported adequately in the paper? Do all the paragraphs support the original idea and "hang together"?
3. Does the essay have a strong and smooth introduction and a conclusion that closes the paper without being abrupt, misleading, or irrelevant?

4. Is the structure of the paper logical; can you follow the thoughts and the line of reasoning easily; do the paragraphs follow each other logically?
5. Is there adequate transition between paragraphs?
6. Are the paragraphs correctly done? Does each paragraph deal with one thought or proof adequately?
7. Does the writer avoid sentence problems? Check for the following:
   A. Sentences that are too long and confusing. Could they be broken into two or more shorter sentences?
   B. Run-on sentences or comma splices that link 2 complete sentences.
   C. Sentence fragments: sentences missing subject or verb.
   D. Sentences that seem to be awkward or ill-written.
   E. Sentences that have a confusing meaning due to a grammatical error.
   F. Short, choppy sentences in a row that might be elegantly combined into a more interesting and complex sentence.
8. Does the writer avoid agreement problems? Do nouns and pronouns always match up? Example: "When one reads this story, we see that Phoenix is very old, and I respect her greatly." Do verbs and nouns agree as to number?
9. Does the writer avoid shifts in the verb tense in the paper? Example: Phoenix <u>walked</u> through the woods and <u>climbs</u> the steps of the hospital.
10. Does the writer avoid excess repetition of specific words or phrases?
11. Does the writer employ words that seem inappropriate or out of place; is a single level of diction maintained?
12. Does the writer avoid the trap of falling into too much plot summary?
13. Does the writer spell words and capitalize correctly?
14. Does the writer use punctuation correctly? In checking this, pay careful attention to colons, semicolons, and commas.
15. Does the writer use enough (but not too much) quotation to support the central idea of the essay?

POST MORTEMS. This type of workshop involves an in-class evaluation of several essays in final form. You can select work from your students that exemplifies the strengths or weaknesses that you wish to discuss. Sample papers may be duplicated (xerographed, dittoed) or projected.

CHAPTER 1

INTRODUCTION: WHAT IS LITERATURE

Chapter 1 is a general introduction to literature and to the skills of writing about it. The chapter also includes four works and, in keeping with the introductory objectives, it proposes a very basic writing assignment on likes and dislikes. All of these tasks may be somewhat imposing if taken at one large bite. You therefore may wish to assign pages 1-5 as a general introduction to the various genres, and then use the stories, the play, and the poem on pages 28-61 as the basis of your introductory discussion about the characteristics of literature.

For emphasis on writing, pages 5-28 make up a unit specifically on the procedure of reading a literary work, and then taking notes on it and going through the prewriting and writing tasks of preparing an essay. Along with the description of this process, there is additional material on the characteristics of good writing. You may wish to coordinate these passages with the assignment on likes and dislikes on pages 61-69. You might use the writing section as a separate introductory unit, but we also hope that you will find it a convenient reference point for your students throughout your course. We believe that the section offers basic advice for students no matter where they may be as thinkers and writers about literature.

The first section, on pages 1-5, is designed to get students thinking about the nature of literature. Classroom discussion may produce other examples. The section on pages 2 and 3, on the power and value of literature, is an attempt to express briefly some of the ideas about reading that students certainly know but which they may never have articulated themselves.

The definition of genres on page 3 is designed as a quick introduction to the types. In discussing it, you might wish to refer quickly to the works on pages 28-61 to illustrate the generic qualities that otherwise may remain abstract in the minds of your students.

The actual studying as opposed to the reading of literature is introduced on pages 3-5. Students sometimes have no very clear understanding of the nature of genuine study. The section thus attempts to explain the need for a regularized set of steps to be followed, more or less in the order suggested, in the process of developing not just a familiarity with literary works but also an understanding of them.

WRITING ESSAYS ABOUT LITERATURE, pages 5-17.

The writing component of the introduction, beginning on page 5, is a most important section for students. You may wish to use it in conjuction with assigning the story "First Confession" (pages 187-193). The step-by-step process may be best understood in reference to this story. The general definitions of an essay on pages 5-7 might also take on more concreteness if you have assigned the story in advance. The process of "brain storming" outlined on pages 9-10, by which students write down their thoughts on the topic as an integral part of thinking, is also important. You might emphasize that once something--anything at all--is on paper, students may work with it and develop it as a part of the essay that they are shaping. The process of establishing a central idea (pages 10-12) is essential to the essay-writing process, because it enables students to focus their thoughts and to rewrite them in a clearly formed way.

The development of a central idea about a work is not a challenge that many students will have met before they get into your class. For this reason

5

you might devote a portion of class time to the discussion of thinking generally. A commonly held misunderstanding is that any kind of mental activity is thinking. Thus, the process of reasoning necessary to develop a central idea should be distinguished from feeling, responding, daydreaming, planning a purchase (although such planning may involve some thinking), determining the day's activities, and so on. The process of abstract thinking will not come readily to the application of reading, however, unless the students can be shown that seemingly disparate details have some unifying, connecting theme. This process, involving the formulation of unifying themes in a work, is perhaps one of the major elements for you to stress in the initial stages of teaching writing about literary subjects.

The section from pages 12-17 concerns the mechanics of shaping an essay and of outlining. The central idea and thesis sentence separation, you will note, is an option presented as a way of dividing the thematic unity of an essay from the actual topics of the essay. Students often become nervous about outlining. One of the most important assurances you can give about outlining is therefore that a formal outline does not need to preceed the writing of the essay. Instead, an outline can be developed as a relatively advanced part of the prewriting process, as a primary means of giving shape to an essay that is already considerably advanced.

SOME COMMON PROBLEMS IN WRITING ESSAYS, pages 17-28.

This section is a brief introduction to the standards by which student essays (and more broadly, all writing) is to be judged. It has been developed over a period of many years in response to innumerable student inquiries about why grades have not been higher on submitted work. Perhaps the greatest problem of students is that they summarize works rather than analyze them. Thus the suggested changing of the order in an essay from the order in the work, for example, is only a rudimentary device that may free students from the trap of summary. Also, the thought that the potential audience will already know the literary work may also help students focus on their own explanations in preference to summarizing. The idea that literary material is evidence is another means to help students break away from the narrative or logical order of the original.

For the section "keeping to your point" (pages 21-24), we have introduced an unfocused paragraph, and then shown, with the aid of the line drawings, how this paragraph may be focused in the light of the topic idea. Students would benefit from your pointing out to them the functional relationship of the underlined parts to the topic. Also, these underlined parts show that the writing of essays on literary topics should emphasize that the writer takes an interpretive, explanatory role with regard to potential readers. There may be no other idea that is so important in the teaching of writing.

The final two parts of this writing section, "Insight, Newness, Growth" (pages 24-26) and "Using Accurate and Forceful Language" (pages 26-28), are presented both as short-term and long-term goals. Students may query the section on "Newness" on the grounds that they should not be expected to produce original criticism as introductory learners. Their question has great validity, but it is quite important to stress that the pattern of thinking originally is to be expected of them even as beginning students, if they are genuinely interested in achieving excellence.

Because the need for accurate and forceful language will always be with everyone who ever takes up a pen or word-processor, you may wish to bring up the point whenever it becomes relevant as a result of student writing in your course. Indeed, many essential problems that students may encounter as they write may be addressed by reference to a number of the subtopics in this section; it is a guide and set of goals to which students may always go for help when they need to conceptualize and execute any writing task.

Gaius Petronius, The Widow of Ephesus, pages 28-30.

      Little is known of Petronius outside of the detail by Tacitus that he was an elegant man and that he committed suicide at the pleasure or command of the Emperor Nero in A.D. 66. The work of Petronius that has survived is The Satyricon, a lengthy narrative, from which "The Widow of Ephesus" is taken. Perhaps better known than the "Widow" is the scene of the banquet of Trimalchio, which is a satire on conspicuous consumption.
      The story, "The Widow of Ephesus," is included here because it is one of the very earliest examples of fiction and also because Chekhov based his farce The Bear loosely upon it (see pages 49-58). There is much in this story that can be used in the initial approaches to literary study. For example, the Widow, within a short space of three pages, undergoes a change in perspective --the change that characterizes the round or developing character. In addition, because the story is brief, it may be quickly studied, and perhaps may even be read aloud in class. Bear in mind that as you explain things, you are actually demonstrating the ways to read and respond to literature. This example may be one of the most thought-provoking and exiting experiences you can share with your students.
      Students may benefit from additional background material: First is the practical difficulty the Soldier would have had in putting the dead husband on the cross. In fact, ancient crosses were laid out on the ground, and they were not raised until the condemned persons were fastened to them with spikes. Crucifixion as a form of execution was outlawed in the Roman Empire during the fourth century, after Christianity became the official religion.

      Answers to the Study Questions, page 31.

      (1) The poet Eumolpus tells the story. He announces that he disikes women. This attitude is embodied in the story, which the speaker tells as an example to support his claim that women are faithless and inconsistant. Eumolpus is introduced as the narrator in the first paragraph, for the speaker of this section (who is the speaker of the entire Satyricon) places himself as one of the group listening to Eumolpus telling his tale. For a similar use of narration within narration, see Twain's "Luck" (pages 245-249). (2) The Widow is known for her love and fidelity to her husband (paragraph 2). She shows her virtue by going right into the vault to stand vigil by her husband's coffin until she dies herself. We learn at the beginning (paragraph 2) that she has a great deal of resolution, and also that she is capable of taking charge of things. When she abandons her resolution and falls in love with the Soldier, she shows that her commitment to life and love is stronger than her vows to the dead (paragraph 12).

      (3) The Soldier is affectionate, and he also has a strong enough sense of duty to feel shame and fear for having been derelict in his task of standing guard (paragraph 11). His first reason for offering food appears to be kindness and compassion, and then, secondarily, desire for the Widow. He shows earnestness and fidelity in his bringing food together with gifts. (4) The Widow's decision to substitute her husband's body is in paragraph 11. Though her new love is sudden, it is sincere, and it therefore is acceptable as an explanation for her decision to give up her husband's dead body to

7

preserve the Soldier. (5) Certainly her decision may be considered a joke, as Eumolpus does. However, her explanation of her love for the Soldier makes the situation much more serious than it was intended.

(6) Whether the story will be liked or not will depend upon individual students. Many might dismiss the story as misogynistic and therefore dated. Others, however, may find that the portrait of the Widow rises above the ostensible exposure of her abandoning her vow of self-sacrifice, and that this inadvertent sympathy makes her worthy of admiration.

(7) The setting and the locations are not precisely described, for only as much is included as will permit the narrative to move ahead. The location of the tomb creates a ritualistic setting for the Widow's vigil, and it also provides a place of secrecy. The scene of crucifixion near the graveyard is also normal enough, for a graveyard would have been the open space closest to the center of town. The corpses of executed felons were displayed as a deterrence to crime. The Soldier was posted to prevent theft of the bodies.

Writing topics: The characters of the Widow or the Soldier. Responses of like or dislike. The nature of the "joke": is it no more than a joke? Does the story sustain the narrator's dislike of women?

Sir Arthur Conan Doyle, The Adventure of the Speckled Band, pages 31-48.

Doyle is best known for his detective stories featuring Sherlock Holmes, though he wrote on considerably wider topics, including a history of spiritualism. "The Speckled Band" is a typical story in the Sherlock Holmes series, featuring, as it does, Watson as the narrator, Holmes as the master detective, danger, and a resolution dependent upon Holmes's powers of deduction. Because students may have become familiar with Holmes before coming to your class, and therefore may already be favorably disposed to him, "The Speckled Band" is a good story to assign as a means of encouraging responses. In teaching the story you will be able to introduce the clear demarcation between Helen Stoner and Dr. Roylott as an important conflict in the plot, to emphasize the importance of Holmes's character as a central protagonist encouraging reader involvement, and to stress the technique of Watson as the point of view narrator--all means of heightening liking and interest.

Answers to the Study Questions, pages 48-49.

(1) Watson tells the story; he is the "I." (2) The introductory paragraphs indicate that Watson and Holmes are good friends along with their sharing of bachelor quarters. They know each other well and respect each other. In paragraph 7 Watson indicates his admiration for Holmes's deductive powers, and in paragraph 8 Holmes introduces Watson as an "intimate friend and associate." (3) Watson is drawn into the case first, because he indicates his pleasure at following Holmes's investigations, second, because he has the time and inclination to go to Stoke Moran with Holmes (paragraph 79), and, third, because he might be needed in order to avert danger (paragraph 198). His quality as a storyteller is that he includes all necessary details of the narration, but does not attempt to interpret them. The story could not work with Holmes as narrator because, to be truthful, Holmes would need to let readers in on his conclusions as he makes them.

(4) The ticket and the mud are discussed in paragraphs 11-15. They show Holmes's power as an observer and also as a person capable of drawing correct conclusions. This episode occurs early because it establishes the ability on a small item that Holmes will use on the much larger item.

(5) According to Helen, Dr. Roylott has a violent and uncontrollable temper (paragraph 26), which caused him to commit manslaughter (paragraph 24). Locally, Roylott is also known as the "terror of the village" (paragraph 26) who has thrown a man off a bridge in a brawl (paragraph 27). He has treated Helen in a threatening way, and has even hurt her physically (paragraphs 71-72). When Roylott first appears in the narrative (paragraph 95) Holmes rebuffs his threats, and indicates by bending the poker back that he, Holmes, is a worthy adversary to Roylott (paragraph 112). (6) The marriage plans first of Helen's sister Julia (paragraph 30), and then of Helen herself (paragraph 67) are important because their marriages would deprive Roylott of the money which he controls in trust for them as long as they are unmarried (paragraph 115). The threat of losing their money is therefore the cause of Roylott's murder of Julia (paragraph 50) and his attempt to murder Helen.

(7) The gypsies are introduced (paragraphs 27, 41, 61-62) as "red herrings" to draw our attention away from Dr. Roylott as the murderer and to cast suspicion on some other plausible but incorrect source of danger.

(8) Holmes is a careful listener and questioner, as is shown in his responses to Helen Stoner (paragraph 31-74); he is also a careful observer, as shown in his investigation of the exterior and interior of Stoke Moran (paragraphs 131-192). Finally, he is intelligent enough to draw the correct conclusions from what he has seen (paragraph 202). By paragraph 172 it is clear that he has determined Roylott as the villain, though he does not wish to announce this conclusion without clearer proofs (paragraph 192). Holmes says (paragraph 249) that he had made all the conclusions about Roylott before he entered Roylott's room. Hence the conclusion is made by paragraph 156.

(9) Briefly, Holmes develops a plan to frighten the snake (the speckled band) by beating it when it appears. Whether he plans to have the snake turn on Roylott is an open question, for Holmes does not so state. His responses in paragraphs 240 and 245, however, indicate that he is not surprised at Roylott's death. We learn about the plan only as it is carried out, because Doyle does not allow Watson to tell us the plan even though the narration is taking place many years after the incident. Holmes also explains his plan in paragraph 249. (10) Therefore, the story is primarily about Holmes, and only secondarily about the mystery. We learn more and more about Holmes as the story progresses, such as his thoroughness in searching records (paragraphs 114, 115, 132ff.), and his bravery (paragraph 235). He is not a flat character because he is constantly learning and adapting to new conditions. Moreover, his plan to foil Roylott by forcing the snake back through the vent suggests his presumption that he may act virtually as judge and executioner.

(11) There are good reasons for liking the story: (a) the clear distinction between good and evil, (b) curiosity (suspense) about how Holmes will solve the mystery, (c) inherent interest (personal involvement) in the character of Holmes, and (d) the defeat of danger and the restoration of security.

Writing topics: The use of suspense as a means of holding the reader's interest. The tension between good and evil in the story. Dr. Watson as the speaker and connecting link with Holmes. Likes or dislikes.

Anton Chekhov, <u>The</u> <u>Bear</u>: <u>A</u> <u>Joke</u> <u>in</u> <u>One</u> <u>Act</u>, pages 49-58.

Born in southern Russia, Chekhov became a doctor of medicine, supporting himself as a student by writing for various humor publications. <u>The</u> <u>Bear</u>, one of his earliest plays, was first staged in 1888, and became one of his most popular. For students beginning to study literature, <u>The</u> <u>Bear</u> has the virtue of being no longer than many short stories. It is thus possible to read the play aloud in class, perhaps even assigning parts to students. In teaching the play you might remark about the swift movement of the plot from the beginning antagonism of Smirnov and Mrs. Popov to their final love. Students may deny the realism of the play because the love happens so suddenly. There is no need to claim fidelity to real life, for you might point out that a major characteristic of farce is unusual or unexpected action.

Answers to the Study Questions, pages 58-59.

(1) At the opening Mrs. Popov is in mourning for her husband, who has been dead for seven months. She has resolved to cloister herself at home for the rest of her life to show her fidelity. Luka's practical advice and his directness immediately show that her behavior is overdrawn, sentimental, and just plain silly. (2) Toby (lines 37, 75, and 407) is a horse that was dearly loved by the dead husband, Nikolai. Mrs. Popov's care of him in 37 and 75 indicates her fidelity. Her abandoning of care (line 407) shows that she has decided to forget Nikolai.

(3) Smirnov has come to collect a debt owed by the dead husband (line 69). He is gruff, loud, and outspoken. He tells Mrs. Popov that he has had his fill of love, having been jilted nine times and having jilted women twelve times (lines 193-220, 383). Mrs. Popov cannot give him the money he needs because she cannot get at her assets for two days. In explaining himself and angering Mrs. Popov, he demonstrates his disillusion with women, summing up his judgment by calling them no better than <u>a</u> <u>common</u> <u>crocodile</u> (lines 209-210). (4) He breaks two chairs (lines 210, 363-364), thus providing comic stage business, one of the major slapstick characteristics of farce.

(5) Mrs. Popov found her husband's love letters in his desk after his death (lines 231-232). She mentions this infidelity earlier, in line 30. Despite this betrayal in his lifetime, she has vowed to be faithful to him eternally (lines 25-32, 235-238). She obviously must have a good deal of anger about Nikolai's infidelity, or else she would not mention it.

(6) Mrs. Popov orders Smirnov to leave (lines 252ff.) and he refuses, insisting first on his money and becoming more insulting. In anger, she calls him a brute and a bear (lines 283-284). His response is to challenge her to duel (lines 292- 293). (7) Once Smirnov is alone after Mrs. Popov has gone to get the pistols, he confesses that he is impressed with her because of the force of her character and anger (lines 317-329). The scene is comic because of the incongruity of his response: When anger and the anticipation of a duel are expected, he begins talking about admiration. (8) Therefore the play's conclusion is sudden and surprising. The appropriate response to the quick reversal (peripiteia) from anger to love should be laughter and happiness.

(9) Mrs. Popov has shown herself to be committed to love and fidelity, and in addition she herself has noted her husband's lifetime cruelty and infidelity (line 30). Smirnov has asserted that he has had many experiences in love, and that he has <u>played</u> <u>the</u> <u>fool</u> (line 196). It is therefore well

within both characters to fall in love at a time of heightened emotion, particularly if they prefer being in love to being angry. The conclusion is therefore more surprising than improbable. A somewhat comparable story to this play is Shirley Jackson's "About Two Nice People" (pages 281-288).

(10) Here, as in most human activities, laughter is unpredictable. Some likely spots are Luka's observation about his dead wife (line 14), about living like spiders (line 16), and about the waving of the fanny (line 23). The play takes off from there. If you choose to read the play aloud in class, you might note where smiles and laughter occur, and then afterward (in the more sober light of analysis) discuss reasons for laughter. (11) There is good reason for the popularity. The subject is love; the mood is good-natured; the widow's pretentiousness is ridiculed; the behavior of Smirnov is funny; the reversal is hilarious; and at no point does the pace slacken.

(12) The widows of both The Bear and "The Widow of Ephesus" give up their fidelity and self-imposed obligations of self-effacement to their dead husbands when a new and lively man appears. Chekhov makes his reversal seem more unlikely by bringing the two characters to the verge of a duel before they fall in love. The focus of Chekhov's play is on the ridiculousness of human beings (both male and female) but also upon their likability, whereas the focus in the tale by Petronius is avowedly on the inconstancy of women.

Writing topics: The transformations of Smirnov and Mrs. Popov. Smirnov's language. The farcical action. The humor. Likes and/or dislikes.

E. E. Cummings, nobody loses all the time, pages 59-60.

Cummings began his writing career in 1922 with The Enormous Room, and continued writing throughout his lifetime. His poetry is unique because of his habit of omitting most capital letters, splitting words, and arranging lines with a zany spacial appearance, to name only the major characteristics. "nobody loses all the time" demonstrates the concreteness of Cummings and also the irreverence that he sometime evidences in his poems.

Answers to the Study Questions, pages 60-61.

(1) Uncle Sol was a talented singer and tried farming, first vegetables, then chickens, then skunks. When everything failed he drowned himself in the water tank. (2) The speaker, a nephew, was apparently not very close to Uncle Sol, and therefore he selects Sol's story to illustrate the half-serious maxim with which the poem begins, "nobody loses all the time." (3) The speaker accurately describes Sol's enterprises but with no evidence that he was directly involved or deeply concerned with them.

(4) The lesson is that "nobody loses all the time," an idea that the speaker proposes with some degree of seriousness. The poem itself offers great amusement, although the serious possibility of beginning to win only after death is not very encouraging.

(5) The comparison with the Missouri, a very large river indeed, is hyperbole, or overstatement. The speaker might offer it seriously, as an expression of the grief of those at Uncle Sol's funeral, but it is too unrealistic for readers to respond with anything but laughter. (6) Words and phrases like splendiferous are probably offered seriously by the speaker, a

11

rather ebullient character who does not have a sense of what language is appropriate to describe Sol's misfortunes or death. The words obviously would not be right if the speaker were sensitive and sympathetic, for they are comically inappropriate where they appear. The insensitive and somewhat pretentious speaker thus becomes a part of the poem's humor.

(7) Suicide is an intensely serious topic, as may be seen, for example, at the end of Arthur Miller's Death of a Salesman (pages 1294 ff.). This treatment, with the funny "moral," is not what one would normally expect.

(8) The unusual line breaks and spatial arrangements suggest that Cummings intended that the poem be seen on the page. The arrangement of lines 34-37, for example, building up to the name Sol, emphasizes the lowering of the coffin, in word patterns of 4, 3, 2, and then 1. The unexpectedness of the line breaks, coming as they do, augments Sol's final comedy.

(9) Students may cite some of the following reasons for liking the poem: (a) the unfortunate comedy of the farming failures, (b) the final "triumph" of Sol in becoming a winner in the grave, (c) the many comic spots in the poem, (d) the grin-and-bear-it philosophy that emerges, (e) the overblown language such as splendiferous, and (f) Cummings's unusual alignment, punctuation, and capitalization.

Writing topics: How are Uncle Sol's disasters made to seem comic? Cummings's use of linear arrangement, parenthesis, and other unusual mechanical devices. Responses to unusual words and phrases in the poem. General likes and/or dislikes.

RESPONDING TO LITERATURE: LIKES AND DISLIKES, pages 61-66.

The reason we have included this discussion is that too often responses are ignored while the business of analysis and thought goes forward. Thus this discussion, coming as a first consideration, is designed to remind students that their responses are important and foremost. We do not propose, however, to admit the de gustibus argument that individual taste is in arbitrary control. Thus we have emphasized on pages 64-66 that responses of disliking may be modified upon thought to become the grounds for the broadened appreciation of literary works. We suggest that in teaching you might wish to stress this section as a reminder that the process of intellectual growth of students will be complemented by a corresponding development of taste. Of special note also is the list of possible reasons for liking a work and in addition the recommended practice of keeping a journal for responses. With regard to first impressions, it is most important to stress the words informed and explained (see page 61). The notebook shold be used as an incentive to the need for students to comprehend all aspects of the work being studied. Responses based on an inaccurate reading will not be valid, and this point should be stressed for their benefit. Sometimes are reader will not like a work despite full understanding. On pages 63-64, we treat this possibility, emphasizing that dislike must be grounded both in proper information about the work and also upon a clearly defined standard of response.

WRITING ABOUT YOUR LIKES AND DISLIKES, pages 66-69.

This assignment is visualized as an excercise in response. It is not to be a full-scale analysis, nor is it to be a reasoned defense of the literary merit of the piece being studied. Rather, the writing is to be based on simple response: What in the work caused the student to like/dislike a work? Thus, of the types of responses for the body of an essay described on pages 66-67, the most common one will be a list of things liked. The sample essay, pages 67-68, illustrates an essay-length treatment along these lines. You might wish to read parts of the essay with your students to demonstrate how each of the admired qualities about Holmes is developed at paragraph length. Perhaps the most important point to emphasize here is that the reasons for liking are developed beyond the simple statement of response.

The other possible developments are also likely, though not illustrated by a sample essay. You might discuss these with your students, noting that the second one described on page 67 is in effect a description of responses upon reading, and that the third and fourth possible essay developments are more fully considered on pages 63-66.

13

ALTERNATIVE STORIES FOR THE CHAPTER TOPICS

To illustrate the various topics of the chapters, you may wish to use not only the stories included but also others. Because any story may serve as the topic of a response, or plot analysis, we have not classed stories according to the first three chapter topics. The lists are designed instead to assist you in making additional choices for chapters 4-10. Thus, to focus on character, you will find that "Miss Brill" (from Chapter 5) and "The Chrysanthemums" (from Chapter 9) are included as good stories for character study. We also include here for your convenience the titles of stories within the relevant chapters, together with the additional stories from pages 375-455. The listing for point of view is designed to be a thorough catalogue of all the stories in this collection, so that you may guide your students confidently through this very complex and subtle topic. In addition, we have included some additional classifications you might use in the classroom.

CHARACTER

A & P
A Worn Path
Blue Winds Dancing
Miss Brill
Act of Faith
The Found Boat
Young Goodman Brown
The Chrysanthemums
Araby

The Horse Dealer's Daughter
Flying Home
The Season of Divorce
Lady with Lapdog
Youth
Slave on the Block
I Stand Here Ironing
Goodbye and Good Luck

POINT OF VIEW

First Person

(A) Narrator as the protagonist or a major character

A & P
Blue Winds Dancing
First Confession
Araby

The Season of Divorce
Youth
Goodbye and Good Luck

(B) Narrator as an observer and/or participant

Adventure of the Speckled Band
Luck
The Hammon and the Beans

The Old Chief Mshlanga (¶s 14-98)
I Stand Here Ironing

(C) Unnamed narrator who is not a participant

The Widow of Ephesus
The Worker in Sandalwood

The Masque of the Red Death

(D) First speaker quotes the first person narrative of another

Youth   Luck

(E) First-person narratives or letters within a story

The Adventure of the Speckled Band   Flying Home
Act of Faith

(F) Narrator speaks of herself in the third person

The Old Chief Mshlanga (¶s 1-13)

Third Person

(A) <u>Limited</u> <u>Omniscient</u>: A major character is the focus of the narrative, together with selected thoughts of this character.

The Necklace   The Found Boat
A Worn Path   About Two Nice People
Maria Concepcion   Young Goodman Brown
The Catbird Seat   The Chrysanthemums
Barn Burning   Flying Home
Miss Brill   Lady with Lapdog
Act of Faith (¶s 90-end)   The Old Chief Mshlanga (¶s 1-13)
A Clean, Well-Lighted Place (¶s 76-85)

(B) <u>Limited</u> <u>Dramatic</u>: Major character are the focus of the narrative, with no revelations of character's thought.

The Portable Phonograph   Slave on the Block
The Fox and the Grapes

(C) <u>Omniscient</u>: the All-Knowing Narrator

The Horse Dealer's Daughter   The Prodigal Son
A Hunger Artist   The Bride Comes to Yellow Sky

(D) <u>Dramatic</u>, or <u>Objective</u>

The Lottery   Act of Faith (¶s 1-89)
The Chaser   Clean, Well-Lighted Place (1-75)

(E) <u>Third</u> <u>Person</u> <u>Frame</u>: Speaker introduces third person narrative of another

The Prodigal Son

SETTING

The Adventure of the Speckled Band	A Clean, Well-Lighted Place
A & P	The Found Boat
The Necklace	About Two Nice People
A Worn Path	The Worker in Sandalwood
Barn Burning	The Old Chief Mshlanga
Miss Brill	Araby
The Masque of the Red Death	The Chrysanthemums
The Portable Phonograph	Flying Home
Act of Faith	Slave on the Block

STYLE

A & P	A Clean, Well-Lighted Place
Blue Winds Dancing	Young Goodman Brown
Barn Burning	The Worker in Sandalwood
Miss Brill	Araby
The Lottery	Slave on the Block

TONE

Maria Concepcion	The Chaser
The Masque of the Red Death	Slave on the Block
Luck	A Hunger Artist
A Clean, Well-Lighted Place	The Old Chief Mshlanga
Young Goodman Brown	A Good Man is Hard to Find
The Worker in Sandalwood	Goodbye and Good Luck
The Hammon and the Beans	

HUMOR

The Widow of Ephesus	First Confession
A & P	Luck
The Bride Comes to Yellow Sky	The Found Boat
About Two Nice People	Goodbye and Good Luck
The Catbird Seat	

SYMBOLISM AND ALLEGORY

A & P	The Masque of the Red Death
Araby	The Portable Phonograph
A Worn Path	Act of Faith
Young Goodman Brown	A Clean, Well-Lighted Place
The Fox and the Grapes	The Found Boat
The Prodigal Son	A Hunger Artist
The Worker in Sandalwood	The Old Chief Mshlanga
The Chrysanthemums	I Stand Here Ironing
The Lottery	

IDEA OR THEME

The Necklace	Araby
Blue Winds Dancing	The Horse Dealer's Daughter
First Confession	Flying Home
The Lottery	Youth
Act of Faith	I Stand Here Ironing
A Clean, Well-Lighted Place	Slave on the Block
The Prodigal Son	The Old Chief Mshlanga

A FUTURISTIC STORY

The Portable Phonograph

ABSURDIST STORIES

A Hunger Artist	The Chaser
A Clean, Well-Lighted Place	

A DETECTIVE STORY

The Adventure of the Speckled Band

FANTASY AND THE MIRACULOUS

The Catbird Seat	The Fox and the Grapes
The Lottery	Young Goodman Brown
The Masque of the Red Death	The Worker in Sandalwood
The Chaser	A Hunger Artist

FABLE AND PARABLE

The Fox and the Grapes	A Hunger Artist
The Prodigal Son	

17

CHAPTER 2

FICTION

The first half of this chapter, pages 73-85, is an introduction to the major concepts and characteristics of prose fiction. We therefore recommend that you assign it first before embarking upon any of the other chapters about stories. The aim of the section is a general coverage of fiction, but not in as much detail as in the chapters devoted to specific topics. Thus, point of view is introduced here in a page (81-82) so that students will have a sense of what to expect as they encounter chapters on plot, character, or symbolism. Should you not have time to use the chapter on point of view, you would still be assured that students would know something about it from their study here.

As you teach this section, you may wish to expand upon any of the parts there. Thus pages 73-74 introduce a brief definition of fiction and narration and also a brief history. You may want to flesh out these pages, as well as develop more fully the description of modern fiction (pages 74-75) and the references to the beginnings of the short story (pages 75-76).

The key elements of character (pages 78-79), plot (79), stucture (79), and theme (80) are all developed more fully in later chapters, so that here you need to be sure only that your students develop familiarity with the concepts. Still, there will be questions that will need answering. We suggest that the two stories included in this chapter, "A & P" and "The Necklace," be used as references, because the problem in this introductory discussion will be maintaining concreteness.

The same will also hold true for your discussion of the major tools of fiction. Thus, narration (page 80), style (80-81), point of view (81-82), description (82), dialogue (82-83), and commentary (83-84) are all readily available in the stories as exhibits for classroom reference. Tone and irony (page 84) and symbolism and allegory (pages 84-85) are cited as appearing in these stories. Hence your discussion may maintain concreteness through continued references to the relevant sections. Obviously, as your discussion progresses, students may introduce their own references as they recall things they have encountered in your course and elsewhere.

John Updike, A & P, pages 86-90.

Updike was born in Pennsylvania. He graduated from Harvard in 1954, and worked for a time for The New Yorker. After his first novel in 1959, The Poorhouse Fair, he published many novels, stories, and poems, and he received the Pulitzer Prize in 1981 for Rabbit is Rich. "A & P" is readily accessible to most students, with the possible exception of those for whom English is a second language. For them you might wish to stress study question 2, on the topic of Sammy's diction. It is significant to note his disregard of grammar at the opening, and his greater care at the end. Even the concluding word, hereafter, is worthy of note in the context of his narration, for it is not of the same wordstock as most of the language he uses.

Answers to the Study Questions, page 90.

(1) The exposition occurs simultaneously with the movement of the girls in the store. We learn about Sammy from his accurate and fascinated description of the girls' appearance, and his observation of Stokesie and Stokesie's expression of doubt about the propriety of being in the store clad in swimming suits (paragraph 9). The basis of the conflict is explained in

paragraph 10, in which Sammy describes the Massachusetts town as a rather staid, respectable place. As Sammy speaks, Updike makes him talk himself alive as a person of perception, sensitivity, and understanding, capable of both annoyance and admiration. (2) From Sammy's language we learn that he has a strong sense of his own identity. His anger at the <u>witch</u> in paragraph 1, for example, indicates an awareness of his own worth when he is taken to task for what he thinks is an inadvertent mistake. His first response to Stokesie, "'Darling,' I said, 'Hold me tight,'" (paragraph 8) indicates a sense of humor, camaraderie, and capacity for enjoyment. Throughout the story, which is presented in a spoken rather than written style, as though Sammy is speaking to a sympathetic and friendly listener, Sammy violates strict grammatical rules. He switches tenses constantly (see, for example, the beginning of paragraph 12), and utilizes slang expressions (<u>gunk</u> in paragraph 12, <u>juggled</u> in paragraph 5), inexact modifiers (<u>kind of</u> in paragraph 32 and elsewere), colloquial phrases ("they all three of them" in paragraph 5, "but never quite makes it" in paragraph 2), misplaced modifiers ("Walking in the A & P . . . I suppose . . ." in paragraph 4). That Sammy also correctly uses a possessive before a gerund ("His repeating this struck me as funny" in paragraph 15), together with other passages of correct English, suggests that he deliberately violates standard English in his colloquial speech.

(3) Sammy's observations, like "two crescents of white" (paragraph 1), suggest his extensive experience as a girl watcher. Also, however, his references to his distaste for older, married women indicate that he has watched them, but not with approval. His remarks reflect his taste for youth and beauty, but also his limited understanding of life as a boy of nineteen. His estimation of female intelligence in paragraph 2 about a "buzz like a bee in a glass jar" and his expressed lack of certainty about how girls' minds work indicate, under the guise of minimizing women, a lack of experience with women on an adult level. His gesture to quit is at odds with his patronizing estimate of women; it shows more respect than he actually expresses.

(4) Sammy describes the community in paragraph 10 as a typically conservative small town, with banks, a church, a newspaper store, and real-estate offices, together with street repair and maintenence. People know each other, for Lengel, the Sunday-school teacher, is friendly wih Sammy's parents (paragraphs 13, 31) as well as his boss at the store. In addition to the conservative establishment, there is also a working-class area, of which Sammy's family forms a part (paragraph 14). The closeness of the community keeps people in line, as in the women dressing decently whenever they go shopping (paragraph 10). This traditional and conservative world is clearly distinguished from the upper-class beach area--the world of the girls.

(5) Lengel is the quintessentially conservative figure suppressing the freedom of the girls to go anywhere in their swimming suits. With his "sad Sunday-school-superintendant stare," he represents propriety (paragraph 15), decency (paragraph 17), and tradition. Sammy reproaches Lengel for embarrassing the girls (paragraph 26), but his values are closer to toleration and a respect for freedom and individual expression.

(6) Sammy makes his sudden decision to quit for reasons that he does not articulate. Probably, however, his <u>thinking</u> (paragraph 21) consists of his viewing his future as a duplicate of Lengel. The meaning to him at the time is summed up in paragraph 31, with his observation that it would be <u>fatal</u> not to go through with his decision. In other words, his sense of identity is on the line, and he must maintain his integrity in his own eyes even if the girls

19

know nothing about his gesture. He realizes that the world will be hard for him hereafter because of people like Lengel who may have power over him.

(7) Sammy's concern with his <u>clean exit</u> (paragraph 31) demonstrates an interest in self-dramatization, a degree of objectivity and awareness about himself. It also suggests his awareness that ethical decisions, such as the one he has made, might break down and maybe even yield to second thoughts if time were to be spent in a long preparation for his exit.

<u>Other Observations</u>: Some details in the story need further explanation. Students may not know that "A & P" stands for the "Great Atlantic and Pacific Tea Company." Hence, in paragraph 9, the name "Alexander and Petrooshki" indicates a vague uneasiness that Russia will control America by 1990. The <u>Cape</u> in paragraph 10 refers to Cape Cod, Massachusetts, a summer resort area filled with beaches. In paragraph 14, "They'll Do It Every Time" refers to a syndicated daily and Sunday cartoon originated by Jimmy Hatlo. In paragraph 31, the <u>Falcon</u> refers to the small car that had recently been introduced by the Ford Motor Company.

Writing topics: A precis of "A & P." The story's plot and/or structure. Sammy's conversational style or character. The theme of the story.

Guy De Maupassant, The Necklace, pages 90-96.

Guy De Maupassant, an apostle of Gustave Flaubert, is known as a careful craftsman who paid great attention to reality of detail. His stories are focused on the difficulties and ironies of existence among not only the working middle class, as in "The Necklace," but also among peasants and higher society. "The Necklace" is notable for its ironic concluding twist, and for this reason is perhaps the best known of his stories.

Answers to the Study Questions, pages 96-97.

(1) There is a sample essay about Mathilde's character (in relationship to the setting of the story) on pages 234-235. Clearly, on balance, she is not negative, for in paragraphs 99-104 De Maupassant describes the massive effort that she exerts to help pay the debt. The attribute of heroism that the speaker uses to characterize her work indicates the admiration that she is to earn in the reader's judgment. The quality of character that is a first cause of the misfortune, however, is her refusal to accept the appearance of her low financial condition and her desire to look well off by wearing the borrowed necklace. (2) Her daydreams are not unusual. It is unlikely that De Maupassant contrived the misfortune as a deserved punishment. <u>Partially deserved</u> would be acceptable as a reason, but not <u>entirely deserved</u>. Thus De Maupassant succeeds in directing sympathy toward Mathilde, together with whatever criticism she deserves because of her daydreams.

(3) Loisel is calm and complaisant; he is satisfied with simple pleasures and is out of his depth at a formal social occasion. He is a hard, sincere worker, however, and sacrifices tirelessly for the sake of his integrity and honor. He contributes to the financial disaster by not insisting on confessing the loss of the necklace to Jeanne. (4) The conversations of Mathilde and Loisel in paragraphs 8-38 indicate that Mathilde tries to pressure Loisel to find solutions to problems, adding a certain degree of accusation and guilt to her requests. Loisel seems desirous to

please, but makes his concession about money and his suggestion to borrow jewels as a means of ending Mathilde's pressure. There is no indication that the married couple has a warm or loving relationship.

(5) The speaker in paragraph 105 states the idea that a little thing may destroy or save. The story bears out the idea, for any number of things could be cited as the cause of the disaster, none of them by themselves of major significance: (a) the invitation, (b) the new dress, (c) borrowing the necklace, (d) the hurrying away from the party (paragraphs 55-59), (e) the failure of Jeanne to tell Mathilde that the necklace was paste. In a discussion about whether fate or chance is the determining influence, one would probably need to emphasize chance, for the idea of fate implies a more systematic pattern of opposition than the circumstances which work against Mathilde.

(6) De Maupassant introduces the idea of "the horrible life of the needy" in paragraph 98, and his description of what happens to Mathilde under these circumstances may be construed as an illustration of economic determinism. The fact that Jeanne Forrestier is "always youthful, always beautiful, always attractive" can be read the same way inasmuch as Jeanne is rich (paragraph 6). The clear contrast, together with De Maupassant's paragraph about "what would life have been like if she had not lost that necklace?" (paragraph 105), shows that in this story at least De Maupassant makes a connection between the economic condition of people and their happiness and character fulfillment.

Writing topics: The character of Mathilde. The structure of the story, including the surprise ending. The use of symbols. The theme. Tone and the irony of situation in the story.

HOW TO WRITE A PRECIS, pages 97-101.

For teaching this section we suggest that a number of elements in the text might need stress and further exemplification. A central idea (page 97) is that a precis does not need to include everything. Students may needlessly lengthen their precis essays if they try to put in every detail from the story. Thus, the section on the need for selectivity (pages 98-99) is also worthy of special mention, for in a precis the idea should be to make a brief rendering of the story, without any attempt at explanations. If you can stress that the precis is to be the basis of later interpretation, then the idea may become clear for the students. Perhaps the word report might help here, for a precis is in essence a simple report, like newspaper reports, of what happens in a story. The newspaper analogy is also helpful because reference to a news article as compared with an editorial might make the distinction between a precis and an analytical essay more clear to students.

For study, the sample essay (pages 100-101) might offer good opportunity for the comparison of the original with the precis. Thus the first paragraph of the sample, containing 97 words, condenses 51 paragraphs, or approximately 40% of the entire story. With such a shortening, it is inevitable that details must be omitted, such as Loisel's planned use for the 400 francs which he gives Mathilde for the dress, and also his taste for inelegant food. In discussing the reasons for omitting such details, you can make a strong point both about essential actions in stories—a point worth making in its own right—and also about what students should plan to include in their essays.

21

CHAPTER 3

PLOT AND STRUCTURE

The first part of this chapter is devoted to discussions of plot (pages 102-104) and structure (pages 104-107). The essential quality of plot is conflict, which creates doubt and tension, and therefore the major interest of each particular story. The discussion of structure makes available the formal five analogies of structure. Discussion should make clear that these are necessary in any story, for without any of them a story would be unfinished. To paraphrase Pope's "Essay on Criticism," the five elements are "nature methodized." The discussion of "Formal and Actual Structure" (pages 106-107) makes the point that the formal elements need not appear in any particular order in the story, but that individual stories may introduce them as natural and necessary for the reader's understanding, and also as they serve the development of the story.

Stephen Crane, The Bride Comes to Yellow Sky, pages 107-115.

Crane was born in New Jersey in 1871, attended college, but spent most of his brief adult life as a writer and war correspondent, dying of tuberculosis in Germany in 1900. He wrote voluminously, and his best-known novel is The Red Badge of Courage (1895). "The Bride Comes to Yellow Sky" is one of his better-known stories. It explores a realistic situation, but one may argue that Crane conventionalizes the two major characters, Potter and Scratchy. Of special interest in the story is the voice of the narrator, whose observations are accurate, perceptive, and wry. In class, students in this day of rapid air travel may need reminding about the comparative slowness of journeying by rail and the consequent need for overnight sleeping accomodations. They might also need reminding of the custom, in the not too distant past, of dressing up when traveling.

Answers to the Study Questions, page 115.

(1) A Pullman was a fashionable railroad passenger car invented in 1859 to make possible long-distance railway travel. Jack Potter and his bride are going to Yellow Sky, having just been married in San Antonio. (2) The conflict between Potter and Scratchy is one of long standing. It is resolved not by an additional, immature gun battle, but by Potter's marriage. Hence the conflict might be defined as one between immaturity and maturity. There are also conflicts in the story concerning the character of Scratchy sober and drunk, and the underlying cruelty of the barkeeper and Scratchy toward the dog. In addition there is conflict in the story between the potential seriousness of gunfighting and the matter-of-fact views toward it of the various characters (including the narrator). (3) The crisis of the story occurs at the beginning of part 4 in the encounter between Scratchy and Potter and his bride. It becomes clear that there will be a peaceful resolution when Potter announces that he is defenseless. Some perceptive students might claim that the peaceful resolution is made clear right at the beginning of the story, however, because of the comic tone established there.

(4) Depending on how one defines the plot, Part I introduces Potter either as an adversary of Scratchy or else as a representative of growth and maturity. Part II is a bridge between Parts I and III, serving, as it does, as exposition about Scratchy and his previous encounters with Potter. The

third part focuses on Scratchy and what he represents, concluding on a mild note of suspense inasmuch as Scratchy is potentially capable of killing with his revolvers. Part IV contains the crisis, climax, and resolution.

(5) Potter is apprehensive not only because of his embarrassment about matters emotional and sexual, but also because he felt himself previously to have been owned and controlled by the town of Yellow Sky. There is a contrast between his concern about facing the citizens and his unflinching courage in facing Scratchy. The code governing gunfights stressed that one could not shoot an unarmed opponent. The fact that Potter is accompanied by his wife while meeting Scratchy is convincing evidence that Potter is telling Scratchy the truth about his new status.

(6) The Weary Gentleman saloon is a typical place of male congregation in Yellow Sky. It is also shown as the scene which will be one of the focal points of Scratchy's bullying of the town while drunk. Because the drummer (salesman) is a stranger, it is natural that Crane uses his unfamiliarity with Scratchy as a cause of exposition about Scratchy's habits. That the drummer travels is of course the explanation for his being a stranger in the town.

(7) Question 7 is designed to start a discussion about the interdependence of all the materials in a story. In real life, Scratchy would be dangerous and unpredictable, but in the story he is accepted as a part of existence. In addition, the amused tone with which the details about Potter and his new bride are presented, together with the companionship in combat established by Crane between Potter and Scratchy, makes it virtually impossible that there could be a death as a result of a showdown. The tone of the story, in other words, is consistently comic.

Writing topics: A plot analysis of the story. The structure of the entire story. The structure of individual parts.

Eudora Welty, A Worn Path, pages 116-121.

Welty was born in Mississippi and attended the University of Wisconsin, graduating in 1929. She is the author of many stories, and was awarded the Pulitzer Prize in 1973 for her novel The Optimist's Daughter (1972). Her stories, usually set in Mississippi, explore the manners and customs of the region. "A Worn Path" was included in her collection A Curtain of Green (1941). The story's main character, Phoenix, is a poor, aging black woman who is experiencing the onset of the afflictions of age (loss of memory, inflexibility of joints, imaginings) while maintaining an indomitable spirit in the face of the hopeless nature of her own plight and that of her grandson. Students may need reminding of the focus upon her character throughout the story up to her appearance in the medical office, where she is seen somewhat more objectively and dramatically.

Answers to the Study Questions, pages 121-122.

(1) The details of the sugar sacks and the rag establish Phoenix's poverty. Among other details that students might note in this regard are the untied tennis shoes and her status as revealed in the medical office. It is clear that her journey is along a worn path, and well worn at that, as she addresses the animals as acquaintances, closes her eyes when she walks the log, and follows her feet rather than her mind to get to the medical office in

23

Natchez. The <u>worn</u> <u>path</u> thus exists both in the world (leading Phoenix from her home to Natchez) and in her mind. She seems accustomed to being alone inasmuch as she is constantly speaking to herself. Her speech to animals and her visualizing the boy suggest the debilitating effects of age. The nature of her speech (such as "I going to the store") shows her lack of education.

(2) The plot (see the sample essay, page 129) is built up as a contrast between Phoenix, on one side, and the focus of poverty, natural obstacles, distance, age, and the illness of her grandson on the other. One might also see the plot in terms of nobility and strength of character standing against forces of destructiveness. These forces are not particularly malevolent, but are shown rather to be a part of the natural course of things. Inasmuch as there is no one actively attending to Phoenix and her grandson, her plight may be seen as reflecting the indifference of a social and political system which ignores the aged and ill, particularly black. The story, however, does not insist on the possible political-economic criticism, but instead reveals Phoenix's character and the pathos of her situation.

(3) Exposition (see also the sample essay, page 129) actually takes place from the beginning until paragraph 94. The complication is of course taking place almost coincidentally, for the difficulties Phoenix experiences are also a part of the virtually impossible conditions of her life. The disclosure about her grandson (paragraphs 78-92) is additional complication. The crisis may be considered as the silence of Phoenix up to her speech (in paragraph 87) for her silence suggests that she may be unable to carry on after having come so far. The climax is her speech in paragraph 94, in which her recognition and determination are revealed. The resolution is her acceptance of the additional nickel and her retreat down the stairs to purchase a toy before returning home. The windmill itself can be seen as a symbol of Phoenix's love and concern as well as an objectification of the child's frailty. The delay in the exposition about her grandson causes a second comprehension of the details prior to paragraph 91.

(4) In considering the confrontation of Phoenix and the hunter, students might bring out her apparent earlier experiences with the arbitrary judgements and punishments that whites have made against blacks. The scene also suggests the young hunter's assumption about his own power and also Phoenix's belief that somehow all white people know about all her misdeeds.

(5) The answers to this question are suggested in the first sentence. Only classroom discussion can bring out an examination of the various possible responses that your students might have.

Writing Topics: As a discussion of plot, the topic of human strength as opposed to poverty, old age, or illness, or, the black-white conflict. The structuring of individual parts of the story, such as the early part describing the walk of Phoenix, the encounter with the dog and the hunter, or the episode in the medical office.

Tom Whitecloud, Blue Winds Dancing, pages 122-126.

In February, 1938, Tom Whitecloud was identified as a Native American Indian living on the Lac du Flambeau Reservation in northern Wisconsin near Woodruff, the town mentioned in "Blue Winds Dancing" (paragraph 20). Though we have made a search, we have been unable to learn more about his life since

that time. The story, or fictionalized autobiographical episode, was awarded
a prize by the editors of Scribner's Magazine, where it was published.

Answers to the Study Questions, page 127.

(1) Paragraphs 1-11 comprise the first part. Exposition in this section
consists of that information which fixes the narrator as a college student in
California yearning for home and questioning the value of continuing his
studies. The complication occurs almost simultaneously as it becomes apparent
that the speaker's nostalgia really represents a deep-rooted rejection of the
values he has been asked to accept at school. The case of claiming that this
first section contains its own crisis and climax, as a virtual story in
little, is that it works up to his decision to return. Thus the rest of the
story is an enactment, or resolution, of that decision. More in conformity
with the entire story, however, is the fact that the crisis and climax are
reached later, in the narrator's fears about family acceptance and in his
belief about the old woman under the ice.

(2) There is much in the first section about the narrator's attitudes.
We learn that he is both homesick and tired, that he has serious doubts about
the values of the white culture, that he has a reverence for Nature, that he
seeks a release from the pressure to achieve, that he resents the feelings of
inferiority of his role as an Indian, that he values the personal closeness of
life at home, and that he is willing to endure hardship because of his
beliefs. He is rejecting civilization as a result of the personal, unhurried,
aesthetic, and passive values of his home, together with a profound sense of
identification with the home as a physical place. The major antagonist in the
story is the set of values of the white culture, but there are also other
antagonists, such as the cold and the threat of Denver Bob. There is also an
inner conflict that develops when the narrator nears home; this conflict is
manifested in self doubt and worry about being received by family and tribe.

(3) Catching a freight meant simply hiding aboard a freight train to
avoid the cost of a passenger train. There was a social stigma attached to
such travel, because it was the habit of hoboes, not the middle class. In
paragraph 12 the narrator makes plain that in the distinction between needs
and wants, he believes that people should only satisfy their needs. Thus he
rejects the value of acquisition. Although he buys presents, they are
personal, and thus belong within his value of personal concerns. There is
therefore no contradicion in his purchases.

(4) Answering this question (the statement is in paragraph 22) depends on
making the proper distiction between the words alone and lonely.

(5) The author invites us to approve the narrator's decision to return
home. The emphasis made on the values of home, together with the negative
expressions about the predominant white culture, make this attitude plain.

(6) Perceptive students will recognize the metaphorical nature of the
dancing of the blue winds, perhaps revealing the feeling and sound of wind on
a sunny day in winter. There is a synesthesia in the combining of color with
dance. In answering the second part of question 6, students may raise issues
of practicality and things aesthetic: in a world devoted to work, profit, and
aquisition, how can non-profit-making values be maintained?

(7) The narrator's return to the reservation and his family suggests a happy resolution of these issues for him, but if confinement on a reservation leads to want and boredom, the narrator's answer will not promote happiness for those who withdraw from the prevailing culture. There is no easy solution to these issues, but "Blue Winds Dancing," along with being a well-crafted and penetrating story, should awaken conciousness. (8) The question about balancing the need for acquisition with the love of family traditions and the natural world should also elicit students' thoughts about the precariousness of these more aesthetic values.

Writing topics: The plot as a conflict between Indian and white values, or between innocence and corruptibility. The structure of the formal elements in the story. The structure of the narrator's trip, which is marked not by American cities, but rather by the locations of Indian nations. The climax of the story, and what is brought to a head there.

WRITING ABOUT THE PLOT OF A STORY, pages 127-130.

This section deals with plot as a laying out of the principal conflict within a story. The conflict and its ramifications may be most readily approached if it can be clearly defined, as in "The Bride Comes to Yellow Sky." When the conflict is that between a person and forces ranged against him or her, students may have difficulty in defining and delimiting the forces. The sample theme, on Welty's "A Worn Path," should be particularly helpful here. If a student attempts to define a plot in terms of abstract forces, say something like "human indomitability versus overwhelming odds," the job of definition will be particularly challenging, but the results might also be particularly rewarding. A particularly tempting obstacle to overcome in the preparation of this essay is that some students, while analyzing plot, may easily slip and use materials from the story not as exemplification but rather as a descriptive end in itself--in short, as a retelling of the story.

WRITING ABOUT STRUCTURE IN A STORY, pages 130-133.

This essay is intended to contrast with the essay on plot. If assigned, it is most instructive to use the same story for both essays, as in the sample essays on "A Worn Path." Students should be reminded that the structure of a work depends on the actual arrangement and placement of materials, in addition to the basic plan of conflict with which the study of plot is concerned. The sample essay, for example, describes the locations in "A Worn Path" as being arranged to coincide with increasing difficulties that Phoenix is facing. It is quite important to stress that this observation is designed to explain the actual placement of plot details--in other words, the structure. It might be convenient to explain the analysis of structure as the attempt to determine the rationale of the arrangement made by the author. Such an emphasis will enable students to provide critical discourse rather than uncritical data.

CHAPTER 4

CHARACTERS: THE PEOPLE IN FICTION

One of the best ways to teach this section is to relate these materials
directly to the experiences of your students. Hence, the characters in their
lives whom they know well are analogous to round characters in fiction. By
contrast, flat characters tend to be those whom they know less well, such as
associates or acquaintances. The concepts of hero, heroine, protagonist, antagonist, and dynamic can all be related directly to the people whom students
know--their friends. The concepts representative, static, stereotype, and
stock are perhaps somewhat more difficult to explain, but if students can show
that the flatness of a character is directly related to the sameness of their
experience with an associate or acquaintance, the point can be made.

To aid this discussion, the concepts representative, static, stock, and
sterotype may be seen as modes of defining flat characterizations. An
interesting idea which often generates much thought and improved understanding
is that we are all round characters to the people we know and love, while we
are simply flat to others whom we do not know.

In teaching the section on probability, the question of "How would a god
(or demon, fairy, goblin, etc.) be expected to behave?" puts the creative act
of fiction in a new light for many students. The goal should be to encourage
students to think about an author's presentation of character in the light of
how they themselves would write in the same fictional mode. To teach the
various sorts of character, you might wish to use the following as a tabular
basis of discussion:

ROUND CHARACTERS

--- Major figures. How many are there? How many details do you learn about
them? What do they do?

--- Hero, heroine (antihero?). Are these terms justified?

--- Protagonist (central figure of interest in the plot). Antagonist? What
role does the protagonist play?

--- Dynamic quality: capable of change and growth. What change(s) can you
observe? Is the change genuinely brought about by the events?

FLAT CHARACTERS

--- Minor characters. How many are there? What do they do?

--- Static quality: no observable changes. How limited are the characters?

--- Stock, stereotype characters. How often do they appear? In what ways do
they seem to have been stamped out of a mold?

Katherine Anne Porter, Maria Concepcion, pages 140-153.

Porter was born in Texas but made her home in many places during her
life, spending considerable time in Mexico. She was awarded the Pulitzer
Prize for Fiction in 1966 for her Collected Stories. The story "Maria
Concepcion" illustrates characters living at the strongest peak of elemental

27

emotions, namely pride, possessiveness, egocentricity, passion, anger, resentment, pair "bonding" and community bonding. In classroom discussion about "Maria Concepcion," care must be taken to delineate the method by which Porter renders character, particularly that of Maria, whose few speeches are brief and pointed. When confessing her crime to Juan, she is not quoted directly; rather Porter leaves readers the task of imagining the gravity of her act. The words between Juan and Maria are almost all Juan's. The result of this method is that Maria, while being fully rounded, is somewat distant and mysterious. The other major character, Juan, is of particular interest as a developing character. His ability as a worker is clearly supported by Givens, and hence his change once he learns of the murder is logical.

Answers to the Study Questions, page 153.

(1) The Indian society of Maria and Juan is closely knit, with the Church as a dominant influence over the lives of the people, but with the sense of community being even more important. The people are Indians; they are poor but hard working. Their attitudes evolve from their Indian identitiy and their personal acquaintance with others of their kind. Because everyone within the society seems to know everyone else, even their own personal annoyances do not prevent them from closing ranks against the forces of law so that Maria Concepcion may be protected despite her having murdered Maria Rosa.

(2) Maria Concepcion is a strong character but she is in need of support. Her behavior when she has been deserted suggests that she is turning inward and brooding about revenge. The Church affiliation preserves her reputation for devoutness and respectability within the community. The value that permits her to be happy at the end, despite having killed Maria Rosa, is a prevailing personal code of honor that supercedes the morality of the Church. Her use of the knife, which Givens observes, suggests that she is capable of killing as a matter of necessity.

(3) Juan Villegas is cocky and egocentric. He is irresponsible at first, and he could not possibly care about Maria Concepcion's reaction to his leaving the village with Maria Rosa. The flat, stock aspect of his character is that he is a type of the brash, macho male. His strength and steadiness combine with his bravado to make him a protector of Maria Concepcion during the investigation. His resourcefulness and decisiveness are brought almost immediately to the front when Maria appears with the knife.

(4) The ambiguity about the fact that Maria Concepcion is not punished results from the conflict between abstract justice and the personal codes of the native society.

(5) The major conflict in the story is that between Maria Concepcion (the protagonist) and the various people and forces against which she must contend. After the murder, Juan joins Maria as a protagonist. The antagonists are (variously, to greater and lesser degrees) Juan himself, Maria Rosa, Lupe, and the forces of law. Interestingly, at the end of the story all the members of the Indian community are united against the law. The crisis of the story extends from the murder until Maria Concepcion sees Maria Rosa in her coffin. A good case may be made for claiming that the climax of the story is in paragraph 91, when Maria Concepcion relaxes upon determining that Maria Rosa is truly dead and that her death was justified. Maria Concepcion is in a strong position at the resolution of the story, for she has been affirmed by the community and has taken her husband's baby as her own.

(6) Givens does not change roles in the story, but remains as a protector of Juan. He is thus a flat character, even though he is fleshed out by Porter in some detail. Lupe, however, actually does undergo change, beginning by antagonizing Maria Concepcion, but supporting her at the end.

(7) Porter utilizes virtually all techniques possible to develop the character of Maria Concepcion: (a) Maria is the point-of-view figure, on whom most of the narrative attention is focused. In this respect, you might profitably study paragraphs 1-3, in which her person is described and also in which the limited omniscience of the narrator reveals Maria's state of mind. (b) Her speeches are relatively rare and unrevealing, except, perhaps, for her remark in paragraph 79, in which her attitude toward the stabbing and her feelings about Juan are suggested. Other quotations are in paragraphs 8, 11, 22, 24, 26, 35, 39, and 80. The small number of these might permit the classroom analysis and discussion of all of them. Obviously, with so few speeches, dialogue is less important for Porter's rendering than her description of Maria's actions and thoughts. (c) The observation and speeches about her are significant (see paragraphs 34, 37, 38, 41, 42, 57 and 116).

Writing topics: Maria Concepcion, Juan Villegas, or Maria Rosa. Lupe or Givens (particularly for shorter essays). Porter's treatment of the character of the Indian community, as manifested in Soledad, the general attitudes of the Indian folk as they speak about Maria Concepcion, and the investigation.

James Thurber, The Catbird Seat, pages 153-159.

Thurber was born in Ohio and made his reputation as a cartoonist and writer with The New Yorker. Late in life, he was troubled with increasing blindness. His stories and drawings are often centered upon quiet, unassuming men yearning to free themselves from the shackles that inhibit their freedom. These shackles are often women. In this respect, "Catbird Seat" demonstrates a typical comic Thurber situation. Erwin Martin's desire for freedom and control becomes actuality, even though the means of achieving them make "The Catbird Seat" a fantasy. The characters appear as exaggerations, but they nevertheless have many realistic traits. The portrayal of Fitweiler is a minor masterpiece, and the description of Dr. Fitch's response to the actions of Mrs. Barrows (paragraph 17) is an understated but pointed dig at scientific qualifications and inconclusiveness.

Answers to the Study Questions, page 159-160.

(1) Martin changes his plan (paragraph 12) in the apartment because he realizes his plot of murder is impossible. The details of his new plan, which takes shape just as he abandons his first plan for violence, are not clear until the very end of the story. Martin's exemplary record during the previous twenty years causes Fitweiler to doubt the report of Mrs. Barrows, whom he has known only a short time. There are two reasons for which the plan is successful: (a) Thurber's clever plotting of the story, and (b) the character traits of Martin and Mrs. Barrows, together with Fitweiler's experience with psychoanalysis.

(2) Martin seems withdrawn and harmless to others; they call him a drab, ordinary, little man and observe that "our most efficient worker neither drinks nor smokes." He also appears to be a man of routein; he calls himself cautious and painstaking and he follows the same schedule every day. Never-

theless, his clever plan reveals his fullness and roundness as a character. His dynamism is shown in his imagination, deception, and subterfuge. Phrases like <u>rub</u> <u>out</u> suggest that he has been assimilating the materials of movies and popular culture generally. His inner life, as evidenced by his "trial" of Mrs. Barrows, is apparently rich and imaginative. His Spartan, rigid habits suggest a person in need of stability, and also suggest why he would feel so threatened by Mrs. Barrows. The <u>catbird</u> <u>seat</u> is defined in paragraph 4, and Martin is certainly one of its occupants at the story's end.

(3) Fitweiler's experience with psychiatry fits in directly with Martin's plan because it causes Fitweiler to see mental illness rather than to consider the truth of what Mrs. Barrows claims. Since the plan depends on Fitweiler's response, one might conclude that Martin accounts for it when the <u>vague idea</u> comes to him (paragraph 12). The precariousness of this prediction is a major element making the story a piece of fantasy rather than realistic fiction.

(4) Mrs. Barrows's career is described in paragraphs 3-6 as a part of Martin's "trial." Only in a comic sense is the death penalty justifiable. The phrases comparing Barrows with a duck, donkey, and horse put her in an unfavorable light. The problem with the scene in her apartment is that for a time she is seen as being relatively tolerant and personable as a hostess.

(5) The story is primarily fanciful and farcical. The potentially serious values putting Martin and Mrs. Barrows in conflict could be classified as (a) a history of pragmatic success vs. unreasonable change, (b) quietness vs. loudness, and (c) the victim vs. the victimizer.

Writing topics: Character analysis of Martin, Barrows, or Fitweiler.

William Faulkner, Barn Burning, pages 160-172.

Faulkner spent his childhood in Mississippi and became one of the foremost American authors of the twentieth century. He twice received the Pulitzer Prize (1955, 1963), and he also received the Nobel Prize for literature in 1949. Throughout his extensive writing, often set in a special microcosmic world which he called Yoknapatawpha County, he treats life in the South as a symbol of humankind generally, emphasizing the decline of culture and civilization in the wake of the Civil War. Often he deals with degraded, sullen, and degenerate characters, and in this respect Abner Snopes of "Barn Burning" is typical. Abner is not violent here but he is portrayed as an ex-horse-thief turned barn burner; the loyalty he tries to exact from his son Sarty excludes any allegiance to morality. Faulkner also treats the Snopes family in <u>The</u> <u>Hamlet</u> (1940), <u>The</u> <u>Town</u> (1957), and <u>The</u> <u>Mansion</u> (1960).

Answers to the Study Questions, pages 172-173.

(1) The time of the story is somewhere between 1891 and 1895, and the scene is rural Mississippi. The date is given in paragraph 15, when the speaker explains the limp of Abner Snopes.

(2) The speaker limits the narration to Sarty, so that most of what we learn is what Sarty himself sees and hears. Thus Abner Snopes is distant, remorseless, and unexplained because Sarty himself is not privy to any of Abner's plans, and it is only through Sarty's responses to the trial at the beginning of the story that we learn that Abner is charged with burning the

Harris barn. Limited though the narrative is, however, the speaker also knows details about Abner's <u>service</u> in the Civil War that no one in the family knows (see paragraphs 15, 27, and 107).

(3) The Snopes family is dominated by Abner. The members are the mother (Lonnie), the aunt (Lizzie), the older brother (elsewhere called Flem), the twin sisters, and Colonel Sartoris (Sarty). The speaker discloses the habitual moving of the family in paragraphs 24 and 40. This constant moving has prevented the family from establishing roots, and it has also made the members dependent upon themselves and particularly upon Abner. The mother and sisters are flat characters. The sisters are permitted to express very little personality, except, perhaps, for paragraph 50. The mother is constantly anxious and apprehensive, for good cause in view of the life of the family and of the contempt which Abner expresses for her. The aunt, Lizzie, is more individual, which is shown in paragraph 98.

(4) Abner Snopes is cold, hard, calculating, cruel, and contemptuous; the speaker in paragraph 25 notes his <u>wolflike</u> <u>independence</u> and <u>latent</u> <u>ravening</u> <u>ferocity</u>. Abner is also manipulative, as is shown in his behavior in court at the beginning of the story. He shows presumptiveness in paragraph 70, when he sues De Spain about the Major's imposition of costs for the spoiling of the rug. That he is also callous and unthinking is shown in his treatment of animals and his family. Abner is not without some redeeming qualities, however, for his sociabiliy is shown in paragraph 82 in the blacksmith's shop, and his sense of family cohesiveness is shown in paragraph 27.

(5) De Spain expects Abner to pay 20 bushels of corn out of the next harvest (paragraph 62). The justice reduces the settlement to ten bushels (paragraph 78). Abner's response seems almost submissive (paragraph 79), but he is also planning to burn De Spain's barn in revenge.

(6) Sarty is young, but has a strong sense of truth and justice, as is shown in paragraphs 7, 29, and 92-103. For a time he supports his father, and thus seems to be taking on Abner's corrupt nature, but even then he wishes his father would reform, indicating his desire to merge his family lies with his sense of justice (paragraph 69). Finally, his commitment to justice predominates; he warns De Spain and then runs away, not looking back (paragraph 108).

(7) Because Sarty is forced by circumstances into making a commitment to law and truth, his growth makes him a natural protagonist. The case for Abner as the protagonist is that he might be viewed as a free spirit under oppression seeking to secure independence. Sarty, though a boy, is more "heroic" than his father, and since he is the center of interest he is more worthy of sympathy than Abner.

(8) The central conflict in the story is between Sarty's commitment to truth and his allegiance to his father. There are lesser conflicts, such as that between brothers (the older brother does not trust Sarty: paragraph 92); between Abner and Lonnie, his wife; between Abner and Mr. Harris, Major De Spain, the justices, the black servant of the De Spains, and Mrs. De Spain; and also between Abner and the law generally. The major conflict is resolved when Abner directs his wife to restrain Sarty, indicating his judgment that Sarty is not reliable. (9) Sarty is round because he grows, determining to follow "truth, justice" (paragraph 29), rather than accepting his father's advice to "stick to your own blood" (paragraph 29).

31

(10) The parallels between the Biblical Abner and Faulkner's Abner suggest that modern persons have lost the heroism of the past. Faulkner's Abner destroys rugs and barns, while the Biblical Abner leads armies. Both have great ability, but Faulkner's Abner is corrupted by selfishness and the desire for booty. Hence the story exposes Abner's corruption and disgrace. Faulkner introduced similar parallels elsewhere--in Absalom, Absalom (1936), for example, where the David-Absalom story is recast; in Light in August (1932), where there is a parallel with the crucifixion; and in A Fable (1954) which also introduces the parallel of the Passion.

(11) At the climax, De Spain rides and shoots. Faulkner does not disclose the results of the shooting because the point of view character, Sarty, is not in a position to learn about them. The mystery about the outcome is hence a direct result of Faulkner's use of a consistent point of view.

Writing topics: Character analysis of Sarty, Abner, Major De Spain, the "lesser" members of the Snopes family, or the justices.

WRITING ABOUT CHARACTER, pages 173-176

Teaching this section is primarily the reinforcing of the essay structures suggested on page 174. The most significant element to stress, no matter what approach your students might select, is that the actions, comments, and speeches should be focused on actual traits of character and should not become retellings of occurrences. Usually organizations 1 and 3 are the easiset types for students to apply. Hence a study of Abner might be developed around the topics of ruthlessness, contempt, and anger--as traits-- or around the campfire, the rug, and the attempted barn burning--as central incidents. Whenever you perceive a change or growth, the second type would be in order. Thus an essay on Sarty of "Barn Burning," or on Juan Villegas of "Maria Concepcion," could be organized to reflect the changes that occur in these characters.

CHAPTER 5

POINT OF VIEW

Because point of view is a new idea and technique for students accustomed to seeking meanings and symbols in fiction (if they have indeed come this far), you will need to emphasize its importance as a mode of presenting and authenticating narrative details. It is still somewhat of a revelation, however, that the author himself or herself is not the direct speaker of a story, and therefore the question "Do you mean the author's point of view?" should be addressed, for it will invariably be asked even after you have spent time in class explaining the meaning of the term. The question offers the chance to explain the difference between point of view and opinions or ideas, a confusion which is not uncommon. The best way to reinforce the point, of course, is to consider a number of stories and to determine the nature of the speaker in each of them. Once students can see that point of view is a means by which modern fiction develops so many individualistic variations, they will be well on their way to becoming capable, disciplined readers.

Katherine Mansfield [Beauchamp], Miss Brill, pages 184-187.

Mansfield was born in New Zealand but spent most of her adult life in England, where her stories earned her a reputation for originality and experimentation. She treats topics of crucial importance in the lives of individual persons, such as those in the stories "The Garden Party" and "Bliss." In "Miss Brill," an insignificant woman who is subjected to a few callously cruel words is deprived of all the dreams on which she had based her life. The story is pointedly and skillfully done, with a quizzical ending that leaves readers wondering whether the heroine can transfer her grief from herself to her most prized possession, her fur.

Answers to the Study Questions, page 187.

(1) The point of view of "Miss Brill" is the third-person limited, with the narrator actually using some of the expressions that the protagonist might have used, such as "dear little thing" and "Little rogue!" (paragraph 1). One is justified in concluding that these are Miss Brill's expressions because there is such a close connection established by the narrator to Miss Brill, and because the narrator allows us to learn much about Miss Brill's life as she herself might have reflected upon it. (2) Had the story been narrated by Miss Brill herself as a first-person involved narrator, it is unlikely that she could explain her own inner reflections without embarassment. The result is that the story, if it could be told at all, would be more like a confession and self-rationalization, and therefore would be unlike the present narrative. A walker in the park would necessarily not know the inner musings of Miss Brill, and hence a dramatic narrative would be more like the observations that Miss Brill herself makes of the woman in the ermine toque.

(3) The change to a dramatic point of view when the boy and girl sit down occurs because these two see Miss Brill objectively, as she actually appears to others; the shift back to the starting limited omniscience does not happen until the last paragraph. This interlude of dramatic point of view enables the reader to conclude that Miss Brill herself is one of the pitiable people whom she deplores earlier in the story. (4) The last paragraph seems to be more consistent with the great bulk of the story than with the previous seven paragraphs. The paragraph brings out the poignancy of Miss Brill's condition,

33

for it demonstrates that she habitually dramatizes her feelings, even this heartbreak, by somehow projecting them into other people and into things.

(5) Few actions occur. Miss Brill goes for her Sunday afternoon in the park, listens to the band, observes the people, and then the young couple appears and lets her overhear their insults, after which she goes home.

(6) Paragraphs 9 and 10 contain Miss Brill's thoughts about her being a participant in a play, even though (paragraph 9) she acknowledges that her role is a small one. Her sense of camaraderie seems to be one of sympathetic observer and interpreter, a member or trouper of the passing throng in the park. She has not articulated the connection in detail, however, for the narrator admits that "she didn't know" just exactly what her understanding is about her fellow actors (paragraph 10).

(7) The ermine toque is rejected by the man she meets (paragraph 8), but she puts on a brave front. The parallel is that she suffers a cruel rebuff just as Miss Brill does.

(8) The question of whether students might like Miss Brill, germane as it is, remains subjective. It is to be hoped, however, that students will see Miss Brill with something like the pity with which Mansfield presents her.

Writing topics: The limited omniscient point of view. The influence of the point of view on the perception of Miss Brill's character. The major conflict in the story.

Frank O'Connor, First Confession, pages 187-193.

Frank O'Connor, the nom de plume of Michael O'Donovan, was an only child of poor parents in County Cork, Ireland. He was a meticulous writer, putting his stories through constant revisions, in some cases as many as fifty times. He revised "First Confession," and the version we present here is the final one as taken from the Collected Stories of 1981. His output was extensive, with 67 stories appearing in this final collection. "First Confession" is both good natured and comic, mildly satiric but also affectionately tolerant. Students may sometimes claim to see anti-religious sentiment in it, because the sternness and rigidity of the father, the sister, and Mrs. Ryan are subject to O'Connor's satiric thrusts. A consideration of the amused but understanding priest, however, will support the contention that the story is anything but irreligious. The story presents a fascinating exercise in the analysis of narration. The point of view is first person protagonist, but the Jackie who tells the story is different (older) than the one in the story.

Answers to the Study Questions, page 193.

(1) With the material of "First Confession," a third-person limited point of view would necessarily be more objective and condescending about Jackie, the protagonist. As the story is now, Jackie the narrator shares some of his amusement about his childhood feelings, although he does not seem aware that he still, as an older narrator, possesses many immature attitudes. A third-person narrative could get at this dual effect only with difficulty. (2) Because Jackie does not state his age at the time of his narration, any lack of maturity shown in the narration (such as the feelings about Nora and the attitudes expressed toward women) might be more easily explained as coming

from an adolescent than an adult. The objectivity and amusement with which the portrait of Mrs. Ryan is expressed, however, suggests a mature narrator.

(3) Jackie as a storyteller is quite perceptive because he transmits (a) his true feelings of amusement about Mrs. Ryan, (b) his continued involvement with sibling rivalry, (c) his quaking fear about the approaching confession, (d) his distrust of women, perhaps because of his experiences with his grandmother, Mrs. Ryan and his sister (although his mother seems to be an ally), and (e) his fondness for the understanding and friendly priest.

(4) Obviously Jackie's confession is good inasmuch as it is totally truthful and detailed. To ask the second part of this question is also to answer it, for clearly O'Connor presents an appealing view of confession as practiced by the priest.

(5) Jackie's attitudes toward his grandmother are common ones for multi-generational homes. Similarly, Nora's behavior toward Jackie does not seem unusual or potentially damaging at all; it represents normal sibling behavior. Greater discussion might develop because Jackie as a narrator is possibly an adult at the time he is telling the story. Many students believe that an adult should make a remark or two indicating that all childhood differences are now reconciled, and they therefore question whether the narrator is a person of mature objectivity.

(6) Many things produce laughter, among which might be Jackie's embarassment at his grandmother's habits, his interest in Mrs. Ryan's half-crown, Jackie's climbing about the confessional, the priest's predictions about how someone will eventually go after Nora with a knife, and Nora's bewilderment after the confession. In discussing the causes of laughter, you can note the relationship of situations such as these to principles of rigidity and incongruity. Thus Jackie in the confirmation class should be considering the state of his soul, but instead demonstrates a little boy's concern for the half-crown. In addition, sober and proper behavior is expected in a confessional, and hence the boy's antics are incongruous.

Writing topics: Mrs. Ryan as viewed by Jackie. Jackie as a narrator. The apparent religious views of Jackie as shown in his attitude toward Nora, Mrs. Ryan, and the priest.

Shirley Jackson, The Lottery, pages 194-199.

Jackson was born in California, graduated from Syracuse University, and lived in Vermont. Her stories generally depict unusual, unreal, or bizarre topics in common settings. "The Lottery," her most famous story, has become a modern classic. It skillfully witholds the gruesome outcome until the final few paragraphs, and ends on a note of horror, even though the author plants clues throughout the story that anticipate this ending. The story provides an especially interesting exercise in the analysis of narration and tone; one goal in teaching might be to get students to see the difference between the narrator's careful neutrality and the author's outrage. You might also anticipate Chapter 6 by discussing setting in the story. The seasonal setting--a fresh and sunny full-summer day in June--is used ironically; the beauty and burgeoning life juxtapose dramatically with the horror of the killing. Similarly, the cultural setting in small-town America, complete with village square, bank, and post office, produces an ironic and jarring displacement.

Fruitful discussion might also focus on the characters and their various attitudes toward the lottery. Mr. Summers, a man devoted to <u>civic activities</u>, conducts square dances, Halloween programs, and the lottery (another jarring context, paragraph 4). He is progressive--suggesting a new box and the shift to paper--but finally committed to tradition. Old man Warner (paragraphs 32 and 34) is a stubborn reactionary who objects to any change whatsoever. Mr. and Mrs. Adams (paragraphs 31 and 33) embody the still (and perhaps always) quiet voice of question and change, but they do not act. Tessie Hutchinson accepts the idea of the lottery gleefully until her family is chosen. Then, her self-centered nature asserts itself. Tessie is not the protagonist; if the story has one, it might be humanity (or the villagers) in general. The antagonist might be unthinking adherence to tradition or conventional wisdom.

Answers to the Study Questions, page 200.

(1) The point of view of "The Lottery" is the dramatic or third-person objective. The narrator seems to be a witness moving invisibly though the crowd, and thus is able to see and hear what is happening and how the people are responding. In addition, the nameless narrator has a good supply of extra information about the background of the lottery and also about the activities of Messrs. Graves and Summers the night before. Consistent with the dramatic point of view, the narrator excludes any opinions or explanations of the activities of the lottery, hence permitting the story's suspense. (2) Either an omniscient or first-person point of view would need to include information about matters such the hesitation of the two men (paragraph 4) and the tradition (paragraph 5) of the lottery. In addition, an omniscient or limited omniscient point of view would probably need to personalize Tessie Hutchinson more than at present, and hence would make the conclusion more brutal.

(3) Upon first reading, the conclusion is a definite surprise. There are many hints throughout about the outcome, such as the piles of stones that the boys collected (paragraph 2), the use of the black box (paragraph 5), the <u>sudden hush</u> (paragraph 19), the discussion of quitting the use of the lottery (paragraphs 31-34), and Tessie's anxiety (paragraph 44 and elsewhere). Upon reading the conclusion, students will see that these hints may be read as expressing double meaning. Thus, the conclusion of paragraph 1, in which lunch is mentioned, may be read as an expression about the callous insensibility of those who could return home after the stoning and sit down to eat as though nothing had happened.

(4) The ritual traces of the lottery are mentioned in paragraphs 5, 7, 13, 32, and 49. Although we recognize the lottery as the remnant of some fertility ritual, no one in the story remembers the resasons for holding it annually. Some examples of common anachronistic rituals might be touching wood, throwing salt over a left shoulder, or fearing the path of a black cat.

(5) The story contains both horror and surprise. The two are not mutually exclusive, for the surprise depends upon delaying the information in the conclusion until the very end, and the horror is coincidental with the ritualized public murder of Tessie Hutchinson.

(6) The fact that the characters in "The Lottery" are just ordinary folks emphasizes the reality of the horror that they perpetrate. If they had been criminals, witches, or even primitive tribesmen, such behavior might be expected. It is the placement of brutal action within seemingly innocent people that magnifies the horror.

Writing topics: The dramatic point of view in "The Lottery." The structure of the story. The meaning of the ritual.

WRITING ABOUT POINT OF VIEW IN A STORY, pages 200-204.

In the classroom use of this section it is essential to emphasize that students are to write about point of view as a technique of narration. One of the most difficult aspects to grasp is the fact that a story's point of view has created the story as it actually is. One of the best ways to bring out this detail, and hence to provide students with the materials to be included in their essays, is to stress study questions 1 and 2, particularly 2, for "The Lottery," and questions 1-4 for "Miss Brill." Once students have become familiar with the possibilities of different kinds of points of view, they can undertake a specific assignment with confidence.

The sample essay on "First Confession" (pages 203-204) will repay careful reading because the details included in each paragraph support the topic sentence there. In classroom discussion, you might stress that any one of these aspects so briefly treated in the sample might be more deeply analyzed and exemplified as the basis for an entire essay. Thus, the scenes at home can be related to Jackie's position as a participant and main mover, his experience at Mrs. Ryan's to his being a listener, his trepidations to his intimate knowledge of his own mind, and his confession to his being an actor and responder. Above all, students will need to be reminded that the immediate purpose of an essay on point of view is to help them analyze not things such as an author's symbols and ideas but rather her or his technique as a writer of narrative.

CHAPTER 6

SETTING: PLACE AND OBJECTS IN FICTION

The goal of this chapter is to define and explain the importance of place, objects, and time in fiction. While the various aspects of setting may be defined and discussed abstractly, it is important that classroom discussion be directed toward the uses of setting in stories that your students have read in advance. Thus "The Masque of the Red Death," "The Portable Phonograph," and "Act of Faith" present abundant materials for the study of setting. To a high degree, the first two stories could not be told without reference to the actual physical locations of setting. A classroom discussion of setting should therefore emphasize this interdependence of plot and place. "Act of Faith" is not entirely dependent on the specifics of post-war France, for the scene could equally have been near Rome, or Frankfurt, or some other army camp. But the setting in time and circumstance does have a bearing on the story, and hence this fact could be brought out.

Edgar Allan Poe, The Masque of the Red Death, pages 209-213.

Poe is one of the foremost writers of American literature. He was born in Boston and educated in Virginia and in England. He always struggled against physical and psychological illness, alchohol addiction, and poverty. To make a living he took on various editorships and wrote constantly. "The Masque of the Red Death," for example, was one of his contributions to Graham's Magazine, of which he was literary editor, in 1842.

In teaching "The Masque of the Red Death," you may find that students have trouble with some of Poe's diction, for example, words like sagacious, seclusion, castellated, and impeded, to select words from only the first four paragraphs. A major objective of studying this story should be Poe's use of setting. The description of the abbey is important to stress, as is the irony of walling in death as well as attempting to wall death out. A stylistic study of paragraph 5 might be used to illustrate the way in which Poe evokes mood through the impressions the clock has upon the otherwise carefree revellers. In addition, one might profitably consider Poe's use of color, particularly the color red in the seventh, black room.

Answers to the Study Questions, pages 213-214.

(1) During the time of the story, a plague is devastating the country. The obvious parallel is the Black Death of the middle ages (and 1665), which was the bubonic plague. Students may need reminding that in 1842, when the story appeared, the bacteriological causes of contagious diseases were not yet known. Louis Pasteur, who made these discoveries, was then only twenty years old. Disease could thus be easily construed as having mysterious origins. Prince Prospero's enclosing himself and his thousand followers within his abbey was hence not beyond imagination. Prospero's withdrawal into the walled abbey with his noble friends suggests that he cares little for the common people and much for himself. (2) The abbey itself is described as an impregnable fortress, totally capable of standing up against the siege of an army. The description helps readers understand the power of Prospero, but also to conclude that his thinking is anomalous when his opponent is not a human but rather a supernatural force.

(3) Prospero's suite consists of seven rooms, a number which often figures in numerology (7 deadly sins, 7 champions of Cristendom, etc.). The

The 7 rooms also suggest the 7 days of the week; they are linked to symbolism of time. The arrangement of the rooms is also significant; they are arranged so that only one room (one day?) can be seen at a time (paragraph 4). They are laid out east to west, with the blue room in the extreme east and the black one in extreme west. Prospero's pursuit of the masked figure (paragraph 13) thus moves from east to west (sunrise to sunset, birth to death). The rooms are, successively, blue, purple, green, orange, white, violet, and black with scarlet (a deep blood color, paragraph 4). Light comes through tinted windows from fires blazing in braziers supported by tripods, so that the light in the green room is tinted green, and so on. Poe's intention here is to invoke a mood of eeriness and unreality, except, perhaps, for the white light in the fifth room, for the monochromatic light reduces everything to the same color, and the revellers change as they go back and forth. (4) The last, most awesome room is black with red trim on its window. These colors suggest the fusion of human blood and the darkness of death.

(5) The black room contains the large ebony clock, which is imposing in appearance and confounding in its tolling of the hours. The guests become disconcerted, pale, confused, and tremulous at these sepulchral sounds (paragraphs 5, 7, 8). Certainly the eerie black light together with the dull sound are sufficient to explain its effect of uneasiness. One might also argue that the clock and its sound are symbolic reminders of time and death.

(6) Poe does not describe the dress of the nobles in much specific detail. Instead (paragraph 7) he describes their garb impressionistically as being grotesque, arabesque, beautiful, bizarre, and terrible. The masked figure is remarkable because he is decked out to resemble a corpse with its face dabbled in blood (paragraph 9), seemingly like a victim of the Red Death (see the description in paragraph 1). Prospero defies and challenges the figure, commanding his servants to unmask him so that the person so costumed may be hanged the next morning (paragraph 11). The reaction of a host to anyone disturbing a party is natural and hence Prospero's anger is to be expected. The figure, of course, is (or represents) death.

(7) The central conflict is Prospero's attempt to evade death. Prospero is the protagonist, and Death or Fate the antagonist. The climax of the story is in paragraph 13, when Prospero falls prostrate in death (the crisis begins in paragraph 8, when the masked figure is first seen). The conflict is resolved with the revelation of the spectral nature of the figure and the instantaneousness death of the guests.

Writing topics: The setting. The symbolic and suggestive meanings of setting. The relationship of setting to action at the masquerade. Setting as an aspect of Prospero's character.

Walter Van Tilburg Clark, The Portable Phonograph, pages 214-218.

Clark was born in Maine but spent most of his life in the western United States. His best-known novel is The Ox-Bow Incident (1940), a consideration of fairness and justice in the Nevada frontier. "The Portable Phonograph" appeared in 1942, early in World War II, when American forces were almost everywhere being defeated in the South Pacific, and two years before the invasion of France. The atomic bomb was not publically known at this time, and hence the desolation envisioned in the story is the result of conventional weaponry of bombs and tanks. Even though the note (page 216) explains the

nature of old-style wind-up phonographs, students may need some additional
information so that the significance and uniqueness of the phonograph may be
understood. Sometimes students miss the significance of the threat by the
musician at the end, because the point of view at this time is limited to what
Jenkins can hear. Clark's narrative technique therefore may need stressing.

Answers to the Study Questions, pages 218-219.

(1) The story is set in a bleak, cold, lifeless prairie that has been a
battleground. Heavy tanks have broken up the old pavement on the roads, and
bombs have left large craters, or pits. The land has not yet been able to
recover and regenerate itself, although there are "young trees trying again"
(paragraph 1). The paragraphs succeed in conveying a tone of desperation,
and an atmosphere of harshness. (2) Adjectives such as narrow, cold, and mute
have in common a quality of stillness, constriction, emptiness, and fragility.
They contribute to the impression of lifelessness and bleakness about the
setting, and therefore characterize the world in which beauty and graciousness
are no more than a dim memory.

(3) Jenkins's home is described as a cell (paragraph 3), implying prison.
The dim fire is a kind of deception; it is petty and acrid, and the burning is
chary (spare and meager) and smouldering (paragraph 4). Blankets are old and
dirty, and the wrapping cord is homemade, being put together with grass. Only
a few utensils are mentioned, and those are of tin, which in 1942 connoted
cheapness and tawdriness. These details all suggest the spare, austere life
lived by the few survivors in this devastated world. (4) The host is Dr.
Jenkins. The speaker's reference to him as doctor suggests that he was a
medical doctor, although some students claim that he was a professor of
literature inasmuch as he thought that he "knew all of Shelley by heart"
(paragraph 37). He values literature and music most highly. His possession
of the books, the records, and the phonograph, together with his management of
his little cell, indicate a person of taste who is also practical enough to
retain what he prizes most even under the worst conditions.

(5) The men agree to hear a Debussy Nocturne, primarily because it is
selected by the musician (paragraph 44), whom they regard as an expert. The
reactions are described in paragraph 45. Three of the men sense tragically
heightened recollection while the musician listens more objectively, hearing
no thing but what is there, but his response when the music is over indicates
his heightened emotion and therefore his appreciation. (6) After the men
leave, Dr. Jenkins hides his valuables and rearranges his bed so that he may
see any intruder, because he has heard noises outside and has seen a shadow
indicating that the musician is waiting to enter his cell and steal the
phonograph and the records. In effect, the doctor is being forced by the
musician to return to a state of nature.

(7) If the protagonist is identified as the doctor, the antagonist might
then readily be seen as the musician. If this story is viewed as a political
tract or prognostication, the protagonist is civilization and the antagonist
warfare. Everyone in the story is then a victim of the antagonist; no one
wins. Then too, the story may be read as a piece realistically depicting the
precariousness of civilization. The protagonist would then again be the
doctor and the music, while the musician would be the antagonist representing
the force threatening the continuance of civilization. The story thus would
be a parable about the need for eternal vigilance. In effect, the story ends
during the crisis and technically is unfinished. Thus, the resolution is Dr.

Jenkins's recognition both of the threat and of the need for continued watchfulness and preparedness.

Writing topics: Setting as postwar devastation. The fusion of action and setting. Setting and the characters of Dr. Jenkins and the musician. The use of artifacts. The importance of scene, temperature, and darkness in the mood of the story. The setting as a symbol of destructive warfare.

Irwin Shaw, Act of Faith, pages 219-231.

Shaw began writing in the 1930's, but did not achieve prominence until his novel, The Young Lions, appeared in 1948. His literary output from that time until his death was considerable. Because he also did much work linked with movies, he reached a wide popular audience. "Act of Faith" is a story combining description, dialogue, and introspection, together with epistolary technique inasmuch as Seeger reads an extensive letter from his father, and this letter introduces the topic of anti-Semitism. The point of view is made complex because of the letter and also because it is not clear that Seeger is the major character until he begins reading it. Setting is of course of major significance. To make the places mentioned seem real, you may wish to use a map to locate them. With regard to these references, the story becomes almost literally global, particularly if one also includes references to the South Pacific and Japan (paragraphs 15, 92).

Answers to the Study Questions, page 231.

(1) The states are mentioned in paragraphs 9 (Seeger: Ohio), 10 (Welch: Kansas), and 16 (Olson: California). In the light of Seeger's letter (paragraphs 90-112), and his thoughts about the anti-Semitic attitudes of the man from Boston (paragraph 123), the naval officer (paragraph 125), the combat engineers (paragraph 126), and those telling the million other stories (paragraph 130), a case can be made that the larger setting of the story is the entire United States, even though the immediate setting is near Rheims.

(2) The framing scene is the military camp stretched drearily over the Rheims plain (paragraph 14). Scenes introduced from the past as a means of tracing the relationships among the three major characters and also of establishing Seeger's motivation are the Normandy Beach at D-Day (paragraphs 126-129), St. Lo and the Siegfried Line (paragraphs 17, 141), Strasbourg (116-120), the town of Coblenz where Seeger shot the German officer (paragraph 84) and the Aleutians, where a Jewish officer was insulted (paragraph 125). Scenes of the future are those in Paris (paragraphs 63, 95, 97), in Pacific Grove, California (paragraph 80), and in the Ohio town where Seeger and his family live (paragraphs 90-112). The interaction of these places is complex. The immediate future in Paris is a goal of the soldiers, but Seeger's view of the future governs his decision about whether this journey will be successful. The places of the past and the events there also govern his thoughts about both the immediate and the distant future. Also, the immediate scene of the camp is the location of all plans and recollections.

(3) The mud and the wet grass are a water-connected frame for the story and also a symbol of the entrapment of war and the slippery, precarious future imagined in postwar America. The contrast between the makeshift army camp and the established structures and places of Paris seems clear to the soldiers.

(4) Seeger's acquisition of the Luger is described in paragraph 84. It represents a victory for him and a symbol of justice (paragraph 121), and it also represents a possible armed response to anti-Semitism (paragraph 122). As a means of gaining the $65.00 that would permit the men to have a good time, it is potentially a source of conflict between Seeger and his friends. The climax of the story (paragraphs 141-148) occurs when Seeger decides to sell the Luger; it causes the resolution which is the <u>act of faith</u>.

(5) The immediate central conflict is that between the desire of the soldiers to go to Paris, with all the camaraderie that this trip signifies, and the barrier of their being without money. The greater conflict in Seeger's mind is about the future of Jews in America; his reliance on the good will of Americans, as represented by the proven good will of Welch and Olson toward him, influences his relatively easy but immensely significant decision to sell the Luger. The soldiers hence resolve the first conflict as a result of the expectation that the second conflict will not need resolving.

(6) The point of view is dramatic from paragraphs 1 to 20, when Seeger goes into Captain Taney's tent, where the point of view becomes limited to Seeger. Once Seeger leaves the tent (paragraph 58) the viewpoint goes back to the dramatic, but it shifts back to limited at paragraph 90, when Seeger receives his father's letter. It remains limited to Seeger after this point, when the issue of anti-Semitism becomes the major focus.

(7) Seeger recalls many examples of anti-Semitism in addition to those mentioned by his father. These are related in paragraphs 115 and 121-130. His recollections of Welch, Taney, and Olson all indicate that they have supported him and saved him (paragraphs 141-142) just as they support him in the present (paragraphs 145-146). His act of faith is the leap of confidence he makes from his past experience of support to an expected future of good will and toleration (paragraph 151-153). (8) You might wish to stress that the three other characters also make acts of faith, which are based on their human associations with each other. The faith is thus trust and friendship.

Writing topics: The setting as a frame. The setting and the theme of trust and faith. The setting and anti-Semitism. The symbolic use of the Luger. The use of other artifacts in connection with motivation.

WRITING ABOUT SETTING, pages 231-235.

The problem to confront in teaching this section is that of moving from the abstract descriptions of possible essays to the specific topics about which students will be writing. The most approachable topic on setting for most students will hence be the first one (pages 232-233), on setting and action. With your guidance, students will be able to determine this relationship and apply it to whatever topic you assign or they select. If you assign some of the other possible types you may need to ask specific questions about stories to get your students to express their observations about the uses of setting. Types 4 and 5 will be the most difficult of the five listed. The sample essay (pages 90-96) is based on "The Necklace," a story in Chapter 2. The use of a sample drawn from elsewhere leaves you free to use any of the stories in this chapter for your essay assignment on setting.

CHAPTER 7

STYLE: THE WORDS THAT TELL THE STORY

In teaching this section, you may find that students need assistance in understanding the examples. Thus, for example, the passage from "The Found Boat" on page 243 may need in-class reading and analysis, with the use of the blackboard to illustrate the "they . . ." sentences. Students may inquire why these repeated patterns are not boring, and you may need to respond that the sentences are of unequal length and content, and that they thus illustrate the principle of variety--an important standard of excellence in style.

A good teaching approach, once you have covered the various concepts to your satisfaction, is to go to a story you have already read and discussed, and pick a passage at random for analysis. If you intermingle student comment with your own insights, such an impromptu consideration can build students confidence about approaching their own analyses of style.

Mark Twain, Luck, pages 245-248.

Mark Twain (Samuel Clemens) is one of the major American writers. His best-known fictional works are Huckleberry Finn and Tom Sawyer. Huckleberry Finn is an acknowledged masterpiece which even today, a hundred years after publication, has been made a subject of controversy. "Luck" is a brief story (Twain calls it a sketch) illustrating Twain's art of comic debunking, a characteristic that he also shows in works such as Innocents Abroad and his essay on "Fenimore Cooper's Literary Offenses." The technique is to get an inside, private view of a person of high reputation, and in effect to show that the emperor has no clothes. Because there are two narrators, you might wish to determine their characteristics early in class discussion. The first is fairly straightforward, while the second is much more conversational in manner and denunciatory in tone.

Answers to the Study Questions, pages 248-249.

(1) Twain includes only enough detail to make his concluding point clear, that Scoresby's an absolute fool. He does not provide specifics about the certain line of stock questions on Caesar's Gallic Wars; he gives only the information that the narrator drilled Scoresby on them. In the description of battle (paragraphs 14-16) he is not interested in detail for its own sake, but gives only enough to show that Scoresby turned blunder into triumph.

(2) Examples of humor in the story are the titles of Scoresby (paragraph 1), the fortuitous passing of the exams in Caesar and math (paragraphs 6, 8), the grown men crying (paragraph 12), and the clumsy victory in battle (paragraphs 14-16). Despite the truth that analysis chills humor, a study of any of these passages will show that the comic response is interconnected with Twain's arrangements of words. (3) After the "look, and look, and look" phrase in paragraph 1, the language is elevated in an effort to inflate Scoresby as a recognized giant. Twain's obvious purpose is to use the rest of the story anti-climactically to deflate Scoresby.

(4) This is really a story within a narration. An unnamed narrator sets up the situation of confidential revelation in paragraphs 1-4. The second point of view narrator, the clergyman, tells the story itself. This shift in point of view, from the unknowing narrator to the knowing counsellor and friend (a man of strict veracity with a good judgment of men [paragraph 4]),

43

is designed to authenticate the exposure of Scoresby's blundering career. The clergyman narrator learns everything that he tells, first, because he was an observer and major mover, and, second, because he was present as a participant and observer. (5) The explanation of how Scoresby passed his exams depends on the clergyman's having been an instructor at Woolwich Academy and thus being familiar with the types of test questions usually asked (paragraph 5). The title of the story, "Luck," explains the rest.

(6) In the plot, the exposition is in paragraphs 1-9; the complication in 10-13; the crisis in 14. The climax occurs in paragraph 14, when Scoresby's blundering charge breaks the Russian ranks. The resolution (paragraphs 15 and 16) emphasizes that "the best thing . . . that can befall a man is to be born lucky." In this way Twain ties together the resolution and the title.

(7) Scoresby, the blundering anti-hero, is characterized as a person of reserve, quietness, and nobility (paragraph 1), goodness, sweetness, and lovability (paragraph 6), stupidity and ignorance (paragraph 6), and inability to understand simple directions (paragraph 16).

Writing topics: Twain's stylistic purpose in the battle description, or in the opening paragraph. The differences in style between the two narrators. The way in which the manipulation of style creates amusement or laughter.

Ernest Hemingway, A Clean, Well-Lighted Place, pages 249-253.

Hemingway, one of the major American writers of the twentieth century, developed a sparce style in keeping with the elemental, stark lives of many of the characters he depicted. "A Clean, Well-Lighted Place" is one of his better-known stories, made memorable by the parody of the Lord's Prayer at the end. Students may raise questions about the meaning of the story. There is no ready-made, easy answer, except to respond by analyzing the states of the three major characters: one a wealthy widower and alone, the second old and with nothing but a job, and the third young with a wife and with confidence. The story uses such contrasts to portray the nihilistic despair that can accompany old age in a world of doubt. It contrasts young and old, clean and dirty, light and dark, faith and doubt, and confidence and despair. In the milieu of disillusionment as represented by the parody, Hemingway is posing possible answers to the questions of basic economy: what human beings need is a clean, well-lighted place, where security is created by proximity if not by friendliness.

Answers to the Study Questions, pages 252-253.

(1) The diction of "A Clean, Well-Lighted Place" is middle, the language used by people in their daily lives. The only unusual words are in paragraph 46: "that omission of syntax." These words may be the only ones in the story in which the narrator permits any personal interjection. The Spanish words in the story suggest the Spanish location, and are designed to remind English-speaking readers that the principal characters are thinking and speaking in Spanish. Other stylistic considerations: Hemingway's style is spare and terse with mostly short sentences, choppy dialogue, and very simple diction. The words are mostly concrete and specific; the key abstraction in the story is nada. You might look at paragraph 1 with students as an example of Hemingway's style. The sentences are long but simple; phrases are strung together with conjunctions such as and or but.

(2) Of the waiters, one is old, and declares that he lacks "everything but work" in his life (paragraph 66). Nevertheless, he wishes to help and serve others, such as the drunken old man. This waiter understands the old man and sympathizes with him. The second waiter has youth, confidence, and a job (paragraph 64), but he is insensitive and self-centered, and he has little sense of obligation toward others. His shallow and selfish attitudes can be shocking; he wishes the old man had killed himself because "I'm sleepy now" (paragraph 17), and he claims that "an old man is a nasty thing" (paragraph 42). Like the other characters, this young waiter lacks a name, thus making him more representative and universalized. The older waiter may represent the wisdom (or despair) of old age; the younger one the callow and selfish demands of youth. The two men may be readily identified by their speeches, one of the master strokes of the story. Identifications would have added length to the story without accompanying clarification.

(3) The first sentence of paragraph 9, one of the longest in the story, describes the cafe and the terrace; it thus delineates the clean, well-lighted place. The other three briefly depict the girl and the soldier. In this way, the paragraph separates the scene from the outside world. The sparseness of these descriptions emphasizes the fleeting, temporary state of the inhabitants of the scene. As in the first paragraph, the first sentence here is long but simple, made up of phrases strung together like beads. The soldier and girl might be construed as emblematic of the modern world: the soldier's brass number suggests dehumanization, while the girl's lack of a head covering (a traditional sign of religious devotion in Roman Catholic Hispanic societies) implies that religious values have been discarded.

(4) The point of view is dramatic up to paragraph 76, when it shifts to limited omniscient as the older waiter closes the cafe, goes to a bar, and seems to recite the parody of the Lord's Prayer. (5) The conflict in the story is more properly a contrast between the two waiters. The older waiter, with his sense of service (or work in the Existen- tialist sense) is tolerant and helpful, while the younger waiter possesses no such sense but nevertheless has confidence. There are other conflicts, or contrasts: (a) between the expected satisfaction of wealth and its actual disappointment (the old man's attempted suicide), and (b) the expected comfort of religion and the conviction that there is nothing. The resolution is the older waiter's determination to continue to serve, even though he has no rest in his life. With the old man who drinks alone in the cafe, the resolution is in the alcohol with which he drives away the memory of bereavement.

(6) The parody of The Lord's Prayer substitutes the Spanish word nada (nothing) in all the key noun positions in the prayer. In light of the termination or futility of what we ordinarily think of as giving satisfaction, Hemingway is using the story to illustrate the minimum needs by which one can define human beings. The title describes the minimum need for habitat. The old waiter illustrates the minimum need for outreach.

(7) The setting is not described in full detail, but is included only to place the ongoing developments of the story. Hence, for example, the bar in paragraphs 77-84 is hardly described at all except as the older waiter considers it as an unpleasant contrast with what he believes people need in life (see the beginning of paragraph 76 for his description). The streetlight (paragraph 9) is introduced only as it illuminates the brass number on the collar of the passing soldier. The other descriptions of places and things in the story are more impressionistic than detailed.

Writing Topics: Hemingway's style in the descriptive passages. His use of style to distinguish the two waiters. The level of diction in passages of action and speech. The use of Spanish words in the story.

Alice Munro, The Found Boat, pages 253-259.

Munro, born in 1931, was brought up in Wingham, Ontario, twenty miles east of Lake Huron. Her output of stories has been copious, and she is today recognized as one of Canada's foremost writers. She often uses settings from small-town life, of which "The Found Boat" is an example. In teaching the story, you may discover that the emphasis on budding sexuality in the story comes as a surprise to many students who believe that the first half is more about the boat than the young people. It hence becomes necessary to study the first part of the story to demonstrate the details of boy-girl relationships established there. You may wish to refer to pages 237-238 and 243-244 for further discussions of Munro's style in "The Found Boat."

Answers to the Study Questions, page 260.

(1) The descriptive passages of "The Found Boat" are specific and accurate, but most also introduce an element of human response and involvement. Paragraph 10 demonstrates this movement from description to character. Also, paragraph 1 focuses on reactions of young and old to the flood.

(2) The level of diction among the boys is generally low, with contractions and interjections (paragraph 4), profanity (paragraphs 7, 8), and grammatical mistakes (paragraph 22). Eva's language is more at a middle level, as is Carol's, although Carol indulges in slang in paragraph 55, and Eva uses an insulting slang term in paragraph 12. (3) Paragraph 10 suggests that Eva has a strong imagination and a yearning for magic worlds of romance. With her becoming the point-of-view character at this point, the style is elevated to reflect her brief romantic reflection. Her taunting of the boys in paragraph 12 is comically contrasted with paragraph 10.

(4) The last paragraph emphasizes the actions of the girls in getting out of the water and in developing their giggling fit. The action verbs and participles are <u>giggle</u>, <u>slapping</u>, <u>splashing</u>, <u>set</u> about <u>developing</u>, <u>showed</u>, <u>snort</u>, <u>start up</u>, <u>make</u>, <u>bend over</u>, <u>grab</u>, and <u>had</u>. Some of these are neutral, but many are graphic and vivid. The verb <u>snort</u>, which usually is used in reference to animals, is probably a perfect choice to describe the giggles.

(5) <u>Truth or Dare</u> is a game which lets the young people objectivize private wishes in a mixed friendly setting. The concluding dare is the command to strip, which is initiated by Frank (paragraph 73). In effect, the game is a ritualized form of the emotional jockeying that has been carried on earlier through insults and the mutual effort of repairing the boat.

(6) Eva and Clayton are clearly though not formally attached to each other, as is shown in paragraphs 51 and 89. All their activities together, including the often deprecatory expressions, indicate sexual attraction.

(7) The plot of "The Found Boat" may be seen as a conflict or contrast between sexual desire and the obstacles preventing it as represented by reasonably moral youthfulness. The complication is the discovery and repair of the boat, which offers the chance for companionship under the guise of

cooperative effort. The crisis is the decision to strip and run to the river, and the climax is Clayton's ejection of water from his mouth onto Eva's breasts. The resolution is that the girls will try to resume their lives as they were before, although their giggling suggests both their heightened emotions and their realization that they are moving toward adulthood.

(8) There are many details of setting in "The Found Boat." The lifestyle and artifacts suggest a poor or working-class environment in the days before electronic entertainments. The town is graphically realized, as is shown in paragraph 47, where the recovery of winter's detritis is described. If the story is considered symbolically as an awakening of sexuality, the cold flood and the promise of warm water suggests the developing maturity of the major characters.

(9) Frank is the planner (paragraph 47), and also an initiator; he is the one who suggests that everyone strip, but he does not seem to be capable of carrying out the action of repairing the boat. Clayton is the doer and the finisher. He knows instinctively what to do (paragraphs 30, 47). Bud is less well realized, and remains flat. Eva, as indicated by her reverie (paragraph 10), her stripping first (paragraphs 83-85), and her suggesting a denial of the frolic (paragraph 97), is clearly the superior of the two girls.

Writing Topics: The style of the descriptive passages. The use of colloquialisms and slang. The relationship of style to character. The style in a paragraph (such as the last one).

WRITING ABOUT STYLE, pages 260-265.

Because writing about style must begin with the analysis of detail, the in-class work with style may be profitably developed from the many questions on pages 260-261. If you select a passage from any story, and show how the questions may produce materials that may be fitted into an essay, students may be guided to see that they too, with these questions as analytical guides, may be able to produce materials suitable for their essays. Because the story chosen for analysis in the sample essay is from Chapter 5 (pages 187-193), none of the stories in this chapter on style has been pre-empted, although the text itself contains illustrative commentaries on two paragraphs from "The Found Boat." The sample essay may be longer than essays your students may write, but it is presented as an example demonstrating how a number of approaches may be used in a single essay. Here the classroom reading of the sample, together with comments, will clarify the writing task for students.

CHAPTER 8

TONE: ATTITUDE AND CONTROL IN FICTION

The aim of this chapter is to introduce tone as a broad concept that includes literally everything that can make up a story. Tone begins with an attitude, and a study of tone should attempt to define and delimit the attitude. But then--and this point is most important--the consideration of tone should analyze and explain how the attitude is transmitted. Hence students need reminding that to study tone is to consider the evidence in the story of the author's awareness of the role externally of speaker, character, circumstance, language, probability of action, and appropriateness of setting, and internally, of audience and also of the author himself or herself.

Americo Paredes, The Hammon and the Beans, pages 274-277.

Americo Paredes is a Hispanic storyteller, essayist, and poet, closely linked with the plight of Mexican-Americans living in Texas. "The Hammon and the Beans," first published in The Texas Observer in 1963, is a poignant story about the death of the narrator's playmate, but in a broad social and economic perspective it is also a portrayal of the plight of poor immigrants.

Answers to the Study Questions, pages 277-278.

(1) Paredes places the grandfather's house near the fort, thus introducing the military and political background of a border town at this turbulent time in Mexico. With this back drop, the connection of the children with the soldiers is made naturally, and Chonita's dependence on them for food is logical. The dirty yellow of the narrator's home suggests that even the better-off Mexican-American residents did not live luxuriously. The shack of Chonita's family indicates poverty (paragraph 12).

(2) The narrator is apparently an adult recalling events that occured in the 1920's. The advanced age might be expected to produce understanding and persepective, but such a perspective is not apparent. Instead, the narrator simply recalls the events, responses, and feelings only as they occurred to him or her as a child. There are similar narrations in Joyce's "Araby," page 339, and O'Connor's "First Confession," page 187.

(3) The fort creates an apparent conflict of loyalties in the people of the town (paragraph 5). Though they live in the United States, they do not identify themselves with the American soldiers in the fort, as symbolized by their feelings of alienation about the flag. The children admire the soldiers but hoot at them because they are, in effect, an occupying army.

(4) The protagonist is, on one level, Chonita, and the antagonist the illness and poverty that destroy her. On another level, the protagonist is the human force present in even the lowest of the low, and the antagonist is the failure of the political system to assimilate and nurture all people.

(5) Chonita is described as a "scrawny little girl of about nine" (paragraph 14) who has a dramatic flair (paragraphs 16-17). Her family consists of her mother, who does washing (paragraph 12) and a stepfather who, though resourceful, is often drunk (paragraphs 12, 32). Chonita's behavior suggests great persistence (paragraph 7) along with incipient craving for recognition as a performer. (6) She is flat because she is a child and makes

no choices. She does come to life, however, and seems real and lovable. She is also representative of her class of Mexican-Americans, for her plight and her death symbolize the results of poverty and neglect. Dr. Zapata is, in effect, Paredes's raisonneur of these ideas (paragraphs 23-42).

(7) The central conflict in the story is between U.S. traditions, represented by the soldiers, the presence of the fort, the food eaten by the men, and the lessons in American history, as opposed to the Mexican-American tradition represented by Chonita, the poverty of her surroundings, the disrespect of the children, and Chonita's death. The climax of the story is in the narrator's thoughts about Chonita in heaven (paragraph 45). The resolution is in the narrator's improvement of feeling.

(8) For Paredes's use of situational irony as a response to this question, please see text pages 271-272. For further explanation of tone, one might consider the pathos exhibited in the sorry plight of Chonita as she receives a scolding before being given food (paragraph 11). Here the technique is the narrator's description, with no additional commentary. Dr. Zapata expresses indignation at Chonita's death, and is supplied by Paredes with substantiating details (paragraphs 24 ff.).

(9) Dr. Zapata's being a physician, thinker, and a caring person makes his anger credible. His claim that he is not a political revolutionary is also consistent with his concern for the personal plight of persons like Chonita. (10) The story explores the problem of cultural assimilation (the attitudes expressed toward the soldiers), poverty (particularly Chonita and her family), inadequate health care (her death), and the Mexican revolutionary movements led by Villa and Zapata. In this political and economic context, Chonita's life and death may be considered as an example of what may happen on a broader scale to children brought up in neglect.

(11) Clearly the tradition of Marion the "Swamp Fox," as quoted from Bryant's poem, is of concern to all United States citizens, but the irony is that the children are not being taught about their own ethnic traditions. (12) The women of Bryant's song are lovely and happy, while Chonita still wears her rags and speaks her pitiful English, even though she flies like a butterfly (paragraph 45). Though the narrator is not specific about his or her own feelings, it is logical that he or she would feel at least some indignation about Chonita's untimely death.

Writing Topics: the techniques used by Paredes to control the tone of the story. Dr. Zapatas impact on tone. The connection between the tone and the economic-political situation. The irony in the education of the children of the town. The tone of the conclusion.

John Collier, The Chaser, pages 278-280.

John Collier (1901-1980) was born in England but wrote in America; he was known for sardonic and macabre but finely crafted stories, and his output was considerable. His use of the dramatic point of view in "The Chaser" needs classroom attention, for the success of the story depends on the privacy between Alan and the old man. The story demonstrates Collier's grim amusement, wry condemnation, and irony. With great subtlety, Collier exposes the folly of romantic posessiveness, and in this respect forces the reader to reconsider human relationships.

49

Answers to the Study Questions, pages 280-281.

(1) The plot is based on the conflict between Alan and his romantic naivety, on the one hand, and the cynicism of the old man. The poison (paragraph 7) is undectable and kills without trace; the love potion (23-37) commits the drugged woman to become a love slave to the man who gives it to her. The connection between the two, according to the insinuations of the old man, is that a man seeking the love potion will eventually demand the poison (the glove cleaner). He makes this connection three times, verbally linking the drugs by speaking about both (paragraphs 7 and 17) and by saying that if he pleases a customer with one item, "he will come back when he needs another" (paragraph 15). (2) In this plot the protagonist is Alan. His problem is that his love for Diana is unrequited. The love potion is the solution to the problem and the resolution of the ostensible conflict; the sale of the potion is the climax of the story.

(3) The irony of the story's resolution suggests that the conflict is between love as a negative, master-slave relationship, and love as affection of equals. Without the irony, the resolution of the plot is that Alan gets his love potion and leaves. The new problem is the old man's au revoir (until later), an indication that Alan will someday return for the poison.

(4) The characters in "The Chaser" are flat and representative, for they do not develop. This characteristic permits the story to focus on the issue of love relationships. In addition, by using this flatness, Collier prevents the sympathy that might result from human and round characters, and therefore he focuses the negative tone against Alan and the old man.

(5) Alan is young and full of desire, and he responds to frustration not by making himself personable but rather by seeking absolute control, which he has confused with love. The old man apparently misunderstands love also, for he offhandedly indicates that wealth might buy love (paragraph 13). Nevertheless, he knows that love is not the slave-like devotion that Alan seeks.

(6) Diana, from what little we learn about her, is popular, engaging, individualistic, understanding, and admirable (paragraphs 24, 26, 28). The old man says that after she drinks the potion she will be totally dependent and submissive, and that she will lose her identity (paragraphs 23-37).

(7) The old man's room is poorly lit, dirty, and drab. Nothing is arranged to be attractive; instead things seem sordid (paragraphs 1-3). Even the entryway suggests nasty furtiveness (dark and creaky stairs, dim landing). This dreariness underscores the mood of secrecy and and conspiracy about Alan's desire to control Diana. The darkness complements the old man's deceptiveness, which he disguises by his apparently sincere speech.

(8) The point of view is dramatic, or third-person objective. This lets Collier present the details without explanation or evaluation, and forces readers to do all the interpretation.

(9) The words here are evocative with regard to tone, particularly because of the story's dramatic point of view. There are few direct reflections of response by the characters; therefore the ones that are present should be viewed carefully. In addition, the old man's control of the conversation should be studied closely to determine how Collier illustrates the skillful and diabolical nature of this character. For specifics, one

could select words everywhere in the story, but in particular <u>nervous</u> <u>as a</u> <u>kitten</u> suggests Alan's youth (paragraph 1); <u>attempting a look of scientific</u> <u>detachment</u> (paragraph 20) indicates a degree of impatience but also indicates that at a future time he will remember the poison. Words suggesting the calculating nature of the old man are <u>Bountifully</u>, <u>insistently</u>, <u>everlastingly</u> (paragraph 19); the old man's reference to the poison as a <u>glove cleaner</u> and his final <u>Au revoir</u> demonstrate his cynicism (paragraph 45).

(10) The success of the story depends on the dramatic irony. Alan does not know where his desire to possess Diana will lead, but both the old man and the readers do. In addition, the old man's condition may be viewed as situational irony, for he victimizes others, but does so because he himself has apparently never understood that happiness might be gained from a good human relationship. The story thereby gains double irony resulting from a victim victimizing others by preying upon their ignorance.

(11) The title is ironic because a chaser may be (a) one who pursues in love, as Alan is doing with Diana, (b) one who hunts with a desire to catch or kill, as he also is doing, and (c) one drink taken to wash down an earlier drink. The concluding words of the story are ironic because they are commonly spoken to mean <u>good</u> <u>bye</u> but literally mean <u>until</u> <u>later</u>. They thus refer to Alan's eventual return for the poison and create a sinister conclusion.

(12) "The Chaser," as we have already stressed in other questions, deals with love and desire. It explores the idea that love cannot be slavish devotion. Indeed, it suggests that such devotion ultimately breeds hatred; it emphasizes that love cannot be coerced without destructiveness, that youth may succumb too easily to thoughtless desire and confuse it for love, and that desire may be destructive if it is not guided by understanding and toleration. The furtiveness and conspiratorial design of Alan and the old man negatively illustrate the need for fusing individuality with romantic commitment.

Writing topics: because the sample essay (pages 291-293) of this chapter treats the tone of the story, and the sample essay in Appendix A on evaluation deals with satiric aspects of the story (pages 1631-1633), you should be careful to devise assignments that are not pre-empted. Some possibilities: the tone of the old man's speech. The character of Alan. The use of irony.

Shirley Jackson, About Two Nice People, pages 281-288.

This story is presented lest students get the idea that Jackson wrote no more than one story ("The Lottery," pages 194- 199) and that she was incapable of humor. "About Two Nice People" offers many examples of the means by which laughter, or at least a happy response, may be evoked. Students may need to be reminded about the importance of the title in the creation of the comic mood, for the action would be less amusing if Walter and Ellen were less appealing. Of special note is Walter's aunt, whose role contradicts Walter's intentions and who serves as the agent hastening the climax of the piece. You may find that this story, which depicts character in a pleasant light and tries to encourage a pleasant view of life, presents a tone unmixed wih irony, anger, disapproval, and the sinister.

Answers to the Study Questions, pages 288-289.

(1) Both Walter and Ellen are carefully described though not highly differentiated: Ellen in paragraph 3 and Walter in paragraph 4, with a short comparison of the two in paragraph 5. Ellen emerges as the rounder or fuller character because she is the center of interest and also is capable of humor (paragraphs 58, 110). Walter is seen slightly more objectively than Ellen. They seem to be sterotypes of young unmarried people, particularly because Jackson does not include many details about their interests. Their marriage is described only in the last sentence of the story (paragraph 113), and it seems stereotypical.

(2) The story offers an almost classic example of structure coinciding with plot: paragraphs 1-5, exposition; 6-60, complication; 61-102, crisis; 103-109, climax; 110-113 resolution. The various pranks of the game occur mainly in the complication, while the crisis is the interview with Mrs. Nesmith. Obviously the game is courtship, without either character seeing this reality until Mrs. Nesmith explains it in her own way.

(3) The setting is the adjoining apartments of Ellen and Walter and the hallway leading to the elevator. The detail of the easily confused phone numbers is also a part of the setting. The jobs and interests of the two main characters make them suitable for each other despite the surface anger of their game. The scene's being on the third floor isolates the action from the rest of the world and therefore prevents any exterior problems or concerns from preventing the story's happy mood.

(4) The central conflict opposes Ellen and Walter, though a case could be made that it is the natural good will of both characters against the state of anger in which they find themselves. There are thus either human or abstract protagonists and antagonists. The complication is developed through the series of pranks. The crisis is in the Mrs. Nesmith scene, and it is resolved as Walter and Ellen confusedly realize that they do not despise each other.

(5) Mrs. Nesmith is round because she goes to Ellen with the assignment of intimidating her, but cannot fulfill this inhuman role in so obvious a human situation. We learn that she is kindly and benevolent though projecting a rough, stern exterior.

(6) The point of view is third person limited, with the emphasis on Ellen. The limited omniscience of the speaker does not, however, reveal any depths of Ellen's character, but instead concentrates on her reponses to the war with Walter. A deeper omniscience would necessarily need to reveal more about her emotions and therefore would make the farcical incidents seem more deliberate and therefore more harmful. At the end, once Ellen has giggled, the speaker again considers the opening topic of anger, and then retreats to the dramatic point of view to describe the marriage briefly.

(7) There is dramatic irony because the characters think they are waging warfare but instead are expressing emotions toward each other that, once established, can readily turn to love. The resolution thus demonstrates the benevolence of nice people. Jackson uses the farcical incidents as a means of showing how Ellen and Walter extend their relationship by devising new means of keeping contact. Because the pranks are not harmful, Jackson keeps readers amused and interested. By thus making the war a limited one with unspoken rules of behavior (paragraph 60), she preserves lightness of tone.

(8) The three possible legal actions are sufficient to indicate the sinister forces that may be generated by arguments over nothing. The story is kept comic and light when Mrs. Nesmith enters because this lady refuses to threaten eviction, and also because she loudly insists that Ellen and Walter are simply playing a love game.

Writing Topics: Jackson's irony (whereby the characters are drawn together by forces that they expressly deny). The tone of the portrayal of Ellen, or of Mrs. Nesmith. The tone of the farcical incidents. The humor.

WRITING ABOUT TONE IN FICTION, pages 289-293.

You might wish to teach this section in tandem with the section on tone in poetry (pages 641-665), where the topic is exclusively the poem. There is a need to emphasize that the study of tone requires an analysis of how attitudes are shaped and controlled, not merely the identification of the attitudes themselves. This point needs contant stressing. Because there are two sample essays in the text on Collier's "The Chaser" (pages 291 and 1631), you might assign this story beforehand, and use it as the reference point for your classroom discussion. Thus, in determining the tone of this story, you might stress how the reader's perspective is shaped by the way in which Collier shows the limitations of the two major characters.

The types of essays you choose to emphasize will be governed by what you might assign. With tone, however, it is probably good to go into a significant amount of detail in class about the particular plan to be followed. It is not out of order, also, to lead a general discussion of the story you have chosen, without dealing with all the specifics of tone. Such coverage liberates many students to consider tone without needing also to create their own interpretations from scratch. Obviously, students who wish to maintain their own readings are always free to do so. As further aid to students for this assignment, you might wish to set up paragraph-length exercises on particular spots in, say, "The Chaser." The benefit of these written exercises is that you can immediately address yourself to encouraging good approaches and correcting misperceived ones.

CHAPTER 9

SYMBOLISM AND ALLEGORY: KEYS TO EXTENDED MEANING

The aim of this chapter is to help students develop a working knowledge of this most fundamental characteristic of literature. In teaching the subject, you may encounter uneasiness about symbols or allegorical patterns. For this reason you may wish to discuss a number of stories with the sole aim of determining whether and why certain elements and actions may be taken symbolically or allegorically. You may also wish to make references to the chapter on poetic symbols (pages 784-813), particularly if you are about to move from fiction to poetry.

Aesop, The Fox and the Grapes, page 300.

Not much is known about the fabulist Aesop. The tradition is that he was a freed slave who lived from ca. 620-560 B.C. Aristotle claimed that he had been a public defender, but there is no other evidence that he existed at all. In fact, versions of some of the fables were known a milennium before his time. Aesop might therefore be considered as much a collector as a creator of fables. "The Fox and the Grapes" has given us the phrase "sour grapes," and you might begin by asking if any of your students know the meaning of the phrase. From there it is a natural step to stress the applicability of the fable to the general attitude of people to the unattainable.

Answers to the Study Questions, page 300.

(1) The fox exhibits normal traits: he needs to satisfy his hunger and he knows that he can get the grapes only by leaping for them. He is also normal enough to maintain his own self-esteem by denigrating the prize when he fails. These characteristics are essential to the moral because the genre of the fable depends on the normal and general qualities of human character.

(2) The plot develops out of the desire of the fox for the grapes, and his inability to get them. The resolution is his minimizing the reward he cannot gain. (3) Obviously his claim is a rationalization. Students may miss the moral that human beings should not justify their own shortcomings by resorting to distortions and lies. Aesop is stressing the need to recognize truth both about oneself and also about the world outside.

(4) The fable as a genre features animals with human traits who carry on a brief action designed to illustrate human truths. The need for animals as protagonists (and antagonists also) is to enable the fabulist to concentrate on the topic without any unnecessary complication.

Writing topics: the fox and the grapes as a symbol. The nature of the fable as a genre. The nature of the action in the fable.

St. Luke, The Parable of the Prodigal Son, pages 300-301.

Although little is known about Luke, evidence in Collossians, Philemon, and II Timothy indicates that he was the beloved physician and travelling companion of the Apostle Paul. His story of the Prodigal Son is told in the words of Jesus. You may therefore wish to claim particular respect for the text, because some students have taken offense at scripture being interpreted away from their own churches. As long as the limits of the discussion are made clear, however, most students will take a lively interest in a literary approach to the work.

Answers to the Study Questions, page 302.

(1) The Prodigal Son is self-indulgent and improvident, but he is also introspective and he has the courage to admit his mistake and to confess his unworthiness. He is round because he does indeed grow to recognize and admit his error. It is necessary that he also be representative to the degree that the religious promise of the parable is designed for all people.

(2) The plot depends on the contrast between the forgiving parent and the headstrong son. The antagonism against which the son strives is also his self-caused poverty and his recognition that he has ruined his life. The religious point of the parable is the father's speech (verses 31, 32), which he makes in response to the angry words of his other son. This older son represents the traditional eye for an eye punishment, and he therefore is to be contrasted with the all-forgiving father. (3) The parable resolves with the father's acceptance of the Prodigal Son and his explanation of why he has rejoiced at the return. There is no "happily ever after" conclusion because the parable stresses the character of the father.

(4) The parable may be analyzed in this way: 11-13, exposition; 14-16, complication; 17-19, crisis; 20, climax; 21-32, resolution. These sections coincide with the development of the plot, except that the resolution takes up more than half the story. It would not be incorrect, in fact, to label the resolution a second story that might be entitled "The Angry Older Brother," for this section has its own brief plot development with its resolution in the father's explanation. In purely technical terms, the Older Brother's anger might be considered a second complication of the parable, except that the resolution of the Prodigal Son's story has already occurred. It is probably best to think of the parable as a form, therefore, in which the structure is governed more by theme or ideas than by traditional demands of plot.

(5) The point of view is limited omniscient in verses 12-21, with focus on the Prodigal Son. In verses 22-32 the point of view is dramatic, featuring the older son and the father. The Prodigal does not appear in these verses. This shift is coincidental with the shift in the structure of the parable. (6) The parable as a form shares many characterisics of fiction: i.e., plot, character development, description, dialogue, and a relatively consistent point of view. The central difference is that the parable stresses theme.

Writing topics: the Prodigal Son as a symbol. The parable as an allegory of the possibility of forgiveness. Shifts in point of view in the parable.

Nathaniel Hawthorne, Young Goodman Brown, pages 302-311

Hawthorne, a friend of the fourteenth president of the United States, Franklin Pierce, is one of the great American writers of the nineteenth century. His most famous work is The Scarlet Letter (1850). Throughout his writing there runs a conflict between freedom and conventionality, with those who choose freedom being subject to the pain of guilt. "Young Goodman Brown" embodies this conflict.

(TEXT PAGES) 302-312

Answers to the Study Questions, pages 311-312.

(1) The protagonist is Young Goodman Brown. The antagonist is ostensibly the devil, the spirit resembling Brown's father (paragraph 13). In fact, however, the antagonist might be Brown's own destructive sense of guilt--the projection of his own sinfulness upon others and his consequent damnation of them. (2) The central conflict seems to be between Brown and his decision to take his journey, or perhaps between Brown and the figure of the devil. The resolution occurs after Brown's climactic denial in paragraph 68. His life is changed after this because his faith in others has been shattered, and he thus alienates everyone around him. The real conflict may be between Brown and his own willingness to see evil in others--his inherently corruped world view.

(3) The level of reality of the story is that Brown's journey is a dream. In psychological terms, he may be schizophrenic, because his view of others is distorted by his own convictions. It is probably best, however, to stress that his gloom results from his religious fanaticism. If his visions came out of his mind, they suggest Brown's willingness to see evil everywhere.

(4) Brown is a round and dynamic character. Beginning as a seemingly good husband with a high estimate of the local minister (paragraph 21), his change into a foreboding, gloomy spirit marks a total alteration. (5) The point of view is limited omniscient. Because Hawthorne stresses Brown's distorted perceptions, this point of view is essential. Either a straightforward first person or a dramatic viewpoint would require much more explicitness, which in turn would upset Hawthorne's intention to expose the vagueness and questionability of Brown's experiences.

(6) The sample essay (page 331) discusses the topic of symbolism. There are additional symbols, such as the withering of the maple twigs (paragraph 38) and the fire at the forest meeting (paragraph 53), to name two. The symbols suggest death and hell. Ironically, though Brown disavows the devil (paragraph 68), these symbols ultimately prevail in his consciousness. (7) In Salem, the details are normal: the threshold, street, bed, meetinghouse, church, pulpit, and grave. The forest setting is much more detailed, with trees, path, and the woodland meeting described as an open space in the dark wall of the forest, the altar-like rock, the blazing pines, the dense foliage, and the vague and sinful hymn, all bathed in red light. One can justify seeing the forest setting as symbolic because it is a focus of Brown's preoccupation with sin, and because there the devilish figure describes his awesome power (paragraphs 63-65).

(8) The sins are commitment to the devil and, as in paragraph 63, sins of seduction, murder, greed, infant murder, and general evil. The common thread of these sins is overpowering self-interest, concealment, and hypocricy.

(9) In terms of allegory, Faith is a guide, holding Brown back from his self-indulgent journey away from honest devotion and into the forest of error and delusion. The journey suggests the moral ambiguity and laxness that people sometimes allow to beset them. All the lesser characters are a part of Brown's journey into evil and of his life afterward. Thus Deacon Gookin and Goody Cloyse meet Brown on the street (paragraph 70), and therefore they touch again the theme of Brown's disaffection with hypocrisy. Here, however, the narrator presents these characters as virtuous, and Hawthorne thus emphasizes Brown's distorted vision. Ironically--and situational irony is a major aspect of this story--Brown becomes evil while pursuing good and supposed godliness.

56

For these reasons together with a number of others, the forest journey is certainly allegorical.

Writing topics: the story as allegory. The network of symbols. The relationship of setting and character. Young Goodman Brown as a symbol.

Marjorie Pickthall, The Worker in Sandalwood, pages 312-317.

Marjorie Lowrie Christie Pickthall was born in England but spent much of her life in Canada. She wrote two novels, and her poems were published post-humously in 1937. Her stories were collected and published in one volume the year after her death. "The Worker in Sandalwood" exemplifies the deftness and exquisiteness of her touch as a writer. The main occurrence in the story is not presented as a miracle that definitely happened. Instead, it comes clouded, as though in a dream, from the distant past. Mysteriousness rather than certainty is the nature of the detail. Students may need to learn something about the apprentice-master relationship, for otherwise they may not understand the absolute power that L'Oreillard has over Hyacinthe.

Answers to the Study Questions, pages 317-318.

(1) The point of view is the first person, an unidentified speaker who has acquired his or her information from Hyacinthe and also has spoken about it with the Cure and Madame. The narrator knows more than might have been learned from these sources, however, because he or she fills in extra details, as in paragraph 15, that would probably not have been supplied by the informant, Hyacinthe, who, as the speaker says, spoke in wood, not in words (paragraph 7). The stress on long ago is one of the devices used to deny the need for total investigative truth that a more recent event would require.

(2) Hyacinthe is a kind and deserving boy of fourteen who has great skill with wood but otherwise has no imagination. His dreams are dumb; his fancies are slow and reluctant (paragraph 7). He has a strong sense of pride in perfecting his work (paragraph 11), and he is generous with his possessions (paragraph 26). He is sensitive, however, and laments his loneliness and personal pain (paragraph 13). He accepts his cruel treatment as his normal lot, and is not at all vengeful. (3) The narrator pities Hyacinthe because he is a growing boy (paragraph 4) who has one of the hopeless despairs of childhood (paragraph 13). This compassion, together with the narrator's focus on Hyacinthe, directs sympathy toward him.

(4) The tone of the story is controlled principally by the narrator's regular emphasis upon her or his sources of information. Thus, Pickthall emphasizes the possibility and plausibility of the miracle without claiming it as an actual event. Also, Pickthall does not state that the visiting boy is actually Jesus, but instead she provides objective details that should lead us to this identification. The tone is thus one of restraint, permitting readers to admire the beauty of the miracle without raising objections about fanciful or unrealistic circumstances. By this means Pickthall undercuts any objection that the story is sentimental self-indulgence.

(5) In contrast to the gentle Hyacinthe, Pierre L'Oreillard is cruel and negligent, spending more time drinking than working. He indulges his sadistic personality by thrashing Hyacinthe whenever things do not go according to his wishes, and his thrashings are cruel (paragraph 11). He does very little work

on the pretext that he is no longer strong (paragraph 9), even though he is strong enough to beat Hyacinthe.

(6) Hyacinthe is a round character, for he is very well delineated and he also develops faith in the strange child who finishes the cabinet. Pierre is well described but flat. The Cure and Madame do not appear sufficiently to rise above the flat stage. The strange child is flat though described with great resonances. The flatness of all the characters but Hyacinthe keeps the focus upon Hyacinthe and therefore emphasizes his deserving nature.

(7) The setting of the woodworking shop on Christmas Eve may be construed as a symbol of religious hope (it also evokes the trades of both Joseph and Jesus). The hurt bird which the boy carries in is a part of the symbol of healing power, as is the clause "where the wild does went to drink" (paragraph 17). These animals are not hunters, unlike the wolves mentioned in paragraph 23, but instead are prey, just as Hyacinthe is subject to Pierre L'Oreillard's exploitation. The symbolism refers to the poor in spirit and the pure in heart who, in keeping with the Scriptural allusiveness of the story, will receive the Kingdom of Heaven and shall see God. (8) The symbols associated with the stranger are all consistent with Jesus as described in the New Testament (Luke 2:42). The training as a carpenter suggests a realistic skill of construction as well as the healing skill of the servant of God, thus providing a scriptural base for the symbolism of the story.

(9) A strong case may be made that the story is an allegory describing the process of difficulty-despair comfort provided by compassion as represented by Jesus and also by any person who provides mercy and assistance. With this kind of reading, L'Orillard represents forces of antagonism both physical and emotional; Hyacinthe represents a deserving person in great need; and the stranger represents the belief that aid and comfort will come to those who have faith.

Writing Topics: The story as allegory. Symbolism. The resonances of the strange child. Biblical allusion.

John Steinbeck, The Chrysanthemums, pages 318-325

Steinbeck attended Stanford University and worked at odd jobs in the 1920's, as he also began his career as a writer. A number of works preceded his best-known novel, The Grapes of Wrath (1939), for which he received the Pulitzer Prize in 1940. His output was steady after this time, and he won the Nobel Prize for literature in 1962. His fiction is often set in rural areas (especially in California) and features a realistic and somewhat pessimistic view of life. A number of his novels have been made into films, the best known of which is The Grapes of Wrath (1940) which starred Henry Fonda.

The elements that may be stressed in teaching this story include (but are not limited to) setting, character, symbolism, and theme. "Chrysanthemums" is a story about character and a statement about society (or social roles, expec-tations, limits). The central character is Elisa Allen; the story focuses on her situation. Steinbeck uses a great deal of symbolism to help define Elisa for us and to underscore her place in the family and society. In teaching the story you may encounter an initial difficulty that students have in following what has happened. Here a stress on symbolism may prove especially fruitful as explanation, for the dark speck on the road (paragraph 108) is the pile of earth in which Elisa placed the chrysanthemum shoots. Sometimes students

claim a dislike for Elisa, but if they can see the story as one about a failed
personal relationship, they can be persuaded to care about her and thus to
find the story interesting. As always, understanding can overcome aversion.

Answers to the Study Questions, pages 325-326.

(1) For the most part, the narrator observes Elisa dramatically (third
person objective), and utilizes omniscience only in paragraphs 108 and 109,
and possibly also in 110. The advantage of this mostly dramatic rendering is
that the reader is left to infer the nature of Elisa's feelings of elation and
therefore of her great disappointment. The method forces us to place our
sympathy, thus making the story stronger than it could otherwise be.

(2) The plot is built up out of a central conflict between the potentially strong, upwelling vitality and sexuality of Elisa, on the one hand, and
the isolated and stultified life she leads, which does not permit fulfillment
or self-expression. Thus, the central conflict is internal: will Elisa escape
(emotionally, physically, psychologically) and achieve fulfillment or will she
remain trapped (by setting, convention, role). Elisa is in a secondary
conflict with her husband, who compliments her but sees her as an economic
asset rather than as a woman. There is also a conflict between Elisa, seeking
approval for her femininity, and the Pot-Mender who like Henry tries to
manipulate her for economic gain. The climax of the story is in paragraph
108, when Elisa sees the pile of dirt and realizes that her emotions have been
thrown down along with the dirt. This climax resolves the central conflict by
making Elisa realize that her feelings cannot be expressed. Her tears in
paragraph 121 thus signify her lost dreams of reaching personal fulfillment.

(3) Henry is flat, though he is by no means made to seem contemptible.
He does not understand Elisa's emotions at all, for he thinks of her gardening
skill as a means of improving his orchards (paragraph 12), and after her hopes
have been dashed he still thinks she is happy (paragraph 112). Henry's major
function in the story is to help delineate Elisa and to underscore the boring
and unromantic nature of her life.

(4) The setting (paragraph 1) is symbolic because it complements Elisa's
isolation as a woman. The time of the year is December, when things have
ceased growing, and the foothills around the valley prevent the sun (a
universal symbol of growth, intelligence, and fertility) from reaching the
farm. The description of the fog, which "sat like a lid on the mountains and
made of the valley a closed pot," suggests limitations and entrapment. The
Allen ranch suggests that everything is finished and put away, with nothing
more to do. The neat, hard-swept and hard-polished house points toward
sterility and compulsive cleanliness. The fence around the flower garden
symbolically implies separation, isolation, alienation, and entrapment. These
aspects of the setting symbolize the bleak prospects for Elisa.

(5) There is a brief illustration on page 1677 responding to this
question. Essentially Elisa is wearing clothes that hide or mask her sexuality and femininity, such as the large corduroy apron, the heavy leather
gloves, the clodhopper shoes, and the man's black hat. The clothes--a symbol
worth exploring in detail--symbolize Elisa's suppressed life on the ranch.

(6) The central symbol is the chrysanthemums, which are described in
paragraphs 6, 8, 12, 27, 50-71 (especially 71), and 108-109. (7) They symbolize Elisa's strong sexual and nurturing power, which is channelled into the

59

flowers (sublimated). The connection with dirt, which she handles with great skill, suggests an earth-mother force. Her description of proper care of the buds in paragraph 71 suggests that she receives satisfaction only in providing care for growing things. Because she does not have children on whom to bestow this talent, she transfers the force to the flowers; she has <u>planter's hands</u> instead of mother's hands.

(8) Elisa at first refuses to employ the Pot-Mender (paragraphs 43-49). He changes her mind by expressing great interest in the chrysanthemums and getting her to make up shoots for his non-existent other customer (paragraphs 50, 58). Elisa gets increasingly excited as she makes up the pot (paragraph 64) because she is exerting some of her creative force. The reason for the accompanying change in her attitude (paragraph 75), is that her love for the flowers easily changes to sexual desire. This renewed sexuality is expressed in a number of actions, including Elisa's removing her hat (paragraph 63), shaking out her hair (63), swelling breasts (72), husky voice (74), and reaching out toward the pot-mender's legs (75).

(9) In the washing and dressing scene (paragraphs 93-98) Elisa wishes to make herself pretty and sexually attractive. The pumice is a normal means of sloughing off dead skill cells and uncovering live ones. For this reason it is a symbolic means of causing her sexuality to emerge, just as her care with her dress symbolizes her desire to be attractive. The scene can be considered as a ritual of purification (clensing before a return to her husband) or a ritual of renewed sexuality and the hope for romance.

(10) Elisa's responses, including her foreknowledge, her hurt, her anger, and her private despair, are described in paragraphs 108-121. The dumped flowers as a symbol indicate the truncation of her creative, sexual desires. Henry sums all of this up by noting that Elisa has <u>changed again</u>. Elisa's questions about prize fights may represent a desire for revenge (men have isolated and betrayed her) or a last grasp for freedom (going to the fights would be something out of the ordinary). At the last, she settlers for wine with dinner, saying "it will be enough." Elisa's "crying weakly--like an old woman" shows us that it is not enough and that Elisa has given up the fight.

Writing Topics: the symbolic value of the setting, Elisa's clothing, the chrysanthemums, or the washing scene. Elisa's plight and women's status.

WRITING ABOUT SYMBOLISM AND ALLEGORY, pages 326-332.

By the time you work on this section you will already have been talking about symbolism and allegory in a number of stories. Thus, students should be well prepared for the assignment. The biggest problem they will encounter, and what they will likely be asking about, is the task of what to say once they have identified a thing or narrative as symbol or allegory. Here the schemes on 326 and 327 might be introduced as aids for the development of subtopics for essays. You might wish to encourage students to develop their own tables or graphs. As you teach the various structures for essays, you might wish to use some of the stories in this chapter. Certainly the sample essay (330-331) offers an approach for an essay based on a number of separate symbols. This structure is easiest for most students. You might also use, say, the symbolism of the flowers in Steinbeck's "The Chrysanthemums." This story is a fine example for showing the extent of a symbol in an entire work. It also demonstrates the relationship of a symbol to character.

CHAPTER 10

IDEA OR THEME: THE MEANING AND THE MESSAGE IN FICTION

This chapter aims at introducing students to the meaning of the words idea and theme, and to the means by which they are made significant in fiction. The earlier chapters have actually been, in their ways, introductions to the use of fiction as idea. Thus point of view (Chapter 5) is one means by which authors dramatize ideas and make them authentic. Symbolism (Chapter 9) is a concrete means of rendering ideas.

Teaching students about the material in this chapter will involve a good deal of discussion about what exactly is meant by the word idea. Related words that might lend clarification are concept, thought, opinion, belief, and meaning. Conception, interpretation, motif, analysis, and explication might also arise, together with others that your students might think about. What is most important is that ideas should be expressed as full sentences or assertions, for stories are genuinely dramatic renderings in narrative form of a moving idea. Thus the complete sentence as a form should be stressed as an initial stage in the perceptions of ideas.

James Joyce, Araby, pages 339-342.

Joyce was born and educated in Ireland, but he left in 1902 and spent most of the rest of his life in Switzerland and France. His best known works are Dubliners (1914), A Portrait of the Artist as a Young Man (1914-1915), Ulysses (1922), and Finnegan's Wake (1939). Much of his work has been called "fictionalized autobiography," and "Araby," one of the stories in Dubliners, is representative. As a young child, Joyce actually lived on North Richmond Street, and the so-called "Araby in Dublin," a "Grand Oriental Fete," was held in Dublin from May 14-19, 1894, when Joyce was the same age as the narrator at the time of the story. Students may wonder why the narrator expresses unexplained chagrin about himself at the end. This question cannot be easily answered without resort to a discussion about the narrator's sense of guilt about his youthful feelings of love.

Answers to the Study Questions, page 343.

(1) The point of view is first person, with the narrator himself (or a younger version of him) as the involved participant. Granted the confessional nature of the story, this mode of narration is the most material and authentic one that Joyce could have chosen, for the narrator himself is the only authority for the inner feelings, the imaginings, and the actions that are disclosed. (2) The narrator is an adult telling about events that occurred when he was an early adolescent. If one considers the story as fictionalized autobiography, the time of the events can be determined as 1893-1894, with Joyce then being a boy of eleven and twelve. It is difficult to determine the age of the narrator when telling the story, except to note that he is not yet mature himself, for he still evidences embarrassment at his childhood feelings (see, for example, the end of paragraph 4). The effect of the distinction between narrator and character is to create a degree of detachment if not total objectivity about the events. The narrator, for example, seems distant enough from the prayerful O Love sequence to share the scene with the readers despite the fact that it is amusing (paragraph 6). For comparison, a similar use of point of view may be found in O'Connor's "First Confession" (pages 187-193).

(3) The details of setting, being derived from scenes of Dublin itself, seem real and authentic. The reality of place lends its credibilty to the story. There are many well-used adjectives. In paragraph 3, for example, are short, sombre, waste, useless, curled, damp, cold, silent, dark, muddy, soft, dripping, odorous, and half-opened, These adjectives are quite accurate, but beyond their creation of vivid images, they also shape a sense of time past, memories preserved through dark and dim light. Very little, for example, happens in daylight. When the narrator goes to market on Saturday evenings he goes through flaring streets and is jostled by drunken men just as he is also thinking of carrying his chalice. The setting in this way is at odds with the narrator's enthusistic dreams of romance. Images of light and brightness would be more in accord with his feelings, but the setting is drab, dank, and dark just like the climax and resolution of the story.

(4) Before the narrator goes to Araby, this bazaar symbolizes for him his adoration of Mangan's sister and also an Eastern enchantment (paragraph 12) of the mystic fulfillment of love. At the end it comes to symbolizes unreality and unreachable hope which has been dashed by his adolescent lack of power and by the passive-aggressive and drunken uncle.

(5) The speaker is smitten with love for Mangan's sister; thoughts of her dominate his imagination. His feelings are normal. His inability to buy the gift should produce unhappiness and disappointment, but the response of being driven and derided by vanity is extreme. This story is marked by its accuracy and craft, and thus you might look with your students at the earlier parts for some sort of preparation for the conclusion. Foreshadowing evidence of guilt associated with love can be found in paragraph 4, where the speaker watches Mangan's sister through the inch-wide gap between the blind and the sash. In other words, the speaker acts with shame well before his concluding pain.

(6) It is telling that the speaker uses the phrase set the boys free in refering to the school, for the words are fitting to a release from prison. The speaker virtually endows the houses with a life that encourages decency, but which does not develop humanness and love. Blind is a normal term for a dead-end street, but it is also appropriate to a group with no understanding of human impulses. The relationship of first to last paragraphs is subtle but real, for the speaker evidences anger not only for himself, as at the end, but also for the culture out of which he came, as at the beginning.

(7) The idea is that youthful love is childish and foolish but that it is also normal, overpowering, and creative. Ideally, such memory as the speaker has should be remembered with fondness. Much of the speaker's memory exhibits just such beauty. If the experience of the childhood crush produced unhappiness at the time it occurred, a mature understanding should be able to filter through the childhood misgivings and remember the affection with joy. The speaker, however, does not indicate that this process has taken place, and hence Joyce is presenting a portrait of a narrator who is still a victim of childhood inhibitions.

Writing Topics: the point of view. The ideas about love and inhibition explored in the story. The relation of setting and theme. The symbolism of the fair. The development of ideas. The dead priest as a symbol.

D. H. Lawrence, The Horse Dealer's Daughter, pages 343-355.

Lawrence was born in an English mining community but received an education sufficient to allow him to become a teacher and writer. He fictionalized
these early years of his life in the novel Sons and Lovers (1913). His most
controversial work, Lady Chatterley's Lover, was printed privately in Italy in
1928, but was not published until the 1960's in the United States. His power
to shock his immediate contemporaries was caused by his emphasis on the vital
role of sexuality and passion in human growth and stability. "The Horse
Dealer's Daughter" is typical of this theme, inasmuch as both main characters,
Mabel and Fergusson, have reached an impasse in their lives by themselves, and
can turn in new directions only when they recognize the power of their sexual
needs for each other.

Answers to the Study Questions, pages 355-356.

(1) Before the story opens, the father of the Pervin family has died in
debt (paragraph 95). The adult children do not have sufficient means to keep
the family enterprise together, and as a result they must go their separate
ways. Some adjectives describing the scene are desolate, desultory, dreary,
strange, sullen-looking, and impassive, all from paragraphs 2 and 3. These
adjectives complement the emptiness and bleakness of the Pervin household now
that it is being abandoned. (2) One of the first of these young adults, Joe
Pervin, is compared to the draught horses in paragraph 7. These are slow but
strong (with a slumbrous strength [paragraph 6]), and are in harness, as Joe
will be once he marries the daughter of the nearby estate steward. Joe is
also compared to horses in his movements in paragraph 20. Another brother,
Fred Henry (paragraph 11), is like horses too, for he is under the control of
the situations of life even though he masters horses easily.

(3) Mabel is rather short, sullen looking with a face of impassive fix-
ity (paragraph 3). She felt the loss of her mother deeply, but enjoyed the
power of ruling the household for the following ten years. She has developed
no friendships with either women or men (paragraphs 95-97), and treats her
brothers with contempt (96). As the story begins, she has has nowhere to go,
no plans, and Lawrence's speaker stresses that she has reached the end
(paragraph 98). Apparently she does not want and will not take temporary
residence with her sister Lucy (paragraph 12). (4) The speaker points out
that Mabel lived for many years "in the memory of her mother" (paragraph 97),
and somehow, vaguely, she believes that the breakup of the family is bringing
her closer to the dead mother (paragraph 98). Her going to the grave also
suggests the increasing power of death over her (paragraphs 99-102).

(5) Jack Fergusson is a doctor whose main friends are the three Pervin
brothers. Now that they are leaving he, too, is at an impasse, for the locale
seems insufferable (paragraph 106). His first responses to Mabel (paragraphs
76, 81) suggest an unspoken and unacknowledged but nevertheless powerful
attraction. (6) In paragraph 103 the speaker notes some mystical element that
touches Fergusson as he looks at Mabel in the cemetery. This power is further
explained in paragraph 104 as having the strength of a drug. When he sees
Mabel attempting to kill herself, he does not feel alarm, but fears that he
might lose her altogether (paragraph 108). These two examples suggest that he
is slowly realizing his emotional tie with her.

(7) The drowning and rescue are described in paragraphs 110-115. The
setting here is wetness, dankness, muckiness, and a foul smell (the smell is
mentioned a number of times later). To determine this setting as a part of
mood, one must conclude that Lawrence is suggesting that unpleasantness is a

necessary part of life, and that at times the environment is ugly and threatening. (8) Despite their obvious reluctance and inexperience with their emotions, both Fergusson and Mabel realize their love, which gives them both confidence and doubt (paragraphs 142, 150, 152, 158, 159, and 191). From paragraph 142 to the end, Lawrence is at great pains to emphasize their ambiguous feelings. (9) In paragraph 150, Lawrence brings out the idea that love is overwhelming and irresistible. To live without love leads people literally to the impasse in which both Mabel and Jack find themselves in the first part of the story. (10) The reason for which Lawrence emphasizes the ambiguity of love is that he is not espousing any easy answers: all problems will continue, as will some of the personal reservations that people have about each other and themselves. Love, however, is the Lawrentian basis of life. The sample essay (pages 372-374) deals further with this idea.

(11) The image of the harness in paragraph 7 has symbolic validity for most of the characters. The brothers will be in harness from henceforth. Because both Mabel and Fergusson are round characters, however, their responses are much more individualized. For the first time in their lives they are being awakened out of their slumbers. Their love is not in their own control, but their problem becomes what to do with their love once they find it. The paradox of love as presented here is that peope like Jack and Mabel must take their own reins--take control of their own emotional lives.

Writing topics: the idea about the barrenness of a loveless life as exemplified in the three brothers. The ideas represented by the horses and the harness. Lawrence's complex ideas about love as shown by the pond. The meaning of the wet, soggy, musty clothing in relationship to love.

Ralph Ellison, Flying Home, pages 356-369.

Born in Oklahoma, Ellison attended the Tuskeegee Institute in Alabama in the 1930's. He has taught at a number of colleges and universities. His major novel, Invisible Man (1952) earned him a National Book Award. Although his topic material is rooted in the plight of blacks, he is also concerned broadly with the condition of all people aspiring to improvement.

Answers to the study questions, pages 369-370.

(1) The point of view is third person limited omniscient; Todd is the center of interest. The advantage of this mode of narration is that we see all the action as Todd sees it. In addition, his thoughts and responses are immediately accessible. Jefferson's narrative can be readily introduced in the story because Todd hears it. Also, when Todd recalls his childhood memory of airplanes, his thoughts may be readily expressed because the narrative method makes them an integral part of the story. (2) The protagonist Todd is opposed by his pain, his sense of guilt at having crashed the plane, the troubles resulting from his color, and Graves. More broadly, the central conflict is the one blacks have in realizing their potential despite both active and passive opposition. (3) The climax of "Flying Home" is subject to debate. It could be Todd's hysterical laughter in paragraph 227, which establishes his identity as a complex person in his own right, or it could be in the very last paragraph, when Todd is carried by Jefferson and Teddy away from Graves's field, thus establishing the need for blacks to pull together and cooperate with each other.

(4) For Todd, flying and airplanes symbolize hope and aspiration, the right to dream about the future and to realize full potential. As a result, his crashing the plane because of the buzzard (or jimcrow) is a symbolic failure because it is not only a crashing of his own life's dreams, but it is also the crashing of the dreams of his race. (5) A number of things in the story are symbolic. The dust on the plane suggests that Todd's idealistic dreams of following a profession face obstacles that derive from the earth itself--namely, his color. The sun, which is high (paragraph 50) and then begins setting (paragraph 213), is a symbol of Todd's being out in the open as a human being, with his errors exposed. The sun is also a symbol of challenge (paragraph 212), aspiration, and opportunity (paragraph 237). The animal references symbolically suggest the low status of blacks. The buzzard being the jimcrow symbolizes the opposition of the white social structure.

(6) As a character, Jefferson is round because in his story he illustrates his individuality despite the commands of the white St. Peter (paragraphs 117, 123). The boy, Teddy, is flat. Both characters illustrate the traditional subservient role of blacks (paragraph 209). (7) Jefferson's story in paragraphs 98-126 is a brief parable and allegory of a black in white society. His assertion that he was the "flyinest sonofabitch what ever hit heaven" (paragraph 126) represents black power and ability, and links this allegory to Todd's aspirations as symbolized by flying. That Todd does not immediately understand the allegorical application of the tale to his own plight suggests that he does not yet believe that other blacks can have aspirations like his own. In other words, Todd is a growing and changing (round and dynamic) character in the story.

(8) The digressions--Jefferson's tale and Todd's memories--are essential to the broader meaning of the story, for they deal with the general aims of blacks and also with the specific aims of Todd. They also add significant resonance to the symbolic value of flying in the story. They are integrated into the action of the story because Jefferson tells his tale to comfort Todd while they wait for help, and because Todd's childhood memories are part of the temporary delerium resulting from his injuries.

(9) When Todd thinks of officers, he associates them with his own failure and fear of displeasing them (paragraph 15). Jefferson (paragraphs 200-211) hates the fact that Graves, the white landowner, is both dependent on blacks and is also arbitrary and cruel in his racial hatred. The attitudes of the two black men are similar because they result from normal aims being frustrated for discriminatory reasons.

(10) The idea underlying the crash, the buzzard, and St. Peter's flying regulations demonstrate the theme that blacks have normal aspirations, that their mistakes will be misconstrued as reflecting on their race (paragraph 93), and that they cannot expand normally because of suppression (see also paragraph 213, when Todd has an image of Ku Klux Klan hooded figures).

(11) Graves (a symbolic name) is flat, static, and representative. His kicking and straitjacketing Todd illustrate the difficulty of the black situation, for he is a menacing racist of the worst sort (paragraph 237). (12) Graves's straitjacket (paragraph 215) is a symbol of the need for whites to lie to explain the normal dreams of a black. The reason given by Graves for the straightjacket is that blacks must be crazy if they try to imitate whites in their choice of occupation (paragraph 220). In paragraph 179 the same idea is raised by Todd's mother, who accepts her inferior role.

Writing topics: the symbolism of flight, or the symbolism of animals. The importance of the names in the story. The meaning of the digressions. The plot as a clash of ideas about blackness and the white power structure.

WRITING ABOUT MEANING IN FICTION, pages 370-374.

In the classroom use of this section, the examples of interpretive commentary on pages 370-371 might provide a good beginning for analysis. Thus the very first example illustrates the method by which details of the text may be directly channeled to the discussion of ideas. You might stress here that the two sentences are designed to show a model of discussion. Obviously an entire essay will be longer and more detailed. But students should be persuaded to see the pattern working of (1) story content, (2) artistic presentation, and (3) interpretive commentary to explicate ideas.

The six models for the body of an essay on page 372 are designed to encourage student experimentation with the ways in which essays may be developed. The aim should be to use as many of these as possible and to query students on the material that might be included in a full-scale essay. The sample essay on pages 372-374 provides an example of how the first model may be developed. The third model suggests how an individual character study may be used as the means of explicating ideas.

If you have enough time, you might discuss parts of the sample essay to show how story materials may be shaped in an essay to substantiate an idea. The fourth paragraph on page 373, for example, relates both Jack's common cold and his accidental seeing of Mabel to his discovery of love and thus to his being restored as an individual. It is instructive to stress how this para- illustrates the pattern students should seek when writing their own essays.

ADDITIONAL STORIES

John Cheever, The Season of Divorce, pages 375-382.

Cheever, sometimes classified as a New England author, also wrote stories about New York city dwellers and suburbanites. His The Wapshot Chronicle (1957) earned him a National Book Award. Usually his stories are based firmly in realistic settings, such as the well-conceived environment of the New York east fifties in "The Season of Divorce." In such settings, Cheever creates unusual and sometime bizzarre situations: a vengeful woman threatens to shoot a man who deserted her; a man narrowly escapes death in a crashing plane, and when he returns to his suburban home nobody pays any attention to the incident; another man begins going home on a route which enables him to take a swim in many of his friends' pools, but when he gets home he discovers that his comfortable life is totally gone.

With such twists on reality, one begins seeking symbols in the work of Cheever, and "The Season of Divorce" is no exception. The passion that Dr. Trencher develops for Ethel in the story could certainly happen in real life in just this way, but the unusual development of the attachment points out that Ethel is to be seen not only as a desirable woman but also as a symbol of women overwhelmed and truncated by marriage, children, and the grind of life. Her outcry in paragraph 77, together with what we learn about her background as a bright student who has studied in France (paragraph 2) points up this combination of realism and contextual symbolism. Her husband, the first-person narrator, seems to be jealously involved in Dr. Trencher's pursuit of his wife, but otherwise he expresses no concern for her--another way in which Cheever accentuates the idea that the grind of married life destroys the spontaneity of early love and courtship.

The story develops its plot by building a number of conflicts. These are (a) the contrast between Ethel's present life as against both the one she had when young and the one Trencher wants to give her, (b) the struggle the speaker and Ethel have in keeping their household going (such as caring for their sick children) and (c) the increasing annoyance the speaker feels for Trencher. The title, "The Season of Divorce," suggests that the story may actually lead to a dissolution of the marriage, but it does not. Cheever's realism here focuses on the daily rounds of life experienced by the speaker and Ethel. An outright divorce would not fit into this pattern. As a result, Cheever sets the story structurally within the frame of dinner and lighted candles (paragraphs 3 and 78). Ironically, the candles at the end seem more like those lighted for the dead than for the elegant little ceremony of dinner for which they were lighted at the story's beginning.

The basic theme of "The Season of Divorce" hence is the the imposition of routine upon normal, desirable, and desiring adults, and the consequences in dissatisfaction, regret, and resignation. Trencher's passion for Ethel brings out this theme: no matter how people may work against restraints, the prospect of chaotic results keeps the principal characters on track, for they are basically responsible people.

Writing topics: the plot as a conflict between the potential and the actual in Ethel's life. Cheever's realistic and symbolic use of setting. The character of Ethel, or Trencher. The first-person narrator as an involved but also detached figure in the action.

Anton Chekhov, Lady with Lapdog, pages 382-394.

Chekhov, best known for his plays, wrote many stories during his brief
career. "Lady with Lapdog" was relatively late, after The Seagull, and just
at the time he began making his big mark with his plays in Moscow. The story
provides an excellent model for the study of plot and structure. The conflict
is between Gurov's reluctance to love and become involved, on the one hand,
and his being drawn into love with Anna Sergeyevna and finally being consumed
with it, on the other. Chekhov neatly divides the story into parts, so that
Part 1 comprises an exposition, and Part II the beginning of the complication.
The divisions after this point are more concerned with the time sequence and
locations of the story, so that the crisis does not occur until paragraph 119,
with the climax in paragraph 120. Some students may point out that the crisis
and climax occur earlier, at the intermission of the concert, in paragraphs
90-104. Either possibility would offer a class the opportunity for discussion
about the shaping of the story.

Perhaps of greatest interest in "Lady with Lapdog" is the character of
Dmitry Dmitrich Gurov. He is the focus of the limited third-person point of
view, with his background, interests, thoughts, self-reproaches, and observations being reported by the narrator, who seems consistently to be
sympathetic to him. Initially Gurov is in the grips of ennui, a womanizer who
gets excitement only from illicit affairs even though at the same time he
holds women in contempt. His alteration because of his increasing love and
obsession for Anna is responsible for the compelling nature of the story.
There are obvious comparisons to be made between Gurov and Smirnov of
Chekhov's own The Bear (pages 49-58), Trencher in Cheever's "The Season of
Divorce" (pages 375-382), and Jack Fergusson in Lawrence's "The Horse Dealer's
Daughter" (pages 343-355). There is a parallel, also, between the conclusion
of both "Lady wth Lapdog" and "The Horse Dealer's Daughter."

Chekhov's characterization of Anna Sergeyevna is less well developed than
that of Gurov, but he does succeed in showing her as a woman living in the
aftermath of too early marital commitment (like Gurov) who is seeking but not
expecting the involvement she finds with Gurov. In a number of ways she may
be compared with Ethel of "The Season of Divorce" and Mabel of "The Horse
Dealer's Daughter," although the parallels of circumstance and character are
not as close as those for Gurov and the male characters just mentioned.

Students may find some difficulty with the setting of "Lady with Lapdog,"
because they might not know Russian geography. The problem is not great,
however, for Yalta is a Black Sea resort town, and most students know that
Moscow is well to the north. Of greater interest is the use that Chekhov
makes of setting. Mostly the settings are metioned insofar as they become
scenes of action. Interestingly, a detail that is not needed, but which
Chekhov mentions, is the long grey fence studded with upturned nails in front
of Anna's home. One is tempted here to look at the fence as a contextual
symbol of the difficulties that Gurov and Anna will face. The dog, too, may
be construed as a contextual symbol, for it is the link that first connects
the two, and in paragraph 84 it dominates Gurov's mind as he reproaches
himself for having travelled from Moscow to see Anna. Thematically, "Lady
with Lapdog" treats the topic of the nature and power of love. Gurov embodies
a number of attitudes, ranging from sexual excitement and involvement, to
boredom and disentanglement, to his ultimate infatuation, obsession, love, and
commitment. With such a range of attitudes linked to one character, students
may find the opportunity for an exciting discussion.

Writing topics: Gurov or Anna as changing characters. The role of the narrator as a commentator in the limited omniscient point of view narration. The nature of the story's conflict. Setting and symbol. The theme of love as both obsession and problem. A comparison of Gurov or Anna with characters from The Bear, "The Season of Divorce," and/or "The Horse Dealer's Daughter."

Joseph Conrad, Youth, pages 394-414.

Conrad, whose full name was Teodor Josef Konrad Korzeniowski, was born in the Ukraine of Polish parents. His family was exiled for political reasons, and he was orphaned at an early age. When 17 he went to sea and remained a sailor until he was 38, having risen in the British merchant fleet to the position of captain. English was his third language, the first two being Polish and French. He claimed that he was captured as a writer by the magic of the English language, and that if he had not known English he never would have written at all.

"Youth" is one of Conrad's longer stories. It was written in 1898 and published in 1902. The basic conflict is one between the individual, Marlow, and the natural barriers to the successful completion of his task. There are general implications as well, for at the outset Conrad's first narrator lets us know that the story is designed to represent life itself (paragraph 12). This representation is often compared to the human situation as presented later in Existentialist philosophy, with its emphasis on freedom and activity as principal aspects of life. Conrad's exact portraiture of shipping, ports, storms, and life about the burning Judea, together with his releasing Marlow to travel to Java aboard his first command--a fourteen footer-- symbolizes the attempt by human beings to find value in the world that they otherwise neither control nor understand. The task of doing all jobs well, such as trimming the forsail even though everyone on board believes that the ship is doomed (paragraph 71), is therefore symbolic of the necessity for controlled action to preserve pride and identity.

The story has two narrators. The first is an authorial first-person speaker, who may or may not represent the author himself, and whose voice is heard in paragraphs 1-3, and 121-125. Once the narrator introduces the setting at the table, he transmits Marlow's tale verbatim, so that Marlow, though a first-person narrator, is actually being filtered through the mind of the first narrator. Marlow's story is told from paragraphs 4-120. Conrad does not preserve this dramatic situation consistently, however, for he endeavors to create a virtual present-tense scene by having Marlow interrupt the story to request wine (paragraphs 16, 24, 32, 53, 58).

Beyond the symbolism of the general situation, "Youth" abounds in symbols. The name Marlow itself has been noted as being close to Maro, the last name of the ancient Latin poet Virgil. The trip aboard the Judea, which contains burning coal, is analogous to the trip to the underworld in Virgil's Aeneid, with Mrs. Beard being a sybil-like figure in this pattern. The name Judea, together with the the smoke and fire, suggests the wanderings of the ancient Hebrew tribes in the Sinai desert. Through such allusiveness, Conrad creates universality in his symbols. He also develops contextual symbols, such as the ship sinking with all its identifying names having been obliterated (paragraph 94). The symbolism is that death is a leveler that blurs all earthly distinctions. The rats leaving the ship also may be read as a symbol in the context for Marlow remarks about it after fire is discovered (paragraph 51). That the boy Abraham goes mad (paragraph 26) could be read as a symbol of how traditional religious answers to life have proved inadequate for contemporary problems (Abraham was the founder of the Hebrew faith and the spiritual founder of Christianity). An ironic symbol is the profanity that Marlow hears from the ship Celestial once he and his small boat crew reach port (paragraph 96). Celestial (the word means heavenly) usually refers to heaven and angels, and therefore the language more appropriate to the infernal regions seems deliberately designed to suggest that faith has undergone a reversal in the modern world. And what about Mahon, pronounced mann, who had never got on (paragraph 6)? One does not need to search hard in "Youth" for these symbols; they literally spring out of the story.

The most significant theme in "Youth" is brought out in the title and throughout the story. You may wish to consider separately the paragraphs where the theme is discussed: they are paragraphs 39, 40, 55, 64, 78, 91, 97, 120, 124, and 125. The topic of youth might be considered as initiation, the commencement of responsibility, and the test of one's abilities. In addition, because of the age of Marlow the narrator, forty-two when he is telling this story about himself at twenty, and also of the first narrator, the view of youth is presented from a perspective of nostalgia, regret, and sadness. You might wish to stress the final word of the story, illusions, in this regard, for throughout, Marlow the middle-aged adult is stressing how the hardships of the voyage are intermingled with his youthful aims and hopes.

By way of specifics, the Judea is a sailing vessel, even though steam-ships were also in use at the time visualized for her voyage. The Somerville, in fact, the vessel that tows the Judea, is a steamer (paragraph 69). The Judea leaves London for Newcastle, and after its early vicissitudes on the water, it sails south around the Cape of Good Hope for Bangkok, in Thailand. Presumably the plan of the voyage was not made with the Suez Canal in mind, even though that Canal was available for shipping after 1870. The Judea sinks south of Java, and therefore the small boats make straight for this land, never reaching the destination of Bangkok, farther to the north. Throughout the story there are many references to parts of a ship, which may be explained with reference to a dictionary. In paragraph 2, Conway refers to the Merchant Navy Cadet School in Anglesey, where naval officers were trained. The P.& O. is the Pacific and Orient Line, which is still in business with headquarters near Trafalgar Square in London.

Writing topics: Symbolism in "Youth." The first-person narrators. The use of setting. The character of Marlow the man of 42 compared with Marlow the man of 20. The theme of youth: its definition, dreams, accomplishments, and impermanence. Conrad's use of allusion. The geography of the story.

Langston Hughes, Slave on the Block, pages 414-419.

James Langston Hughes was born in Missouri. He received a BA from Lincoln University there in 1929, and when he came east he became one of the leading figures in the Harlem Renaissance, which included Countee Cullen, Jean Toomer, and Claude McKay. He wrote extensively, producing volumes of poems and stories, and he also wrote a number of plays.

"Slave on the Block" is one of the stories from The Ways of White Folks. It is representative of this collection, dealing with themes of condecension, exploitation, and developing anger. The setting of the story lends realism to the incidents, for the Carraways live in Greenwich Village (a district of Manhattan south of Fourteenth Street) but frequent areas of Harlem (from 110th to 155th Streets). At the beginning, the narrator demonstrates the life style of the Carraways by referring to their taste in art, music, and literature, and also to their social pretentions (meeting W.E.B. DuBois, sociologist, novelist, black leader, and one of the fouders of the NAACP, and wishing to kow Carl Van Vechten, a white patron of the Harlem Rennaissance). Throughout, Hughes introduces passages from songs of blacks (paragraphs 38, 48), and also refers to a popular tune "You Rascal You" (paragraph 51). Students may understand Michael's mother's annoyance if they know that the complete line in the song is "I'll be glad when you're dead, you rascal you."

The story may be considered a satire on the patronizing attitudes of some whites toward blacks in the 1930's. Thus the Carraways embody the failure of whites to understand blacks in human terms. Both Michael and Anne see Luther, for example, not as a person but as a potential painting (paragraph 7) or song (paragraph 6), and they see Mattie as no more than a servant. When Mattie and Luther start exhibiting human qualities that are totally normal (paragraphs 43, 45, 46) the Carraways are annoyed principally because their art objects have come to life.

This view of the Carraways leads to some of the qualities of style of the story. The third-person omniscient narrator frequently presents indirect quotations from the Carraways, and it is in these that the narrator's tone of disapproval is made most plain (see, for example, paragraphs 1, 4, 12, 18, 29, 44, and elsewhere). These indirect quotations reveal not only the words and sentiments of the Carraways, but also, presumably, the rhythms and inflections of their speeches. Much of Hughes's satire is conveyed in these passages.

The plot of the story may be defined as the development of a conflict in perspective, namely the failure of the vision of the Carraways as opposed to a more human vision. Exposition dominates paragraphs 1-32 and complication occurs in paragraphs 33-52. The crisis develops when Luther confronts and insults Michael's mother, and the climax, in paragraph 63, is Luther's decision to leave. The resolution may seem weak, but the point is that Anne, on whom much of the story is focused, does not undergo any change as a result of the action. Instead, she remains a flat character, in keeping with the satire of the story, and concludes as she began, with the view that blacks are objects of art and nothing more. Thus she laments only the loss of the model for her painting, not the departure of a human being from her household.

Writing topics: Michael and Anne as characters. The satiric tone of the story. The characterization of Luther or Mattie. The use of setting. Style in the story. The involvement of the third-person omniscient narrator.

Franz Kafka, A Hunger Artist, pages 419-425.

Kafka was a Jewish writer who lived in Prague but wrote in German. He published little during his lifetime, leaving a number of works unfinished. In Hitler's Germany his works were proscribed because of his Jewish identity; as a result he was not well known by Germans until after 1950. He was also forbidden in Stalinist Russia. In Britain and America his works received wide attention after 1930 in the translations of Willa and Edwin Muir, the translators of our version of "A Hunger Artist."

71

Kafka's work is characterized by an unreal and fantastic premise, such as a young man turning into an insect (The Metamorphosis, 1915), or a man being arrested and put on trial for no reason at all (The Trial, 1913). There is everywhere in his work a sense of the absurd, aimless, bizarre, and grotesque --all to be found in "A Hunger Artist," which was one of the works on which he wished to base his reputation (the others being "The Judgement," "The Stoker," "The Metamorphosis," "In the Penal Colony," and "A Country Doctor"). This story was one of a collection of four published in 1924, which Kafka proofread on his deathbed, and each one exhibits unreal premises. In one, a trapeze artist is happy nowhere but on his trapeze ("First Sorrow"). In the second, a man feels threatened by a woman who compulsively tries to change his ways ("A Little Woman"). In the third, a singer is so excellent that her coming death will terminate the existence of music ("Josephine the Singer, or The Mousefolk"). The premise of "A Hunger Artist," similarly bizarre, may be phrased as follows: what if the world placed a premium on the technique of fasting, admired practitioners of the art, but then lost interest? The plot is a conflict between the pride and integrity of the unnamed hunger artist, on the one hand, and the fading away of the demand to see him, finally resulting in nothingness, on the other. The hunger artist, always thin, becomes virtually invisible by the story's end, for those seeking him have to locate him in the straw of his cage. The grim irony of his situation is that at the very end even he minimizes his own achievement (paragraph 9).

With such a bizarre story, one is compelled to look for meaning in symbolism and allegory. Thus the hunger artist may be seen as a symbol of all artists, or perhaps of human identity, which like sound has no reality unless it is understood and supported by others. As allegory, the story may be seen as a brief reflection upon human history or upon the fleeting value that we tend to place on artistic endeavor. In this reading, the high point of the hunger artist's performances symbolizes human achievement in politics and art. The retreating recognition by the artist's public may be the increasing sense of anomie, doubt, and alienation that has occupied many modern philosophies. Conversely, it may represent the human preference for violence and immediate sensation over aesthetic contemplation. There is nothing hard and fast about this allegorical reading; it may be put forth only as a point of departure for class discussion. Your students will doubtless advance their own ideas.

Within this pattern of meaning, the story has a normal enough structure. The exposition takes place in paragraph 1; the complication in paragraphs 2-8. The crisis and climax are both in paragraph 9 (the paragraphs are remarkably long), and the resolution in paragraph 10. The characterization of the hunger artist, even though he is nameless, is detailed and full. He is a meticulous, proud person, offended by the suspicions of others, but who nevertheless lives only because of public recognition and admiration. He undergoes the change that makes him round, for his confession at the end is an admission he never made when he was at the height of his fame.

The setting of the story is adequately detailed, with the various loca-tions of the hunger artist's cages having both realistic and symbolic value. The placement of his cage on the way to the menagerie indicates his loss of prominence, and finally his anonymity and invisibility. The limited point of view (with brief excursions into omniscience in the collective responses of the artist-viewing public) carefully traces all details of the hunger artist's career, an also focuses often on the artist's responses. Although the limited point of view does reveal many traits about the main character, however, he does not emerge as real. Rather, he is an abstraction, an effect achieved because there is no conversation quoted until paragraph 9, when the artist whispers his dying confession to the overseer. Thus, for most of the story, the character of the artist is totally controlled by the narrator.

Writing topics: the level of realism. Symbolism and allegory. The character of the hunger artist. The theme of identity as embodied in the career of the artist. Ideas explored about the way humanity values art.

Doris Lessing, The Old Chief Mshlanga, pages 425-433.

Doris Lessing [nee Taylor] was born in Persia, and at age 5 was taken by her parents to Southern Rhodesia, where she grew up. She took a number of non-literary jobs after leaving school at 15, and in 1949 she went to England to take up the writer's craft. Her best-known novel is The Golden Notebook (1962) and she has written many stories and novels since then. "The Old Chief Mshlanga" is from That Was the Old Chief's Country (1951), a part of her African stories, and it reflects her early career as a writer.

The story is particularly powerful and moving, even though it may seem slow at first. The themes are those of the cruelty and insensitivity of colonial white settlers to the natives of southern Africa, the usurpation by whites of native land, the destructiveness and also the ugliness of colonial agricultural methods, the incommunicability of white and black cultures, and the monumental difficulties of effecting any change in the relationships between black natives and whites.

To make these points, Lessing introduces a female first-person narrator who recounts first her childhood and then her young adult experiences in Rhodesia. The story is unique, however, because the initial point of view is third-person limited, with the narrator obviously speaking about herself in the third-person before shifting to the first-person in paragraph 14. You might want to discuss this duality of point of view with your students. It would seem that the narrator, who is tolerant and seems ashamed of many of the cruelties of the story, thinks of her own early childhood as a period detached from her present conciousness, and uses the third-person to convey this idea.

The narrator herself is one of the major subjects of the story. Her conflict is between her upbringing and her developing sensitivity. Her descriptions of her reading and of her inherited callousness about native people (paragraphs 9-13) establishes one pole of her personality. In contrast, her increasing tolerance and sympathetic growth are detailed in paragraphs 21, 31, 35, 38, 41, and 69. In addition to the subject of the narrator, the story of the Old Chief Mshlanga powerfully and poignantly dramatizes the case against white colonial cruelty and exploitation. The climax of this conflict occurs in paragraphs 85-95, in the confrontation of the Chief with Jordan, the narrator's father, and in the cruel and heartless decision to displace the Chief and his people to a proper Native Reserve (paragraph 96).

Aside from the narrator, who is a thoroughly drawn character, Lessing has sketched characterizations skillfully though briefly. The narrator's mother is only briefly quoted (paragraphs 44-49) but her impatience and intolerance are made plain. The father is not just intolerant, but defiantly insensitive and pitiless. His decision to keep the goats of the Chief's tribe is of minor significance to him, but a death blow to the Chief's people (paragraphs 80-88). By contrast, Chief Mshlanga is shown sympathetically. He grows to the point of defying the narrator's father. Similarly, his son also grows by translating the Chief's words and then by leaving his ill-paying job in the Jordan household. A major achievement in rapid and skillful characterization is the policeman (paragraphs 43-45, 95) who speaks of native government with derision, and also mentions the uprooting of native habitat and a morning's tennis game as though they were of equal importance.

The setting in colonial Rhodesia (now Zimbabwe) is the principal reason for the reality and power of the story. Lessing introduces colonial Dutch words to describe native African places, namely <u>vlei</u> (a slough, pond, valley), <u>kopje</u> (a small hill, usually covered with vegetation and rocks), <u>kraal</u> (a native village including huts and surrounding land), <u>Kaffir</u> (a perjorative word for the various Bantu dialects), and <u>mealie</u> (corn). The descriptions of meeting natives, and the cruel harassment through the siccing of dogs, are a memorable and also unpleasant vison of the ways of life reflected in the story. Lessing also uses the setting symbolically, particularly in paragraphs 54-57 where the beauty of the unspoiled native area as contrasted with the <u>harsh</u>, <u>eroded</u> white farmland symbolizes the ugliness of colonialism.

Writing topics: the theme of anti-colonialism. The shift in the point of view. The growth of the narrator. The setting as reality and symbol. The impact of diction (especially the non-English words).

Flannery O'Connor, A Good Man is Hard to Find, pages 433-443.

Mary Flannery O'Connor was born in Georgia, graduated from the Women's College of Georgia, and received a Master of Fine Arts from the University of Iowa in 1947. Regrettably, she contracted lupus, a degenerative disease, and was an invalid for the last ten years of her life. Despite her illness, she wrote extensively, publishing two novels and many short stories. Her first collection was <u>A Good Man is Hard to Find</u> (1955). A posthumous collection, <u>Everything That Rises Must Converge</u>, was published in 1965, and <u>Complete Stories</u> appeared in 1971. Her works combine flat realism with grotesque situations; violence is encountered without apparent reason or preparation. Quite often her characters appear to be odd, eccentric, and bizarre.

In this respect "A Good Man is Hard to Find" is representative of her work. She selects a third person limited omniscient point of view (let us put a stress on limited), so that all the characters remain at a distance from the reader. The focal character is the unnamed grandmother, but she also distant. The paragraphs in which we are let in to her thoughts are 1, 10, 29, 63, 65, and 69, although an examination of these paragraphs will not reveal much information about her thoughts or her personality. Essentially, she is portrayed by O'Connor as a contradictory, superficial, somewhat whimsical, manipulative, and forgetful person. After the Misfit and his cohorts appear, the point of view is almost totally dramatic or objective, but in the Misfit scenes the grandmother is still the center of the story.

The plot of "A Good Man is Hard to Find" is grounded in situational irony, a conflict between ordinary folks and both chance and evil. The forces of chance are built up by an almost overwhelming set of coincidences leading to disaster. These are: (a) the decision to go to Florida; (b) the decision of the grandmother to go too even thugh she said she did not want to; (c) her hiding the cat in the car because she didn't want to leave it at home; (d) her remembering the house she wanted to see, and exciting the children by making up a <u>secret</u> <u>panel</u> (paragraph 45); (e) her realization of her error just at the wrong moment; (f) her upsetting the basket with the cat in it; (g) the cat's jumping on Bailey's neck and hence causing the wreck that makes the family vulnerable; (h) the Misfit's being close by when the accident occurs.

The Misfit represents evil; he is a psychopathic killer and a person of mindless cruelty. Contradictions in his personality are shown in his apology for Bailey's language (paragraph 85) and in his apparent uneasiness at wearing no shirt (paragraph 99), even though he thinks nothing of killing the grand-mother and having Bailey's family killed. If reasons for his evil are sought, his experience and preoccupation with punishent may be a partial answer (para-graphs 113, 123), as is his tenuous grip on reality (117). His blank accept-ance of his own ruthlessness, however, exceeds explanations (99). It seems clear that the Misfit is not only a heartless psychopath but also a symbol of the harm and pain that may be inflicted on humans. The bizarre discussion of Christology that takes place from paragraphs 129-136 perhaps is intended to remind readers of the errors of religious perception that can lead people to disaster. The grandmother waffles philosophically, trying to use Jesus as a means of saving herself even though she evidences no other understanding of Jesus, prayer, or religion. Certainly everyone in the story is in need of redemption. Thus Bailey's automobile is a symbol, a microcosm, of people who experience anger, annoyance, humor, deception--all the ills that flesh is heir to. Allegorically, the trip is a voyage toward arguable and arbitrary goals, and the disastrous diversion and encounter suggest the need for a more rigorous modern teleology. Without a clearer vision, the story is suggesting, people will continue to be subject to the whims of chance and the irony of their situation.

Writing topics: the character of the grandmother or the Misfit. The basic conflict of the plot. Chance and situational irony. The grotesqueness of the characters. Symbolism and allegory.

Tillie Olsen, I Stand Here Ironing, pages 444-449.

Tillie Olsen was born in 1913 in Nebraska. Early in her life she worked in domestic service, but then married and became the mother of four daughters. When she began writing she fictionalized her life's experiences. She became an advocate of feminism and minorities, and has lectured frequently at colleges and universities. "I Stand Here Ironing," if one judges it as being related to her own experience, is visualized as happening in about 1951, when Emily is 19 and the mother is 38.

The setting is particularly significant and realistic. The year 1932, when the mother indicates that she herself was 19, was the time of the Great Depression, before the Roosevelt administration introduced the WPA (Works Progress Administration) to aid families on relief, or welfare. During this time sound movies were new, and a favorite child star was Shirley Temple (paragraph 35), who sang and danced to divert filmgoers from their troubles. Many mothers of the time tried to model their daughters on Shirley Temple, and many other mothers regretted that their daughters resisted such molding. In World War II (1941-1945), wives and girlfriends were encouraged to write V-Mail (paragraph 45) to loved members of the armed services. From 1945 to 1952, many students developed a fatalistic attitude about atomic weapons (paragraph 53), before nuclear weapons became an even more ominous reality. In the 1930's a single parent like the narrator would have experienced just such difficulties with preserving a secure home as the narrator describes, and things would have improved during and after the war. All these aspects of setting make the story real, almost like genuine autobiography.

For this same reason, the point of view is authentic and convincing. The narrator is a woman of 38 doing the domestic chore, in those days before permanant-press clothing, of ironing. Her narration is not so much a story as a meditative recollection prompted by a presumably recent telephone call from a college counsellor. We can also think of the narrative as an interior monologue or conscious musing, designed for a specific listener, but never heard or seen by him or her. At one point in the narrative (paragraph 16) the narrator becomes so affected by her recollection that she puts her iron down. At the end, she considers the iron again and it suggests to her a negative comparison with her daughter (paragraph 55)--that she, Emily, is an individual with life and free choice, unlike the dress being ironed.

The mother/narrator and Emily are major, rounded characters. The mother, like most parents, is vulnerable to doubt about the way she raised her child. In the story, she cites many of the occasions of regret--illnesses, instances of negligence and even neglect, separations, and fears. Her narrative is full of poignant memories of pain and helplessness (see, for example, paragraphs 9, 22, 24, 29, 30, and 35). It is these which make plain that the conflict in the story is the ideal vs. the actual upbringing of Emily, the daughter, with the complementary conflict being the expected ill, negative results in a vital, talented young woman. The affirmative paragraphs near the end (46-50) are not totally negated by the moderately pessimistic concluding paragraphs (54, 55), for these last two may be considered a function of the anguish and self-doubt that never leave a caring parent. The mother, in this respect, is totally real and probable. Her daughter, Emily, is also real. The child's solitude (paragraphs 9, 12), fear of separation (paragraph 14), and humor (paragraph 15) are well portrayed. Her success at being an entertainer in pantomime (paragraphs 18, 46) is anticipated in her early silent though deeply felt protests at being sent out for day care (paragraph 16). Her conversation with her mother as quoted in paragraphs 51-53 is a demonstration of her growing spirit and also an illustration of a major theme of the story, namely the resilience and adaptability of human character.

Writing topics: the character of the mother/narrator or the daughter. The depression and war years as setting. The point of view as part response and part meditation. The ideas explored about human resiliance, parental regrets, or the mother-daughter relationship.

Grace Paley, Goodbye and Good Luck, pages 449-455.

Grace Paley was born in the Bronx and educated at Hunter College in New York City. She has taught at Sarah Lawrence College, and has written many stories, publishing notably in magazines such as the Atlantic and Esquire. She has published three major collections, the first being Little Disturbances of Man, subtitled Stories of Men and Women at Love, from which "Goodbye and Good Luck" is taken. The second is Enormous Changes at the Last Minute, which in 1985 had undergone its fourteenth printing. Her most recent collection is Later the Same Day (1985). Though this total output might be considered small, she has earned a solid reputation for her insight, her boldness, and her meticulous craft as a stylist.

The setting of the story is the background of the Yiddish theater of the lower East Side of Manhattan, which was supported by east European first and second generation immigrants. Although some of these knew a national language along with Yiddish, most knew only Yiddish, and it was their common bond. The children were brought up bilingually; they spoke Yiddish at home and learned English at school and in American society. The strength of the Yiddish culture, however, enabled the Yiddish theater to flourish for many years. Though now there is not wide support for it, it still exists to some degree, still in the lower East Side of New York, where it grew. The point of view is first person protagonist. Aunt Rose is the speaker, with her niece Lillie, her sister's daughter, as the listener. Only on one occasion, however, does Lillie enter into the discourse, when she has apparently taken exception to Rose's insinuation about the easiness of modern girls (paragraph 52). Otherwise, the story is a monologue in which Rose describes her life-long love for Volodya Vlashkin, the principal actor in the Yiddish theater.

Rose's speech relects the Yiddish idioms of her childhood. In fact, most of her communication with her mother, and with Vlashkin and others connected with the theater, would have been in Yiddish. The English that Rose speaks to to Lillie, who is third-generation and assimilated into American culture, is thus laced with Yiddish rhythms. Students enjoy trying to describe the unique syntax of the story resulting from the submerged Yiddish. The tone of the story is shaped by the rhythms and, for want of a better term, quaintness of the language. With the speech being almost comic, it is difficult to stress the intense seriousness of the emotions that Rose would have felt. Thus the tone seems both warm and tranquil. When Rose thinks of a goodbye to Vlashkin, for example, she says to herself that he is a <u>dear</u> <u>friend</u> and <u>topic</u> of her life (paragraph 70). By such language Paley keeps the story light, and away from the edge where it might possibly, in other cicumstances, sink.

Though Rose admits to being fat, she denies having been lonely; her character seems strong, patient, and resilient. She does not admit to Lillie any of the grief she might have felt, but Paley suggests in a number of spots that her feelings nevertheless run deep (see paragraphs 16, 30, 46, 53, 62, 70, and 94). These offer hints and suggestions, but not developments. It is important here to stress that Rose is speaking to her niece, who is not, one supposes, a person to whom she is accustomed to reveal her sentiments.

Rose's story is a normal enough plot of "Men and Women at Love." The obstacles are those of custom and time. Vlashkin cannot marry Rose until he is free culturally to do so, and thus the relationship stretches out for many years. Ironically, it is Vlashkin's wife who sues for divorce, but her reason is a comic application of the old saying that a woman marries "for better or for worse, but not for lunch." Once Vlashkin is around the house full time, his wife chooses to use the grounds of adultery she could have used at any earlier point. The time that elapses in the story is not clear, but Rose's sister has been married for thirty years (paragraph 1), and Lillie has grown to adulthood, while Rose has been unmarried. Thus the conflict is not the usual one of misunderstanding or intrigue, but rather is one of freeing the affection that has been restrained by difficult circumstances (Rose twice indicates that she does not see herself as a homewrecker (paragraphs 46, 94).

Writing topics: the style. The setting of the Yiddish theater. Paley's control over tone. The character of Rose, as determined by both what she says and does not say. The plot as a love story. Rose as a first-person narrator.

POETRY

COVERAGE OF THE MANUAL

We provide information and suggestions for every poem in <u>Literature</u>: <u>An</u> <u>Introduction to Reading and Writing</u> except those poems that are explicated extensively in the text. For each poem with study questions in a chapter, we provide a brief overview and introduction, some observations on teaching, the answers to the study questions, and one or two suggested topics for writing. For poems that are unencumbered with questions in the text, such as those in Chapter 26 and in "Additional Poems," we also provide a series of questions that can be used for teaching or study. You have the option of using as much or as little of the material here as you like; it is not our intention to tell you how to teach poetry. All the material that follows simply suggests some approaches; others are equally valid and rewarding. As with the rest of the manual, this material is designed to help (where necessary) rather than to prescribe.

ORGANIZATION OF THE POETRY SECTION

We have attempted to organize the 16 poetry chapters in a logical order, moving from less to more complex concepts. We chose to include this many poetry chapters because we felt that omnibus chapters tend to be too confusing and make too many demands on students. Thus, for example, we include three separate chapters on imagery, metaphor and simile, and other rhetorical figures, rather than dealing with all these techniques in a single chapter. The poetry section begins with a chapter that offers an introduction to poetry and an overview of the elements of a poem. Here, we ask the student to consider whole poems. In subsequent chapters, we focus on specific elements of poetry, but we encourage instructors to consider the whole poem whenever possible. At the end of this section, we provide two chapters--25 on theme and 26 on poetic careers--that pull all the elements back together in a consideration of the full meaning and methods of poems. We do not expect instructors to use every poem in a chapter or even every chapter. The material in any given chapter may be taught using only one or two poems from the chapter, or even poems from other chapters or from the poems for further reading. Nor do we expect that instructors will necessarily use the chapters in sequence; the text is designed so that the chapters may be taught in almost any order and number. To ensure that such a reordering of material will not confuse students, we have provided a great many cross-references and a glossary and index of technical terms. In addition, we repeat crucial information or guidelines where it will be helpful.

ORGANIZATION OF EACH POETRY CHAPTER

Although there is a great deal of variation, each chapter in the poetry section follows the same general plan. Each begins with an introduction to the topic or aspect of poetry under consideration in the chapter. This material may be assigned as outside reading and reviewed quickly in class or not, as time permits. In the course of this introduction, or at its close, a poem (or several poems) are usually discussed in some detail. Earlier chapters tend to offer more and fuller explications; the aim here is to show the students the processes through which poetry can be understood and experienced with pleasure. In later chapters, the illustrative explications become more limited in number and scope.

In each chapter, this introductory material is followed by a selection of poems for study that illustrates the issues raised in the introduction. The number of such poems usually ranges from five to eleven; most chapters include a great deal of variety so that the instructor may choose to teach what he or she likes. There are, however, three chapters that provide a much larger selection of poems: metaphor and simile (17 poems), form (30 poems), and poetic careers (51 poems). These large numbers of poems are offered to afford flexibility and choice; in the case of the chapter on form, however, they are necessary to illustrate all the forms that are discussed.

The poems in each chapter are followed by a discussion of writing about whatever aspect or feature of poetry the chapter takes up. This section includes a discussion of prewriting strategies, formulation of central ideas for essays, the identification of supporting details, and organization. It also provides a sample essay and a brief commentary on the sample. In every case, the sample essay deals with one of the poems included in the chapter. For chapters in which you are not assigning an essay or a writing exercise, you will probably want to omit this discussion from your students' reading. You might want to consider assigning the sample essay, however, as an additional example of explication.

REPRESENTATION

Literature: An Introduction to Reading and Writing includes 379 poems, 239 in the poetry chapters and 140 in the poems for further reading and study. All poems in the text have a date of both publication and composition (in parentheses) if possible. In terms of historical coverage, the poems break down numerically as follows:

Medieval Poetry	6 poems
Renaissance Poetry	57 poems
Restoration/Eighteenth Century Poetry	17 poems
Nineteenth Century Poetry	83 poems
Twentieth Century (before 1960)	123 poems
Twentieth Century (after 1960)	93 poems

Modern and contemporary poetry is heavily represented, but the text also contains a healthy sampling of older masterpieces that have withstood the test of time. Over one-fourth of the poems in the text--98 to be exact--are by women; they are represented in every historical period except medieval and Renaissance.

We have provided, in Chapter 26, an extended look at the poetry of John Donne, Emily Dickinson, and Robert Frost for instructors who want to concentrate on the work of a single poet or several poets. Should instructors want to concentrate on other poets, we have included a substantial number of poems by significant poets throughout the text. The poets who are most heavily represented in the text (and the number of poems by each) are as follows:

Emily Dickinson	25 poems
Robert Frost	17 poems
John Donne	16 poems
William Shakespeare	10 poems
E. E. Cummings	7 poems
John Keats	6 poems

William Blake, Thomas Hardy, George Herbert, Ogden Nash, Alfred, Lord Tennyson, William Wordsworth	5 poems each
T. S. Eliot, Robert Herrick, Gerard Manly Hopkins, A. E. Housman, Theodore Roethke, Dylan Thomas, William Carlos Williams, W. B. Yeats	4 poems each
Robert Browning, Langston Hughes, Randall Jarrell, Ben Jonson, John Milton, Sylvia Plath, Edwin Arlington Robinson	3 poems each

We have also included a substantial selection of poetry by writers who represent America's ethnic and racial minorities. Instructors who are especially interested in teaching the work of Black, Hispanic, or Amerindian Americans can refer their students to the work of Leonard Adame, Maya Angelou, Imamu Baraka, Arna Bontemps, Gwendolyn Brooks (2 poems), Angelico Chavez, Lucille Clifton, Countee Cullen, Paul Dunbar, James Emanuel, Mari Evans, Nikki Giovanni (2 poems), Frances Harper, Michael Harper, Robert Hayden, Roberta Hill, Langston Hughes (3 poems), Etheridge Knight, Don L. Lee, Ben Luna, Claude McKay (2 poems), Amerigo Paredes, Dudley Randall, Luis Salinas, Sonia Sanchez, Leslie Marmon Silko, Anne Spencer, Jean Toomer, Tino Villanueva, Alice Walker, Margaret Walker, and Phyllis Wheatly.

TEXTS AND TITLES OF POEMS

The texts for all poems in the book are drawn from editions of the poets' work or from standard anthologies. Where a poet has provided a title for his or her poem, it has obviously been maintained. Untitled poems are identified in the text, index, and manual by their first line. Poems that are often identified by number, such as Shakespeare's Sonnet 55 or Donne's Holy Sonnet 6, carry both the number and the first line as a title.

SPELLING AND PUNCTUATION

For the most part, we left the poems as we found them, complete with spelling eccentricities, Britishisms, and ideosyncratic punctuation. We did, however, adjust some of the spelling and punctuation in medieval ballads and in some Renaissance poetry. In all instances, these adjustments served to simplify the students' reading of the poem (and avoid another gloss) without changing the syntax, diction, or sense of the poem.

GLOSSES AND NOTES

The poems in the text feature both side glosses and notes following the poem. In the side glosses, we attempted to find a reasonable median point between glossing all "hard" words and glossing only foreign or obsolete words. Our aim was to be as helpful and unobtrusive as possible. You will probably still find it useful to encourage students to read with a dictionary at hand. We use the notes that follow a poem to provide various kinds of relevant information, including extended definitions of words, explanations of some allusions, and identification of many historical, mythological, and literary figures and events. Occasionally, we employ the notes to explain a possible meaning of a particularly difficult phrase or line. In these instances, we have tried to provide a straightforward (rather than interpretive) reading.

SUGGESTIONS FOR TEACHING POETRY

Students tend to be more afraid of poetry and resistant to it than they are to any other form of literature. They may often believe that they simply cannot read poetry and "get anything out of it." One of your first tasks in the classroom is to overcome this fear.

The fear is often the heritage of years of having interpretations delivered "from on high" by various teachers. This kind of teaching makes poetry a mystery and fosters the "deep hidden meaning" approach. In order to overcome this problem, you will have to show students that poems mean what they say and say what they mean. It is thus very important to show them how and from where conclusions about a poem are derived. This may mean spending an entire class period on one poem, but the time will be well spent. What you are actually teaching here is a method or process of discovery about poetry (and literature in general). In some respects, the process is much more important than the number of poems covered in a single class or even in a semester or quarter.

There are many teaching strategies that can be helpful in demystifying poetry for your students. One effective method is reading aloud in class; you or a student might read the poem aloud, sentence by sentence. The class could discuss (or you could ask questions about) the sense and the effect of each sentence. Questions (rather than lectures) about specific aspects of the poem will allow the students to see where ideas are coming from and will provide bits of data about the poem that you can put together with the class to develop a larger view of the poem.

Analysis of this type can be followed by synthesis: a set of questions designed to allow the class to pull the whole poem back together into a coherent moment of experience, thought, and emotion. Again, by using questions and allowing (or insisting that) the class to respond, the students will be able to watch and learn the process of interpretation and understanding. At the close of discussion, you might have a student (perhaps the same student) read the poem aloud again. Hopefully, this second reading will reflect the intervening process of discovery and experience.

CHAPTER 11

MEETING POETRY: SIMPLE THEME AND FORM

The aim of this chapter is to introduce students to poetry and to the processes of analysis, interpretation, or explication. The opening pages raise some questions that you may want to discuss briefly in class. The heart of this opening material is the five questions (pages 463-465) that can be used as students begin to study poetry. Although the chapter makes some tentative beginnings at a definition of poetry, such a consideration might best be delayed until the end of your classwork on the genre.

The chapter contains poetry that most students will be at least partly familiar with already. This should help set them at ease. Indeed, many students might think that they already understand most of these poems. Reading and classroom discussion should help these students reappraise their own degree of understanding. Four poems are discussed at some length in the early part of the chapter. You may opt to go over one or more of these in class to illustrate the process of discovery embodied in each discussion.

Randall Jarrell, The Death of the Ball Turret Gunner, page 461.

Anonymous, Sir Patrick Spens, pages 465-467.

William Shakespeare, Sonnet 55: Not Marble, nor the Guilded Monuments, 468.

A. E. Housman, Loveliest of Trees, pages 470-473.

Emily Dickinson, Because I Could not Stop for Death, page 473.

Dickinson's poem presents an extraordinary perspective on death and the process of dying. It can almost be taught as a story, dealing with the narrative details in the order in which they occur in the poem. The speaker was too busy, too involved in life, to consider death; there is a note of self-directed irony or mockery here. Death is characterized as a gracious and polite gentleman caller; the key words here are <u>Kindly</u> and <u>Civility</u>. This characterization is extremely unconventional; Death here is clearly not the traditional grim reaper. The carriage might be considered a hearse. On the journey, the carriage passes children at play, the gazing grain, and the setting sun. These might suggest three stages of life: youth, maturity, and death; the setting sun, at least, is a traditional symbol. In line 13, the carriage (and time) apparently stops, since the sun passes the speaker and death. The <u>chill</u> (line 14) implies the cold of the grave; the gown and tippet suggest a shroud. The <u>house</u> (lines 17-20) is probably the grave (or vault). In the last stanza, we discover that the speaker is long-dead and speaking from timeless eternity. This accounts for her distorted perspective on time.

Other elements that work well in class include diction and tone. Words like <u>strove</u> (line 9) and <u>Gazing</u> (line 10) have interesting connotations in connection with children at play and grain. The tone is polite, grim, and a bit self-deprecating. Like many of Dickinson's poems, this one can be sung to several hymn tunes; get your class to try it to the tune of "Amazing Grace." Writing topics: the characterization of the speaker or of death. The use of symbols. Ideas about death that the poem explores.

Thomas Hardy, The Man He Killed, page 474.

This is an anti-war poem that questions the impersonal slaughter of modern warfare. One way to teach the poem is to bring the class to understand the difference between the speaker's hazy understanding of the problem (i.e., what's bothering him about his own actions) and the poet's much clearer understanding. The title sets up this distinction and the speaker's odd understanding by using "He" instead of "I."

The speaker is a common soldier; he previously made the transition from a simple life to the military. His enlistment was not motivated by patriotism or idealism, simply the need to do something (lines 13-16). He recalls a situation in battle in which he killed a man "because he was my foe." The speaker confusedly considers the morality and validity of this act. His diction indicates that he is simple and uneducated; his language is full of colloquial phrases and slang. The repetition of because (line 9) and the word although (line 12) indicate the speaker's confused reaction to war and killing. He realizes that his "foe" was probably much like him, and he does not understand the "quaint and curious" demands of war.

The poem's implications about war are much clearer; it underscores the impersonal and senseless destruction of warfare. Other interesting areas for class discussion include the tone, rhyme, meter, and imagery. The tone is simple and confused; the speaker is not altogether clear about his ideas. The rhymes clinch ideas, especially foe and although. The sing-song meter underscores the speaker's simplicity without detracting from the poem's ideas. The imagery, especially of civilian life, is concrete and familiar, suggesting the aberration of war. Writing topics: the the characterization of the speaker or his foe. The ways diction is used to shape the character of the speaker. The ideas about war explored in the poem.

Robert Frost, Stopping by Woods on a Snowy Evening, page 475.

Frost's most familiar poem dramatizes a number of alternatives that students may not readily see: life verses death, action versus contemplation, involvement versus withdrawal. Life, action, and involvement are embodied in "promises"; death, contemplation, and withdrawal in the dark, cold, silent woods and the snowfall. In teaching the poem, you can aim to open up some of these darker and less accessible ideas to students through questions that focus on speaker, setting, and situation.

The speaker is in familiar territory; he is riding through the woods during a snowfall and has stopped to watch the "woods fill up with snow." The setting begins to bring forward some of the darker implications of the poem; the woods are lifeless--no farmhouse near, a frozen lake. The time--"the darkest evening of the year"--suggests both the mystery of the woods and the darkness within the speaker. The silence reinforces the isolation implicit in the setting and action; the speaker is attracted to the "lovely, dark, and deep" world of withdrawal and contemplation. He is also embarrassed by his attraction to this world; he acknowledges (is glad?) that the owner of the land will not see him, and he projects his own feelings about the queerness of stopping onto his horse ("must think it queer"). In the last stanza, the alternatives are brought into sharp contrast: the woods versus the promises. The speaker opts for life, involvement, and action; all this is embodied in the single word but (line 14).

Technically, the poem lends itself nicely to classroom considerations of sound and rhyme. Alliteration on the s and w sounds (lines 11-12) reinforces the silence and the sweep of the wind. The sounds are comforting and attractive; they invite withdrawal. The rhyme scheme is aaba, bbcb, ccdc, dddd; it provides for linking or interlocking each stanza with the next. To end the poem, Frost sticks to a single rhyme sound throughout the last stanza and repeats the last line. Writing topics: the implications of the setting and situation. The alternative attitudes or courses of action implied in the poem. The effects produced through sound, rhyme, or meter.

James Wright, Two Hangovers, page 476.

Like Frost's poem, this one presents two perspectives on life. In this instance, however, the alternatives are laid out much more simply, and the distinction is less monumental. In teaching the poem, you might concentrate on the speaker and the ways in which his mental state controls the way he sees the world. Similarly, you might focus on the images and on the way each grows out of the intensity of the respective hangovers. Some of your students may have first-hand experience with these states of mind; you might approach the poem through that familiar avenue.

In hangover "Number One," the speaker feels miserable; he slouches in bed and looks out the window at the world. His mental state shapes his vision of this world; the trees are bare, and the world is depressed and dying. Visions of poverty and death--the old man, the grave, graveyard, fresh graves, dead moon--reflect the speaker's own hungover misery; he feels as though he might as well be dead. The sun (lines 15-19) is an image or symbol of the speaker's own condition; its stumbling and mumbling reflect the speaker's inability to deal with the day. In the second hangover, the speaker feels better and his vision of the world reflects this improvement. The vivid image of the bluejay in the tree, and the speaker's conviction that "the branch will not break," indicate a positive reaffirmation of life. Both the tone and the imagery here are much more affirmative. Writing topics: the impact of the images of death in hangover "Number One." The attitude toward life expressed in hangover "Number Two."

PARAPHRASING POETRY, pages 477-479.

The aim of this section is to explain to students how to paraphrase poetry and to suggest some reasons why paraphrasing might be useful. In teaching paraphrasing, you can stress the idea that a paraphrase is always reductive. Indeed, paraphrasing can heighten students' awareness of the skill in the original poem. All the poems in this chapter are likely candidates for an exercise in paraphrasing, and the skill will be useful as students continue to study poetry. The sample paraphrase (page 478) and the commentary (page 479) provide an example and a bit more guidance for students.

CHAPTER 12

CHARACTER: THE PEOPLE IN POETRY

The goal in this chapter is to introduce students to the various kinds of characters that can appear in poems: speakers, listeners, and other actors. The most important concept to get across in teaching is the difference between the poet and the speaker; students have an almost unconquerable impulse to conflate the two. Poems like "The Passionate Shepherd" (page 484) and "The Nymph's Reply" (page 486) are ideal in this respect since Marlowe was clearly not a pastoral shepherd and Raleigh certainly not a nymph. Once students begin to understand that the speaker or persona in a poem is no less fictional and no less a character than the narrator in a short story, they will be in a much better position to understand poetry and discuss it in class. We discuss the characters in four poems at the beginning of this chapter (pages 484-495). Some of these poems are fairly accessible to students on their own. Others, like "My Last Duchess," may require extensive discussion in class as well as outside reading.

Ben Jonson, To The Reader, page 481.

The voice here is not the poet, although it is very close. It is, rather, a persona that Jonson sustained in much of his poetry: the curmudgeon-critic who tells his readers how his poems should be read.

Robert Herrick, His Prayer to Ben Jonson, page 481.

Again the speaker and the poet are close, but the persona always remains a fictional character. To complicate matters, this speaker's name is Herrick.

Christopher Marlowe, The Passionate Shepherd to his Love, page 484-485.

An ideal poem for teaching speaker and listener since both are named in the title. Poems for comparison include Raleigh's "Nymph's Reply" (page 486), Lewis's "Song" (page 499), and Donne's "The Bait" (page 880).

Sir Walter Raleigh, The Nymph's Reply to the Shepherd, page 486.

It might be interesting to review this and Marlowe's poem as a pair in class and to contrast the tones. Marlowe's shepherd is passionate, supplicating, and sly; he knows that spring and youth do not last. Raleigh's nymph is honest, realistic, and cynical; she ruthlessly exposes the flaws in the shepherd's argument.

Robert Browning, My Last Duchess, page 488-489.

Although Browning did not invent the dramatic monologue, he refined and developed it into one of the most characteristic idioms of modern poetry. The Duke and his last Duchess are portrayed in the poem (explicated, pages 489-492). Students often feel that the Duchess must have been guilty of something more than inappropriate smiles or blushes; they usually suspect infidelity.

This can be an effective point of discussion, because Browning seems to leave the suspicion as a very tenuous possibility in the poem. Writing topics: the character of the Duke or the Duchess. The symbolism of the works of art.

Thomas Hardy, Channel Firing, page 492-493.

Again, the poem is explicated rather fully in the text (pages 493-495). It is a good one for teaching character because it includes so many speakers, and the central persona is so clearly distinct from the poet. Aside from the characters, other topics that lend themselves well to class discussion and to writing include (1) the effect of the last stanza, (2) the characterization of God, and (3) the attitude that the poem expresses toward humanity. Good poems for comparison include Donne's "Batter My Heart" (page 556), Blake's "The Lamb" (page 556) and "The Tyger" (page 581), Eberhart's "The Fury of Aerial Bombardment" (page 562), and Hopkins's "God's Grandeur" (page 703).

Anonymous, Bonny George Campbell, page 495-496.

This popular ballad (Child number 210) tells of the death of George Campbell and the reactions of his family. You might consider with your students why the poem focuses on the image of Campbell riding away, the image of the riderless horse, and the survivors, instead of focusing on the actual death (or murder). The poem is narrated in the third person; the speaker is "outside" and detached. The three characters in the poem are Campbell, his mother, and his wife; none are described in any detail. Although we get a sense that the family is well-off and perhaps noble, details do not seem to matter; the poem focuses only on the climax of a series of actions.

The first two stanzas, which describe Campbell's riding forth and the horse's return, are devoid of emotion; they simply report the facts. In the 3rd stanza, however, we see the intense grief of the mother and the wife. The 5th stanza presents interesting possibilities for discussion; it is spoken by a character other than the narrator. Students can usually make a good case that the speaker here is either the wife or the ghost of Campbell. The repetition in the poem (stanzas 2, 4, and 6) repeats the critical action three times, thus focusing on the discovery of death. Writing topics: the effect of the emotional detachment of the speaker. The image of the riderless horse. An analysis of the 5th stanza. The repetition.

George Herbert, Love (III), page 496-497.

This three-stanza lyric is a meditation on the relationship between God (Love) and the soul ("me," the speaker) expressed in an extended metaphor in which Love becomes an innkeeper and the speaker becomes a guest at the inn. The two characters are thus Love (God) and the speaker (the soul). The primary speaker is the "I" of the poem or the soul; this voice narrates all the action. All the actual dialogue, however, is in quotation marks.

The speaker feels that he is an unworthy guest since he is "guilty of dust and sin"; he considers himself sinful, unkind, and ungrateful. In other words, he feels spiritually corrupt and unworthy of Grace. Love (or God) makes two crucial points in welcoming the speaker (soul). In stanza 2, Love points out that He is responsible since He created the soul (line 12), and in stanza 3 He points out that He "bore the blame" (line 15) for the soul's imperfections. Thus, Love alludes to His roles as creator and redeemer (through the crucifixion). Love's meat, the body and the blood of Christ, is the sacrament of communion--the conduit of divine Grace. In discussing this poem, you might have your students compare the image of God developed here to the one presented in "Channel Firing" and the poems listed there for comparison. Another approach is to have students think of the poem as a very short play, complete with dialogue and action. Writing topics: the character of the speaker or of Love. The extended metaphor (conceit) of the inn and innkeeper.

Alfred, Lord Tennyson, Tithonus, page 497-499.

This dramatic monologue, spoken by Tithonus, embodies the mythological figure's feelings of isolation and alienation from both humanity and the gods. Students must know the mythology to understand the poem. Tithonus, a mortal, was loved by Eos, the goddess of the dawn. Eos gained from Zeus the gift of immortality for her lover, but she forgot to ask for the gift of eternal youth. Thus, Tithonus grows ever more decrepit and aged, but he cannot die; Eos remains eternally young and beautiful.

The poem is spoken by Tithonus, now an incredibly old and weak immortal who can no longer endure immortality. The listener, referred to in the second person throughout, is Eos. In lines 1-4, Tithonus portrays the cyclical nature of the world, and in line 5 he separates himself from it; he "only" is consumed by immortality "at the quiet limit of the world." Isolated from humanity, he is also isolated from the "immortal youth" of the gods by his "immortal age" (line 22). In the first flashback, Tithonus explains the history of his present situation. In the second (lines 50-63), he recalls what his love for Eos was like when it was fresh and new.

Eos's tears (45) indicate that she is helpless in the matter; "The Gods themselves cannot recall their gifts." Some students will argue, with good reason, that Tithonus wants to die. While this is not wrong, it does miss the point that he primarily wants to return to the world and to the natural cycles of life and death introduced in the first 4 lines. Tithonus makes this point in lines 27-31, and he begs Eos to release him in lines 64-76.

"Tithonus" lends itself to the exploration of contrasting states of being such as youth versus age, mortality versus immortality, natural versus supernatural, and community versus isolation. All these, as well as an analysis of the speaker or the listener, would make effective topics for writing. This poem can also be used successfully in conjunction with Chapter 24.

C. Day Lewis, Song, page 499.

This lyric is a parody of Marlowe's "The Passionate Shepherd" (484) that reflects the conditions of modern life, complete with pollution and poverty. Like Marlowe's poem, it is an invitation to love. But like Raleigh's "Nymph's Reply" (page 486), the speaker here presents the world with all its flaws and warts. The speaker--a man--invites the listener--a woman--to share the pleasures that "chance employment" might provide. The life that the speaker offers is meager and uncertain, full of "chance employment," care, pain, toil, and hunger. Lewis's diction underscores the ironic uncertainty of modern life. Phrases like "dainties on the docks" and "a wreath of wrinkles" undercut the pastoral assumptions of Marlowe's poem and the connotations of dainties and wreath in a wry combination of words. Instead of having summer frocks or hearing madrigals, the speaker offers only the chance to read about dresses and the hope to hear songs. Writing topics: the connections among this poem, Marlowe's "Passionate Shepherd," and Raleigh's "Nymph's Reply." The character of the speaker. The diction. The image of the modern world created in the poem.

James Merrill, Laboratory Poem, page 500.

This is a wonderful poem to show your students that poetry need not confine itself to "poetic" images or situations; the vivisection of living turtles to experiment with their hearts is a long way from the proverbial "hearts and flowers" that many students associate with poetry. In teaching the poem, it might be helpful to have your students explain, in as much detail as possible, what is actually going on in the laboratory. The poem is spoken in the third person; the speaker is outside, detached, and uninvolved, although he or she has access to Charles's thoughts. The two characters, Naomi and Charles, are lovers (line 18). Naomi, the scientist, is cutting open living turtles, removing their hearts (an action that involves "taking heart" in more ways than one), and experimenting with "solutions tonic or malign" on the heart muscles to evaluate the effects. Charles, more a philosopher than a scientist, watches Naomi, gags at the blood and the "blind twitching," and considers the implications of her experiments.
The poem, set in a research laboratory, offers a little dramatic scene (lines 1-12) and then one character's meditations on the scene. Merrill uses diction, metaphor, and pun to make the language exact and to broaden the meaning; "taking heart" (line 1) can refer to the experiment, courage, or love. The heart becomes the central image of the poem, and it comes to embody science, human endeavor, courage, and love. Charles's meditation (13-18) establishes these possibilities. He considers that the heart leads people into exquisite disciplines (science, love, risk) and, if the turtles' hearts are any indication, they are all fated to expire. Writing topics: the character of Charles or of Naomi. The impact of the setting and action on meaning. Merrill's use of the heart as a central image.

Randall Jarrell, The Woman at the Washington Zoo, page 501.

This dramatic monologue, a woman's lament for her sterile and constricted life, is the subject of this chapter's sample essay (pages 506-508). If you teach the poem without using the writing section, you may want to have your students read the essay anyway. Writing topics: the most compelling writing topic here is an analysis of the speaker--the subject of the sample essay. The poem also lends itself well to analyses of setting, diction, metaphor, and simile.

Maura Stanton, The Conjurer, page 502-503.

This is another dramatic monologue, spoken in the first person by the conjurer or magician; he (or she) is the central and most fully revealed character in the poem. The poem is spoken directly to us--the readers--and the conjurer is both defensive and pugnacious about what he has done to the people in the mayonnaise jar. He claims ignorance (line 3), misunderstanding (line 8), and prudent care as defenses for his action, and he cites ingratitude (lines 16, 25) as the reason for his growing irritation with the little folk. The conjurer's dream (lines 28-33) may embody his suppressed knowledge that he has created an evil situation. In any event, his final "trick" will certainly be detrimental to the miniature people. It might be interesting to discuss what this trick might be with your class; the conjurer's defensiveness and irritation suggest that he is going to make the people "disappear."

The other characters in the poem are the "tiny people" in the mayonnaise jar. Although the conjurer has attempted to dehumanize them through the magic of shrinking (tyranny, repression), they remain fully human in their desires and reactions. They both resent and fear the conjurer, and he is irritated at this response. The poem's ideas are quite complicated. On the one hand, it works as a character sketch of the conjurer; it explores his defensiveness, guilt, rationalizations, and irritation. On the other hand, it may be an exploration through symbolism of the dynamics of tyranny and repression. Writing topics: a character analysis of the conjurer/speaker or of the tiny people. Exploration of the poem's ideas about tyranny or manipulation.

WRITING ABOUT CHARACTER IN POETRY, pages 503-508.

If you assign an essay about character in poetry, this material will help your students formulate, organize, write, and revise their papers. In class and in the written assignment, you might emphasize the importance of a clear central idea, a clear topic or thesis sentence, and the need to choose details that support the central idea. The sample essay on Jarrell's "The Woman at the Washington Zoo" and the commentary (page 508) illustrate and emphasize these principles.

CHAPTER 13

WHEN, WHERE, AND WHAT: SETTING AND SITUATION

The aim of this chapter is to introduce students to the fact that place and time are interrelated with thought and expression. Students usually find it easy to understand the places, periods, and artifacts of poetry. Indeed, some may be able to provide actual sketches. It is harder to get them to recognize how character and attitude are shaped by the objective surroundings described in poems. You may therefore find it essential to emphasize that the setting is important because the poet uses it to transfer the totality of responses, attitudes, and thoughts from the poem to the mind of the reader.

James Dickey, Cherrylog Road, pages 510-512.

Dickey is the author of Deliverance, which has been made into a film. If your students have seen this film, you may wish to discuss it briefly with them before you talk about the poem. Study Questions: (1) The scene of the poem is specific, although generalizations about life and experience arise out of the concreteness. Note the exact description of the place (Highway 106 at Cherrylog Road), the speaker's progress to the center of the yard (the weedy heart, line 16), the names of the cars (Ford, Essex, Chevrolet, Pierce-Arrow), the colors (red, blue, red-haired, gray), and the temperature (body heat).
(2) The speaker has come to meet Doris Holbrook (note the concreteness, in both given and family names), who gets away from home at noon, on the pretext of collecting useful junk. Note the disparity between the declared purpose of her errand and its real purpose. (3) The speaker imagines that the '34 Ford was used by moonshiners to carry whiskey (lines 5-6), that sitting in it is like being in a stock-car race (line 24), that he is an envoy or movie star leaving a car (27-28) or that he is a wealthy old woman with black chauffeur, driving out to an orphanage to dispense largesse (lines 35 ff.).
(4) The two must go through one car after another. Evidently the scene is that the cars are jammed tightly together, and it is not possible to walk around them. The cars are rusted and hot, and some are covered with vines. The meeting is therefore private but also uncomfortable. (5) The father would apparently not hesitate to beat his daughter or to come after the speaker with a gun if he knew about the meetings. Doris has to escape from him by pretending to be on an errand. (6) Both go in opposite directions through cars to different roads heading off to different destinations. Doris will bring back junk that she has scavenged from the junked cars (lines 55 ff.).
(7) The emotional ties are not fully explained in the poem, and seem to be simply the powerful sexual hunger of young people. The speaker wants her to come to him enough to pray for her arrival; both want to be together enough to take all the risks involved and endure the attendant discomforts. (8) He is wild because in becoming part of the junkman's wreckage, he is also transforming it by using it for life, not death. Amid that wreckage he experiences powerful pleasure and release, and the thrill of danger overcome; in so doing, he and Doris affirm life amid a scene of uselessness, desolation, and abandonment, thereby denying them all. Writing topics: setting and action. The contrast between the wreckage and the speaker's lust for life. The setting and the structure. The auto junkyard and the mood and atmosphere.

Robert Browning, Soliloquy of the Spanish Cloister, pages 514-515.

This poem is a masterpiece in the mode of the dramatic monologue. As the speaker talks himself alive, he also reveals himself as a fish out of water, a man filled with anger and contradictions. The poem is simultaneously comic and frightening; the speaker reveals himself to be a monster of envy. We can assume that under other conditions, however, he might be more at peace with his surroundings and close associates. Good poems for comparison include Browning's "My Last Duchess" (page 488) and Tennyson's "Tithonus" (page 497).

Study Questions: (1) The speaker is a monk in the same order as Brother Lawrence. He hates him, and is jealous of his serenity and a faith which manifests itself in happy service instead of in trifles (making a cross of silverware in a plate, drinking in three sips to parallel the three aspects of The Holy Trinity). The speaker believes that Lawrence's apparent indifference to lovely women is in fact a cover for lechery. In point of factr, the speaker is probably projecting his own lechery onto Lawrence. (2) The speaker is in the cloister of the monastery, watching Lawrence care for his flowers, herbs, and melons. As Lawrence works, the speaker reflects on what he thinks Lawrence's actions reveal about Lawrence and about what he himself has done to disturb him (clipping off the flower buds [lines 47-48], etc.).

(3) The speaker is quite perceptive and observant, but clearly the disparity between his outward actions and his ugly feeling illustrates that it is the latter which really count. (4) He intends to hide a pornographic novel, open to a particularly juicy part, amid Lawrence's harvest, or to try to get him to misinterpret a particular text on his deathbed, thereby damning himself. Failing that, he might even make a pact with the Devil, hoping to leave himself a loophole, but using the Devil to damn Lawrence. The plans would not succeed; Lawrence's faith and goodness are proof against this kind of machination, and damnation does not consist in an occasional fleshly thought. The speaker, by contrast, clearly exists in a constant state of hatred and repressed lust.

(5) The disparity between the intensity of the hatred and the pettiness of the speaker's actions against Lawrence is comic, as is the inadvertent humiliation of his character. To be so mistaken about oneself and about another can be seen as a comic illustration of human blindness and rationalization. But the projection of one's own unacceptable emotions and thoughts onto another demonstrates an alienation from the self which can be characteristic of a serious emotional disturbance. Writing topics: the speaker's character as a person and as a monk. The significance of artifacts. The references to places, times, and things, and the poem's organization.

Christina Rossetti, A Christmas Carol, pages 517-518.

This poem is also a well-known Christmas hymn, with music by Gustav Holst (1874-1934) whose best-known orchestral composition is The Planets (1916). You may be fortunate enough to have students who know the tune of A Christmas Carol and who also have the bravery to sing some of it. Study Questions: (1) The time is Christmas day, here shown as in the coldest depths of winter, the place allegedly Bethlehem. Yet Rossetti is describing an English winter (ice, frozen ground, snow falls, etc.). The bitterness and bleakness are intended to contrast with the warmth of the love and the glory of the event. (2) The location—a stable, the manger, the adoring Magi, shepherds, and animals—is part of the story of Jesus's birth as the Bible describes it and as legend embroiders it. The simplicity is essential, theologically, to present the human vulnerability of the God/Man and yet to remind the readers that the person born in such poverty was the King of Kings.

(3) Both angels and the mother are present to love and honor the child. They stress human involvement in the event. Christmas being a time of gift giving, the speaker sees the newborn child as God's gift to humankind, and responds with gratitude and courtesy, wishing to offer a gift in return. (4) The speaker considers the gifts (gold, frankincense, myrrh, and, presumably, a lamb), which were offered by poor and rich alike. Being poor, she opts for the gift of herself. Since the heart is both the traditional seat of love and the center of one's whole being, her gift is total; no one could offer more. Writing topics: Winter and warmth. Historical and legendary scenes of the birth. The link between the speaker and the traditional adoration. The references to rich and poor.

Andrew Marvell, Bermudas, pages 519-520.

This poem blends discovery and wonder. For comparison you might consider it with Keat's "On First Looking Into Chapman's Homer" (page 592). For still further comparison, the last paragraphs of Fitzgerald's The Great Gatsby also consider the relationship of discovery and awe at the wonders of the world. Study Questions: (1) In seventeenth-century England, most people lived and died in the same place in which they were born. Very few people crossed the Atlantic, and doing so was a difficult journey which took months and was filled with dangers and the real possibility of shipwreck, illness, or death. (2) A small boat, propelled by rowers and filled with English sailors, is moving over a protected area of water in Bermuda. (3) The speaker and his or her companions are in the boat and are rejoicing over the gifts of God that characterize the newly found island. It is not necessary that they have been in Bermuda, for the details are easily imagined, and the song of praise is less concerned with details than with their value as evidence of God's generosity to human beings.
(4) The parallels between the Bermudas and the Garden of Eden are strong: in both, God's plenitude and benevolence are basic to the fecundity of the land and the intended joy of those meant to live there. As in Eden, the inhabitants do not need to work, for food simply meets their lips or drops at their feet. (5) Therefore, the list of things which justify praising God includes: God's kindness in leading the sailors to safety, the safety of the island, its springs, its beauty, the food, and the gifts of the Gospel and of a temple in which to worship. Writing topics: setting and structure. The levels of perceivable reality in the structure: real, reported, and imagined. The Bermudas as a new Eden. The integration of setting and idea.

Thomas Gray, Elegy Written in a Country Churchyard, pages 520-523.

Gray's "Elegy" is one of the major lyrics of the eighteenth century, and one of the representative poems of the graveyard school of poetry. Students might wonder about the power of death as a theme. You might stress the importance in this poem, as in many poems touching on death, of how life is to be lived in the light of inevitable death. Carpe Diem poems like "To His Coy Mistress" (page 849), together with Christina Rossetti's "Echo" (page 725), Donne's "Death, Be Not Proud" (page 724), and Cummings's "Buffalo Bill's Defunct" (page 769) might create a grouping of comparative approaches to the theme. As a biographical note, you might point out that Gray himself was the only one of his parents' children to grow to adulthood. A concern with death is therefore not unexpected.

Study Questions: (1) The time of day of the poem is twilight. The cattle
are heading back to the barn and milking, the farmer is returning from the
fields, the sun is setting, and the curfew bell is ringing from the church
tower. (2) It is natural to shift from the close of day to the sleeping
forefathers because it is easy to associate the end of the day with the end of
a life, or of many lives. In addition, a country churchyard would contain or
be right next to the Graveyard used by the villagers and their ancestors. (3)
The people buried here are essentially humble, rural folk. Yet the speaker is
at pains to show that they are not to be objects of contempt because of their
simplicity; instead he emphasizes their useful toil and homely joys, pointing
out that death is the great leveler, and that "the paths of glory lead but to
the grave." Some of those buried here might have made good rulers, musicians,
defenders of the people's rights, or poets as great as Milton. The speaker
balances the missed opportunities for good buried here by pointing out that
they never had the chance to do evil on a grand scale either.
    (4) The thee of line 93 is the author of the frail memorial . . . erected
high which in unlettered fashion attempts to record and honor those buried
here. He was the natural poet, a loner, lover of nature and its beauties, one
not quite at home in life, perhaps "crazed with care, or crossed in hopeless
love" (line 108). He too has died, and is buried here. (5) The setting (the
rural landscape with its animal sounds, the churchyard and cemetery, the
closing of day and the tolling of the bell) establishes immediately a mood of
intensity, heightened by the approach of night with its suggestion of the
night/death nexus. Times of passage and change (dawn, nightfall, festivals
marking changes of season) are often viewed as moments when the natural and
supernatural are most open to one another. Writing topics: time of day and
the passage of time. The setting in the graveyard. The effect on life of the
presence of death and the dead in cemeteries.

William Blake, London, page 524.

    Blake was distressed because custom and politics suppressed the human
spirit. His idea was that humanity could flower if institutions could be
eliminated or at least redirected. Songs of Experience, from which "London"
is taken, was a collection of poems on this basic theme. Blake published the
work in 1794 with his own engravings, at the time of the French Revolution.
    Study Questions: (1) London represents a fallen world. Every person the
speaker observes has been blighted or plagued, and the midnight streets
heighten the darkness, misery, and danger. (2) The speaker mentions cries,
both of adults and children, public pronouncements, the cry of the Chimney
Sweep, the sigh of the Soldier, and the curses of young prostitutes. These
are sounds mainly of sorrow and poverty, or rage and debasement.
    (3) Chartered suggests the privilege of those who can hire (charter) the
river Thames itself for their use and whose lives contrast with the misery of
the poor. It also suggests that all of this is chartered (mapped), and thus
the city itself has violated natural beauty by creating artificial streets,
and assigning even the river to commerce and ownership. Marks in line 4 means
permanent marring of people's faces by grief; in line 3 it simply means to see
or observe. In stanza four the reiteration of the bl sound gives each word
emphasis, as does the position of this sound in stressed syllables.
    (4) The poem may be considered revolutionary because it stresses the need
to correct the misery that the speaker describes. Those who are degraded
ought instead to be healthy and wholesome. By contrast, we are reminded of
privilege, soldiers, and palaces, all of them aspects of oppressive authority.
(5) The poem purports to be based on the personal observation of the speaker,

the I who sees these abuses and horrors with his or her own eyes. Having made these observations, the speaker is qualified to speak from experience. Writing topics: the use of actions and sounds as setting. Political order as superimposed on the human spirit. The relationship of the setting to the mood of indignation.

William Wordsworth, Tintern Abbey, 525-528.

A critic once said that writers of the Romantic movement wrote poetry, not poems. "Tintern Abbey" fits this description. Note that Wordsworth himself calls the work as Lines, implying that he did not have specific limitations of form in mind when he composed it. "Tintern Abbey" also illustrates the Romantics' idea that the source of poetry was mysterious and also virtually holy. Thus Wordsworth says that the poem came to him as he finished his walking tour in 1798. When he committed the poem to paper, he says that he changed nothing, thus observing the sacredness of his own inspiration.

Study Questions: (1) The speaker visualizes the scene as taking place in the present moment. He is lying beneath a sycamore on the banks of the Wye River, surrounded by steep cliffs and an agricultural landscape. In the distance there are farm houses from whose chimmneys come wreaths of smoke. (2) The scene is specific because the speaker claims to describe it as he sees it, and has located it clearly at a particular place on the Wye near Tintern Abbey. During the past five years he has often been in towns and cities, and there, in his lonely rooms, the memory of these scenes has given him great pleasure. (3) The speaker believes that experiences of natural beauty, and the pleasure they give both as they occur and as they are remembered, directly cause human beings to be moral, kind, and loving. He clearly finds in nature a transcendent experience, a motion and a spirit, that unites all created things with the life force of the universe. (4) The speaker believes that this experience will be life and food for future years (lines 64-65).

(5) The speaker's argument is subtle. He believes that a spirit both in and beyond nature speaks to humans at moments like the one he is describing. It is a two-way street: the individual must be willing both to see and listen, knowing that eye and ear also help create the experience which allows the speaker to find this presence in the world around him. (6) Beginning with line 111, the speaker shifts the discussion by addressing a friend (thought to have been his younger sister, Dorothy Wordsworth).

(7) The speaker believes that nature has the power to create scenes of beauty which, in their overwhelming power and effect upon the mind and senses, bring the receptive viewer to a state in which "we are laid asleep / In body, and become a living soul," (lines 45-46) and penetrate to the essence of reality and life itself. The cheerful faith (line 133), shared by the speaker and his friend, is that nature will never fail to provide them with this joy if they continue to love and to be receptive to her; that with the strength given by this happiness they can withstand life's disappointments or human betrayals, and that everything around them is full of blessings (line 134). (8) The setting is fully integrated into the speaker's philosophy. Without the two way relationship--the speaker brings his thoughts, experiences, and responsiveness to the scene while nature provides the beauty from whch many of his intellectual and emotional responses spring--the philosophy would not have the immediacy and emotional power which it manifests. Writing topics: The setting as an actual perceived place. The effect of setting upon the speaker's ideas. The contrast between remembered perception, present perception, and future perception.

Matthew Arnold, Dover Beach, pages 529-530.

"Dover Beach" is Arnold's best-known poem, for many reasons, not the least of which is the powerful conclusion. Arnold perceived a loss of absolute religious faith in his time, and hence he stressed the need for an intensive search to recover absolutes--an indefinite time of searching, inquiry, and what he called <u>criticism</u>. "Dover Beach" reflects the loss of faith, while at the same time it stresses the need for integrity.
    <u>Study Questions</u>: (1) The unnamed speaker is an educated, thoughtful person, fully attuned to the intellectual (and particularly the religious) currents of the time. The speech may begin as a kind of soliloquy, but by the middle of the first stanza the speaker is addressing another person, someone dear enough to be called <u>love</u> in the last stanza. (2) The time is evening, the place a room overlooking the sea and the beach. Because the night is clear and moonlit, one can see all the way across the English Channel to the French coast. The reference to the withdrawal of the Sea of Faith places the poem in the mid-nineteenth century, when European Protestantism in particular was reeling under the combined effects of scientific developments and the application to Biblical texts and teachings of new scholarly techniques and discoveries. Words useful in establishing the setting include <u>sea</u>, <u>moon</u>, <u>straits</u>, <u>cliffs of England</u>, <u>window</u>, <u>night</u>, and <u>pebbles</u>.
    (3) The speaker and listener are in a room on the English coast near the white cliffs of Dover. They hear the rhythmic, unending sound of waves throwing water and pebbles against the <u>moon-blanched land</u>. This causes the <u>cadence</u> in which the speaker hears <u>the eternal note of sadness</u>. (4) The speaker's eye moves from distant (the sea and the French coast) to near (the English shore). (5) The first effect of the sounds is that the speaker connects them with sadness. Because of the age and continuity of the ocean, the sounds also suggest eternal, never-ending sadness. (6) The speaker claims that this same sound (on the shore of the Aegean) was a reminder to Sophocles of the "ebb and flow / Of human misery" (like Wordsworth's "still, sad music of humanity"). By comparing Sophocles's thoughts to the present, the speaker suggests the timeless and inevitable unhappiness of the human condition.
    (7) The setting symbolizes the human situation, in which individuals find that much of life and its sorrows are inherent and beyond control. (8) The only kind of faith that remains is personal fidelity, based on love between two individuals. Nothing else is sure; the beauty, joy, and other human experiences which we wish were certitudes--all these are illusory. Basically, what remains is an act of will: a determination to be faithful and by fidelity to be victorious over all that is transient and vulnerable in life. Love is specifically listed as one of the illusions of the world. (9) In the last 3 lines we see war and its confusion--battles taking place in darkness and ignorance. We cannot (and do not need to) know what these <u>ignorant armies</u> are; the image carries the meaning. Obviously the speaker has little respect for governments' actions, at least in matters deemed grounds for war. With the public world thus dismissed, the private world of the little room assumes the full weight of human life and freedom. Writing Topics: structure and setting. Setting and mood. Setting and idea. Mood and references to sound. Setting and response/attitude/reflection in "Dover Beach."

Thomas Hardy, The Walk, pages 530-531.

"The Walk" represents Hardy's mastery, within a short compass, of deeply felt dramatic situations. His long experience as a novelist had sharpened his skill at perceiving human interactions, a capacity he also exhibits with great skill in, for example, "The Workbox" (page 647). In "The Walk," he captures the sadness and poignancy of love, age, and encroaching death.

Study Questions: (1) The relationship between the speaker and the person being addressed appears to be long-standing, for the second person's failure to join in the walk has been going on for some time (of late). They are close enough for the speaker to know the state of the other's health. (2) The companion is weak and lame. The speaker, at least at first, appears unaffected by the other's absence, saying "I did not mind" (line 7). (3) The poem thus seems to be saying that age or illness will inevitably affect a relationship, although to the degree that one memeber can resist thinking of the other as left behind, there is a sense in which they are still together. (4) The final two lines give the poem its intriguing ambiguity. All has proceded as is customary--the speaker walks alone as he or she has now frequently done--until these final lines, when the powerful thought of "the look of a room on returning hence" brings home to the speaker the reality of the changed situation. Their old walking place is now closed to the homebound companion, and a part of life is ended for both of them. Writing topics: the idea of emotional unity amid physical parting. The use of setting as a symbol of aging and separation. The effect of the concluding lines.

Richard Hugo, Degrees of Gray in Philipsburg, pages 531-532

This poem is typical of many of Hugo's works, concentrating, as it does, upon a derelict or ghost town. With this subject matter, Hugo, who lived in Montana for the last eighteen years of his life, dwells upon themes of economics, psychological stability, and the interdependence of life.

Study Questions: (1) Philipsburg is characterized as a virtual ghost town. The economic boom which gave it its reason for being is over, the young people have left or are leaving, and all of its promises have petered out. The past was a boom caused by the mining of silver, creating the need for bars, hotels, businesses, and churches. But for some reason the demand for silver dropped (line 16), and the town's prosperity vanished. The you is the speaker, in stanza one and throughout, speaking to himself or herself. (2) The speaker calls rage the town's present principal business--rage against the mines, the mill, the repeal, and the absence of the pretty girls who have left town. Life is boring and empty, without much hope. (3) By contrast, a living town would not live on rage: the pretty girls would stay, and there would be blondes, good jazz, and booze (line 30).

(4) At lines 25 ff. the speaker suggests that many towns other than Philipsburg are at risk from this kind of malaise. (5) In the last stanza the speaker talks about depression, and even shares the old man's desire for death. Yet for all its grayness, the town is hanging on, and rage is at least a human emotion. There are other good things: the speaker's car runs, he has money, and he likes the red-haired girl. Therefore, even in the midst of despair, some things awaken the human heart. (6) The color gray relates to the color of all the items listed, suggesting depression, sameness, and a lack of spark or exitement. It is also, of course, linked to the color of silver and magnesium. It symbolizes the fading of the town and of the human hopes needed to build it. But the red hair lighting the wall in the last line keeps the gray from being total. Writing Topics: the specifics of the setting. The ghost town setting as a symbol of endurance. The use of gray in the title. The things necessary for community and urban life.

James Wright, A Blessing, pages 532-533.

"A Blessing" demonstrates a flat, common portrayal of experience. The skill of the poem is its restraint in the rendering of experience, and its sudden, climactic expansiveness at the end. In this respect "A Blessing" may be compared with Virginia Scott's "Snow" (page 786).

Study Questions: (1) Just before the narration begins, the two ponies have come out of the woods, as if to welcome the two representatives of another order of beings (the speaker and friend). The present tense gives the poem immediacy, so that the greeting appears to be happening right before the speaker's eyes. (2) The setting is specific: the event is located in place and time, moving from physical concreteness and specificity into the speaker's more intense but less easily described feelings of satisfaction and joy. (3) The realization which overtakes the speaker is that of the kinship, perhaps even the oneness, of all living things (thematically, the poem may be compared with Robert Frost's "The Tuft of Flowers" [page 901]). Filled with love for the animals, the speaker delights in the touch and feel of the pony. At that point the speaker experiences a realization that could he or she transcend the human body and its limitations, the true expression at the moment could only be a transformation into a burst of blossoms. (4) The first 21 lines are essential because they bring the reader along into the speaker's experience. The care with which the landscape is drawn, the description of events in the present tense, the shift from what the ponies do to how the speaker is responding—all this gives and immediacy which sets the stage for the speaker's concluding revelation. Writing Topics: the importance of the details about natural setting. The stucture leading up to the last lines. The significance of twilight and darkness in connecting speaker, animals, and natural scene.

WRITING ABOUT SETTING IN A POEM, pages 533-538.

In this section we suggest a series of approaches for the discussion of setting in poetry. The listings on pages 534-536 describe possible develop- ments for essays. Many of the suggested writing topics may be adapted to these structures. Thus the action of "Cherrylog Road" may be fitted to type 1 (page 534). Any setting in the poems may be treated in terms of type 2 (organization, pages 534-535). The structure of "Dover Beach," for example, may be described according to its setting. Type 3 (page 535) is a natural for Browning's "Soliloquy of the Spanish Cloister." Setting and Mood, type 4 (pages 535-536), would work well for Wordsworth's "Tintern Abbey," Hardy's "The Walk," and Hugo's "Degrees of Gray in Philipsburg." The Sample Essay (pages 536-537) illustrates how the reality of place as perceived or conceived by the poet may be integrated with a major idea.

CHAPTER 14

THE WORDS IN POETRY

The goal of this chapter is to introduce students to the importance of individual words and of word order in poetry. In teaching the concepts here, you can stress the relatively heavier load that each individual word must carry in a poem. The example at the opening of the chapter, Yeats's sequential revisions of the first line of "Leda and the Swan," illustrates the poet's struggle to find the most effective and compelling combination of words. If you choose to discuss this example at length, you may want to have your students read the whole poem (page 819). In teaching denotation and connotation (540-542), you may want to call on your students to provide more examples of words that have acquired negative or positive connotations; advertising can be a gold mine for strongly connotative words.

Robert Graves, The Naked and the Nude, pages 542-543.

This poem, which is discussed in some detail (pages 543-546), explores the impact of denotation and connotation on poetry, language, and human behavior. The last study question invites the students to associate "naked" with Old English vocabulary and diction--usually quite straightforward--and "nude" with the elevation and artificiality of Latinate diction.

The discussion of diction (pages 546-549) may also be expanded in the classroom by calling on the students for examples. This can be especially effective with jargon and slang. A good illustrative field here is computer jargon, which is quickly moving into "mainstream" English. Jargon is especially important in discussing the poems by McHugh, Reed, and Eberhart.

Heather McHugh, Language Lesson, 1976, pages 549-550.

Again, we discuss the poem at some length in the text (pages 550-552) and answer most of the study questions. If you deal with the poem in class, you may want to ask your students about the simultaneous shift in tone, subject, and scope that occurs when the speaker jumps from language to love. The poem shifts from a public setting and tone to a private world and an intimate, warm tone as the subject shifts from language and society to love. Like Marlowe's "Passionate Shepherd" (page 484) and Lewis's "Song" (page 499), this is an invitation to love. You might ask your students to compare all three, and decide which is the most convincing.

Ben Jonson, On My First Son, page 555.

Jonson's poem, in iambic pentameter rhymed couplets, is both a lament on the death of a son and an attempt to find consolation in the knowledge of salvation and heavenly bliss. It is full of interesting instances of connotative words, special language, and odd syntax that add to its impact. The speaker, a poet and father named Benjamin Jonson (but not exactly identical with the poet), addresses the poem to his dead son. The phrase "child of my right hand" puns on the Hebrew name Benjamin and evokes an Old Testament ethos at the opening. Jonson develops a metaphor in which the speaker becomes a

98

borrower and the son a commodity or sum of money lent (by God or fate) for a specific period. Words like lent, pay, exacted, and just augment the metaphor. The day is "just" because the debt is due and because God's actions are always "just." Other denotations and connotations of just also come into play: fair, righteous, exact, legal. The word order in "I thee pay" reflects the idea that the father is paying back God with the son (thee = the payment rather than the recipient).

In lines 5-8 the speaker attempts to deal with his grief and rage through the consoling awareness that his son is in eternal bliss ("the state that he should envy") and has escaped the miseries of age, the world, and the flesh. Here, lament contrasts effectively with both envy and rage. "All father" is a condensed phrase that may mean all fatherly affections, emotions, and griefs. In the last four lines, "rest in soft peace" and "here doth lie" are both instances of graveyard jargon (Requiescat in pace and Hic Iacet), the phrases (in English or Latin) we commonly see on tombstones. The name "Ben Jonson" refers to both the father and the son. Since the word poet is derived from a Greek word that means maker or creator, the father-poet-speaker can call his son his best piece of poetry (or his best creation).

Writing topics: the ways in which Jonson uses jargon, diction, and connotation to convey the speaker's attitude toward the son's death. The dilemma posed by the speaker's love and earthly hopes for his son and his concurrent awareness of the Christian ideal of salvation and eternal bliss. Good poems for comparison are Housman's "To an Athlete Dying Young" (page 727) and Dryden's "To the Memory of Mr. Oldham" (page 758).

John Donne, Batter My Heart, Three-Personed God, page 556.

This sonnet is a meditation on the speaker's inherent sinfulness and his desire that God purify him. The "three-personed God" is the Trinity; the active verbs in the first quatrain suggest a violent and powerful God. Knock and break can be associated with God the Father, breathe and blow with the Holy Spirit (spiritus = spririt, breath, wind, blowing), and shine and burn with God the Son (the pun lurking here is the traditional play on son and sun). The two central quatrains are based on traditional metaphors. In lines 5-8, the speaker compares himself to a town captured (usurpt) by evil forces, the governor (Reason) having failed to defend it for the king (You, God). In lines 9-12 the speaker becomes the bride, Satan the enemy to whom the speaker is engaged, and Christ the bridegroom who must "break that knot again." The couplet states the clinching paradox; the speaker will never be free of sin unless God enthralls him and he will never be chaste (cleansed of sin) unless God ravishes him. Free and chaste paradoxically oppose enthrall (enslave) and ravish (rape), but the paradoxes can be resolved through diction or theology. Enthrall means both enslave and captivate; ravish means both sieze by force and fill with joy. Spiritually, of course, both suggest their opposites; to be enthralled or ravished by God implies freedom from sin and absolute purity.

Writing topics: the way that the diction creates a specific image of God in this poem. The speaker's conceptualization of his own spiritual state. Good poems for comparison regarding images of God include "Channel Firing" (page 492), "The Lamb" (page 556), "The Tyger" (page 581), and "The Fury of Aerial Bombardment" (page 562). An excellent poem for comparison of the treatment of the sinful soul's relationship to God is Herbert's "Love (III)" (page 496).

William Blake, The Lamb, pages 556-557.

This poem is useful in discussing the effects of simple diction and repetition in creating tone and meaning. The childlike diction reinforces the simplicity of the speaker and the listener and emphasizes through connotation the loving and mild nature of the creator portrayed here. The repetition stresses the same childlike qualities and makes the structure of the poem simple and clear. The speaker is a child and the listener a lamb (line 20); they are linked in their mildness, simplicity, and symbolic value as alternate images of the creator (Jesus as a child and the Lamb of God, the agnus dei).

The first stanza asks the poem's central question four times: "who made thee?" The diction implies an answer; words like lamb, delight, softest, wooly, tender, and rejoice suggest a loving and cherishing creator. The second stanza answers the question, equating the creator (God) with both the lamb and the child (lines 13-18). The creator, like the lamb and the child, is meek and mild, loving and gentle, simple and caring.

Writing topics: the effect of diction and repetition in the poem. The image of the creator presented here. The character of the speaker. Good poems for comparison are listed immediately above in the discussion of Donne's "Batter My Heart."

Lewis Carroll (Charles L. Dodgson), Jabberwocky, pages 557-558.

This poem proves, unfortunately, that we can understand poetry to some extent without knowing the meanings of all the words. Like Alice, we can get the drift without being able to pin down the exact meaning of any lines. Carroll depends on the suggestions that sounds create for meaning here. The speaker narrates an adventure story; a young man goes forth, defeats the monstrous Jabberwock, and returns home victorious.

The unpacking exercise can work very well in class, especially if you ask the students to prepare something in writing beforehand. When you make the assignment, you might ask the students to consider how they can tell what part of speech (noun, verb, adjective) a specific word is supposed to be. The answer, of course, is that Carroll's syntax defines the role of each portmanteau word absolutely. Here are some of the more obvious unpackings you might offer as examples: slithy = slippery + slithery + lively + lithe; toves = toads + doves; gimble = gambol + nimble; manxome = maximum + noxious + fearsome; galumphing = galloping + lumbering + lump.

Edwin Arlington Robinson, Richard Cory, page 559.

This poem is discussed in some detail in the sample essay (pages 566-568). Even if you choose not to use the writing material in this chapter, you may want to assign the essay in connection with the poem. The repetition of And at the beginning of six lines keeps the poem moving at a rapid tempo, driving us on from line to line, and suggests that all Richard Cory's qualities are connected. Beyond the topic explored in the sample essay, possible writing exercises include the characterization of the speaker and the ideas about the human condition that the poem explores.

Wallace Stevens, Disillusionment of Ten O'Clock, pages 559-560.

The poem contrasts the sterile and colorless lives and imaginations of the townspeople (the white nightgowns) with the vivid and bizarre imagination (life) of the drunken sailor. In teaching the poem, it might help to begin by having the class discover this contrast. The people (nightgowns, ghosts) are colorless, boring, without imagination, regular in their habits. They retire at 10 p.m. (implied by nightgowns and dream) and always wear white nightgowns (not green, purple, yellow, multi-colored, ringed). Stevens's strategy in lines 3-11 is negative; he tells us what the townspeople do not wear or dream.

All the vivid colors, bizarre images, lace socks, beaded ceintures, baboons and periwinkles disassociated from the townspeople in these lines are ultimately linked to the old drunken sailor who dreams of catching tigers in red weather. The lace and beaded ceintures suggest finery (piracy, exotic places, strange people); the baboons hint at African ports and jungles, and the periwinkles evoke the sea. The sailor has what the townspeople lack: imagination, imagery, color, vividness. The disillusionment of the title may refer to the absence of illusions (dreams, imagination) or to the poet's revelation that the people in white nightgowns lack any imaginative life.

Writing topics: the speaker's attitude toward the people in white nightgowns or toward the drunken sailor. The contrast established in the poem between the people in white nightgowns and the drunken sailor. Stevens's use of color or connotative words in the poem.

Theodore Roethke, Dolor, page 560.

In this poem, Roethke combines general and abstract words for sadness or grief with concrete and specific words that describe the details of day-to-day life in the offices or institutions of the modern world to portray the empty and unhappy lives led in such places. In teaching the poem, it will be useful to let your students separate the two classes of words and let them see that the specific-concrete terms define and focus the general-abstract terms.

The general terms here are sadness, dolor, misery, desolation, and pathos. With the exception of sadness, all are Latinate (or Greek) and elevated. In each case, the general term is defined by concrete and specific words and images. Misery, for example, is linked to "manila folders and mucilage." The real problem to address with this poem in class is why the specific items or objects that Roethke describes embody dolor, misery, or desolation. What do his lists suggest about public places, institutions, businesses, administrations? At the close of the poem, the people (or at least their nails, eyebrows, hair, and faces) join this long list of enumerated objects. The implication is that the world of business and institution can turn living people into unhappy objects, on a level with dust, pencils, glue, and file folders.

Henry Reed, Naming of Parts, pages 561-562.

Reed's gentle anti-war poem, which balances the parts of a weapon against an altogether different set of parts in nature, can work very well in class discussion. Try to elicit from your students a description of the situation: an old sergeant is droning on to a group of young recruits about the parts of a weapon. The lecture is boring. It is a lovely spring day, the gardens are nearby, and one thoroughly bored recruit's mind keeps slipping away from the lecture to consider the burgeoning fertility and sexuality of the spring.

The two voices that we hear in the poem are the instructor's lecture and the recruit's musings about nature and the garden. Ask your students to establish exactly when (or where) one voice stops and the other begins in each stanza. The two sets of parts named in the poem are pieces of a weapon (probably a rifle) and objects in nature, such as the Japonica, the branches,

blossoms, and the early bees. The recruit "slides" one set into the other in
his mind as he picks up words and phrases from the lecture and applies them,
often with a double and sexual meaning, to the garden or to himself. The poem
is rich with sexual allusions and implications; the jargon of weaponry becomes
sexually charged as the young recruit picks it up and applies it to the world
of natural impulse and inclination. The ideas explored here are neither
profound nor cosmic; the poem suggests that young men in spring would prefer
to follow their natural instincts rather than listen to boring military
lectures. A good point for writing or discussion might be to consider if the
poem's implications can be pushed any farther. Is one set of "parts" better
than the other? Does the speaker (or the poet) imply that nature and natural
impulses are better than lectures on weaponry (and thus war)?

Richard Eberhart, The Fury of Aerial Bombardment, page 562.

     Eberhart's poem, like Hardy's "Channel Firing" (page 492), uses the
occasion of war to consider questions about the nature of God and humanity.
In the classroom, you might begin by asking your students to describe the
differences they see between the first three stanzas and the last.
     The speaker, as we discover in the last stanza, is a military instructor
("late in school"); the "you" can be the reader, one, or humanity in general.
The diction of the first three stanzas is general and abstract. The speaker
asks unanswerable questions about humanity and God: why does humanity continue
to wage war? Why doesn't God put a stop to it? Is humanity stupid? God
indifferent? Is warfare the only "eternal truth"? In the last stanza, the
speaker shifts to specific and concrete terms and names: Van Wettering,
Averill, list, lever, pawl. He also shifts from abstract considerations
("infinite space," "eternal truth") to specific facts: the names of young
soldiers who have "gone to early death" (notice the lovely play of "early
death" against "late in school"). This shift does not answer the earlier
questions, but it does focus the poem and bring it to an effective conclusion.
The jargon in this closing stanza works perfectly; it provides the
concreteness of objects and weaponry even if we cannot identify the objects.

WRITING ABOUT DICTION AND SYNTAX IN POETRY, pages 563-568.

     This kind of writing assignment can be very difficult for students; they
are not used to thinking about words as carefully as such an assignment
usually requires. The material here should help solve at least part of the
problem. The opening discussion considers ways to begin this sort of
investigation, to develop ideas, and to formulate a central idea for an essay.
If you decide to have your students write this sort of essay, you might take
them through the investigative and thesis-formation processes in class with a
specific poem. You could then have them write about that poem or any other in
the text. The sample essay on "Richard Cory" (pages 566-568) illustrates many
of the principles and processes discussed in the chapter. These are
highlighted once again in the commentary on the essay (page 568).

CHAPTER 15

IMAGERY

The goal of this introductory section is to acquaint students with the various types of images—visual, auditory, olfactory, gustatory, tactile, kinetic, and kinesthetic—which account for the appeal and validity of poetry. Real images in a poem lend reality to the poem's assertions. The logic of understanding imagery is this: readers have seen many of the same things that poets describe (sun, moon, stars, ocean), and have also perceived or experienced many similar things (roses, boats, fish, sweethearts, singers, songs, jewels, hair, and so on). Therefore, references in poetry to these things create a bond of perception authenticating the presuppositions, responses, attitudes, thoughts, and ideas of poetry.

John Masefield, Cargoes, page 571.

"Cargoes" is a fascinating image-picture in which things are almost graphically rendered in poetry. Students usually respond easily to the language. Indeed, the poem's great value is that its diction, being so real itself, leads naturally into a general discussion of degrees of reality as represented by language. Study Questions: (1) Stanza 1 offers splendid and exotic images. They convey color and oriental grandeur, as well as the values of a world now long gone. All the objects are appropriate to Solomon's time, whether as gifts to be used to amuse the court or as building materials. They evoke the nostalgia with which we view this lost world. Stanza 2 and the values it contains are closer to our world. Finally, stanza 3 shows us what it has all been for—so that a dirty coastal ship can carry fuel and cheap products for sale in the modern world. Gone are the splendor, the color, and the beauty; utility and trade are all. (2) The images are primarily visual. Almost all suggest colors and textures, though some also suggest aromas (cedarwood, cinnamon) and some suggest nasty smells (smoke stack, coal). The blazing colors of stanza 2 are preceded by somewhat less color in stanza 1 and followed abruptly by an almost unrelieved grey-brown-black palette of color in stanza 3. There is little stress on auditory images, except that one may imagine the apes chattering and the peacocks calling.
(3) The repeated use of the participles intensifies the impression that the poem is a word picture: it is not a description of action but a verbal rendering, almost like a painting of ships. (4) Rowing suggests human action, and one visualizes the unified motions of men and oars; dipping suggests flight, like that of a bird; butting suggests struggle, and the determined action of a stubborn and tough animal like a mule or a goat. (5) The supposition is very possibly accurate, but Masefield obscures that line of thought by his deliberate use of verbals and pictures rather than expository language. Writing topics: Masefield's images of sight. The relationship of image to mood. The allusiveness of the imagery.

Wilfred Owen, Anthem for Doomed Youth, pages 572-573.

Wilfred Owen was killed in France in 1918, a week before the Armistice that ended World War I. Today he is considered one of the foremost anti-war poets. "Anthem for Doomed Youth" may be compared with Seeger's "I Have a Rendezvous with Death" (page 999), Jarrell's "The Death of the Ball Turret Gunner" (page 461), and Owen's own "Dulce et Decorum Est" (page 644).

Study Questions: (1) The predominant images in the octave are those of sound. Lines 1, 4, 5, 6, and 8 refer to sounds of peace, while 2, 3, and 7 ironically displace these peaceful sounds with sounds of war. Thus the passing bells are not bells but gunfire, and the prayers (orisons) are made up of rapidly rattling rifles. In line 8, the sound of bugles from sad shires suggests the solemnity of military burials. In lines 9–14 the images are primarily visual--held candles, shining eyes, pale brows, flowers, and the repeated drawing of window shades. It is as though a cease-fire calm had descended. (2) The contrast and tone are set in the first line, where the image of the death of cattle stands for the death of men in combat. The image suggests that the men are not valued as human beings. Similarly, the comparison of rifle fire to prayers, and the wail of shells to the sound of demented choirs, underlines the monstrous lack of dignity with which these men died.

(3) The boys may be English choir boys; the girls may be sweethearts left behind; those who draw the blinds are not named, but may be the wives or families of the dead. The shining eyes may reflect candle light or perhaps tears or both. (4) The poem would not be as effective if it were more strident. As it is, the images focus on the irony and pathos of war. In this way the poem stresses the needless and purposeless loss of life, together with never-ending sorrow. Writing topics: the auditory images. Images conducive to sorrow. The use of irony or ironic reversal in the images.

Elizabeth Bishop, The Fish, pages 574–576.

This poem has been a particular favorite among lovers of Nature and the environment. It was so often requested for anthologies that by the early 1970's Bishop did not grant permission for it to be printed, on the grounds that she wanted readers to learn the wider range of her subject material. In its stress on vivid details and flat, scrupulously plain diction, "The Fish" may be compared with Wright's "A Blessing" (pages 532–533).

Study Questions: (1) The actions imaged in the poem are (a) the catching of the fish and holding him out of the water by the speaker, (b) the fish's absolute passivity (line 7), (c) the movement of his gills as he breathes, (d) the speaker's careful observation of this trophy, (e) the fish's tiny eye movements, (f) the expansion of the speaker's sense of triumph, (g) the development of the rainbow colors in the boat, and (h) the release of the fish. The images are both ordinary and unusual, since it is the internal motion (the growth of the sense of victory) which pulls the reader into the poem's movement and excitement.

(2) The fish is very ugly. It is described in such detail to give us a sense of its identity and therefore its value. (3) The fish has been caught before and has, on 5 previous occasions, broken the line and gotten away. It is a fish of almost legendary prowess in the battle with human enemies. (4) The rainbow is a floating oil stain, but to the speaker it represents the shimmering excitement of victory.

(5) The action is abrupt, but in the light of the fish's unusual passivity (a fish hooked and pulled out of water fights and wiggles desperately) and its almost Olympian refusal to meet its captor's eye, the release is the only appropriate act.

(6) Letting the fish go signifies both the speaker's respect for this old fighter and the speaker's realization that to have caught the fish is victory and achievement enough. Writing topics: the fish and the rainbow as symbols. The kinesthetic images. Images of endurance and indomitability.

George Herbert, The Pulley, page 577.

This poem is an excellent one to use because of its graphic title, which presents the master image of the whole poem. If any of your students know about the mechanical advantage of pulleys, you may be able to call on them to furnish the literal basis of the image.

Study Questions: (1) The dramatic scene of the poem is apparently The Garden of Eden or somewhere on earth at the time of the Creation. God is deciding what blessings to bestow on humanity. (2) These blessings include strength, beauty, wisdom, honor, and pleasure. All are blessings because they give joy and happiness as corrolaries of living. (3) God decides to withhold rest or repose, fearing that we human beings will otherwise have all we need and will have no reason to seek for God. Herbert may be thinking of the frequent Biblical references to the need for rest (e.g., Lamentations 5:5; Revelation 14:11), and particularly to Matthew 11:28 (Come unto me, all ye who labor and are heavy laden, and I will give you rest"). (4) Words such as dissatisfacation and anxiety all suggest human uneasiness; to them might be added insecurity, loneliness, lovelessness, lack of acceptance. (5) Herbert is building the poem on the faith that God accepts humankind unconditionally; his phrase repining restlessness (line 17) describes the anxiety prior to this acceptance. Herbert emphasizes weary and weariness here as the accompanying condition of the search. Again, weariness is a recurring Biblical word and concept. See, for example, Isaiah 28:12 ("give rest to the weary"). (6) The image of the pulley is unusual though also ordinary. When we realize that pulleys are mechanical devices, that they hold exceedingly firm, and that they sustain and lift great weights, we may see the appropriateness of the image. Writing topics: the image of blessings as part of a liquid in a glass. The poem's allusiveness. The image or emblem of the pulley (in what ways does it imaginatively connect the various parts of the poem?).

William Shakespeare, Sonnet 130: My Mistress' Eyes, pages 579-580.

This sonnet, from the 1609 edition of the sonnets, is one of those (numbered from 126 to 152) which supposedly refer to a "dark lady," about whom there have been many attempts at identification. More to the point of the sonnet is that in it Shakespeare openly ridicules some of the poetic conventions that the English inherited from the Italian, Petrarchan writers.

Study Questions: (1) The speaker makes the following comparisons: eyes to the sun, lips to coral, breasts to snow, hair to wires, cheeks to roses, breath to perfume, voice to music, and walk to the progress of a goddess. Then he concludes that no part of the lady can properly be compared to the object chosen. The negative comparisons are visual, olfactory, auditory, and kinesthetic. (2) Shakespeare is mocking a style of hyperbolic comparison and rhetoric popular in his age. The point he makes by puncturing this particular balloon is that a human woman, who "when she walks, treads on the ground," is the ideal for a real lover. (3) Although students often think that the speaker is mocking his mistress, this is clearly not the case; he is mocking bad, exaggerated, and trite poetry. The images are not insulting because so many of the comparisons are preceded by "if . . . then" constructions (note that the word reek carries unfortunate connotations in modern English that it did not have in Shakespeare's time). The point is quite the contrary, for the conclusion stresses that the mistress has attributes which are rare. Writing topics: the nature of the images. The reversal of convention in Shakespeare's images. Humor and seriousness as a result of the images. The literary criticism inherent in the poem.

105

Richard Crashaw, On Our Crucified Lord, Naked and Bloody, page 580.

There are a number of Biblical allusions in this short poem. In line 1, interested readers may consult Mark 15:24 and John 20:23. In lines 2-4, the reference is to the Roman soldier who pierced Christ's side with a lance after he had died (John 20:34 alone includes this detail). Also, the robe given to Christ after the beating was purple (Mark 15:17; Matthew 27:28). The two dominant images in the poem metaphorically equate Jesus's blood with a royal garment and the cut in his side to a wardrobe (clothing closet).

Study Questions: (1) The speaker first refers to the bloody garment worn by Jesus after the scourging. The other garment, according to the speaker, is the blood which ran from the wound in his side. There was likely blood elsewhere too: from the crown of thorns on his head, and on his body from the scourging with sticks and whips. Since the blood presumably covered the body, the speaker considers it as though it were clothing.

(2) To consider blood in this way is ironic and contradictory, since it would neither warm, protect, nor conceal the body. But the speaker asserts that Jesus is so rare a being that no human garment could be fine enough to clothe him except for his own blood. (3) The phrase this garment in line 2 refers to the blood, as does Thee with Thyself in line 3. These lines indicate the speaker's indignation that the soldiers should have so profaned the person whom the speaker believes to have been the son of God.

(4) Although the emphasis on blood may seem excessive, the concern is appropriate to the Christian tradition which has always seen the blood of Christ as life-giving. Writing topics: the double meaning of robe and garment or the image of the wardrobe. Color imagery. Allusiveness. Images as causes of worship.

William Blake, The Tyger, page 581.

"The Tyger" is one of Blake's best-known poems, usually contrasted with "The Lamb" (page 556). The large predator as a symbol of evil is readily understood, although some students today, aware of the ecological need for the predator-prey relationship and also of the endangered state of many predators in the world's diminishing wilderness areas, regret Blake's choice. In all other respects, however, Blake's poem is timely. This poem and "The Lamb" finally deal with the same concept--the creator. When the poems are looked at together, we see either two distinct creators or two very different sides of the same one. The poem articulates this quandry in line 20.

Study Questions: (1) Burning carries associations of heat, brightness, intense danger, and the capacity to spread and engulf all. The fire shows up more brightly at night and, like everything else, seems more dangerous than in the daytime. That night has forests makes it all the more dangerous and wild. (2) The immortal hand or eye suggests a creator, who envisioned and fashioned all things. In stanzas 3 and 4, this creator is metaphorically imagined as a cosmic blacksmith. (3) Creation is a kinesthetic image; other such images include burning, flying, seizing, twisting, hammering, and grasping. These images all suggest powerful, strong muscularity.

(4) The question posed in the poem is whether God is the source of both good (the lamb) and evil (the tyger) in the world, and the poem therefore raises the issue of how an allegedly all-powerful and beneficent creator permits evil at all. Writing topics: the meaning the tyger and the lamb. The kinesthetic imagery of creativity. Darkness and night as images.

Samuel Taylor Coleridge, Kubla Khan, pages 582-583.

This poem is a virtuoso piece in every major respect, even though we have what Coleridge claims is only a fragment of a much longer work that he was in the process of writing (many critics claim that this assertion is a fictional narrative frame and that the poem is, in fact, complete). If this is not the case, we can only regret that the knock on the door, which drove the rest of the poem from Coleridge's mind, did not occur several hours later. As "Kubla Khan" exists, however, it possesses its own unity, being a perfect representation of the Romantic theory of inspired composition that attributed the source of creativity to a "penetralium of mystery," in Keats's phrase. Of particular note is the indulgence in sound. Lines 17-24 form a unit that illustrates the device of onomatopoeia, and so also do lines 25-28.

Study Questions: (1) The romantic setting of the poem is a fictitious and exotic locale (Xanadu), complete with palace, deep caverns, a sacred river, gardens, incense, and greenery. (2) Many of the imagined scenes are panoramic, especially those in stanzas 1 and 2. They could be sketched or visualized, although the sounds of the mighty fountain would be missing, and they are essential to a full sense of the excitement and splendor of the scene. The damsel with the dulcimer is a close-up image, as is that of the wailing woman. (3) The auditory images convey excitement, sorrow, danger, and supernatural involvement in the action of the poem.

(4) The poem does not seem unfinished, although the switch at line 37 from landscape description to the far more simple, human, and quiet images of the damsel, being abrupt, suggests a new, incomplete direction. Yet clearly the speaker is showing that inspiration, whether it be from a vision or from the milk of Paridise, is essential to inspire the sort of creative energy that shaped Khan's palace and its gardens and landscapes. (5) Sun and ice together appear to be contradictory, but to combine them as sources of pleasure suggests a mysterious (and oxymoronic) union, beyond everyday reality. (6) To the speaker, this magical union is represented by the image of the singing maid; she is an incentive to him to aspire to goals that he has not yet seen but has only imagined. The poem concludes with the image of a group of persons, who are in awe of the person of inspiration, who dance around the speaker three times to protect themselves through ritual. The kinesthetic images recall the earlier images of motion, but here they have brought the movement into human terms.

Writing topics: the visual imagery. Images appropriate to natural scenery. The effect on the poem of auditory imagery and onomatopoeia. The image of the Abyssinian maid and the speaker.

Gerard Manley Hopkins, Spring, page 584.

"Spring" is a poem of celebration--celebration of the time of year, the existence of the world and the universe, the glorious sounds of English words, and the Resurrection. Like "Kubla Khan," it is a virtuoso piece of sound. Even students who are not particularly perceptive about sounds can appreciate the repeating segments, as in patterns like weeds-wheels, long-lovely-lush, and strikes-like-lightnings, to cite just a few of the many ringing examples.

Study Questions: (1) Images supportive of the beauty of spring include lushly growing weeds, bird songs, blue skies, and leaves and flowers. Except for the weeds they are not unexpected. What seems unusual is the language of movement in which the speaker expresses them.

(2) Imagery of motion is the thrush song like lightnings, the leaves brushing the descending blue, the blue being in a rush, and the lambs racing.

107

These are dynamic images, suggesting that the speaker is surrounded by a season of moving color and sound. (3) This pristine beauty is like Eden before the fall, and is equally at risk because of sin (line 12). But for now it is all new, clean, and lovely.

(4) For many non-Christians the references to Christ, and the assertion that this Edenic world is worthy of him, may make the poem seem nothing more than an intellectual exercise. But the fragile loveliness of the first 11 lines is fully accessible to all who respond to color, movement, and word painting. (5) If one contrasts "Spring" with Marvell's "Bermudas," Marvell's images are more conventional, and more of his poem is devoted to praise of God. Hopkins's poem brings in the specific religious connotations only in the last few lines, and then to suggest the inevitably mixed quality of all things human. Writing topics: images of nature. Visual images. Images of motion.

Ezra Pound, In a Station of the Metro, page 585.

This poem, an example of the "Imagist School" that heavily influenced modern sensibility and taste in poetry, is an experiment because it does not embody traditional form or even traditional grammar. The impression, the image, is what Pound expresses, on the presupposition that poetry exists in the transference of mood from the poet to the reader through the creation and apprehension of strong and direct images.

Study Questions: (1) The image of the petals is complex: are they part of a full blossom? Have they dropped off the flower? Are they sticking temporarily to the wet bough? Do they suggest that, even in rain and clouds, some remnants of beauty are still visible in human experience? If they were petals on a sunny tree they would be positive and less ambivalent.

(2) Another aspect of ambivalence is apparition, which is usually a ghostly figure, but which may be simply an unexpected sight. (3) Although short, this is still a poem because it works entirely in images, not logical development. Writing topics: the poem as image. Imagery and mood.

H.D. (Hilda Doolittle), Heat, page 585.

"Heat," like Pound's "In a Station of the Metro," exemplifies imagism in poetry. Through image and analogy, it shows how something may be understood not through the intellect but through the senses. "Heat" was published in Sea Garden (1916), Doolittle's first collection of poems

Study Questions: (1) The speaker presents heat as being solid and palpable, as strong and as oppressive as heavy canvas that can be moved only by a powerful, shredding wind. (2) The oppressiveness of this heat is such that it lies like a solid weight, pushing on soft things like fruits and putting them out of shape. (3) In the plough image we see soil (as in a farmer's field) being cut apart to open a furrow. Again, the poem is stressing the solidity and resistance of the heat.

(4) The poem thus catches those days of suffocating summer heat in which one longs for a wind (remember that in 1916 there was no air conditioning). It presents an unusual and yet extremely effective series of images, all the more effective because the poet does not push the images too far, and also because she keeps the poem brief. Writing topics: visual images. Images rendering sensations of heat. The images of cutting, rending, and ploughing.

WRITING ABOUT IMAGERY, pages 586-589.

The aim of this section is to provide guidance for students who otherwise might not know what to do with an assignment on imagery. The major principle is that students deal with what they find in the poem, and then develop their essays in the light of their findings. Thus, the poem "Cargoes" may be the basis of a type 1 essay stressing images of sight, just as a major image of sight may be discussed in "In a Station of the Metro." By contrast, H.D.'s poem "Heat" highlights kinetic imagery, and a type 1 essay would stress this imagery foremost. For type 2 essays, the text (page 587) cites Shakespeare's Sonnet 130 as an illustration. "Cargoes" is an obvious example connecting images and mood, and "The Tyger" is another example. For type 3, the text (page 587) cites three poems which might be fitted. The fourth type might be useful for essays on "To Our Crucified Lord," "Kubla Khan," and "Spring."

CHAPTER 16

RHETORICAL FIGURES: METAPHOR AND SIMILE

This chapter aims at introducing students to the concepts and uses of metaphor and simile, certainly one of the most important topics in the study of poetry. Students will have some familiarity with similes, and can usually identify one when they see one, but with metaphor they will usually have less familiarity. Thus the use of many examples, together with accompanying explanations, will be most fruitful.

John Keats, On First Looking into Chapman's Homer, page 592.

Students may be interested to learn that Keats did not set out at first to be a poet, but instead was trained as an apothecary-surgeon. In the year he wrote this poem, 1816, he received his licence to practice, and also gave it up to pursue a life of reading, thinking, and writing. The poem conveys the emotions that can be awakened by literature in metaphors related to exploration and discovery.

Study Questions: (1) Keats uses the image realms of gold (line 1) as a metaphor for literature and its many delights. Literature can take us to new places, and Keats presents these places as goodly states and kingdoms, western islands, and Homer's demesne (lines 1-6). (2) The cause of the speaker's excitement is Chapman's translation, which is so striking that the translator is virtually speaking out loud and bold to the speaker. (3) The serene in line 7, both a political and ecological metaphor, refers to the clear air, and to the freedom and control, of Homer's poetry.

(4) The similes in lines 9-11 and in 11-14 convey the thrill of being the first person to see an unknown planet or an unknown ocean. With that thrill comes the awareness that the world is larger and more amazing than had been dreamed. Keats has found exactly the right similes for this enlarged sense of the world. (5) In these similes, the description of the planet suggests a purposeful entrance, while the other words suggest chance and a far less active and deliberate motion. (6) Although Keats mistakes his history here, few readers will condemn the poem for this reason. Cortez as a model voyager and discoverer is still an excellent metaphor. (7) The poem speaks about the discovery of the excitement, wonder, and beauty of literature--a new world with no apparent limit. Writing topics: the similes of discovery. The value of reading as expressed in the metaphor of Homer's territory as a ruler. The metaphor of fealty and the condition of the writer.

Robert Burns, O My Luve's Like a Red, Red Rose, pages 595-596.

This poem was done for the Scots Musical Museum, a collection of old and new Scots songs in the eighteenth-century traditions of William Thomson's Orpheus Caledonius and the poems of the elder Allan Ramsay. Students can understand the poem with a minimum of annotation, for the diction is not over-burdened with localisms, and the sentiments and expressions are quite clear.

Study Questions: (1) The situation is that the speaker is declaring his love for his bonnie lass (line 5), vowing his love's continuation, bidding her good bye, and promising to return. This situation is similar to the one created in Donne's "A Valediction: Forbidding Mourning" (page 599), except that the social class and level of education of this speaker are imagined as lower. (2) Stanza 1 may be regarded as a brief soliloquy or meditation, in which the speaker reflects on the lady's charms. But by stanza 2 he is addressing her directly. (3) The initial two similes of the poem, and much of the rest of the speaker's language, are commonplace. However, the charm of the poem lies in its evident sincerity and boldness, even if the language is unexceptional. (4) The speaker asserts that seas must dry and rocks must melt before his love will end. Since neither is likely to happen soon, the lady can be assured of his fidelity and his return. Writing topics: The rose as a simile. Structure. Hyperbole. A comparison with Donne's "Valediction."

William Shakespeare, Sonnet 30: When to the Sessions, pages 595-596.

This is one of those sonnets, beginning with when, that Edward Hubler praises on the ground that the when subordinate clause requires a logical development and an integrated couplet (The Sense of Shakespeare's Sonnets, 1952). To this interesting idea you might add that Shakespeare in the sonnets is fond of integrating connected systems of imagery as the basis of his metaphors and similes. See text pages 596-597 and the sample essay, pages 618-19, for a consideration of the matters raised in the study questions (page 596).

John Donne, A Valediction: Forbidding Mourning, pages 599-600.

It is impossible to date this poem, and hence all we can do is surmise that it may have been inspired by an occasion of a trip, when the poet found a need to answer objections that might have been raised to his going. More to the point here is the extensive use of metaphorical language, together with the renowned concluding metaphysical conceit (an extended metaphor or simile) comparing lovers to a geometric compass. In the course of the poem, the speaker employs five conceits to define the quiet and calm that should characterize his departure: (a) the death of virtuous men, (b) movement of the celestial spheres, (c) the assurance of love that is more than physical, (d) the expansion of gold beaten to foil, and (e) the legs of a drawing compass.
Study Questions: (1) The situation of the poem is a valediction, literally, a saying of farewell (ask your students if they know what a valedictorian is). (2) Stanzas 1-2 form a simile developing the following idea: Let us part the way virtuous persons die, quietly and easily. The two phrases tear-floods and sigh-tempests are exaggerations designed to tease the listener out of weeping, and then to emphasize the remaining parts of the poem, which are quite serious. (3) The simile about the dying men sets a serious tone, and makes clear that the parting is genuinely painful, both for speaker and listener. (4) The metaphor of stanza 3 refers to parting and disruptions: Earthquakes destroy earth and the dwellings on it. Movement of the spheres disrupts the smooth, circular movements of heavenly bodies; it is far more significant than earthquakes, but it cannot be felt by humans. Thus, the parting of the lovers should be like the trepedation of the spheres: significant but quiet, insensible to others, and innocent.
(5) The basis for the speaker's claim in lines 13-20 is that the love of ordinary lovers (sublunary [which means subject to change], line 13) is only physical, and that for this reason they cannot retain love at a distance. By contrast, the love of the speaker and the listener is not just a physical love, but is also an interaction of minds; therefore a separation of the physical does not threaten the love since it does not imply a separation of the mental. (6) The subject of the metaphor begun in line 17 with the word refined is the refining of gold, in which all dross and impurities are removed and only the purest and most valuable material remains. (7) The speaker also

refers to the malleability of gold to suggest that even when lovers are apart they are still united, just like a sheet of delicate gold foil (line 24). This metaphorical language supports the conviction that this love is deep and lasting. (8) See text pages 600-601 for a consideration of the compass simile. Writing topics: the apparent dramatic situation occasioning the poem. The extended simile of the compass. The idea of love expressed in the poem.

William Shakespeare, Shall I Compare Thee to a Summer's Day, pages 602-603.

About this sonnet there is little that one can say except that it is one of the foremost poems in the language. Though ostensibly it is an elaborate compliment, its range extends into the realms of time and eternity. We recommend that all students learn it by heart. Study Questions: (1) The speaker of the poem wants to tell the lady that she is surpassingly beautiful, and that his love and art will give her eternal life in the memories of all those who read the poem. A possible dramatic situation is that the speaker has been challenged to develop an elaborate comparison, and the poem is his response. It is possible that laughter might be sought early in the poem, because the speaker is clearly demonstrating his ingenuity. However, more thoughtful and sober responses are appropriate as the poem becomes more serious. (2) The opening comparison is not unusual, but the speaker's pattern of metaphor is memorable. (3) The metaphors (lines 1-8) assert that natural beauty fades or dies. This assertion is essential to the point of the sestet that only art (eternal lines, this very sonnet) can give immortality.
(4) Temperate as used in the sonnet means moderate, not extreme. Summer days can be blisteringly hot; by contrast, the lady is always pleasant and even tempered. The buds of May (line 3) are the first signs of summer, and they are dear (darling) and cherished both because they are pretty and because they signal the end of winter. Like most lovely things, buds are fragile, and are valued because they are so rare. (5) Also in keeping with shortness is Shakespeare's language of rental for a fixed period ("summer's lease hath all too short a date"). (6) In lines 5 and 6, the sun can be too hot, or it can be hidden behind clouds (dimmed). Human beings too can lose their beauty or their desirability. (7) At line 9, the speaker begins to assert that, unlike natural objects, the lady's summer (i.e., the beauty of her disposition) cannot fade, and that even Death (line 11) cannot claim her as long as she is the subject of the lines of the poem. Here the speaker is complimenting the power of his own poetry as well as the lady.
(8) Lines 13-14 (the couplet) climax the poem's argument. Here the speaker asserts that the poem will endure as long as human life endures, and that as long as people can see (to read), the sonnet will give life to the lady. It is the immortality of art that the speaker exalts over the transience of life. Writing topics: the metaphor of summer and the brevity of beauty. The seriousness of the poem. The poem as a dramatic utterance. The idea of immortality conferred by art.

Thomas Campion, Cherry Ripe, pages 603-604.

Campion himself set many of his poems to music, this among them. Those listening to a musical rendition, however, would need to pay close attention upon first hearing, for the text demonstrates the complexity of the Jacobean lyric. Study Questions: (1) The metaphor of the of the garden stands for the lady's beauty. The roses are her cheeks, the lilies her skin. (2) Comparing her mouth to paradise, the speaker suggests the lady's desirability. The

phrase pleasant fruits of line 4 suggests that every sweet and natural thing
one could desire to taste is in her face. (3) The orient pearl refers to her
teeth. Perhaps it is important to remind students that four centuries ago,
many people had missing, decayed, or stained teeth. Women in particular often
suffered tooth loss during pregnancy. Thus, the lady's full number of white
teeth makes her unusually lovely.

(4) The eyes were thought to be windows of the soul. Since the lady's
eyes are like angels (line 13), her virtue is underlined, while her arched
brows will protect her as a bow and arrow would against unwelcome approaches.
(5) The metaphor of cherries draws upon the sweetness and desirability of the
fruit. The cry cherry ripe was apparently used by fruit sellers to advertise
their wares. Here it suggests that no one may have the fruit (i.e., kiss the
lady's lips) unless she herself declares that she is willing, perhaps when she
is mature, perhaps when in love. The unusual aspect of the poem is that the
decision clearly rests with the lady to manage her own life. In stanza 2 she
is free to resist men of rank and power, in stanza 3 all (line 16) fall into
this category. Religious language (angels . . . sacred) suggests the moral
significance of her decisions.

(6) The poem thus opens conventionally, and the girl's prettiness at
first appears to be for sale. But by the last stanza we have seen that her
beauty brings the need for wise decisions about where she will give her love
and her physical favors. The poem is a morality lesson, one which shows
surprising respect for the woman's freedom to choose. Writing topics:
conventional metaphors of beauty. Morality in the poem. The structure of the
poem.

Henry King, Sic Vita, page 604.

Students will need to know that sic vita means thus is life or such is
life. The poem itself is virtually a tabular arrangement of metaphorical
language, and is memorable for this reason.
Study Questions: (1) Lines 1-6 of the poem present a series of similes;
lines 7-8 finish the comparisons; lines 9-12 comment on the comparisons. (2)
There are six similes, ranging from the objects in the night sky to drops of
dew on leaves and grass. All are comparisons from nature, and all describe
motions which come to an end. (3) In lines 7 and 8, human life is presented
as light, and night then becomes death. Human light or life is borrowed, and
can and will be called in for payment; that is, death. The source from which
life is borrowed is God or Nature.
(4) Lines 9-12 are not logically essential, but without them, lines 7 and
8 would have to bear the weight of the poem, and the balance would be skewed.
By adding these lines, King not only underscores his point, but does so in
rhythms which give the poem stateliness, importance, and closure. (5) The
poem emphasizes human brevity, but similes like that of the falling star and
the rippling of water suggest that human life is beautiful, desirable, and
admirable, despite its shortness. Writing topics: the philosophy of the poem.
The development of the similes. Borrowed light in relationship to life.

Edmund Waller, Go, Lovely Rose, page 605.

This is a lovely and haunting poem. It establishes the image of the
rose, a conventional comparison with writers of love lyrics, but it uses the
rose as a metaphor of the beauty, fragility, and impermanence of life. It is
a perennial favorite of readers, and has often been set to music.

Study Questions: (1) The poem suggests a dramatic situation in which the speaker addresses a rose which he is about to send to a woman. Both rose and woman possess short-lived beauty. (2) In stanza 1 the speaker attributes youth and beauty to the rose. (3) In stanza 2 the speaker responds to the young woman's apparent reticence. He asks the rose to remind her that, had it grown in an isolated desert, no one would ever have seen its beauty. The message is logical: asking a rose to deliver it is somewhat more fanciful. (4) The imputed darkness in which the lady lives is her self-imposed privacy. In lines 13-15, the speaker asks the rose to invite the lady into the open, since beauty unseen is little valued. He is not asking her to abandon her modesty, merely to accept the normal relationship of men and women.

(5) In lines 16-20 the poem makes clear that both the flower and the lady must die. The comparison is apt inasmuch as the assertion is true, but it falls short because (a) the flower's life is shortened by its having been cut, and (b) a flower's life is briefer and simpler than the life of a human being. (6) Thus the poem is more a philosophical reflection than a sensual invitation which carpe diem suggests. The poem is sensitive to the woman's feelings; the speaker applauds her not just as pretty and healthy but also "wondrous sweet and fair" (line 20). Writing topics: is the poem about life or death or both? The metaphor of the rose. The dramatic situation. The carpe diem theme.

George Gordon, Lord Byron, The Destruction of Sennacherib, pages 606-607.

This poem is perhaps the best known of the poems in Byron's Hebrew Melodies (1815), the last major work he published before he left England, to remain in virtual exile until his death. "The Destruction of Sennacherib" demonstrates virtuosic metrical skill, being almost entirely in anapaests, with occasional amphibrachs and iambs as substitute feet.

Study Questions: (1) The opening simile, comparing a wolf attacking a sheep fold to the Assyrian army attacking the Hebrews, is striking, filled as it is with the implication of the innocent and helpless sheep and the vicious attacker. (2) In lines 3-6, human power appears mighty and menacing. By contrast, Divine power is not only total but it is also part of the order of the universe, as inexorable and irresistible as the changing of the seasons. (3) In lines 9-20, the details about the Assyrian deaths are not excessive given the style, with its intense visual and rhythmic stresses.

(4) Both "Sir Patrick Spens" and "The Destruction of Sennacherib" concentrate in their final stanzas on the women left widowed by the deaths of their husbands. Were Byron to concentrate the entire stanza on them here, the poem could be diverted to the sobering and realistic note that the Assyrian soldiers were people too, with homes and wives and responsibilities. But by returning quickly to the supposed falsity of Assyrian religion, Byron ends by resonating the main string of his theme once more: God's protection of the Hebrews against injustice. Writing topics: the simile of wolf and sheepfold. The narrative structure. The metrical pattern and its variations.

Ogden Nash, Very Like a Whale, pages 607-608.

This poem is amusing for students who have just studied Byron's "The Destruction of Sennacherib." It is also instructional, however, for it invites readers to consider the justness and appropriateness of comparisons, as well as their meanings. The technique of Nash's humor here is the logical fallacy known as reductio ad absurbum. Virtually any simile or metaphor, if pushed far enough, can seem inappropriate or even silly, and some, like the mice and the petticoat, are silly from the start.

Study Questions: (1) In Hamlet, Hamlet makes fun of Polonius by showing the courtier's willingness to agree to any suggestion made by his prince, and to see anything he thinks will please. Nash is protesting a tendency of some poets--and readers--to push their imaginations too far. (2) In lines 1-4, the speaker lays out possible objections to metaphor and simile; lines 5-22 illustrate the objections, using Byron's poem as the example; lines 23-26 lay out what the speaker thinks should have been said--without simile and metaphor, had Byron been willing to dispense with them; lines 27-30 are the speaker's reflection on the need for reality as opposed to metaphor. (3) It is hard to know how far Nash's speaker is going in his campaign of reform. We can only be sure that he objects to far-fetched, inappropriate metaphors. (4) Nash's persona is a down-to-earth, suffer-no-fools-gladly fellow who, rather than being impatient with persons unable or unwilling to use their imaginations, holds their literal-mindedness up as admirable. Such a stance is unlikely for a teacher of literature, however, since taking it might well complicate teaching. (5) The speaker's complaints about images comparing ladies to lilies make clear that certain comparisons may no longer work. A metaphor acceptable in the past may now be a cliche. Students thus need to develop a capacity to read with historical understanding. (6) Mice are unpleasant rodents to most people, and few like the idea of mice running about their feet. Nash picks up on that discomfort. Suckling is, among other things, complimenting his lady on her small feet, and hinting at the eroticism of a living thing under a woman's skirt. Snails too, as in Herrick's poem, are unattractive, and the metaphor could therefore be criticized. (7) In the same vein, Nash's speaker shows the metaphor of the snow-blanket to be silly on the literal level; many, perhaps most, metaphors would fall if taken literally. Used as aids to the imagination, however, they add richness by opening up unexpected comparisons and pointing toward heretofore unobserved similarities and complexities. (8) Nash's humor results from the poem's literalness, its reduction of the simile of the wolf to a real wolf on all fours saying "woof woof woof," its rag-tag collection of quotations and allusions, and its outlandish rhymes and rhythms.

Writing topics: does the speaker mean everything he says? The poem's humor. The relevance or justice of the criticism of simile and metaphor. The use of the poem as a guide for judging metaphorical language.

Langston Hughes, Harlem, page 609.

This brief poem is best known for having provided Lorraine Hansberry the title for her play, A Raisin in the Sun (1959). The similes here are quite compressed. In class, they can occasion a vigorous discussion about the psychological effects of denial and frustration upon individuals who have been given promises but no opportunity to better themselves.

Study Questions: (1) The dream deferred is the dream of equality, equal opportunity, and of a society based on mutual respect. The use of the word deferred may be an allusion to the saying in the law that Justice deferred (or delayed) is justice denied. See also Proverbs 13:12, "Hope deferred maketh the heart sick." (2) The structure of the poem, like Shakespeare's sonnet 18 (pages 602-603), depends upon an opening question. But whereas the sonnet ends confidently, Hughes's poem ends with an ominous question. (3) The similes refer to things left alone to change--to dry up, fester, stink, or crust over. All become unusable and unpleasant. (4) The metaphor in line 11 is that of a bomb. Here the dream deferred is not like a bomb, it is a bomb.

115

Thus the rhetorical figure carries the climax of the poem. Writing topics: the meaning of the similes. The concluding metaphor as climax. The types or classifications of the similes.

Fray Angelico Chavez, Rattlesnake, page 610.

This poem creates a contrast, embodied within the two stanzas, between awe and respect and fear and rejection. Students understand the reasons for fear, but are somewhat surprised at the admiration and virtual worship in stanza 1. Study Questions: (1) The first two phrases, line of beauty and in-laid band, stress the beauty of the snake, as does the word cloisonne in the poem's last line. But we cannot forget that a hive (line 4) contains both patterned honeycomb and potentially harmful bees, while a coil (line 8) is something that can ensnare and entrap. (2) The speaker thus responds to the snake's beauty in stanza 1 and to its dangerousness in stanza 2.

(3) The metaphor of stanza 1, stressing the word scrawled, suggests that the snake is God's handiwork, but was done carelessly or quickly. This metaphor is appropriate, since the living snake is not artistically arranged, but is stretched out or moving over sand like an accidental scrawl, or like a doodle. Since modern views of creativity involve both chance and cataclysmic change, the sense of almost accidental creation is not inconsistent with a concept of God's handiwork. Both scrolling and scrawled sound alike, but scrolling suggests a constant process of motion, more careful and controlled than a scrawl. (4) The poem is impressionistic, since it does not give a scientific or realistic description, but builds on the viewer's impressions of the snake's beauty and its deadly threat.

Writing topics: the ambivalence of the speaker toward the snake. The use of metaphor to convey impression and thought. The concept of God and creation as represented by the snake.

Sylvia Plath, Metaphors, page 610.

A posthumous recipient of the Pulitzer Prize in Poetry (1981), Plath wrote highly personal, revelatory poems. "Metaphors" is one of her happier efforts. Study Questions: (1) The only clue that the speaker is a woman, and a pregnant one, is at line 7 ("I'm . . . a cow in calf"). (2) The nine syllables are the nine months of pregnancy. The pregnant woman is a riddle because (a) even today there is much unknown about pregnancy, and (b) traditionally, the results of pregnancy are not known until birth. The poem is a riddle because one has to determine the identity and condition of the speaker. (3) The metaphors suggest size, ripeness, increase, and wealth. They all suggest normal feelings of pregnancy, especially the expectant mother's awareness that she cannot get off the train she is on (line 9). (4) Some of the metaphors--the melon and tendrils, the elephant--are funny, for however big she might feel, a pregnant woman is not elephantine. None of the metaphors are shocking or demeaning; indeed, the speaker's sense of herself as having fine timbers or being a full purse conveys her self-satisfaction.

(5) The aspect of early pregnancy suggested by the green apple metaphor is morning sickness, while the metaphor of the stage (i.e., part of a process) shows the speaker's awareness that she is the means by which the race continues itself. The train metaphor conveys the speaker's sense that she is being carried along by forces beyond her control. Writing topics: the metaphors of ripeness. The difficulty of the riddle (and what, if anything makes it difficult). The humor or seriousness of the poem.

Linda Pastan, Marks, page 611.

Students can take great delight in discovering the metaphor of this poem. Some may want to take the conclusion seriously, and it is therefore important to stress that this part can be read in context as a joke or quip. Even so, however, the poem contains an underlying note of annoyance that can provoke a vigorous class discussion. Study Questions: (1) The extended metaphor is that of school and grades. Housework is like taking a course: the speaker has been given a varying report card, including an A for cooking and an incomplete for ironing. The son and daughter offer overall grades based on a superior-average and a pass/fail system respectively. (2) In cooking, ironing, lovemaking, and mothering, her family does not give her the highest grades. (3) The son, like a teacher, calls for improvement. (4) The speaker suggests that she is dropping out because she's tired, and because dropping out is an option often used by students. The way she phrases it, "Wait 'til they learn," is an implied threat, but granted the tone of affectionate banter throughout the poem, the threat is a joke rather than an actual decision. (5) The poem thus explores the speaker's sense that she, like most people, is constantly being rated, and that even those who love her find her not fully adequate. The playful metaphor, which puts this situation in a new light, is accurate, vivid, and memorable. Writing topics: tone. The metaphor of student life as applied to being a wife, housekeeper, and mother. The humor of the poem. The last lines as a serious/comic climax.

Marge Piercy, A Work of Artifice, page 612.

This poem embodies a deeply effective metaphor which is straightforwardly detailed and applied, and a tone that one student has described as controlled fury. Study Questions: (1) In lines 1-17 the subject of the poem seems to be the bonsai tree; then, it shifts explicitly to women. The metaphor is apt granted the poem's view that traditional attitudes toward women do not encourage their development. A full growth (eighty feet tall, line 3) could result only from equality of opportunity with men. (2) In lines 12-16, the gardener's song represents society persuading women to be content with being dwarfed and with feeling fortunate when and if they find a pot to grow in (a home) and a singing gardener (a husband). Note that the gardener does both the stunting and the brainwashing. (3) At line 17 the poem switches to a series of direct observations on women dwarfed in their growth. Thus distorted, they are concerned with their looks (curlers), they have allowed their abilities and minds to become crippled, and they occupy themselves only with love. The image of the bound feet (an old Chinese practice of stunting the feet of women) is a powerful symbol depicting the traditionally unnatural treatment of women. Writing topics: the bonsai tree as metaphor. Piercy's critique of women's traditional roles. Irony in the last lines.

Judith Minty, Conjoined, page 613.

Alert students will notice the irony in the poem's subtitle, "a marriage poem." Like Eliot's "Prufrock" (page 947), which is called a love song but ironically has nothing to do with love, this poem's subtitle suggests a celebration of marriage, but instead expresses great misgiving if not hostility. Study Questions: (1) Literally, the two parts form a double onion; metaphorically, the parts are husband and wife. The two things could be the body and soul of one person (since to cut them apart might kill [line 13]), but

117

husband/wife is more plausible. (2) In the metaphors of the onion, the twins, and the calves, the three were intended to be separate, but instead they are freaks of nature, monstrous accidents that allowed them to live but to live abnormally. The speaker suggests that this situation is like marriage. (3) In lines 12-13, the speaker suggests that freedom (divorce, separation) might kill one partner, as it sometimes kills a Siamese twin. Note that the one who might not survive is not specifed. The metaphor thus represents a recognition of reality. (4) An increasing number of men now slice onions, but men, more often in charge of power and money, usually lay out the grounds of a relation- ship. Hence it is often asserted that women must be alert to hidden dynamics (body language, looks) to protect themselves emotionally, while men may be more direct and less subtle. Writing topics: the irony of the subtitle. The view of the marriage bond. The metaphors of the onion, twins, and calves.

Seamus Heaney, Valediction, page 614.

This poem, from Heaney's Death of a Naturalist (1966), creates a mood of solitude, regret, uneasiness, and sorrow. Study Questions: (1) The opening word, Lady, reminds us of more formal poetry such as that in the love poetry of the sixteenth and seventeenth centuries. Other, more intimate words would have given a much different tone and image. A lady, after all, has both status and power, and a high degree of grace. (2) The words has hurt stress the close ties between mental processes and the emotions--in this case, pain. Metaphorically, the phrase compares hurt feelings to a physical injury. (3) The expanded metaphor in lines 5-16 is a ship at sea: time rides easy at anchor; absence creates a stormy sea with the ship of love being cast adrift without anchor. Thus the speaker suggests that he is being tossed about emotionally as if in a storm at sea. The metaphor is more effective than simple assertions because it is more complex and more dramatic, more suggestive of the mystery of human life. (4) All three poems are about a leave-taking. In both Burns and Donne, the speaker intends to return, while in Heaney, there is no such happy ending on the horizon. In addition, it is the Lady who has left the speaker of "Valediction," and the emphasis is on the speaker's grief and disorientation. The only suggestion of a return comes at Heaney's line 15, but this line contrasts oddly with line 3 ("you have left the house"). Writing topics: the ship as metaphor. Hurt thought as metaphor. A comparison of this poem and Minty's "Conjoined" (page 613). An extended comparison of this poem with Donne's "Valediction" and/or Burns's "O My Luve's Like a Red, Red Rose."

WRITING ABOUT METAPHORS AND SIMILES IN POETRY, pages 615-619.

Four possible essay developments are outlined on pages 616-617. Most students will probably use type 1, with perhaps some reinforcement from type 2 as is shown in the sample essay on pages 618-619. The third type of essay (page 617), because it attempts to select characteristic metaphors, may be most useful if students study more than a single poem by a particular author (see Chapter 26, or consult the index, for such materials). The fourth type (page 617), in addition to being a study of metaphor generally, also brings in tone. The sample essay (pages 618-619) is useful as a guide to any of the suggested writing topics for this chapter because, throughout, it stresses the topic of metaphor. In such an essay it is easy to get diverted from the rhetorical figures and begin a general discussion. You can encourage students to concentrate on the assigned topic (and method) of this or any other essay.

CHAPTER 17

OTHER RHETORICAL FIGURES

The topic of this chapter is sometimes omitted by instructors who are pressed for time. Because it is important that students know at least some of the figures, however, we have structured this introductory section so that you may assign as many of the figures as you think important or for which you have time. Each of the discussions is self-contained: students may benefit from as many of them as you assign. The other figures, with pages, are these:

Thus, for example, if you wish to assign paradox, personification, and the pun only, you can single out these sections of the chapter for your students.

Sir Thomas Wyatt, I Find No Peace, pages 620-621.

See text pages 621-622 and the sample essay (pages 638-639) for discussion of this poem. Possible writing topics include the nature of the speaker and the ideas about love explored in the poem.

John Gay, Let Us Take the Road, page 625.

The poem is discussed on page 625. You may wish to amplify some of the points, like the work of the alchemists. In addition, the word road (line 1) refers to grand theft that occurred on the open highways of eighteenth-century England. Even today we still use the phrase highway robbery, which originated in this aspect of eighteenth-century life. Writing topics: the imagery appropriate to theivery. The use of puns. The use of rhyme.

William Wordsworth, London, 1802, page 627.

This Italian sonnet, an extended apostrophe to John Milton, bemoans England's apparent loss of manners, virtue, freedom, and power and sets up Milton as an ideal. Study Questions: (1) In this apostrophe to Milton, the speaker views Milton as the moral conscience of the nation, one who can recall a selfish population to the virtue, freedom, power which once was its own. The speaker reminds the readers that Milton wrote on major issues such as freedom of expression (in Areopagitica) and on the relationship of God and humankind, as in Paradise Lost. (2) By the metonyms altar, sword, and pen, the speaker refers to clergymen, soldiers, and writers, all of whom, in his judgment, are failing their country in time of need. Milton, by contrast, is seen as one who concerned himself with the moral habits of his country. (3) Overstatements abound: calling England a fen of stagnant waters, the sweeping rejection of the three professions referred to above, the reference to Milton's voice where sound was like the sea, and the whole presentation of

119

the quite human John Milton as a model of saintly perfection. Their effect is
to underline the seriousness of the national malaise, and to establish Milton
as an ideal moral guide. (4) Milton's moral stature is underlined by the
statement, "Thy soul was like a star, and dwelt apart," suggesting that the
best qualities of his intellectual and moral nature were as far above those of
ordinary mortals as a star is. His heart, by contrast, suggests his physical
nature and the cheerful acceptance in his daily life of common duties and
obligations. Thus Wordsworth, drawing on his audience's undoubted knowledge
of Milton's life, of his literary and political career and the physical and
moral courage which characterized both, and of his religious steadfastness
despite the undoubted suffering occasioned by his blindness, calls up to the
reader a moral exemplar of unquestioned validity to Protestant England.

Writing topics: the use of overstatement. The nature of the apostrophe
to Milton. The use of synecdoche in the poem.

John Keats, To Autumn, pages 628-629.

Because this poem is so effective and lovely, readers may ignore the many
figures that Keats employs. Indeed, the poem is loved by many who might ask
if knowledge of the figures can add anything to their appreciation. The fact
remains, however, that Keats created the figures as an integral part of the
poem, and therefore to understand them is one way of following the processes
of his poetic art.

Study Questions: (1) In stanza 1, Autumn is presented in his prime,
actively conspiring with his close bosom-friend, the sun, to bring to fruition
all growing things. Here Autumn is the busy, active producer of the copious
harvest. In stanza 2, Autumn is a laborer who sometimes forgets the task of
gleaning and making cider and sits down and dozes in the midst of the work
day. The change suggests the passage of time: the actions of stanza 1 produce
the crops; stanza 2 is concerned with reaping them and the resulting fatigue.
(2) The poem progresses in accord with qualities or powers given to Autumn.
In stanza 1, Autumn is an internal force, expanding and making the world grow.
In 2, Autumn is manifested in human beings, replete and satisfied in the
security of the harvest. In 3, the attribution is that Autumn is a bringer of
sounds and evening songs, all heard through the air illuminated by the rosy
sun. There is twist on convention here, for Autumn in the tradition of
pastoral poetry is often a time of death and decline. Keats's emphasis on the
fruition and satisfaction of the season hence illustrates the security offered
by Autumn as personified as the grower and harvester.

(3) Keats uses both synecdoche and metonymy in each of these two stanzas.
Specifically, metonyms in stanza 1 are the thatch-eaves, which represent the
people who live in the houses so protected, and the clammy cells of line 11,
which, because they are the location of honey, stand for the honey itself and
the sweetness of the season. In stanza 2, synecdoches are hair (line 15),
which figuratively represents the dust of harvested grain and therefore the
grain itself; laden head (line 20), which represents the persons working in
the autumnal harvest both as laborers and as planners of the season, and
oozings (line 22), representing specifically cider but generally the
substances made from the year's produce. These figures give insights into the
intricacy of growth, harvest, and manufacture, and also along with the
personification of autumn, the intention of nature and life to nurture human
beings. (4) The images throughout the poem suggest ripeness, harvest, rest,
and beauty after labor. The trees are loaded with apples; the machinery
(cider press, reaping hook) is that which is used at the time of harvest; the
light is red and mellow--rosy--and is seen over plains of cut grain; and the

sounds are those of twilight and night--not threatening but restful.
     Writing topics: the structure of the poem. The use of metonymy and
synecdoche. The images of ripeness and fullness. The personification.

Alfred, Lord Tennyson, Break, Break, Break, page 629.

     Tennyson's great long poem, occasioned by the death of his friend Arthur
Hallam in 1733, is In Memoriam (1850). "Break, Break, Break" is a spearate
piece with the same sense of regret and mourning. Critics have pointed out
that Tennyson's major talent was in the lyric rather than narrative and
dramatic modes. "Break, Break, Break" is evidence of this great talent.
     Study Questions: (1) The scene in the poem is a craggy shoreline, with a
heavy surf and harbor scenes. Thus the apostrophes to the sea with which the
poem opens and closes are part of the scene, and also form a structural frame.
The sea suggests the permanance of time and the impermanance of life, as it
does also in Arnold's "Dover Beach" (page 529). (2) The bay, the sister, the
sailor lad, and the ships in lines 5-10, through the function of synecdoche,
stand for family relationships, the growth toward a career, and the business
of commerce. All these are connected with life, unlike the hand and voice
which stand for the dead person for whom the speaker is mourning. The day of
line 15 refers to the past times of friendship. Thus the contrast is between
life and death, the present and the past. (3) The breaking of the waves
symbolizes the disruption and emptying of the speaker's plans and feelings.
The heart, because it is popularly considered to be the center of emotions,
and therefore a metonym for feelings, is thought to break when a person goes
through extreme emotional pain. Thus the breaking of the waves is appropriate
symbolically, though the speaker certainly does not emphasize the connection.
     (4) Students may provide their own answers to the question of what makes
the poem beautiful, if they so consider it. One may respond by citing the
balanced structure and the contrast between life and death in the poem. Lines
11 and 12 are particularly touching and memorable. In addition, the poem
captures a balanced mood of regret and sorrow that avoids sentimentality. The
poem has a sense of finality about it. Beyond all these specific reasons,
however, the poem is genuinely moving. Writing topics: the contrast between
life and death. The emotional balance or sentimentality of the poem. The use
of synecdoche. The structure of references to the sea.

T.S. Eliot, Eyes That Last I Saw in Tears, page 630.

     This poem is not one of those on which Eliot's reputation rests (i.e.,
The Waste Land, "Prufrock," etc.); it is unusual in his work because it is
considered to be quite personal, likely a reflection of the pain he apparently
experienced in his marriage.
     Study Questions: (1) Eyes as a synecdoche stand for a person who was
obviously in close communication and in an intimate relationship with the
speaker. The word tears as an instance of metonymy indicates emotions of
grief and sorrow. (2) The tears result from division, a rupture of the
relationship. The meaning of eyes outlasting tears is apparently that people
cannot sustain deep emotion. Eventually they go on to do other things, and,
though they do not forget causes of sorrow, the emotions become less painful.
The eyes holding us in derision (line 15) do so perhaps because hurt feelings
can lead to anger. Perhaps, also, the speaker is here expressing guilt for
having caused the tears. The meaning of the eyes being of decision (line 9)
suggests that the grieving person has made personal choices that will lead to

121

a new way of life. It is in the nature of these references that they cannot
be expressed too specifically. (3) The eyes but not the tears is paradoxical
because the speaker seems to be remembering the eyes, without tears, as in a
golden dream; that is, he thinks of the person as she was before the division
occurred. The paradox is that the relationship seems over, but the fond
memory is not. The affliction, about which the speaker remarks in lines 6 and
7, is apparent inability to close off the memory.

(4) The entire poem might be considered a paradox because of the complex
awarenesses of the speaker; he sees a golden vision but knows it is a dream;
he knows of the tears but cannot see them when he recalls the eyes; he looks
forward to less division in death than he experienced in life, but expects
that ultimately all human beings (us) will be held in derision by persons for
whom all former arguments are now irrelevant; he would like reconciliation but
knows that there can be none. (5) The references to the two kingdoms of death
are obscure and likely allusive. They may be explained perhaps as allusions
to classical states of dreaming and death. Thus Homer (Odyssey, 19:562)
explains that an ivory gate opening to the region of dreams permits the issue
of false dreams, while a gate of polished horn is the entry way of true dreams
predicting the future. Death is viewed not as an end but a continuation of
consciousness. The kingdom of death, ruled by Hades, was reached through an
entrance, or door. (6) The repeated words and phrases (i.e., eyes, tears, a
little while, This is my affliction) create an effect of incantation, a
ritualistic attempt to face the truth of the situation through repetition.

Writing topics: the personal topic matter. Paradox and contradiction.
The meaning of eyes and tears.

Ogden Nash, Exit, Pursued by a Bear, pages 631-632.

"Exit, Pursued by a Bear" is not like much of Nash's other poetry because
it stresses the destructiveness of a nuclear war. The source for the idea of
animals overrunning locations of former wealth is Fitzgeralds's translation of
The Rubaiyat of Omar Khayyam, which Nash directly echoes in lines 17 and 21
(please see the textual notes).
Study Questions: (1) The allusion to Shakespeare's stage direction as the
title of the poem creates emphasis of irony and understatement. The bear
refers to the animal that roars at and eats up Antigonus in 3.3.58 of The
Winter's Tale, and it can also refer to the danger added to the world by the
proliferation of nuclear weaponry by potentially hostile countries. (2) The
setting is one of extreme wealth--likely a private home as shown by the
artifacts contained there, all suggested by the identifying (proper or trade)
names as metonyms. The home is now vacant, for the owners are presumed to
have been killed as a result of nuclear warfare. (3) Because the building is
no longer maintained, animals have gained entry and now use the artifacts for
their lairs. The situation has apparently lasted for a long time, for mold
has had a chance to grow on the the rare and expensive books (line 15). (4)
One paradox in the poem is that the collector's items, usually not used by
people because of their value, are used indiscriminately by animals once the
people are gone. Another paradox is that the people who valued the museum
pieces and took good care of them did not take enough care of humanity to
negotiate for their ultimate security--the elimination of the nuclear threat.
(5) The fireball is a nuclear bomb. The idea is that war can no longer be
limited, but with atomic weapons is global and totally destructive. By
comparison, the danger in Yeats's "The Second Coming" is one of increasingly
brutal and dictatorial regimes. In Jeffers's "The Purse Seine" the threat is
the pollution resulting from increasing industrialism. "The Second Coming"

envisages suppression, however, while "The Purse Seine" implies slow but
inevitable self-strangulation and "Exit, Pursued by a Bear" holds up the
spectre of sudden annihilation. Writing topics: the names of museum pieces
and collector's items as metonyms. Setting. Allusion. Paradoxes.

Elizabeth Bishop, Rain Towards Morning, page 632.

This poem, which is personal, impressionistic, and symbolic, may be
contrasted with Bishop's much more specific "The Fish" (page 574). Both poems
speak of freeing living creatures, but the effect of the liberations is
different: in "The Fish" the cause is love for Nature. Here, the freeing of
the birds signifies the solution of a problem or difficulty.
    Study Questions: (1) The poet does not allow us to know any specific
details about the situation, except to say that the liberation of the birds
has brought about a release of intense feelings. (2) The overstatement of the
million birds suggests the magnitude of the previous unhappiness or
frustration. The kiss (line 8), which is a simple action--not an overwhelming
act of love of extensive duration--suggests that simple things produce great
results. Both overstatement and understatement are equally effective, so long
as they are used appropriately. (3) The great light cage can only be taken
suggestively or impressionistically. It likely indicates a publicly known
problem of a suppressive or enslaving nature. The puzzle may refer to the
sometimes contradictory and incomprehensible attitudes and motivations of a
human being.
    (4) The synecdoches of face, kiss, and hands suggest that another person
is involved, who has been hostile, mysterious, or otherwise alienated, but
that this person, through a kiss, has opened up and freed the relationship.
(5) Rain usually accompanies gloomy moods. Once the character (is it the
speaker?) has been freed from worry and anxiety, however, even rain seems to
be brightening (no longer frightening) and cheerful. Writing topics: the
personal meanings. Paradox. Overstatement. Synecdoche.

John Fandel, Indians, page 633.

For many years, because of cowboy movies, American Indians were perceived
in the popular imagination as a threat. More recently this view has been
changing as a result of increasing awareness of the plight of Indians as a
minority people. Fandel's "Indians" shares in this awareness.
    Study Questions: (1) The speaker is perceptive and sympathetic. His
thoughts are prompted by the mention of Indians by Margaret. He indicates the
irony of the fact that his present residence was once owned by Indians, but he
does not mention that the Indians were driven out by his forebears. Lines 3-4
and 16-22 particularly indicate regret about the loss of Indian civilization.
(2) In lines 12-20 synecdoche is used in wigwams, canoes, arrows, summers,
hills, and meadows as brief references to indicate the travel, mode of defense
and hunting, development of agriculture, and pantheistic religion of the
Indians. Suns was an Indian way of reckoning years; here, as a synecdoche, it
suggests the duration of Indian civilization.
    (3) The poem may be considered, structurally, as a meditation developed
by association. The opening indicates the initial cause--the reference to
Indians. The repetitions in lines 5 and 6 emphasize that the speaker knows
little about Indian civilization, and they also begin the train of thoughts in
the rest of the poem. The hesitations are suggested by the repeated use of
words in the couplets. These repetitions cause a "double-take" as the reader

checks to make sure that the ear heard what the eye saw. The effect is a deliberate slowness which emphasizes the uncertain, hesitant state of the speaker's knowledge and also the sympathy which evolves in the poem.

Writing topics: references to Indian ways of life. The effect of verbal repetitions. Structure and development.

Mark Strand, The Remains, page 634.

Strand, born in Canada, often develops themes of alienation and unusual states of mind. Study Questions: (1): the paradox is that the speaker tries to forget the past and move into the future, but discovers that the past still exists inside. Therefore, lines 11 and 12 indicate that changing a life is not simple. (2) The poet uses synecdoche to signify the following: friends and associates (names), personal possessions (pockets), previous preparation and experience (shoes), past jobs and habits (road), and present age (hours). Thus these simple references suggest almost everything from the speaker's earlier life.

(3) The major idea is the paradox that the road to self-fulfillment, necessarily involving internal growth, forces a person to become distant from everything and everyone in the past. Thus change requires a constant saying of goodbye. Time tells the speaker what he or she is, because individuals change or develop only within their histories. Past experience, part of memory, is also part of the present, though it has vanished on all other counts. It is therefore still within the speaker (my life remains, line 12) despite all changes (line 11).

Writing topics: paradox. Is the poem about alienation, or human growth? The use of synecdoche in the poem.

Diane Wakoski, Inside Out, page 634-635.

Wakoski is a poet of great imagination and insight. This poem exhibits her originality to the highest degree. There is humor here, together with a keen understanding of both the depth and the limitation possible in the relations of women and men.

Study Questions: (1) The speaker, a woman speaking to a man who is apparently a painter, talks of a personal and intimate relationship. The two share knowledge of many domestic details, such as screen doors, Kool-Aid, and a commonly owned cat. One may conclude that the two have been living together and have developed a bond of common knowledge and shared experience. (2) The details of the listener's anatomy are the eye (line 1), the mind containing old songs (line 11), hands (line 11), mouth (line 15) and veins (line 20). The title, taken with these details, suggests that people who are close together genuinely do become part of each other. There is also a suggested reversal here of sexual roles: as the act of love involves the male's being within the female, the condition of love also involves the female's being metaphorically within the male. The notion of inside out hence indicates the nature of human intimacy. (3) The eye and the veins suggest through synecdoche the mind and the emotions of the you, while the paintings and the old hat may be transferred as metonyms to refer to the you's accomplishments and personal habits.

(4) These examples are all highly fanciful. Their precise meaning may not be possible to determine unless the reader exerts the kind of playful application intended by the poet. Hence the tire prints would give pain, and by transfer suggest not physical pain but rather emotional annoyance at

responsibilities taking the couple away from their own personal world. Similarly, the mouth containing ground-up pigments transfers by synesthesia to taste and therefore to ideas about art. The ostrich feather which is used like a brush to paint on the moon suggests showiness and flamboyance but also delicacy of touch, and therefore the feather transfers to something like a vivid imagination. The moon and the mouth are appropriate to romantic moods. In the context, transfer by synesthesia suggests that the speaker's thoughts become inspiration for the you who is the painter.

(5) In lines 19-24, the speaker denies the possibility that she can or should remain within the you for too long. The idea is that individuals, even in an intimate relationship, must have their own identities. The paradox is that lovers must be close, but cannot be too close, on the principle of "too much of a good thing." The silver bullet therefore suggests this need for individuality as well as union. (6) The paradox of lines 1 and 2 is that a red carpet is used for royalty, while a butter server is used by a servant. The speaker is here, apparently without irony, suggesting the dual role of her relationship with the you.

Writing topics: personal intimacy. The uses of (1) paradox, (2) synecdoche, (3) metonymy, (4) synesthesia. The playfulness of the poem. The difficulty of the references.

WRITING ABOUT RHETORICAL FIGURES OTHER THAN SIMILE AND METAPHOR, pages 636-640

Some of the figures discussed in this chapter are difficult and subtle. For this reason we recommend that you assign with care any or all of them. In the recommendations for writing, we have suggested that paragraph-length assignments may be useful, in addition to full-length essays. If you have noted a number of figures in the poem, however, the type of essay described second at the bottom of page 636 would answer the need. The type of essay illustrated in the sample on pages 638-639 requires that students detail the pervasiveness of a single figure throughout the assigned poem.

CHAPTER 18

TONE: THE CREATION OF ATTITUDE IN POETRY

Tone is both easy and difficult. It is easy because the beginning and ending of a discussion of tone is the formulation of attitudes present in a poem, or a statement about the appropriateness of diction, imagery, or metaphor to the content. Usually these judgments are readily described. Tone is difficult, however, because a full discussion requires not only the formulation of an attitude but also the analysis of how the poem permits the reader to draw conclusions. Thus, any investigation of tone is complex, requiring students to show the interaction of poet, material, reader, situation, word choice, fairness, completeness of development, truthfulness, and structure, together with anything else that might have a bearing on the proper interpretation of attitudes. When you ask students to describe the dominant tone in a poem, they may respond by saying irony, humor, phoniness, indignation, fury, pathos, or a number of other descriptive terms. The problem for them then becomes explaining the means by which the poem enables these assessments.

Cornelius Whur, The First-Rate Wife, page 643.

The commentary on this truly obnoxious poem (page 644) addresses many of the study questions. Possible writing topics include the nature of the speaker and the tone with respect to women and men.

Wilfred Owen, Dulce et Decorum Est, pages 644-645.

The commentary (page 646) deals with most of the study questions. Writing topics: the tone of the speaker toward the listener. Attitudes about warfare. The irony of the title in the light of the poem's meaning and end.

Thomas Hardy, The Workbox, pages 647-648.

Introductory remarks about this poem are found on page 649. Study Questions: (1) The speaker is mostly the husband, a village cabinet maker. The tone develops here as much in the rhyme scheme and rhythm used--variations on the ballad form--as in other devices. Here the poem tells a story, and though there is no refrain there is a parallelism of actions or words stressing the poem's concerns (e.g., look white, line 21; wan, line 37; a face held or turned aside, lines 22 and 38; the intimate address of little wife and my dear, lines 1 and 21). Thus the form suggests that a significant drama will occur, and that the poet wants us to be attentive, for much is suggested and not made explicit. (2) The dialogue in lines 21-40 indicates that the wife knew the dead man, John, and had established a close relationship with him (have your students consider how close). We can assume that she denies the previous connection because she had never told her husband about it. She is thus covering up an earlier lie. The last stanza (lines 37-40) insinuates that in some way she had knowledge of the causes of John's death. The mystery is preserved about the death (lines 12 and 40) so that the irony of the poem may be maintained.
(3) The irony of the little workbox is that it is, in effect, a miniature coffin, and what the husband meant as a gift of love becomes its opposite--an occasion for pain each time the wife sets about to sew. (4) A more sinister

126

possibility, of course, is that the husband knows the full story, or more likely that he suspects it, and has deliberately fashioned the workbox either as a test or as a punishment for his <u>little wife</u>. The deeper irony is therefore that the husband, by his suspicions, is probably destroying forever any possibility of future truth and intimacy with his wife. The wife's rejection of the husband's suggestion that she is <u>shocked</u> is also ironic. Whether she makes the denial to preserve her mystery or to defend herself from further probing is part of the poem's intriguing ambiguity. (5) The opening speech of the narrator establishes the dramatic situation of the poem. Of the narrator's concluding four lines, the first two are dramatic, and the last two (lines 39-40) indicate his own conclusion about the wife. These lines could possibly be eliminated because they are not consistent with the objective viewpoint of the rest of the poem. Better lines would be descriptive ones, more like lines 37 and 38.

Writing topics: the use of irony. The problematic nature of the wife's relationship with the dead man. Irony of situation. The narrator's role.

Alexander Pope, Epigram from the French, page 650.

This epigram may also be described as a squib, lampoon, or barb because of its shortness. The rhetorical structure in lines 2 and 4 is that of chiasmus or antimetabole: <u>poet</u>, <u>fool</u>; <u>fool</u>, <u>poet</u>. The characteristics of satire present are the qualities of (a) attack, and (b) humor. Insult alone is not enough to create interest in such a poem, but with the wit shown in the speaker's attack, the poem nicely captures the reader involvement and assent necessary in successful satire. Writing topics: The speaker's nature. The speaker's attitude toward the listener. The poem as satire.

Alexander Pope, Epigram. Engraved on the Collar of a Dog, page 650.

This barb is an even more brief illustration of satiric technique, yet it accomplishes much within so short a space. Students who have had acting experience might be able to mimic the superciliousness of the speaker, and thereby demonstrate the skill with which Pope has brought this putative canine to life. Here, satire is illustrated within the speaker himself or herself: the speaker embodies the attitudes being satirized. Writing topics: the speaker as subject of satire. The use of satire to attack attitudes. The dramatic situation.

Anne Bradstreet, The Author to Her Book, page 652.

Anne Bradstreet's brother-in-law had arranged for publication of her manuscript poems in 1650, and did so without her knowledge and corrections (see lines 3-6). The volume, entitled <u>The Tenth Muse</u>, was the first poetic publication in England by anyone living in colonial America. Apparently a second and corrected edition was considered in about 1666, and "The Author to Her Book" was composed in this expectation as a prefatory poem. The new edition did not appear, however, until after Bradstreet's death.

<u>Study Questions</u>: (1) That the speaker refers to her book as <u>ill-formed</u> shows modesty about it. The metaphor is the birth of a child (<u>offspring</u>), a comparison that is more natural for a woman than a man. The metaphor is developed throughout the poem (see, for example, lines 8, 22-23, among others). (2) The tone of the speaker's references to her friends eager to

publish her work is one of both disapproval and disavowal, but at the same time she acknowledges their fidelity by labeling them <u>true</u> (line 3). The negative aspect of the tone is governed by the words <u>snatched</u>, <u>less wise</u>, and <u>exposed</u>, all of which suggest the speaker's ambivalence or ambiguity. (3) The speaker's excuse for issuing the poems is stated in lines 11-12, where she talks of amending <u>blemishes</u>; that is, she wishes to have her reputation depend upon corrected and accurate copies of the poetry. The tone is conducive to humor because of the continuing metaphor of the child. Thus, the images of washing off spots, stretching joints, and improving clothing are all comic. The concluding application of the metaphor, in effect equating the birth of the poems with the birth of an illegitimate child is amusing. Thus the tone throughout makes the collection of poems, the <u>book</u>, seem like an external object, to be laughed about by both poet and reader. (4) In this way, the speaker's attitude about herself is that of conventional self-depreciation. Readers are expected to neglect this attitude as being no more than ordinary modesty expressed by anyone who has ever made a creative effort.

(5) The speaker's portrayal of herself as a busy and harried but also affectionate mother, trying to improve the appearance of a difficult child, encourages an amused response. The details promote understanding and sympathy, along with amusement.

Writing topics: the speaker's attitude toward herself and her work. The attitude toward the well-meaning friends. The tone created through the metaphor of the illegitimate child.

Anne Finch, Countess of Winchelsea, To the Nightingale, pages 653-654.

The nightingale is one of the popular birds of poetry because of the sweetness of its call. The song is often metaphorically equated to poetry. Perhaps because of the associations with night, the bird has also often symbolized the mysteriousness of poetic inspiration, treated by both Finch and Keats ("Ode to a Nightingale," pages 761-763).

<u>Study Questions</u>: (1) The speaker expresses ambiguous ambivalence about the nightingale; it is <u>sweet</u> in line 1, but is a <u>trifler</u> in line 27. The tone is therefore mixed. (2) The speaker praises the bird's song for its wildness (line 7), unintentionality (8), feeling (13), division or harmony (23), and superiority to human song (25). The tone of the description in lines 14-25 is built up out of the envious notion that the poet cannot find words as easily as the bird can sing. The speaker's censure in lines 26- 29 thus reflects both anger and envy. Apparently the poet intends these lines to represent human imperfection and therefore to suggest regret but also understanding.

(3) The tone of the connection made between the nightingale's song and poetry is one of yearning, a desire to imitate in poetic form the song that the bird expresses naturally. The idea underlying this wish is that the poetic spirit is both difficult and mysterious, a function of a <u>spirit of the brain</u>. (4) The metaphor of the thorn causing song is that the poetic spirit is brought out best through the experience of pain, and, by extension, deep feeling. The implication for the speaker is that she too is best inspired when she feels pain, even though she does not describe any of her personal circumstances. (5) In lines 30-35, the speaker concludes the poem on a note of self-reproach, the idea being that those who cannot reach perfect expression envy those who can. The speaker makes the generalization about <u>we poets</u> in order to include her own judgments within a broad range of human response. Writing topics: the bird as a model for the poet. The tone of admiration. The tone of envy. Structure and development.

Arthur O'Shaughnessy, A Love Symphony, pages 654-655.

This poem ties the subject of romantic adoration to images of flowers, birds, and sea--topics which are often included separately but not often all together. Those who wish to speak about the so-called pathetic fallacy may wish to use this poem in illustration, although the tone of the poem makes the comparisons seem true and genuine, not sentimental. The flowers in stanza 1 are all appropriate to the purpose of praise. With regard to stanza 2, both the thrush and the linnet were birds that for many decades had been associated in songbook and miscellany collections with the beauty of nature. In this scheme, the blackbird is slightly problematic.

Study Questions: (1) The symphony of love is the blending of all colors and sounds to make up a song that, in the speaker's fancy, speaks of praise for the listener. The tone is conditioned by the selection of locations and appropriate flowers and harmonies. Thus the bindweed (line 6) becomes a means of complimenting both the beauty and personal care of the beloved's hair. If these references were to be more fully developed they might fall over the edge into sentimentality, but here, because of the directness and simplicity, they work, particularly because of the you were more formula of lines 8 and 16.

(2) The tone of the phrase ancient mystery . . . you (lines 19-20) is designed to reflect the amazement of the speaker at the paradox that love is both old and past, on the one hand, and ever present, on the other. On mysteriousness, all three poems, by Donne, Finch, and O'Shaughnessy, use the concept of religious mystery to describe the power and force of love. Here, O'Shaughnessy uses the idea as a straightforward descriptive statement. Anne Finch uses the idea to contast the often expected state of married people (coldness and indifference) with the state of her speaker's marriage (page 797, line 93). The mystery makes Finch's couple draw inward toward their own private world. In Donne's "The Canonization" (page 478), the mystery is both sexuality and love, with the idea moving from a playful pun on die to the seriousness of the canonized union. Both Donne and Finch thus treat the concept more fully than does O'Shaughnessy. (3) Lines 23-24 suggest not closeness but admiration and praise, not intimacy, but worship and adoration. The phrase fled back to your feet suggests the distance of a statue, with the concluding location of the speaker at the statue's feet.

Writing topics: the meaning of the symphony of love. The attitude of the speaker toward the listener. The idea that love is like a religious mystery, as expressed by O'Shaughnessy alone, or as contrasted with Donne and Finch.

E.E. Cummings, she being Brand / -new, pages 655-656.

This poem is characteristic of Cummings in many ways. It demonstrates his use of popular material, in this case the breaking in of a new car. It also shows his frankness, sexual explicitness, and sense of fun, together with his poetic arrangement of poetry as unusual arrangement on the page. Modern students, accustomed to cars with self-starters, may not know that in 1926, the date of the poem, cars were started with a hand-crank (lines 9-10), gears did not always engage smoothly when the foot clutch was released (line 12), and the spark and choke were worked by levers (line 16) that were moved up and down, to be held in place on a heavily notched dial.

Study Questions: (1) The sexual double entendre of the poem depends on the equation of breaking in a new car and a first experience with sex. Once this premise is admitted, most students are adept at determining the extensive double meanings in the poem. The excitement and discovery invariably cause students to remark that the poem is enjoyable and fun, though this aspect of the poem should probably not be emphasized if there are students who express any dismay about it. (2) Cummings's spacing and alignment assist in the visualization of the experiences both of sex and of driving a new car. The slowness caused by the specific line [again slo-wly; bare,ly nudg. ing (my] is appropriate to the tentative nature of testing out the apparatus of a new car. Similarly, the run-together word greasedlightning suggests that once working, the gears of a car may move smoothly. Need we be so explicit with regard to the double meaning? (3) The poem is better called frank, open, happy, or unabashed rather than bawdy or off color. The ostensible narration of the poem--the difficulties of breaking in the car--keeps the poem on the level of surface innocence. The frankness develops from the verbal irony and ambiguity realized in the process of reading the poem.

Writing topics: the frankness and joy of the poem. The double entendre. The spacing, alignment, and punctuation, and their effect on the tone.

Langston Hughes, Theme for English B, pages 656-657.

See the sample essay (pages 662-664) for a discussion of the tone of this poem. For a discussion about Hughes, see page 70 in the Manual.

Theodore Roethke, My Papa's Waltz, page 658.

Roethke was born in 1907 in Saginaw, Michigan, where his father operated a greenhouse. His first collection of poems was The Lost Son (1948), which included "My Papa's Waltz." He achieved wide recognition before his death in 1963. He not only distinguished himself, but he taught other poets, numbering James Wright and Richard Hugo (both anthologized in this volume) among his students at the University of Washington.

Study Questions: (1) The opening description of the father is conducive to the speaker's boyhood sense of ambiguity and anxiety. The phrases like death and such waltzing are opposed; either one or the other is inappropriate, or else the speaker is being ironic. Given like death, however, the term waltzing is likely an understatement. The tone then suggests apprehension and anxiety, although the assertion that the father's whiskey breath could make a small boy dizzy is a tempering overstatement. (2) The waltz is a drunkenly boisterous mock dance done by the speaker's father, with the speaker as a boy being the partner. The tone of the description suggests the mixture of emotions conveyed in the opening stanza. The roughness and grossness of the father is brought out in the references to his battered knuckle, his lack of coordination, the scraping his buckle gives the speaker's ear, the drum beats on the boy's head, and the dirt-caked palm. The lack of control is made mildly amusing by the sliding of the pans and the frowning mother. The potential pain and fright that might be experienced by the boy are mitigated by the light iambic trimeter and the trochaic rhyme of lines 10 and 12.

(3) Countenance in line 7 is an instance of overstatement because the word is inconsistent with the diction in the rest of the poem. In context, and along with the use of unfrown, the word countenence suggests the mother's annoyance and disapproval but not outright anger or fear. (4) The tone of the speaker's treatment of the father suggests that a sense of powerlessness accompanies his memory. Whatever pain the boy experienced is not mentioned in the poem, even though the descriptions indicate that he would have felt at least some (such as having time beat out on his head, his right ear scraping the buckle). Thus the speaker's recollection emphasizes that he is attempting to understand and to objectify his memory of his father, with the

less pleasant aspects being diminished.

Writing topics: the tone of the descriptions of the father. Tone through overstatement and understatement. The speaker's attitude toward the childhood memory. The function of rhythm and structure in the tone of the poem.

WRITING ABOUT TONE IN POETRY, pages 659-665.

In teaching this section you will need to remind your students that tone can be a slippery topic if they consider no more than the attitudes they find in the poem. Always, it is important to emphasize that to write about tone is to explain how the attitudes are built up. Just to define the attitudes is not enough. Therefore, the five approaches suggested on pages 660-661 may be stressed as providing ways for students to explore tone. The sample essay on pages 662-663 illustrates that the approaches are by no means mutually exclusive. Thus a discussion of tone emphasizing the poem's situation will invariably include a section on diction, as the sample essay does in paragraphs 5 and 6. Probably the best thing to stress in teaching is that students should be prepared to adapt their approaches for their essays to the circumstances of the poems on which they will write. Once students are so forewarned, they should be able to control their handling of tone in poetry.

CHAPTER 19

THE RHYTHM OF POETRY: BEAT, METER, AND SCANSION

This chapter aims at presenting a great deal of fairly technical material with as much clarity and ease as possible. While not all instructors will be comfortable with the degree of detailed analysis required here, metrics and scansion are a central and integral part of all closed-form poetry. Students may not need everything in this section to carry on a competent discussion of metrics. Some students can easily perceive light and heavy stresses, and can therefore produce good essays with no further instruction. Many students have difficulty, however, and therefore they may need to go back to basics about the syllable (pages 668-669). Also, many students quickly recognize variations in rhythm, here called rhetorical substitutions (pages 678-679). If they have difficulty, however, you may wish to have them study the section on cadence groups (pages 667-668), for this portion of the text deals with this particular problem. Also, the section on the various feet and types of measures is longer than you perhaps will have time for in a one-semester course. As a result, the most essential material--on the two-syllable feet (pages 671-673)--will serve most students first becoming acquainted with prosody. This material deals with the metrical feet that are the most common for poetry written in English.

In teaching the caesura (page 677), you may encounter surprise again about the role of pause and spacing in the development of meaning and rhythm. Most students understand junctures and use them properly. The problem comes when they are first asked to systematize their knowledge, and then to determine the effect of juncture or caesura in poetic rhythm. Punctuation is a great help here, for students will usually pause naturally at a comma or period. The problem will come in the determination of where internal open juncture and caesura coincide. It may take much practice for many students to perceive caesurae occurring in these circumstances. Here, as elsewhere, practice, together with your supervision, will help.

William Shakespeare, Sonnet 29: When in Disgrace with Fortune, pages 679-680.

This is one of the better-known sonnets, and it is noteworthy because it shows a departure from the usual Shakespearean sonnet structure: lines 9-14 form a unit--a sestet. In the classroom teaching of the poem for rhythm, it is important to stress the poem's iambic regularity, so that the substitutions can be perceived as Shakespeare's subtle manipulations of the form.

Study Questions: (1) In lines 1-8, the speaker cites circumstances in which his self-doubts overwhelm him. Knowing the exact causes would not help the reader's understanding of the depressed mood described in these lines. In lines 9-12 the speaker notes that the remembrance of the thee who is the listener of the poem, a memory occurring almost at random, lifts the speaker's spirits. (2) The idea explored in lines 9-12 is that love is necessary for emotional well being. The analogy is that of the soul departing from earth and singing as it passes into heaven. The simile also indicates that the speaker's joy is like the return of the lark's song at the beginning of day. The sentence structure here is in conformity with the structure of ideas: the incompleteness of the speaker's condition is complemented by the incomplete, dependent state of the grammar. The complete sentences in lines 9-14 suggest that the independence of the speaker's spirit is genuinely restored.

(3) Formal substitutions abound as emphasis, as, for example, in the opening trochee (When in), which accentuates disgrace, or in the spondee which

132

concludes line 1 (<u>men's eyes</u>) and therefore which stresses the speaker's regret that his disgrace has been made public. Other substitutions are <u>heaven</u> (trochee), line 3; <u>wishing</u> (trochee) and <u>more rich</u> (spondee), line 5; <u>featured</u> (trochee), line 6; <u>man's art</u> and <u>man's scope</u> (spondees), line 7; <u>these thoughts</u> (spondee), line 9; <u>despising</u> and <u>arising</u> (amphibrachs), lines 9 and 11; <u>haply</u> (trochee), line 10; <u>sings hymns</u> (spondee), line 12; <u>sweet love</u> and such <u>wealth</u> (spondees), line 13.

(4) Shakespeare varies the caesurae in the poem. Sometimes it occurs after the fourth syllable, as in lines 1 and 2 (there is also a caesura after the first syllable in line 1), and sometimes after the sixth (as in lines 3, 4, and 8). In line 13 the caesura falls after the seventh syllable. Though all lines are end-stopped but line 11, Shakespeare moves the thought along by developing grammatical units which are coextensive with the lines. Thus the <u>I</u> in line 2 is the subject of the verbs <u>trouble</u>, <u>look</u>, and <u>curse</u> in lines 3 and 4. The participial phrases in lines 5-8 all modify the <u>I</u> of line 2. Writing topics: formal substitution or the use of caesurae in the poem. The poem's continuity despite the end-stopping.

William Shakespeare, Sonnet 73: That Time of Year, pages 680-681.

"That Time of Year" is one of the best known of all the sonnets. In the best of all possible worlds, students should memorize it. The sonnet explores the connection between mortality, death, and love.

<u>Study Questions</u>: (1) The topics of the quatrains are these: lines 1-4, autumn; lines 5-8, sunset and night; lines 9-12, a dying fire. The common link is diminution or dying. The concluding couplet is tied to the previous twelve lines by the demonstrative pronoun <u>This</u>, which begins line 13, and which turns the thought to the need for strengthening love.

(2) In all instances the spondees create emphasis by slowing the speech and thereby thrusting the ideas into prominence. Also, the frequency of spondees in this sonnet suggests the heaviness of a slow march or respectful walk appropriate to a funeral procession. The phrases <u>those boughs</u> in line 3 and <u>that well</u> in line 14 should be added as spondaic substitutions. (3) Line 2 connects to line 1 because it begins a subordinate adverbial clause, just as line 3 begins an adverbial-prepositional phrase in which the headword <u>boughs</u> is modified by the adjective clause <u>which shake against the cold</u>. The completeness of each line is hence caused by the pause produced between the verbs and the modifying elements. Much the same applies to the movement from line 5 to line 6; here, however, the modifying element in line 6 is an adjective clause modifying the noun <u>day</u> (or is it <u>twilight</u>?).

(4) The caesurae in the lines are placed as follows: Line 2, after syllables 4, 6, and 8. Line 5, after syllables 2 and 7. Line 6, after syllable 5. Line 9, after syllables 2 and 7 (the same as line 5). These pauses cause emphasis or continuity where they appear. In line 2, the effect is one of slowness and heaviness. In lines 5 and 9, which are grammatically and rhythmically identical, the similarity is a means of tying together the two four-line units describing the setting sun and the dying fire. Line 6 is regular, divided in the exact middle by the caesura. This regularity throws emphasis on the eternal sameness of the setting sun. In the last two lines, the rising caesurae (in both 13 and 14, after the fourth syllables) stress the positive qualities of the love which is the subject of the lines.

Writing topics: the use of spondees as the main substitute foot. The relationship of caesurae to the ideas in the poem. The repetition of rhythms (principally the use of the <u>in me</u> patterns, and the adjective clauses).

(TEXT PAGES) 681-683

John Keats, Bright Star, page 681.

The sample essay (pages 690-691) deals with most of the issues raised in the study questions (page 682).

Robert Browning, My Star, page 682.

Robert and Elizabeth Browning eloped and were married in 1846, and they lived in Italy until Elizabeth's death in 1861. This poem is somewhat unusual because there are not many poems by speaker-husbands praising wives. With "My Star" may be compared O'Shaughnessy's "A Love Symphony" (page 654) and Anne Finch's "To Mr. Finch," (pages 794-797).

Study Questions: (1) Granting that the star refers to Elizabeth, the images are appropriate because they refer to light, the colors of the prism, birds, flowers, and the world itself. All these images, as metaphors, suggest intelligence, variety, conversation, beauty, and intimacy. (2) It is difficult to establish a metrical norm for this poem because it changes from dimeter to more complex meters after line 8. For the first eight lines the pattern could be called an anapaest followed by an iamb (the feet of lines 2, 4, and 5-8). After this pattern, however, the lines resist being pinned down, because the poet presents the same variety in the meter than he is stressing in the subject. Line 9, for example, may be schematized as spondee, amphibrach, iamb, and anapaest (My star, / that dartles / the red / and the blue!). Also, in line 13, there are ten syllables (as in line 9), but the first two feet are trochees, the next two iambs, and the last a trochee. The lines, in other words, are alive, like the spirit of the star. (3) The first eight lines are short, and therefore caesurae are not significant in them. For lines 9-13, the caesurae fall after these words: Line 9--star, red. Line 10--bird, flower. Line 11--themselves. Line 12--me. Line 13--me. The use of the caesurae, together with the end-stopping of the lines (except for line 13), prevents the anapaestic rhythms from building up to a sing-song beat. These pauses, together with the substitutions, keep the poem conversational despite Browning's departure from the normal iamb, which is the most conversational of poetic feet. Writing topics: variation as the rhythmical norm of the poem. The relationship of meter and subject. Use of caesurae.

Francis Thompson, To a Snowflake, page 683.

If poetry can be thought to dance, the lines of "To a Snow flake" dance. The topic of God the Shaper is heavy and serious, but the created object--the snowflake--is light and beautiful.

Study Questions: (1) The speaker, an undefined and indefinite person who is perceptive and sensitive, is speaking to an individual snowflake; the snowflake is personified in its relpy in lines 11-22. The metaphor dominating the poem is God as a skilled sculptor and metalworker. The poem may hence be considered a religious tribute because God, rather than producing a heavy statue, delicately creates the lightest and most fragile of things--the snowflake. (2) The dimeter, a short, light line, is appropriate to the subject because a snowflake too is small and light. (3) The most common foot in the poem is the amphibrach, although there are many trochees intermixed for variation. These feet are appropriate to the subject of snow because they both end on lightly accented or falling syllables. Theoretically, iambs would be less appropriate because they end on stressed, heavy syllables, and therefore an iambic poem on snow would likely be less light and more overtly philosophical. The last three lines of "To a Snowflake" switch the amphibrachic-trochaic norm of the poem to an iambic-anapaestic pattern. The reason is likely that the poet wishes to shift our attention from the lightly dancing snowflake to the more enduring power of God. (4) In comparison, "To a Snowflake" is more like "The Lamb" than "The Tyger," although all three raise questions of created things about their Creator. The snowflake and the lamb are alike because they represent the lighter, less sinister parts of creation, while the tyger is used as a symbol of evil in the world. "To a Snowflake" is not like either of the Blake poems in the respect that there is no complication or irony about the snow; snow is clean and innocent, without qualification. Writing topics: the use of falling rhythms in the poem. The use of dimeter. The metaphor of God the Creator in the poem.

T.S. Eliot, Macavity: The Mystery Cat, pages 684-685.

Eliot, often considered a hyper-serious poet of either negative or religious themes, published Old Possum's Book of Practical Cats in 1939. He was what is called by cat-fanciers a "cat person." There is a 1928 photo of him with a cat named "George" (George V was king at the time), and among some of his other cats were "Wiscus" and "Pettipaws." There were many other cats, no doubt, which he owned or with whom he was acquainted. His poems about felines achieved popular fame in 1981, with the musical play Cats, freely adapted from Old Possum's Book. Cats was spectacularly successful on both the London and New York stages.

Study Questions: (1) Macavity's crimes are detailed in lines 21-34. The speaker expresses fear and amazement at the crimes, which in a human being would indeed have been heinous. The misdeeds occasion humor, however, because they are part of the overstatement on which the poem is built: to attribute felonious behavior to a cat is automatically incongruous and therfore comic. (2) The line length, according to a conventional scansion, is septameter or the septenary, with iambic feet as the norm but with occasional lines commencing with anapaests (e.g., lines 9, 10, 12, 19, etc). (3) Once one begins reading and getting into the swing of the lines, however, the dipodic foot takes over, so that each line contains four major stresses accompanied by a number of minor stresses, as in, He always as an alibi, and one or two to spare. In this line, the dipodic feet throw heaviest stress on al (in always), al (in alibi), one, and spare, even though more formally (and more slowly) the line contains seven iambic feet. Because the poem is really on a nonsense theme, the transformation of the serious verse form into the bouncier, thumping rhythm adds to the ridiculousness that Eliot is creating. (4) The poet to whom Eliot is referring in the quotation is Edward Lear (1812-1888), whom he greatly admired. Some students may know Lear either as the author of "The Owl and the Pussycat" or as the popularizer of the Limerick form (see pages 746-747). In discussing the quotation, you might note (or get your students to note) that Eliot stresses enjoyment as the major standard of judgment. However, students might also note that "Macavity" is a well-formed poem with an introduction, characteristics of the hero, accomplishments, refrains, and a climax. There are allusions to large matters of criminal law and international politics, and through out there is a constant use of overstatement and anti-climax. The poem is also enlivened by a number of oblique and direct literary allusions to Arthur Conan Doyle's stories about Sherlock Holmes. The two crimes noted in stanza 6--the stolen treaty and the lost plans--both allude to specific Holmes stories. More to the point, Holmes frequently refers to his archenemy, Doctor Moriarity, as the Napoleon of Crime (line 42). Thus the nonsense is tightly controlled. Writing topics: the

135

dipodic foot. The development of humor. Macavity as a normal cat or as a villain. The effect of literary allusions in the poem.

Gwendolyn Brooks, We Real Cool, pages 685-686.

Winner of the Pulitzer Prize for Poetry in 1950, Gwendolyn Brooks in later years has stressed the topic of race in her writing. "We Real Cool," with its strong sense of pathos, is a part of this emphasis. Study Questions: (1) The major idea of the poem is that an aimless existence leads nowhere. The speakers are young men whose life pattern is based on diversionary and fruitless activity. They do not mention any obligation toward constructive service, but speak glowingly of enjoyable but destructive habits, which they describe as cool. The last sentence is a climax because it recognizes the outcome of the way of life depicted in the poem. The poet's attitude is clear because of the poem's situational irony: the opportunities for those who waste their lives at the Golden Shovel pool room should be improved in all respects.
(2) The rhythmical stresses on all syllables are strong. The absence of weak stresses, making the poem totally strong-stressed, is achieved because all the words are of one syllable, and because there are no definite or indefinite articles and no prepositions. Thus, every word carries a great deal of weight as a subject, verb, object, or predicate adjective or adverb.
(3) The repetition of we at the ends of Brooks's lines creates emphasis on the following verbs and therefore on the destructiveness of the activities of the speakers. In Cummings's "In just," by contrast, there is a pun on whee, as though the speaker describes a genuinely happy and soon-to-be-fruitful time.
Writing topics: the use of strong stress in the poem. The relationship between the metrical beat and the main idea of the poem.

James Emanuel, The Negro, page 686.

This poem is somewhat more cryptic than the dramatically presented "We Real Cool" of Gwendolyn Brooks. In classroom discussion, students can bring out the ideas of the poem, but they may need some leading questions to do so.
Study Questions: (1) The single most important attribute of the black described in lines 1-4 is principally that of invisibility. In other words, the black is not visible because he has never had a chance to develop knowledge, character, and identity. Lines 5 and 6 bring out the traditional servile role in which blacks have been cast. Lines 7 and 8 refer to the time-wasting and destructive ways of life that many blacks have followed because they were denied more fulfilling opportunities.
(2) The-ness in line 9 (with the definite article) refers to the definite and circumscribed role of the black. A-ness in line 11 (with the indefinite article) refers to freedom and the opportunity to grow as an individual without the restrictions imposed by race. (3) The predominant metrical foot of the poem is the trochee, with the concluding light stress missing in lines 2, 4, 10, and 12. The trochee, with falling rhythm, is here suitable to the poem's irony of situation. A rising foot, specifically the iamb, would suggest a more complete, fulfilled life than the poet is dealing with here.
(4) The variants are bossir and flicking in lines 6 and 8. These words dramatically reflect the speech and activity of blacks in their stereotypical roles. The lines with which these variants may be compared (2, 4, 10, and 12) all contain comments by the speaker, so that the lines end on stresses to indicate definite statements about indefinite existences.

Writing topics: the main metrical foot of the poem. The use of metrical variation. The use of short dramatic quotations in lines 5-8 to symbolize the condition of blacks.

WRITING ABOUT RHYTHM IN POETRY, pages 687-692.

Although this writing project is quite specific, it offers problems for some students. Success in the essay depends on a successful rhythmical analysis (or scansion) of the poem at hand. If they make no errors in their rhythmical analyses, then their essays will go forward well. If there are errors of analysis, however, then the essays will embody the errors. With normal analytical essays, errors are not quite as crucial, for students may make a good argument even for a misinterpretation. In the study of rhythm, however, it is difficult to make a well-reasoned discussion compensate for a mistake. There are two ways to get around this difficulty. The less demanding solution is for you to present students with mimeographed or xerographed copies of a poem fully analyzed and annotated for meter and rhythm; the students will then write an essay based on this prepared data. The problems with this approach are obvious: it prevents the students from doing any significant metrical analysis on their own and it tends to produce a large number of identical papers. Nevertheless, it does provide an exercise in the organization of information and, of course, another opportunity to write. The second solution (more demanding for you and the students) involves checking over each student's worksheet before he or she begins to write the essay.

In using the sample essay (pages 690-692) as a possible model for your students, you might direct them to the fact that even here there is a strong connection between the central idea and the development. Thus in paragaph 3 of the sample, you might note the thematic importance of words like regularity, balance, idea of steadfastness, again, also, to echo, and unify. No matter what central idea students may make about the rhythms of their assigned poems, the same need for overall connection will prevail.

CHAPTER 20

SOUNDS AND SEGMENTS

This chapter is designed to introduce students to the way sounds and patterns of sound can create effects in poetry. The material here builds on what students can hear readily but may never have thought about or studied either systematically or cursorily. It therefore may be necessary to spend time in illustrating the concepts of segments, and in verifying these in speech. Many students enjoy discovering, by using their own mouths, the positions of the tongue and lips in forming the various consonant sounds, and it is a revelation to them to follow the tongue downward and backward as they form vowel sounds ranging from ee and ay to ah, oh, and oo.

Once your class has studied segments, the principle of distinguishing sounds from spelling should be established (pages 693, 697). You may discover that some of the students, even against their own hearing, will identify sounds on visual rather than spoken evidence. It is therefore good to select a poem or short passage and have the class analyze the written words for the sounds themselves. One student might truly believe that the s's in sure, silver, and resemblance spell out the same sound. You will need to raise consciousness about the differences in these and in other words. Sometimes students have a special problem with digraphs, identifying the t in the with the t in type, the t in thick, or the t in Betty. The principle of the differences is not difficult, but it is often difficult for students to develop the habit of actually perceiving what they are hearing and seeing.

As exercises in segments, the following nonce sentences might prove useful for your students. You may add to these as you wish, or omit them:

VOWEL SOUNDS

He sees deep fields of green freaks.
Palely made cakes are aided by savory flavors.
Swift Camilla skims the pillowed plinths.
The fresh fellow offended Ted's sense of method.
Afterward, a lanky lad ambled by with angular ankles.
Often he saw faults that caused awe.
She told of foes openly loading goalposts.
Puny new tunes are few in the pews on Tuesdays.
The fooling troupe coolly sat on stools.
I find the sky quite high in my mind's eye.
His foible was joining in toil not to foil but to spoil.

CONSONANT SOUNDS

The beau in the bed was bored with his beard and his billboard.
The dark darter dashed toward the dawn.
The kiln cooked while the king counseled quiet.
The pals panted palpably and probably panicked.
His task was tasting tangy but tart tangerines.
The game was to glide gallantly in galloping galoshes.
The ocean shore shifted the nation's passions.
Azure closures measure beige rouges.
Chinese chimpanzees chirped cheerfully in chimneys.
George generally enjoyed judging jellies and jams.
With special skill, Smith smashed several small smelt.
Zebras and zephyrs zigzagged in the zoo zones.

Phil fancied fabulous financial finds following funny but fantastic failures.
Vales of vexatious vampires vanished in vapors of vinegar.
He was thumped and throttled thoroughly by the thin but thriving thresher.
The other brother then bathed the feather.
Nervously nattering nabobs of negativism need nice new nutrition.
Red railroad ramps recede refulgently and refreshingly.

Robert Herrick, Upon Julia's Voice, page 697.

This poem is one of Herrick's poems on the qualities of generalized,
conventionalized women, including also Corinna (pages 955-956). The idea of
the poems is not so much to describe specific details about a woman as to
demonstrate the poet's sharpness and poetic skill. Study Questions: (1) The
speaker praises Julia's speaking voice, but commends it for its melodious
qualities. Silv'ry and amber are euphonious words as well as rich
commodities, and therefore they reflect the speaker's high opinion. (2) The
joke of the poem is that Julia's voice is beautiful enough to overcome the
devil's power of torment, so that damned souls would stop their screams of
pain from hell fire to listen to her. (3) The alliterations in the poem are s
(so smooth, so sweet, so silv'ry), n (no noise), m (melting melodious), and l
(melting, melodious, lutes). The m sounds complement the praise for the
voice, because m, being a bilabial nasal continuant, brings the mouth into
obvious use. Writing topics: the poem as an elaborate compliment. The use of
alliteration and euphony.

Jonathan Swift, A Description of the Morning, page 698.

For most of the time from 1701-1714, Swift lived in England as a special
envoy of the Irish church and also as a writer for the Tory government. This
poem was one of the many satiric pieces that he wrote during the time. It is
often considered a companion piece to the "Description of a City Shower" (page
1012). Study Questions: (1) All the images in the poem are anti-heroic, being
derived from the seamy and unromantic aspects of life, such as the lazy
apprentice, the dirty kennel's edge, and the noisy charcoal seller. The
attitude toward his lordship is sarcastic; the lord symbolizes form without
substance. (2) Alliteration may be found in lines 1 (h), 2 (p), 3 (b and f),
4 (s), 7 (m), 8 (c), 9 (wh and w), and 16-18 (l and s). The effect generally
is emphasis, as in softly stole in line 4, which stresses by sound the furtive
quality of Betty's movement to her own room. (3) Assonance may be found in
lines 2 and 4 (o), 3 (eh), 7 (aw), 9 (oo), 10 (eh), 12 (il as in shriller), 15
(er in turnkey, returning), 17 (ay), and 18 (ae as in lag). Because the poem
is in couplets, these closely connected patterns (at least nine of them)
create unity of sound and therefore emphasis within this brief scope. Writing
topics: the use of segmental devices in the poem. The negative images of
life. The use of realism.

Alfred, Lord Tennyson, The Passing of Arthur, pages 699-700.

One of Tennyson's preoccupations was the legendary King Arthur. He began
publishing Idylls of the King in 1857. The book initially consisted of twelve
connected poems on Arthurian topics. Tennyson continued to add more material
as time went by. The completed version of Idylls was published in 1891, the
year before Tennyson's death.

(TEXT PAGES) 699-702

Study Questions: (1) Bedivere carries the dying Arthur from a series of
ridges to the water, where a barge awaits. Arthur is then taken aboard to the
lamentations of three queens. Tennyson develops the mood of depression by
including images of cold, darkness, shrill winds, dust, and a shattered
column. (2) The sample essay (pages 708-712) analyzes segments in the section
from lines 349-360. Further study could produce additional patterns, such as
dark, scarf and stem, stern (line 362); were, ware (line 363); decks, dense
(line 364); and dream, these, three, queens (lines 365-366). These patterns
of assonance and alliteration unify these passages and make them particularly
suitable for spoken delivery.
        (3) The onomatopoeia in lines 349-360 is discussed in the sample essay
(pages 708-712). The content of lines 369-370 concerns the sounds of
lamentation being likened to shrill winds in an empty land. Here Tennyson
uses a number of syllable-lengthening consonants, principally l, n, and m, to
enable the words to be extended in virtual imitation of wind. Words thus
stretched are lamentation, wind, shrills, land, one, and comes. In lines
380-383, Tennyson emphasizes the tears of the tallest queen falling upon
Arthur, and also the streaks and spots on him as a result of his mortal battle
wounds. Tennyson achieves onomatopoeia here through the use of one-syllable
words to emphasize the individual drops (line 380, for example, consists of
ten one-syllable words) together with the use of stop sounds which also
emphasize the drops (in the words striped, dark, blood, greaves, cuisses,
dashed, and drops). When he describes Arthur's face he uses words with fewer
stop sounds (face, white, colorless, withered, moon, springing), which when
mingled with the monosyllabic words succeed in creating a word picture.
Writing topics: Tennyson's use of assonance and alliteration in a selected
portion of the fragment. The means by which Tennyson creates onomatopoeia.

Edgar Allan Poe, The Bells, pages 700-702.

        "The Bells" strongly evokes the connection between sound and mood. If
students come to the poem searching for ideas as such, they will be sadly
disappointed. Instead, in "The Bells" the idea is mood, or rather the
separate moods evoked by Poe's descriptions. In making this stress upon
emotion as a mode of knowledge, this poem, noisy and percussive as it is, is
not unlike Emily Dickinson's "There's a Certain Slant of Light" (page 892).
Dickinson, remember, speaks about the heft of cathedral tunes.
        Study Questions: (1) The stanzas discuss (a) silver sledge or sleigh
bells, (b) golden wedding bells, (c) brass alarm bells, and (d) iron funeral
bells. The metals are appropriate because of their colors and textures.
Certainly silver and gold suggest happiness and security, while brass and iron
are more suitable for the fearsome, somber, and bizarre uses to which Poe puts
these bells. The stanzas, particularly the third and fourth, become longer
because the situations of alarm and death being described are more complicated
and far-reaching than sleighrides and weddings, and perhaps more congenial to
the poet's temperament.
        (2) In stanza 1, the major assonance is the short i, and there are a
number of repeated t and d sounds in alliteration. For the wedding bells in
stanza 2 there is more of a mixture of sounds. Thus one may note assonances
in eh (mellow, wedding), oh (molten, golden), short i (liquid, ditty,
listens), and a number of oo sounds (through, tune, euphony, voluminously,
future). There are more nasals (m and n) here, and liquids (l) than in stanza
1, so that brittleness gives way to something more like the mellow sounds to
which Poe refers in line 15. Stanza 3 introduces a number of r sounds to
emphasize the noise of terror (as in scream out their affright). In the first

140

part of the stanza there is also the plosive <u>t</u>, and the <u>k</u> sound is introduced in line 53. Stanza 4, about funeral bells, introduces the fricatives <u>s</u> and <u>sh</u>, presumably to imitate sounds of sighing and weeping. From line 89 to the end, however, the poem moves from the suggestion of sorrow and shivering into a bizarre, mad dance by a King of the Ghouls. Repetition here is princpally on the word <u>bells</u>, which is a percussive counterpoint to sobbing, moaning, and groaning, which the bells also are doing. (3) The word <u>bells</u>, used sixty-one times in the poem, as a refrain and as the repeated word in lines, is a one-syllable word that begins with the voiced stop <u>b</u> and then moves to <u>eh</u>, <u>l</u>, and <u>z</u>. It suggests a constant hammering and ringing sound. Musical notation (because several lines can be laid out simultaneously) would be better able to capture Poe's desired effect than lines of poetry alone can do. Writing topics: the relation of segments to content (any stanza). The progress or change in sounds in the poem.

Gerard Manley Hopkins, God's Grandeur, page 703.

If one did not read the poem word by word, but merely looked at its form, it would appear to be a traditional Italian or Petrarchan sonnet, with an extra iambic foot in line 3. To read the poem aloud, however, is to recognize the tension between the formal and the actual, which is caused by Hopkins's use of "sprung" rhythm. Briefly, he achieves the vigorous spoken effect through the frequent juxtaposition of single-syllable words together with alliteration. Thus the regular light stresses are replaced by stronger stresses, which "spring" out of the lines.

Study Questions: (1) Lines 1-4 praise God, concluding with a question about human disobedience. Lines 5-8 contain a brief review of the speaker's judgment that human beings are enslaved to commerce. The sestet develops from this octave because it stresses the world's beauty, and suggests the possibility that improvement, like a new dawn, is awaiting those who are open to God's power. (2) To emphasize God's grandeur and power throughout all creation, Hopkins speaks about God as a resident of all the universe, as a ruler, and as the all-pervasive Holy Ghost who resembles traditional images of angels (with <u>bright wings</u>). As a means of illustrating divine omnipresence, he introduces metaphors of electricity or flame, the freshness of creation, the dawn, and guardianship.

(3) There are many alliterative patterns in the poem, which coincide with positions of rhythmical stress and therefore also with important words and ideas. See, for example, line 2, which emphasizes <u>f</u> in <u>flame</u> and <u>foil</u> and <u>sh</u> in <u>shining</u> and <u>shook</u>, and line 7, with its <u>sm</u> pattern in <u>smudge</u> and <u>smell</u>. (4) For assonance and internal rhyme, see, for example, lines 4 and 5: <u>men</u>, <u>then</u>, <u>reck</u>, and <u>generations</u>, where the <u>eh</u> sound predominates. There are other internal rhymes: <u>seared-bleared-smeared</u> and <u>wears-shares</u>. (5) It is probably not enough simply to say that Hopkins creates emphasis though his use of segmental textures. He is rather bringing the energy of language itself into prominence along with his message and his images. Writing topics: Hopkins's use of (a) alliteration, (b) assonance, (c) internal rhyme, (d) the Italian sonnet form, and (e) "sprung" rhythm.

A. E. Housman, Eight O'Clock, page 704.

Housman, a classical scholar, is best remembered for <u>The Shropshire Lad</u>, a collection of poems which he published privately in 1896. Frequently treating topics such as life's brevity, human insignificance, and death, these

141

poems also feature a sense of stoical resignation. In all these respects, "Eight O'Clock" is a representative Housman poem, with its central figure being a man about to be hanged, for the poems usually focus on an individual caught and often foiled by situations beyond anyone's control.

Study Questions: (1) The unnamed and representative he of the poem is a condemned criminal. When the clock strikes eight, the trapdoor on the gallows will be sprung, and he will be hanged. (2) The st and k consonant sounds and the monosyllables of the poem may be considered complementary to the slow ticking of a clock, which as the symbol of time signifies the vast, impersonal force from which individuals cannot escape. This individual, of course, is especially aware of the inexorable passage of time. (3) The placement of in the tower out of its expected position enables a build up to the direct object, strength, and by this deferment to suggest the tension before the clock's springs release the toll of eight, and also the tension before the springing of the trap door. In addition, the grammatical structure enables Housman to place strength and struck, with the double alliteration, in the last line as the poem's climax. Writing topics: the use of alliteration. The irony of the protagonist's situation. The grammatical and segmental buildup to the last line of the poem.

Dylan Thomas, The Force That Through the Green Fuse, pages 704-705.

In his brief life, Thomas became popular on lecture and reading tours, and was famed for his vigorous voice and acute ear for sound. Indeed, so good was his creation of sound that some critics have stated that he sometimes sacrificed sense in favor of his ringing, rolling cadences. In "The Force That Through the Green Fuse Drives the Flower," students may perceive the Thomas sound. With regard to the content and structure of the poem, the development at times seems imagistic, and sometimes paradoxical.

Study Questions: (1) In this poem the speaker states that the powerful forces of his life are also leading him to death. Drive refers to a force like a pile driver or screwdriver--a powerful, undeniable, inexorable wave that nothing can stop. Images of decay and death, the inevitable result of life, are blasts, destroyer, fever, wax, quicksand, hangman's lime, leech, sores, and crooked worm. (2) As comparison, both Thomas in "The Force" and Shakespeare in "That Time of Year" comment on the movement of life toward death. Shakespeare's speaker, however, uses the occasion to affirm love for the listener, while Thomas's speaker has no listener for whom to affirm anything, but describes only perplexity and muteness at the finality and also the repulsiveness of death (brought out in lime and worms).

(3) In this poem Thomas creates a network of repetitions, repeating force, drives, green, mouth, hang- (-ing and -man), crooked, and the clause I am dumb. He uses alliterations and assonances in fairly close connection with these repetitions as a means of emphasis. For example, along with the mouth repetition he introduces the ow diphthong of mouth in how and mountain (lines 9, 10). In the same way, in lines 1-7 the word drives is used four times, and the d sound beginning this word is also present in destroyer and dumb, and the word dries provides an example of consonance as well as assonance. (4) The stanza from lines 16-20 is perplexing, but it can be understood if taken as images of the speaker's negative and paradoxical views of existence. The alliterations here, on l, t, and w, cause a vigor in the reading, as though life and the life force were still strong even though the world itself seems contradictory and beyond human imagination. Writing topics: the patterns of repetition in the poem. Uses of alliteration and assonance. The poem's paradoxical view of life.

David Wagoner, March for a One-Man Band, pages 705-706.

Born in Ohio, Wagoner has taught since 1954 at the University of Washington, where he knew Theodore Roethke. He has been extremely productive both as poet and novelist. This poem is a short virtuoso piece, which mixes iambs and anapaests together to work up an infectiously rhythmic but also slightly chaotic tetrameter.

Study Questions: (1) The speaker enjoys the one-man band being described: not with awe or respect, but with amused acceptance of an amusing situation. The noise is so outlandish that irrational is a better word than national to describe the anthem he plays. (2) The italicized words poem are all echoic; that is, they are onomatopoeic or imitative in origin, having sound-effects as their meaning. The accompanying rhythyms are swinging, bouncing, or thumping, designed to imitate and illustrate in words the noisy, desperate motion and sound of one person working all the instruments with hands, feet, knees, and mouth--a frantic, wild spectacle of sight and sound. (3) At the end of the speaker's description, the bang recalls the so-called "button" note which punctuates the second beat of the last bar of a march (hear, for example, the conclusion of Sousa's "The Stars and Stripes Forever"). The one-man band's bang presumably ends the national anthem, creating an amusing sound where none at all ought to be, a sound that is not at all inappropriate if one considers how "The Star-Spangled Banner" is sometimes performed at many sporting events and public spectacles. (4) In both Poe and Wagoner, the echoic words transmit real sound to the printed page. Wagoner of course uses more variety than Poe, for while Poe speaks only of bells, Wagoner mentions drums, cornet, harmonica (the wheeze?), cymbal, whistle, and perhaps a few other "instruments" thrown in for good measure. Writing topics: Onomatopoeia in the poem. Rhythm. Poe's "The Bells" and Wagoner's "March for a One-Man Band."

WRITING ABOUT SOUNDS AND SEGMENTS IN POETRY, pages 706-712.

As in teaching the essays on rhythm and rhyme, you will need to stress correctness of analysis as your students begin to work on an essay dealing with sounds and segments. Thus, the development of an accurate and thorough worksheet (see pages 709-710) is most important for students to prepare in the prewriting stages of their essays. And as with the essay on meter, you really have two options here--to develop a set of data for the students or to let them develop their own analyses. If you provide them with a completed worksheet, the exercise will clearly focus on the organization of evidence and the writing itself. If, on the other hand, you ask the students to do their own analysis of sound effects, you may need to give them classroom time so that their observations may be checked. Have they correctly recorded the sounds? Do they have any doubts or questions? Especially important is that students have not confused spelling with sound. If, in the poem you have assigned, there are any possible chances for confusion, you may wish to use selected lines as the basis of exercises and queries. Invariably, you will find students who will set up incorrect correspondences of sound and sense. The best time to make corrections and clarify understandings is at those times when students can see where they are likely to be going astray.

When you use the sample essay (pages 708-712), it is important to note that the claims there for relationships between segments and content are modest. Only in the section on onomatopoeia is there a strong connection, and here the assertions go no further than can be supported by Tennyson's descriptions.

CHAPTER 21

RHYME: THE ECHOING SOUND OF POETRY

The goal of this chapter is to introduce students to the ways that rhyme can function in poetry with as much clarity and fullness as possible. In many texts, rhyme is handled along with sound, meter, or form. We felt that the device was important and interesting enough to warrant its own chapter. In a regular semester or quarter, the chapter may be assigned independently or in conjunction with any of the chapters noted above.

Because rhyme is one of the aspects of poetry with which students are often quite familiar, the technical material in this chapter should be relatively easy to teach; it is fairly limited and straightforward. Brief in-class explanations of exact rhyme, rising and falling rhyme, slant and eye rhyme might be helpful. The section on describing rhyme schemes (pages 717-718) is a bit more demanding since it calls for an understanding of meter. Of course, you might allow your students to define rhyme schemes simply by reference to the sounds (i.e., abab, cdcd). If you do use the whole formulation in class, be sure to remind the students to look for the dominant meter and not to be misled by variant lines.

Alexander Pope, from An Essay on Criticism, pages 718-719.

Our discussion of this poem (pages 719-722) illustrates one way that rhyme can be discussed. It also demonstrates the close connections among rhyme, sound (such as alliteration and assonance), and meter. Because the extract is so rich in musical devices and effects, you might want to go over it in class as an introduction to rhyme and a review of sound and meter.

Anonymous, Barbara Allan, pages 722-723.

This popular folk ballad (Child number 84) shares with most other ballads in this text an external and detached speaker, dialogue, and a focus on a tragic incident. The poem can be taught effectively by focusing first on the story, then the characters, and finally on poetic devices such as repetition and rhyme. The story is quite simple; you might ask a student to summarize it. Sir John Graeme is dying of love for Barbara Allan; he sends a messenger to fetch her. She comes to him slowly (notice the way slowly is repeated here to slow down the poem) and she refuses his love because he slighted her once while drinking toasts (lines 17-20). Graeme dies for love, and Barbara Allan predicts her own death the next day. Graeme comes across as headstrong, willful, and romantic; Barbara Allan seems to be loving but proud and spiteful. Her pride and anger at Graeme's earlier behavior lead to both deaths.

The first stanza, which establishes setting, foreshadows the ending of the ballad. Three specific phrases--Martinmas time, the green leaves were a-fallin', and the West Country--connote death through their connection with seasonal cycles and sunset. It is also helpful in teaching the poem to have your students identify the various speakers quoted by the narrator: the messenger (lines 7-8), Graeme (lines 13-14, 23-24), the death-bell (32), and Barbara Allan (12, 15-20, 33-36). In the last stanza, Allan's reference to a soft and narrow bed is a traditional formulaic phrase indicating a grave.

The rhymes are particularly interesting because they hold the poem together and underscore, through sound, the idea of death (falling off). Only the second and fourth lines of each stanza rhyme (abcb, dbeb, fbgb, and so

on). The b rhyme is repeated in stanzas 1, 2, 3, 4, 5, 6, and 8. In almost
every case, the poem repeats Allan as the second rhyme word of each of these
pairs. The repetition unifies the poem and creates an ongoing focus on
Barbara Allan. In addition, all these rhymes are falling (trochaic, double)
and slant. Normally, this might produce a humorous effect, but here it
stresses through sound the idea of dying (falling). The pattern of repeated b
rhymes is abandoned in stanzas 7 and 9, the two crises of the poem. In stanza
7 Graeme dies, and the rhyme forces our attention on him. In 9, Barbara Allan
announces her death, and the rhyme stresses when this will occur.
     Writing topics: the character of Barbara Allan or of Sir John Graeme.
The images associated with death. The effects produced through rhyme.

Michael Drayton, Since There's No Help, pages 723-724.

     This English sonnet, spoken by a male lover to his mistress, captures the
moment in which the relationship is about to fall apart. While the poem may
present some difficulties for students, it deals with universal feelings with
which they should be able to relate. The poem can be examined twice in class,
once to discuss the situation, the speaker's argument, and his attitude, and a
second time to deal with the rhyme. In the first quatrain, the relationship
seems doomed and the speaker resigned (and even glad) about it. The key words
are no help (line 1) and Nay (2); the nay indicates the speaker's resistance
to any rapprochement. The second quatrain continues in the same vein. Here,
however, you can begin to lead your students to the realization that the
speaker "protests" too much; he sounds too glad, too exaggerated, and too
final in his position. The hyperbole is expressed in the speaker's all-encom-
passing claims like forever, all our vows, and not one jot.
     We get a clearer sense of the speaker's real feelings in lines 9-14,
where he claims that the woman could save the relationship. Lawrence Perrine
(CEA Critic, 25 [1968]:8) points out that there is an allegorical death-bed
scene in lines 9-12. The speaker's Love-Passion lies speechless on his bed of
death attained by Faith. We can tell this is the speaker's love because of
the masculine pronouns used to refer back to Love-Passion. The woman's
Innocence (line 12) appears to be forwarding the death by "closing up his
eyes." The allegory suggests that the speaker considers the failure of love
to be the woman's responsibility and that he is neither resigned nor glad
about the situation. The couplet makes his hopes quite clear.
     As in most English sonnets, the rhyme scheme here subdivides the poem
into three quatrains and a couplet (abab, cdcd, efef, gg) which organize the
speaker's thoughts and argument. The rhymes are all exact and rising, thus
adding force and focus to the poem. Pairs of rhyming words are effective in
clinching ideas; some of the pairs that warrant class discussion include
part-heart, me-free, breath-death (an especially nice antithesis), and
over-recover (an eye/slant rhyme that is also an antithesis). Writing topics:
the effects of rhyme. The speaker. An explanation of the allegory.

John Donne, Death Be Not Proud, pages 724-725.

     Donne's sonnet is a meditation on death and salvation; its apparent
paradoxes are all resolved with reference to the idea of death as the
beginning of eternal life. In teaching the poem, you might concentrate on
Donne's image of death as a powerless slave; this usually frightening force is
personified and then convincingly ridiculed. A good class discussion might be

generated by contrasting Donne's image of death with the one in Dickinson's "Because I Could Not Stop for Death" (page 473).

As in Drayton's sonnet, the rhyme scheme here organizes the poem into three quatrains and a couplet. Here, however, the first 2 quatrains are linked together by repeated rhymes (iambic pentameter: abba, abba, cddc, cc). In the first quatrain, the speaker characterizes death as needlessly proud, and points out that it cannot really overthrow or kill anyone. The second quatrain presents two interesting put-downs of death. The speaker claims that death is only a larger version of rest and sleep, both sources of pleasure (lines 5-6). Then, he argues that the best men go to death soonest (lines 7-8), implying that it is an enviable state. The speaker continues to belittle death in the third quatrain, observing that it is controlled by (a slave to) "fate, chance, kings, and desperate men" as well as "poison, war, and sickness." The paradox in the couplet resolves in the realization that death is the way to eternal life; the sonnet thus explores the idea that death is powerless and insignificant compared to salvation and divine Grace.

The rhymes in the sonnet are mostly exact and rising, thus contributing to the poem's force and conviction. Interesting (and often antithetical) rhyming pairs for class discussion include thee-me-be-delivery, dwell-well, and eternally-die. This last rhyming pair, which occurs in the couplet, sums up the basic opposition that runs through the poem. Writing topics: Donne's characterization of death. The effects of rhyme.

Christina Rossetti, Echo, page 725.

This three-stanza lyric, spoken by a lover to the spirit of his or her dead beloved, is discussed in some detail in the sample essay at the end of the chapter (pages 735-738). Dante Rossetti's "The Blessed Damozel" (page 993) makes a nice companion piece since it also deals with the relationship between a living and dead lover. There, however, the primary voice is the dead lover, speaking from heaven. Thus, the perspective is neatly reversed. Besides an analysis of rhyme in the poem, possible writing topics include a discussion of the speaker and of the poet's use of repetition.

Emily Dickinson, To Hear an Oriole Sing, page 726.

Simply put, this poem fleshes out the old adage that "beauty is in the eye of the beholder," but it does so in terms of sound rather than sight. In classroom discussion, it is helpful to identify the attitudes of the speaker and the listener as quickly as possible. The listener (the skeptic) argues that the Tune is in the Tree. The speaker, who presents virtually a whole aesthetic theory in 15 lines, asserts that the tune (music, poetry, art) is In Thee (the ear of the listener, the mind of the perceptor).

The poem is written in triplets, rhyming aaa, bbb, ccc, and so on. Only the rhymes in the fifth stanza are exact throughout; the rest contain at least one slant rhyme (the fourth contains 2). The slant rhymes emphasize and illustrate the aesthetic point that the poem explores. If they work at all as rhyme, it is because our ears (eyes, imaginations, perceptions) make them work. Thus, the song of the poet, like the Oriole's song, is (works) in us rather than in the world at large.

Writing topics: the character of the speaker or the listener. The rhymes. The ideas (the aesthetic theory) explored in the poem. The degree to which the rhymes of the poem reflect and reinforce the poem's theme.

A. E. Housman, To an Athlete Dying Young, page 727.

Housman's seven-stanza lyric illustrates the brevity of fame and the advantages of dying young, before a hero can become a has-been. The ethos of the poem is classical rather than Christian. In discussion, you might ask the class to come up with examples of people who outlived their glory and became obscure failures later in life. A stanza-by-stanza examination of the poem will probably yield the best classroom discussion.

Stanza 1 presents the athlete's moment of glory, when he won the town race and was carried home by the cheering mob. Stanza 2 is the present--the athlete's funeral. The <u>road all runners come</u> is life's pilgrimage to death; the coffin is carried <u>shoulder-high</u> and the <u>stiller town</u> is the graveyard. The last five stanzas comprise the speaker's meditation on the advantages of dying young. The speaker calls the dead athlete <u>smart</u> to leave before all his records and glories are eclipsed by younger and better men (lines 9-12). In death, the athlete will not see others outstrip him or hear the cheers (lines 13-16); he will not become a has-been (lines 17-20).

The poem is in rhymed couplets with no rhyme sounds repeated (iambic tetrameter: aa, bb, cc, dd, etc.). All the rhymes are rising and exact, lending the poem seriousness, a steady tempo, and focus. Rhyming pairs are employed to clinch ideas and underscore meaning throughout; especially interesting pairs are noted in question 5. The poems by Jonson and Dryden noted in question 6 also deal with people who died young. Dryden's "Mr. Oldham" is closest to Housman's poem in its classical orientation and its emphasis on the advantages of early death. Jonson's poem alludes to these advantages (lines 7-8), but is far more complicated in tone and content by grief, by the father-son relationship, and by the speaker's awareness of the Christian perspective. Writing topics: the ideas about life, glory, or death that Housman's poem explores.

Edwin Arlington Robinson, Miniver Cheevy, pages 728-729.

This portrait of "Miniver Cheevy" illustrates the futility of seeking an escape into the romanticized and idealized past. An effective classroom strategy might be to focus on (1) the portrait of Miniver, (2) the speaker's attitude toward Miniver, and (3) the poetic techniques that Robinson employs to make Miniver all the more pathetic and ludicrous. Miniver's problem, defined in the first three stanzas, is that he disdains the present and longs for an heroic and idealized past. His longings encompass ancient Greece (<u>Thebes</u>) and Troy (<u>Priam's neighbors</u>), the Middle Ages (<u>Camelot, iron clothing</u>), and the Renaissance (<u>the Medici</u>). His dissatisfaction with the present and longing for the past are both passive and useless; they lead him only to sickness, dreaming, and drinking.

Robinson uses a broad array of poetic techniques to make Miniver look ridiculous and to convey the speaker's scornful attitude toward him. Any one of these techniques might serve as the basis for a writing assignment that examined either the portrait of Miniver or the tone of the poem. These devices include (1) repetition, especially of <u>Miniver</u> and the beginning of ten lines and of <u>thought</u> in lines 27-28, (2) alliteration, as in <u>Cheevy-child</u> (line 1), <u>Miniver-mourned</u> and <u>ripe-renown</u> (line 13), and <u>Miniver-Medici</u> (line 17), and (3) inappropriate diction, especially <u>neighbors</u> (line 12), <u>fragrant</u> (14), and <u>iron clothing</u> (24). Along these same lines, rhyme effectively communicates both the speaker's disgust and Miniver's pathetic silliness. The falling (double, dactylic) rhymes in the 2nd and 4th lines of each stanza underscore Miniver's ridiculous situation through sound.

Ogden Nash, The Turtle, page 729.

Nash's humorous quatrain on the sex life of the turtle provides an ideal example of the ways in which alliteration and rhyme can establish the tone and impact of a poem. This one must be read aloud in class. You might start discussion with a very general question: why is the poem funny and why does it sound funny? Alliterative patterns that contribute to the poem's humor include the t (turtle, twixt, plated, fertile) and the x (twixt, decks, sex, and fix). The rhymes--decks-sex and turtle-fertile--shift from rising (lines 1-2) to falling (lines 3-4). The falling rhymes in the last two lines clinch both the tone and the central idea of the poem. Writing topics: the effect of rhyme in the poem. The effect of alliteration.

Barbara Howes, Death of a Vermont Farm Woman, page 730.

Do not let the title mislead your students; the poem is not about death. It is primarily a portrait of an individual and a way of life; the speaker is a sixty-year-old farm woman whose life has been a constant for survival. She has worked the farm, given birth four times, outlived three of her sons, and now looks for peace (perhaps death). The setting is established in the opening lines; it is late July and fall is approaching. The fields, like the speaker, are old but still productive; the long green evenings will delay death for both the fields and the farm woman. But the season shifts toward winter (and death); this is inevitable. We are reminded of the next winter by the speaker's recollection of the last (lines 6-9). She may have thought that her death was approaching then; she was wrong. In the last stanza, the speaker looks back over her whole life; it seems short and difficult. Now she seeks rest, peace, and death; she asks again, "Is it time now?"

Howes uses rhyme with remarkable skill, tying the whole poem together with two repeated rhyme sounds and isolating the speaker's central question with a third rhyme that is repeated in lines 9 and 15. The rhyme scheme is aabba, aabc, aabbac. Most of the lines end with the a or b rhyme, thus creating an ongoing network of repeated sounds that holds the poem together tightly. In this pattern, the double use of long (lines 4 and 13) does not weaken the poem; quite the contrary, it stresses the sense of age, struggle, and exhaustion linked to the speaker. Similarly, the repetition of now as the c rhyme underscores the speaker's readiness for peace and rest in the present moment. Writing topics: the character of the speaker. The setting. The seasonal imagery. The connection among setting, imagery, and theme. The impact of the rhymes.

Isabella Gardener, At a Summer Hotel, page 731.

Gardner's short poem provides an instance in which rhyme (and sound) seem to undercut the serious ideas explored. When you teach this poem, you might begin with the larger questions, such as the nature of the mother-daughter relationship and the source of the speaker's anxiety. You might then ask your students to consider whether the poetic devices--alliteration, repetition, internal rhyme, and end rhyme--work to emphasize or undercut the major thrust.

The speaker here is a mother at a Summer Hotel by the sea with her daughter (How old is the daughter? See what your students can do with bountiful beautiful womanful). The mother is passive; she sits on the veranda and worries (uneasy). The daughter is active and immersed in nature: gold in the sun, bold in the dazzling water, drowsing on the blond sand and in the daisy fields. The speaker wants to relax; she wants to be soothed by the sea not roused by the roses roving wild. But the "beautiful bountiful womanful" daughter induces anxiety. The source of this anxiety is revealed in the closing allusions to Europa, Persephone, and Miranda; all three women attracted violent sexual attention. The speaker finally seems uneasy about her daughter's sexuality and the vulnerability associated with it.

Gardner employs a number of musical devices to unify the poem and emphasize the ideas. In some instances, these seem to undercut the ideas rather than advance them. The poem includes a great deal of alliteration: the b sound in beautiful and bountiful (the three ful endings form another kind of repetition), the s sound in soothed and sea, the r sound in roused, roses, and roving, the g sound in girl and gold, the d sound in gold, bold, dazzling, drowses, blond, sand, daisy, daughter, and dreams. This may be too much of a good thing. Internal rhyme--as in gold-bold (line 3) and blond-sand (line 4)--also holds lines together but produces a faintly humorous effect. The end rhymes are also a problem in this respect. Child-wild is an exact, rising rhyme that neatly captures some of the daughter's qualities and the mother's anxiety. Water-daughter and veranda-Miranda, however, are falling (double, trochaic) rhymes that ring in the humorous. Like the first rhyming pair, water-daughter captures some of the speaker's anxiety, especially if we see the water as even faintly sexual. Veranda-Miranda can only be amusing.

Writing topics: the effects of rhyme, alliteration, or repetition. The character of the speaker or the daughter. The poet's use of allusion. The idea(s) about the mother-daughter relationship that may be obliquely established in the poem.

WRITING ABOUT RHYME IN POETRY, pages 731-738.

The introductory material here (pages 731-734) explains the way in which students can develop an essay on rhyme, from an initial reading of the poem to writing and revision. A key point to stress in class and in assignments is that any consideration of rhyme must be linked to analysis of another element such as character, tone, or meaning. An essay that deals only with rhyme will be merely descriptive; it will not make any useful or interesting assertion about the poem. Since the same caveat holds true for essays that deal with meter or sound, one useful way to use this section of the chapter on rhyme is to combine it with the writing sections of those other chapters (Rhythm, pages 666-692, Sound, pages 693-712), and to use a single paper assignment to cover all three topics. Thus, you might give your students the option of writing about the effects of meter, sound, rhyme, or any combination of those elements in any one poem (it might be helpful to select a single poem or a group from which they can select one).

As with the essays on meter and segments, successful writing here depends on correct analysis. The analysis of rhyme, however, is less fraught with difficulty than either of the other processes. In this case, we suggest that you have students prepare their own worksheets, and then look them over briefly before the students actually begin to write. Essays that seek to combine analyses of rhyme, segments, and/or meter will require a very detailed and sophisticated worksheet. The sample essay in this chapter (pages 735-738) focuses on the impact of rhyme, repetition, and sound on meaning in Christina Rossetti's "Echo." The essay and the commentary emphasize the principles and processes of selectivity and organization discussed previously in the chapter.

CHAPTER 22

FORM: THE SHAPE OF THE POEM

This chapter is designed to introduce students formally to the idea of form and structure in poetry. It makes no attempt to describe or define every possible traditional form; such an undertaking would require a book all its own. Your students may come to the idea of form in poetry with pronounced prejudices or resistance. They may assume that all closed forms are artificial and imposted (or invented) by poets in collusion with teachers. While this is at least partly true (poets invent forms, we identify them), a quick look at several ballads or lyrics will reveal the natural and organic connection between singing, memory, patterns of repetition, and form. More sophisticated students might condemn all closed forms as too restrictive or all open forms as too sloppy and disordered. Classroom discussion and emphasis can deal with these extreme prejudices.

The key distinction in this chapter is between closed and open forms; this central distinction can be reiterated in class. At the same time, you can encourage your students to consider the ways in which each form partakes of the other's qualities. Closed-form poets seek the greatest freedom and innovation within rigid structures of form. Open-form poets undertake an equally difficult task; they must impose order, shape, and meaning in new ways. Encourage your students to appreciate each type of form for its strengths, rather than condemning it out of hand.

The discussion of the building blocks of closed form (pages 740-743) considers one-, two-, three-, and four-line units. The one-line unit (blank verse) is exemplified by a speech from Hamlet (a sample essay explicating this passage is on pages 1375-1377). Other poems in the text you might use to illustrate blank verse include Tennyson's "Tithonus" (page 497) and Wordsworth's "Tintern Abbey" (page 525).

Couplets are illustrated by two poems in the chapter (pages 758-759) and by the epigrams. Other useful poems that exemplify couplets of various lengths include "My Last Duchess" (page 488), "Bermudas" (page 519), "The Destruction of Sennacherib" (page 606), "Very Like a Whale" (page 607), "Macavity" (page 684), "We Real Cool" (page 685), "An Essay on Criticism" (page 718), and "Ars Poetica" (page 844).

The three-line unit (triplets, tercets) is exemplified in the chapter by "The Eagle" (page 742), "Ode to the West Wind" (page 764), and "Do Not Go Gentle into That Good Night" (page 766). Two other poems that illustrate the usefulness of the tercet are Dickinson's "To Hear an Oriole Sing" (page 726) and Roethke's "The Waking" (page 933, another villanelle). Poems that illustrate the versatility of the quatrain can be found throughout the text; they are far too numerous to mention.

The discussion of types of closed-form poetry (pages 743-748) deals with some of the major forms that have remained popular for centuries and a few minor forms. Out of necessity, a number of forms are omitted. We do not, for example, discuss syllabic verse such as haiku. If you wish to examine haiku with your students, examples can be found on pages 585 and 964. Most of the closed forms introduced here are exemplified by one or two poems later in the chapter (pages 756-768). Beyond these, examples of most closed forms are scattered throughout the text. Here are some alternate examples for teaching:

ITALIAN or PETRARCHAN SONNETS: Keats, On First Looking into Chapman's Homer, page 592; Wyatt, I Find No Peace, page 620; Wordsworth, London, 1802, page 627; Hopkins, God's Grandeur, page 703; Yeats, Leda and the Swan, page 819; Browning, How Do I Love Thee, page 934; Millay, What Lips My Lips Have Kissed, page 977.

ENGLISH or SHAKESPEAREAN SONNETS: All sonnets by Shakespeare; Keats, Bright Star, page 681; Avison, Tennis, page 927; Cullen, Yet Do I Marvel, page 940; McKay, The White City, page 976. For modifications of the form, see Donne, Batter My Heart, page 556; Owen, Anthem for Doomed Youth, page 572; Spenser (the Spenserian sonnet), poems on pages 851 and 1010.

BALLADS: Sir Patrick Spens, page 465; Bonny George Campbell, page 495; Barbara Allan, page 722; Edward, page 922, Lord Randall, page 923; Keats, La Belle Dame sans Merci, page 797.

COMMON MEASURE: Many of Emily Dickinson's poems, pages 889-898.

SONGS and LYRICS: Housman, Loveliest of Trees, page 470; Rossetti, Echo, page 725; Herrick, To The Virgins, page 850; Donne, poems on pages 875-886; Cohen, Suzanne, page 936; Shakespeare, Fear No More the Heat o' the Sun, 1001.

ODES: Wordsworth, Intimations of Immortality, page 853; Keats, Ode on a Grecian Urn, page 859.

Pope, Coleridge, Cummings, Cunningham, Epigrams, pages 745-746.

These epigrams share brevity, wit, and a satiric thrust. Pope's epitaph is part of a set of three commemorating the deaths of Hewet and Drew. The other two that he wrote are longer, more decorous, and mock-heroic. This one is terse, witty, and bawdy. Coleridge's epigram is a superb definition of an epigram. Cummings pokes fun at politicians, and Cunningham at human nature and sexuality. Epigrams are related to heroic couplets and to the couplets that end Shakespearean sonnets in that they clinch ideas with a very rapid poetic thrust. Couplets and epigrams contain whole thoughts put with economy and skill. Two additional epigrams can be found on page 650.

Anonymous, Limericks, page 747.

You should not have to say much about limericks in class; they remain a very popular form of children's poetry in their less bawdy form. The rules are described on page 746. As an exercise, you might ask your students to write a few topical limericks; such an assignment can serve as a pleasant and easy introduction to the idea of writing verse within a fixed form.

E. C. Bentley, Two Clerihews, page 747.

Clerihews are almost always humorous or satirical; they attack or at least mock the figure named in the first line. The form has relatively few requirements: four lines rhymed a a b b; the first line must name a famous character or literary figure. Like limericks, the clerihew is a closed form that most students can handle reasonably well. You might have your students write a few as an exercise and share them in class.

Anthony Hecht, Nominalism, page 748.

Arthur W. Monks, Twilight's Last Gleaming, page 748.

Double-dactyls, also called Higgledy-Piggledies, were very much in vogue in the late 1960s. Like epigrams and clerihews, they are usually humorous or satirical. The form is rigid and demanding, requiring two quatrains. The first line must contain two rhyming nonsense dactylic words; the second consists of a name (or title and name) that can be read as two dactyls (e.g., Moses Maimonides, Judas Iscariot, Emperor Oedipus). The third, fifth, and sixth or seventh lines must be two dactylic feet, while the fourth and eighth lines must be short (a dactyl and one stressed syllable) and rhyme. Finally, the fifth or sixth line must be a single word that scans as two dactylic feet (e.g., antepenultimate, octogenarian, quasitheistically). These are not easy to write. Nevertheless, you may want to have your students give it a try. The exercise will give them a much stronger sense of the difficulty of writing at all in closed forms.

William Shakespeare, Let Me Not to the Marriage of True Minds, page 749.

Please see the discussion of this poem in the text, pages 749-751. Writing topics: imagery and meaning. Form and meaning.

Walt Whitman, Reconciliation, page 752.

This poem is also discussed at length in the text (pages 752-753). Hardy's "The Man He Killed" (page 474) is an excellent poem for comparison. In addition to contrasting an open- and closed-form poem on the same subject, there is clear contrast in speakers and tones. Whitman's speaker is a good deal more sophisticated and clear about his own feelings. The two poems make a good comparison-contrast writing assignment. The focus of such an essay could be form, tone, speaker, imagery, diction, or meaning.

George Herbert, Easter Wings, page 755.

This splendid and skillful example of shaped verse is well worth class discussion. Teaching can be organized around questions of content and then shape or structure. The ideas are expressed in four movements: humanity's fall, personal salvation, personal fall, and personal flight. The shape of the poem suggests angel's wings (visually suggesting grace, Christ, resurrection, salvation), an hour glass (suggesting elapsed personal and cosmic time, the end of time), and fluctuation (illustrating variations in flight, spiritual status, and song). Some readers also see birds' (or larks') wings in the image. Each line also visually reflects its own meaning through its length (wealth, richness).

John Milton, When I Consider How My Light is Spent, page 756.

In this Italian sonnet (iambic pentameter: abba, abba, cde, cde), Milton employs the octave-sestet structure to organize the poem's movement and meaning. In the octave, the speaker complains about the failures and frustrations in his life, only one of which is blindness. In a limited sense,

the one talent refers to the speaker's skill at poetry and political writing
(Milton was a brilliant propagandist for the Puritans during much of the
Interregnum). As an allusion to the parable in Matthew, however, talent
refers to the active and energetic preparation for the Lord's return. The
speaker's frustration includes both physical and spiritual blindness--a crisis
of faith in which he is unsure about God's expectations and assumes that he
will be rejected. The speaker almost asks if God exacts "day-labor, light
denied" (light here means sight, faith, inspiration), and he admits that it is
a foolish question. The problem is resolved in the sestet, where the
speaker's (personified) Patience prevents him from asking the question by
explaining God's expectations. Patience makes it clear that God is
self-sufficient; he does not need "man's work or his gifts." The proper and
best service to God is to accept divine will ("bear his mild yoke"), and that
can be done by those "who only stand and wait" (wait suggests a series of
ideas including wait on, wait for, attend, and expect).
    Writing topics: the connection between form and meaning. The character
of the speaker or of Patience. The image of God. Two good poems for
comparison-contrast, both dealing with salvation and the relationship between
the individual and God, are Herbert's "Love (III)" (page 496) and Donne's
"Batter My Heart" (page 556).

Percy Bysshe Shelley, Ozymandias, pages 756-757.

    This is a modified Italian sonnet (iambic pentameter: abab, acdc, ede,
fef). The octave-sestet structure organizes the poem's images and ideas; the
statue is described in the octave, the inscription in the first triplet, and
the surrounding desolation in the second triplet. The modified rhyme scheme
has an effect similar to that of Spenser's adaptation of the Shakespearean
sonnet; it allows each unit of the poem to be interconnected with the next
through sound. In class discussion, you might focus on the image of Ozymandias
and what he represents, and then on the many ways in which his vanity (and the
grandiose claims of all tyrants) are ironically undercut.
    The image of the face and the inscription convey Ozymandias's arrogance
and vanity. The artist recognized this vanity; it was his hand that mocked
the king's passions and heart. The vain arrogance is undercut throughout the
poem. A single shattered statue has outlasted the whole empire. The sonnet
reshatters the statue; the pieces are scattered about verbally (legs in line
2, visage in line 4, pedestal in line 9). Ozymandias's words are undercut in
two ways. First, they point to works that no longer exist. Second, they are
distanced by layers of narrative filters. Ozymandias dictated the words to
the artist who carved them. Centuries later, the traveller (line 1) read the
words and repeated them to the speaker; the speaker relates them to us. Each
of these narrative filters pushes Ozymandias (and his vain boast) farther away
from us and makes him less significant. Thus, the sonnet illustrates the
vanity of human tyrants and the power of time and change.
    Does the poem say anything about art? You might ask your students if the
poem implies that anything lasts. There are at least two positions. The
sonnet implies that the lone and level sands will eventually cover everything.
In the present, however, it is the artist's skill rather than the tyrant's
power that endures. Writing topics: the relation of form to meaning. The
ideas explored about tyranny, time, or art.

Claude McKay, In Bondage, page 757.

McKay was born in Jamaica, emigrated to the United States in 1912, and settled in Harlem in 1914, where he became an important poetic voice in the Harlem Renaissance. "In Bondage" is a straightforward Shakespearean sonnet (iambic pentameter: abab, cdcd, efef, gg). McKay uses the three quatrains and the couplet to organize his ideas. In teaching, it is important to get your students to see the radical shift (or disjunction) between the hypothetical (lines 1-12) and the actual (lines 13-14), indicated by would and but.

Would signifies the hypothetical nature of the world envisioned in lines 1-8, a world of freedom, leisure, fairness, and time. The third quatrain draws back from this world and explains its importance--life is more important and enduring than petty and short human conflict. All this is sharply undercut by the couplet, which jerks us back to the reality of Blacks in the United States during McKay's life. Here, the rhyming words--grave-slave-- pound home the image of what is instead of what should be.

Writing topics: the relation of form to meaning. The ideas explored about life, reality, humanity. The effects of rhyme, especially in the couplet. Another sonnet by McKay is on page 976.

John Dryden, To The Memory of Mr. Oldham, pages 758-759.

Dryden's elegy for John Oldham is in heroic couplets (iambic pentameter: aa, bb, etc., with a triplet in lines 19-21). In class, you can focus initially on the speaker's links with and attitude toward Oldham, and then the ideas about early death explored in lines 11-25. Discussion of rhyme, form, and allusion can follow.

In the opening ten lines, the speaker describes his affinity with Oldham, noting that their souls were near allied and that they both wrote verse satire. The allusion to Nisus (line 9) puts the friendship in a classical and poetic context. This classical ethos dominates lines 11-25, where the speaker discusses the advantages of dying young. As in Housman's "To An Athlete Dying Young" (page 727), the consolations of early death are entirely pagan and classical (rather than Christian and redemptive). The speaker asserts that Oldham might have learned more even metrics (numbers) had he lived longer, but this is not necessary for satire. Time might have mellowed Oldham's rhymes, but his verse already showed quickness and wit. Marcellus (line 23) implies that Oldham would have succeded (Dryden?) as a brilliant poet; the laurels suggest that he has already achieved greatness.

The poem's end-stopped heroic couplets give it a dignified and stately tempo, appropriate to its elegaic tone. Dryden uses an alexandrine (line 21) to slow the poem still further before its final "hail and farewell." Rhymes are useful in clinching ideas and linking concepts; you might ask your class about pairs like mine-thine, shine-line, and prime-time-rhyme (the triplet). See if your students think the repetition of the young-tongue rhyme (lines 13-14, 22-23) helps or hurts the poem.

Writing topics include an analysis of form, rhyme, diction, or allusion in connection with character or meaning. Housman's "To An Athlete" would provide a splendid focus for a comparison paper, with reference to tone, form, speaker, allusion, or ideas. "Oldham" can also be taught as an elegy, with reference to Gray's "Elegy in a Country Churchyard" (page 520).

Jean Toomer, Reapers, page 759.

Toomer was born in Washington D.C., studied at five colleges, and eventually settled in the Black community in Sparta, Georgia. An important

voice in the Harlem Renaissance, his only book, Cane, was published in 1923.
"Reapers" is in iambic pentameter rhymed couplets that are enjambed rather
than end-stopped. The enjambment, especially in lines 1-2 and 7-8, moderates
the effect of the couplets and keeps the poem moving quickly.

The auditory images of the poem contrast the silence of reaping to the
sound of steel on stones and the squealing of the field rat. Alliteration on
the s sound links all these together, but squealing is shocking; it breaks the
relative silence of the poem. The visual images form a linked chain that
relates to death: black reapers, scythes . . . silently swinging, black
horses, the bleeding field rat, and the Blood-stained blade. Like the squeal,
the blood (lines 6-8) shocks by contrasting vivid red to the dominant black of
the poem. What is implied about the reapers? Are they, like the field rat,
mowed down and destroyed by impersonal and inexorable forces? This is a
traditional reading. To what extent might the reapers also symbolize death,
or at least embody an inexorable force? A good poem on a similar subject for
comparison is Arna Bontemps's "A Black Man Talks of Reaping" (page 932).
Writing topics: the impact of the rhymed couplets on meaning. The reapers as
metaphorical images of life or of death. The play of colors (especially black
and red) in the poem.

George Herbert, Virtue, page 760.

This wonderful lyric explores the differences between transient worldly
things and the immortal soul. The poem is discussed at some length in the
sample essay in this chapter (pages 781-782). Writing topics: the degree to
which form organizes meaning. Rhyme and meaning. Meter and meaning. The
imagery (especially the day, rose, and spring).

Robert Frost, Desert Places, page 761.

Frost employs repetition, alliteration, and rhyme in this lyric to create
a network of related images and sounds that reinforce meaning. Reading this
aloud in class may help your students pick up the repetitions of snow, the
alliteration on f (falling, fast, field, few) and the web of sounds/words
linked to loneliness. The four stanza lyric (iambic pentameter: aaba, ccdc,
eebe, ffgf) moves from the landscape to animals, and finally to the speaker's
meditations. It is about moments/places of loneliness, and desolation.

In stanzas 1 and 2, the snow covers and isolates, turning the earth into
a desert place. The speaker is included in this loneliness unawares because
he is too "absent-spirited to count." In the third stanza, the speaker begins
to meditate on this desert of loneliness, and implies that there is nothing
within or without (nothing to express) to mitigate the desolation. The snow,
landscape, speaker, and nature are all benighted (unenlightened, in the dark,
cursed, spiritually void). Finally, the speaker contrasts the vast and vacant
interstellar spaces of the galaxy to the empty spaces within himself; he finds
these internal desert places far more terrifying. Thus, desert places include
external nature, cosmic emptiness, and internal desolation (lack of spirit,
despair). The falling rhymes in the last stanza--spaces-race is-places--do
not lighten the poem's tone; they add a twist of grim irony.

Writing topics: an analysis of form, repetition, rhyme, or sound in
connection with tone, speaker, or meaning. The "snow" imagery here and in
"Stopping by Woods" (page 475) would make a good topic for a comparison-
contrast essay.

155

John Keats, Ode to a Nightingale, pages 761-763.

This is not an easy poem for students or teachers, yet it says what it means and exemplifies the closed-form of the ode. We suggest a stanza-by-stanza classroom approach. The stanza form Keats employs throughout is a truncated Italian sonnet (iambic pentameter: abab cde 3cde).

The first stanza establishes the speaker's mental and emotional state; he is unhappy and pained. Key metaphors relate this condition to poison (hemlock) and narcotics (opium), but it is the nightingale's song that has produced the lethargy. The speaker (in stanza 2) wants a drink of wine (vintage, warm south, Hippocrene, inspiration, spirit) so that he can join the nightingale and "fade away into the forest dim." He wants to escape (stanza 3) the ills of the world: sickness, age, time, change, death. In stanzas 4 and 5 the speaker's tone and imaginative status change; he claims that he will join the nightingale through the power of poetic inspiration/imagination ("the viewless wings of Poesy"). In his imagination, he makes this transition to the nightingale's green, fragrant, murmurous, and dark world of nature; the sensual images here are visual, olfactory, and auditory. The speaker notes (stanza 6) that he has considered easeful Death as a means of making the transition from the world of pain and change to the timeless realm of imagination. The rub, of course, is that he would lose the song (inspiration, poetry). In the seventh stanza, the heart of the ode, the speaker establishes the symbolic value of the nightingale's song as immortal and universal poetry (or inspiration), heard by emperors, clowns, faeries throughout time. The song expands to fill all time and history. In a world where beauty cannot last, the song (poetry, inspiration) is timeless and eternal. After this climax, the speaker sinks back into his own world, wondering if he has had a dream or a vision (both exercises of imagination/inspiration).

Writing topics: the organization of the poem's ideas or argument through form. The impact of rhyme or diction. The ideas about the world, poetry, or imagination explored here. Shelley's "Ode to the West Wind" (page 764) is an excellent poem for comparison.

Percy Bysshe Shelley, Ode to the West Wind, pages 764-766.

Like Keats's ode, this poem may present difficulties to students and instructors. Again, we recommend a careful stanza-by-stanza approach. The poem shares with "Ode to a Nightingale" a focus on the need for poetic inspiration. The ode is in five fourteen-line stanzas of iambic pentameter terza rima concluded by a couplet, as follows:

       aba, bcb, cdc, ded, ee
       fbf, bgb, ghg, heh, ee
       iji, jkj, kck, cec, ee
       ele, lml, mnm, non, oo
       pqp, qrq, rsr, sts, tt

The terza rima interlocks and unifies each stanza through sound; the repeated b, c, and e rhymes help unify the entire ode. The three e couplets tie stanzas 1-3 together and separate 4 and 5, although the initial repetition of the e rhyme in 4 creates a bridge. The stanzaic structure organizes the poem's ideas quite rigorously; stanzas 1-3 deal with the West Wind and nature, stanza 4 with the speaker's problem, and stanza 5 with a solution.

In stanza 1, the wind blows (moves, affects) the leaves and seeds; it is both a destroyer and preserver, and the images reflect death and rebirth. In the second and third stanzas, the wind similarly drives clouds and waves. In each instance, the wind represents power, movement, death, and rebirth. The speaker calls on the wind (O hear) at the close of each stanza. In the fourth stanza, the core of the poem, the speaker presents his problem; he wants to be moved (affected, inspired) by the wind as he was in his "boyhood." Life and change have destroyed his ability to respond to the wind; maturity and time have chained and bowed him down. The speaker wants to be lifted as a leaf, wave, or cloud; he wants to become the wind's lyre (voice, stanza 5).

Like Wordsworth's "Intimations of Immortality" and Keats's "Ode to a Nightingale," this poem is finally about the failure of poetic inspiration or spirit. The wind, like the nightingale's song, becomes a symbol for inspiration. Writing topics: an analysis of the interconnection between form and meaning. The symbolic value of the wind. The character of the speaker. Question 6 also suggests a good topic for a comparison essay.

Dylan Thomas, Do Not Go Gentle into That Good Night, pages 766-767.

Thomas revitalizes the rigid form of the villanelle, making each repeated rhyme and line work with meaning and impact. The poem reflects the poet's dismay at his father's emotional and physical decay (Thomas's father had been a strong and authoritarian teacher; in his 80s, however, he became blind and ill). The speaker addresses the poem to this father (line 16); he wants him to remain fierce and independent, to resist a passive or "gentle" ending. He wants his father to emulate "wise men" (lines 4-6), "Good Men" (7-9), "Wild men" (10-12), and "Grave men" (13-15), all of whom "rage against the dying of the light" and don't "go gentle into that good night." The poem is enlivened by puns on good night (dying and "farewell") and grave (serious and dead).

The ideal writing topic here is an exploration of the relation between form and meaning. The poem constantly returns to two rhyme sounds and two repeated lines (iambic pentameter: aba aba aba aba aba abaa). Line 1 is repeated (the form allows for minor changes) as lines 6, 12, and 18; line 3 is repeated as lines 9, 15, and 19. All this repetition of words, rhymes, and lines turns the poem into something of an incantation or prayer; each repetition underscores the speakers hopes, fears, and demands.

Dudley Randall, Ballad of Birmingham, pages 767-768.

In 1965, Randall founded the Broadside Press, an important and valuable publisher of modern Black poetry. One of the first poems he published as a broadside (a single sheet) was this ballad. The poem demonstrates that the ballad survives as an effective and moving poetic form. It is highly traditional in form and subject matter. The rhyme scheme (abcb, etc.) and meter (iambic tetrameter and trimeter) reflect medieval practice, as do the use of quotation and the sensational and disturbing events. The quoted speaker in stanzas 1 and 3 is the child; the mother is quoted in stanzas 2, 4, and 8. This dialogue slows the ballad down and delays the climax.

The story of the bombing is related through dialogue and third-person narration. The speaker remains dispassionate; emotion is conveyed through description and dialogue. The daughter wants to participate in a freedom march; the mother considers this too dangerous, and sends the daughter to safety in church. The irony here--a splendid writing topic--operates at several levels. The mother is ironically wrong about safety. American society is also presented in an ironic light; in the world of the ballad, it is safer to face "clubs and hoses, guns and jails" than it is to go to church.

157

The little girl's shoe (line 30), like the hats of Sir Patrick Spens's crew (page 465), is a more gruesome and ironic symbol of death than the actual body would be. Writing topics: the relation of form to impact, the characters, tone, and ideas about society. The character of the mother, daughter, and/or speaker. Comparison-contrast assignments dealing with form, rhyme, tone, or repetition might focus on this poem and on "Sir Patrick Spens" (page 465) or "Barbara Allan" (page 722).

Walt Whitman, When I Heard the Learn'd Astronomer, page 769.

This open-form poem (no stanzas, meter, or rhyme scheme) explores the idea that our experience with nature and the cosmos should be personal, immediate, and mystical. Whitman employs lists in the first four lines to signify the impersonal and boring approach of the astronomer: proofs, figures, columns, charts, diagrams. This setting is noisy and crowded; the astronomer's approach to the cosmos is dry and limiting, full of meaningless manipulations of numbers ("add, divide, measure"). The repetition of "when" at the beginning of lines 1-4 gives the poem an oratorical flavor and underscores the droning boredom of the lecture. The cadences here are short, and the language colloquial. In the last four lines, we see the speaker's rejection of this world and this approach to nature. He became "tired and sick," wandered "off by myself," and "Looked up in perfect silence at the stars." The repeated sounds in "mystical moist night air" add to the sense of quiet and mystery in this personal communion. The poem thus contrasts personal, mystical, moist, silent, and eternal with communal, statistical, dry, noisy, and limited. The cadences in the last four lines grow longer and more sweeping, until Whitman glides into a surprising line of iambic pentameter in the last line. Writing topics include questions 3 and 4 as well as analyses of setting, tone, and speaker.

E. E. Cummings, Buffalo Bill's Defunct, page 769.

This poem can lead to a spirited class discussion. It is certainly a portrait, but your students will have to decide if it is admiring, mocking, or something in between. You can also discuss what is portrayed: Buffalo Bill as person, institution, business, or myth. The form is also worth extended discussion. Lines made up of single words or names (1, 5, 7, 11) depend on typography and space to emphasize the images/ideas. Buffalo Bill's and Mister Death, as the opening and closing lines/names, are balanced and opposed against one another (Does this make Bill a symbol of life?). Defunct usually describes a bankrupt business; the term's connotations may imply that Bill was more (or less) than a human being. Nice touches are produced through the typography and onomatopoeia of words run together, such as watersmooth-silver (very smooth) and onetwothreefourfive or pidgeonsjustlikethat (suggesting rapidity). Handsome man (line 8, with a play on "hand") is balanced against blueeyed boy (line 10). Writing topics may be developed from each of the study questions. Additional topics include an examination of tone and of the image of death developed in the poem.

William Carlos Williams, The Dance, pages 770-771.

Williams captures in verse the movement and energy rendered visually in Breughel's painting. The poem makes no profound assertions; it is a verbal portrait of a painting. The key question for class discussion--and the most effective writing topic--is how Williams recreates the essence of the painting in the poem. Since the painting is reproduced in the text, page 770, students have no excuse for not looking carefully at both poem and image). Answers are legion. The repetition of the first line at the close creates a circular movement; the poem could start all over again. The identical lines also create a frame, like the edges of the canvas. The repetition of sounds, syllables, and words drives the poem faster and forms internal connections (notice, for example, the web created by "round . . . round . . . around . . . round . . . impound . . . sound"). Williams employs onomatopoeia to suggest/duplicate the sounds of the instruments (squeal, blare, tweedle). While end-rhyme is lacking, internal rhyme (around-impound or prance-dance) pulls different parts of the poem together and speeds up the movement. The participles (tipping, kicking, rolling, swinging, rollicking) suggest the confusion and energy of ongoing activity. While Williams avoids a traditional meter, he frequently combines two unaccented syllables to suggest an anapestic or dactylic rhythm; the two light stresses create a rapid and dancing cadence. The absence of initial capital letters produces visual enjambment. Similarly, the unstressed or split words that end lines (and, the, thick-, those, such) push the reader on from line to line. For another poem by Williams about a painting see "Landscape with the Fall of Icarus" (page 831).

Allen Ginsberg, A Supermarket in California, page 771.

This tribute to Walt Whitman imitates several features of Whitman's style, including his poetic cadences, enumerative lists, and long sentences. The speaker is alone at night looking for images. The neon fruit super market is the contemporary (1955) America of conspicuous consumption and wealth; the enumerative lists (which imitate Whitman's style) reflect this abundance. Lorca and Whitman (both poets and homosexuals) are the speaker's spiritual progenitors; they also pull the past into the present. The speaker, like the Whitman presented in the poem, is an outcast and a wanderer on a journey without a destination. For both figures, the key terms are childless, lonely, solitary, and silent. Whitman's journey to death (Charon, Lethe) is as silent and lonely as the speaker's journey through the night. The "lost America of love" could be the past (in contrast to the supermarket present), but the past seems no more hospitable than the present to poet-dreamers. Writing topics: the impact of setting, form, diction, or imagery on meaning. The link between the speaker and Whitman as poets in a hostile world. The ideas about modern America and its values explored in the poem.

Nikki Giovanni, Nikki-Rosa, page 773.

Short lines and cadences alternate with longer ones here to punctuate ideas; conjunctions at the openings of lines speed up the tempo. The central point for class discussion and writing: the contrast between the speaker's good memories of childhood and the assumptions that the speaker claims they (biographers, line 6) will make about the childhood. The poem is full of positive and loving images of childhood, even when they are linked with hard times. The speaker's central assertion is in the last four lines; he or she claims that no white person will ever understand that Black love is Black wealth. Other topics for writing include the speaker or the tone (self-assured and a bit condescending; the speaker, in retrospect, can assume fame), and the ideas about childhood and understanding. Possible points of

159

controversy: does the poem reflect the way whites understand blacks, or the way blacks think that whites understand blacks? Are the speaker's assertions about black childhoods and black love in fact universally true?

May Swenson, Women, page 774.

This poem is open-form rather than shaped or concrete; the typography is suggestive, but it does not displace the words in importance or form an image. The poem can be read at least two ways: down the left column and then the right, or in ten-line two-column units divided at lines 10 and 20; the second method may provide a more coherent reading. The undulating typography suggests curves, movement, and pliancy--all consistent with the textual images of women "moving to the motions of men" as "rocking horses rockingly ridden." You can begin an effective class discussion by looking at the verbal images of women developed here. They are envisioned (defined) as "pedestals moving to the motions of men," as "painted rocking horses," and as "immobile," always "waiting willing to be set in motion"; they are the "gladdest things in the toyroom." These images are sexual and ironic; women are ironically presented as passive objects (toys) to be used and then abandoned by men ("the restored egos dismount and the legs stride away"). The speaker's irony suggests that the social/sexual formulation is wrong. The poem also implies that men, given this dynamic, are children (childish). Questions 2, 3, and 5 can be developed into good writing topics.

Mary Ellen Solt, Forsythia, page 775.

Solt's "Forsythia" is an example of concrete poetry; words give way to image completely. The image on the page evokes forsythia; the yellow background (in the original printing) reinforces the visual effect. The dots and dashes between the letters are Morse Code for the letters of "forsythia." They visually reinforce the "telegram" concept in the (minimal) text. The central topic for discussion and writing: Is this poetry? Let your students debate the question; the answer lies in the eye and mind of the beholder.

Edwin Morgan, The Computer's First Christmas Card, page 776.

The poem looks like a column of words generated at random by a computer; the typeface is reminiscent of early computer printers. As a poem (if your students will accept it as one), the words provide interesting linked sound effects and images we might associate with Christmas. Combinations like "jollymerry" or even "boppyjolly" might work, but those like "hoppyBarry" or "moppyjelly" wander pretty far afield. Nevertheless, sound holds the entire list together until the end, when the "computer" goes completely off the subject and generates "asMERRYCHR / YSANTHEMUM." Writing topics and points for discussion: the reasons why this can (or cannot) be considered a poem. The effects of sound produced in the work. The extent to which this makes fun of Christmas cards, computers, and/or Poetry.

John Hollander, Swan and Shadow, page 777.

This poem works as shaped verse, but not quite as well as Herbert's "Easter Wings" (page 754); there is no multiple image here, and every line length does not reinforce meaning. The poem is about perception, memory, and time; the swan is only the convenient example. The image awakens recognition in the beholder, creates illumination in the mind, and then fades into memory. The relation of swan to shadow is parallel to present and past, image and reflection, perception and memory. Typography and shape produce some interesting effects. The what when where (lines 10-12) are all answered in the same lines of the body--a perceptual leap. Line 18 divides swan from shadow, present from past, perception from memory. It is the "perfect sad instant now." A single rhyme (light-sight) frames and emphasizes the transition. At the close, Hollander introduces a visual/verbal pun. The "swan / sang" is an allusion to the swan song, the myth that a swan sings once in its life immediately before dying. The single word sang visually embodies that dying and fading away, a last glimmer of memory.

WRITING ABOUT FORM IN POETRY, pages 778-783.

Although the sample essay (pages 781-782) deals with a closed-form poem, the discussion on writing about form provides approaches that will work effectively for either closed or open forms. If you use this part of the chapter and make a writing assignment, you should stress in class the need to consider the relationship between form and content (speaker, tone, meaning) rather than simply the form. If you select a poem for your students to write about, choose one in which form impacts significantly on content. Closed- and open-form poems lend themselves equally well to this sort of assignment.

161

CHAPTER 23

SYMBOLISM AND ALLUSION: WINDOWS TO A WIDE EXPANSE OF MEANING

If you have already taught symbolism in fiction (Chapter 9), you may wish to use this introductory section simply as a review. If you omitted Chapter 9, however, there will be much here that is new. Particularly important is that poetry, being more compact than fiction, does not go into as much detail with symbols as one is likely to find in fiction. Students should thus be sensitive to the rapidity with which symbolism is often rendered in poems, through words, actions, setting, character, and situation (pages 788-789).

Allusion (pages 789-791) is sometimes difficult for students because they may not have built up the background needed for recognition. Even with good explanatory notes, they need guidance, so that they may understand the context and therefore the meaning of allusions. On pages 791-793 we address one of the perennial problems of students: how to recognize symbols and allusions. Often we ourselves may take these things for granted, but students are less sure of their ground. A discussion about how students may try independently to determine the presence of symbols and allusions is thus often helpful.

Virginia Scott, Snow, page 786.

The matters raised in the questions about this poem are considered on pages 787, 790, and 792-793 of the text. Writing topics may deal with any of the questions listed on page 787.

George Herbert, The Collar, pages 795-796.

Herbert's poems, many of which dramatized his conflicts about God before becoming a priest, were not published during his lifetime. "The Collar" gives us a man in conflict with his calling. At the end of the poem, the voice of God reasserts the normal and proper relationship between God and humanity.

Study Questions: (1) At the beginning the speaker describes a moment when in frustration he beat a table (the communion table?) and began the train of inward debate contained in the rest of the poem. The speaker is thinking about the reasons why he should resist or abandon his calling to divine service. (2) The title of the poem is a multiple symbol, because it involves an elaborate pun. It represents the speaker's anger (choler) against what he considers the yoke (collar) of service for which God (the caller) is calling him, and also the power of service because the clerical collar is round and therefore enveloping and enclosing. Because of the way the poem concludes, the calling by God and the collar as an enclosure are dominant.

(3) The symbols of the poem may be classed as follows: (a) positive religious symbols are thorn, blood, wine, and the parent-child relationship. (b) Positive secular symbols of independent self-fulfillment are bays, flowers, and garlands. (c) Negative religious symbols (prompting the speaker's anger or choler) are cage, the death's head, and the rope of sands (symbolizing the many complex, endless, and never-to-be-finished duties of the clergy). (4) The speaker cites the following reasons for pursuing his own secular goals: freedom, impatience, earthly reward capacity and opportunity to do other things, independence, and possible adventure. The sole reason in favor of the clergy role is God's call (line 35), and this is overwhelmingly persuasive. (5) The thorn and the wine as symbols allude to the crucifixion and communion. The parent-child relationship alludes to the New Testament

idea that God is like a father, close and personal to the obedient child (see
Mark 14:36; Romans 8:15; and Galatians 4:6). These allusions are important in
the argument of the poem because they stress the Biblical authority of the
calling to service that the speaker is resisting.

Writing topics: the use of <u>collar</u> as a multiple symbol and as a pun. The
conflicting symbols. Herbert's use of allusion.

Anne Finch, To Mr. Finch, now Earl of Winchelsea, pages 794-797.

Like George Herbert, Anne Finch wrote her poems privately. She did,
however, arrange for publication, and her verse was printed in 1713. Many of
the poems are about her personal "melancholy," but in "To Mr. Finch" she shows
great wit, charm, and affection.

<u>Study Questions</u>: (1) The occasion of the poem is explained by <u>Ardelia</u>,
the speaker, as a day's task requested by her husband, <u>Flavio</u>, when he had to
be away on business. The fictional journey is begun as Ardelia sends a
messenger to the Muses on Mount Parnassus to request their aid in composing a
poem in her husband's praise. As the poem progresses, Ardelia seems to be on
hand to record the responses of the Muses. Hence she apparently takes the
imaginary trip herself. She exhibits both persistence and wit in pursuing
her request for aid. Her love for Flavio is considered unusual and unique by
the Muses. (2) The structure of her mission takes the following form: (a) the
Muses agree to hear the request, and they ask its nature, lines 13-36. (b) In
council, the Muses refuse to grant the aid, but they cover themselves by
offering false excuses, except for Urania, who tells Ardelia that sincere
words do not need divine inspiration, lines 37-78. The narrative shifts in
line 79 to focus on Ardelia's self-analysis. (3) The response of the Muses is
comic because they claim that no married woman has ever asked before for the
inspiration to praise her husband. They want to supress Ardelia's request on
the grounds that it is in bad form, and would be embarrassing if it became
known among the worldly-wise people frequenting clubs and chocolate houses
(chocolate was a fashionable and expensive drink at the time). The convention
to which Anne Finch is alluding is that marriages among the higher social
classes were arranged as business deals, not as unions of loving couples.

(4) In lines 43 and 44 the speaker alludes to Griselda, Andromache, and
the wives of Douglas and Percy--all characters in past epics or ballads.
These references symbolize a former style of marriage in which wives and
husbands loved each other. The beaux of line 49 symbolize a view of life in
which clothing is more important than personal relationships. The situation
of Ardelia and Flavio is symbolic inasmuch as they themselves are the only
ones who are interested in their relationship. Hence their life is private
and therefore like a religious mystery. Writing topics: the humor of the
poem. The use of allusion. Symbols reflecting attitudes about married love.

John Keats, La Belle Dame Sans Merci, pages 797-799.

Because of Keats's letters, we know the precise date when he wrote the
first version of this poem (April 21, 1819) and also the circumstances (soon
after he had taken care of the personal effects of his dead brother, Tom).
Critical biographers have tried to demonstrate the influence of this situation
on the poem, together with Keats's own uncertainty about his love for Fanny
Brawne. Despite the wealth of information about the circumstances of composition, and also despite attempts to relate the poem to a linkage of death and
life in the poet's psyche, "La Belle Dame Sans Merci" has an independent

existence that defies categorization. All poems of course require great perception and care in reading, but this one demands special care.

Study Questions: (1) The first three stanzas contain the first speaker's questions. The remaining eight stanzas contain the knight's narrative about his encounter with the lady, the "Belle Dame." (2) The knight's narrative is structured according to the meeting, the first loving, and the magical journey (stanzas 4-7). In stanzas 8-11, the knight goes with the lady to her grotto; they make love and the knight falls asleep and dreams the ghostly dream, only to awake on the hillside. Stanza 12 is the knight's answer to the speaker's question in the first stanza. The source of the knight's information about his thralldom is only his own dream, his own imagination. (3) That the knight's narrative is a dream requires that it be read as a symbol. The meaning, however, is not easily determined. Is it disillusionment with love? A sense of doom about life itself? A disparagement of the regrettable power of the human imagination to misconstrue and negate positive experiences? Sorrow about the hauntingly brief nature of happiness? Your students might wish to consider any or all of these possibilities. (4) Relish, honey, and manna are all magical, unreal symbols. Manna, particularly, is the food provided by God to the ancient Israelites (Exodus 16). Keats probably intends by it no more than a magical nourishment. The pale kings and warriors are the previous victims of the Beautiful Lady without Mercy; they symbolize powers of doubt and negation. (5) The multiple setting of sedge, meadows, herbs, and grotto all symbolically complement the knight's dazed state of mind.

Writing topics: the narrative structure of the poem. The puzzle of the meaning of the poem's major symbols. The nature of the fairy lady, apart from the knight's perception.

Thomas Hardy, In Time of "The Breaking of Nations," page 799.

With this poem, students may wish to discuss whether the topic is people or politics. Another interesting subject is whether such a poem could be written today, with the possibility that nuclear warfare could penetrate even to remote corners of the earth where maids and their wights are together.

Study Questions: (1) The man and woman are a universal symbol of love. The man and the horse are also a universal symbol. The smoke coming from the grass, however, is contextual; the poet must arrange the stanza to make the smoke symbolic. As images, these symbols refer to sight, sound (whispering) and smell (smoke). (2) Hardy emphasizes the symbolism of the phrase breaking of nations by speaking of dynasties and war's annals in lines 7-8 and 11-12. The Biblical allusion adds the sense that wars and political changes have been going on for milennia, but that human life has been predominating and will prevail, because strength is in human affection, not anger. (3) Stanza 1 is descriptive, whereas in stanzas 2 and 3 only the first halves are descriptive. In developing his assertions, Hardy refers to these halves as this (line 7) and their story (line 12). (4) Hardy's speaker makes his evaluation by citing the quietness and permanence of his pictures of life among the people, the folk. He dismisses the great business of war and dynastic change by relegating it to the second parts of the stanzas, and by negating it in favor of common life. Writing topics: the visual symbols. The importance of the Biblical allusion and the quotation marks in the title.

William Butler Yeats, The Second Coming, pages 800-801.

The issues in the questions are treated on page 791 and in the sample essay (pages 811-813). Writing topics: The structure of the poem. An analysis of one central symbol in detail (e.g., the gyre, the rough beast).

Robinson Jeffers, The Purse-Seine, pages 802-803.

One of the dominant themes in Jeffers's poetry is the capacity of human beings to self-destruct. Many of the poems go on to suggest, however, that a restoration of the pristine beauty of the natural world may come out of such destruction. "The Purse-Seine" deals with this theme, although in this poem Jeffers is not concerned with the potentially positive aftermath. In teaching the poem you may need to spend time with the speaker's assertions in stanza 3, for the validity of the poem itself depends on these assertions.

Study Questions: (1) A purse-seine is a fishing net that contains floats at the top and a draw-cable at the bottom. When drawn, the net does not allow any fish to escape. In stanza 2, the speaker responds to the seining by claiming that it is terrible because of the certainty of capture, but he also stresses details about the beauty of the fish as they struggle to free themselves. (2) In stanza 3, the speaker shows the symbolic nature of the purse-seine by equating it to the inability of industrialized nations and humanity to survive independently. He points out that the draw cable may take the form of dictatorship, revolution, repression, anarchy, or mass disasters, from which there is no escape. The sardines hence symbolize the present world population, and the seine symbolizes destructive political forces. (3) Both Jeffers and Yeats agree that a sinister force will soon become powerful. To Yeats, however, things happen in 2,000-year cycles, with the possibility of a better cycle replacing the evil one now approaching. The idea of Jeffers is less systematic than that of Yeats, for Jeffers makes plain that repressive political processes will mark the death of world civilization.

(4) Progress is capitalized to emphasize the fact that it is a complex idea that is often understood to mean improvement and historical change. In the poem, Jeffers is referring apparently to increasingly complex systems in areas such as food delivery, health care, and communication which make people totally dependent and in fact helpless in the event of systems failure. The irony of his usage is thus that progress is a movement not toward betterment, but toward self-destruction. (5) The concluding assertion (line 31) about death being the end of life is both a recognition and a resigned acceptance. Because the fish are described as caught (line 9), the poem does not offer the possibility of escape for human beings. The speaker is clearly concerned, if not fearful, about the loss of beauty represented by the city and its lights (line 17). (6) The sighing watch of the sea lions in line 12 may be seen as a symbolic lament for the loss of the freedom and natural beauty represented by the fish. The you of the concluding lines is the reader being drawn in to the scene of the poem as a virtual witness, who would need to be insensitive not to sigh at the prospects of destructiveness symbolized in the poem.

Writing topics: the symbolism of the purse-seine. The symbolism of the lighted city and the fish. The cataclysmic views of Jeffers and Yeats compared and contrasted.

T.S. Eliot, Sweeney Among the Nightingales, pages 803-805.

This poem is one of Eliot's early "quatrain poems" published by Virginia and Leonard Woolf. Students often experience difficulty with it because the narrative is obscured and because of the allusiveness. Some of the difficulty can be removed, however, if you point out that Eliot embodies an idea about the complexity of experience: one event does not happen in isolation, but is a part of world and even universal history. Thus the broadness of references is designed to illustrate the integration of life, the reenactment in the present of things that have happened in the past and are happening elsewhere.

Study Questions: (1) Sweeney symbolizes the broad, coarse, unthinking mass person of drives and instincts who is devoid of thought. The animal attributes accentuate these gross features. The epigraph--Agamemnon's outcry--demonstrates the continuity of human brutality from ancient to modern times. (2) The constellations, one of which refers to a mythic hero who was killed (Orion), suggest the galactic scope of brutality. Corvus, the crow, also signifies bad luck or ill omen. All the references, both real and mythical, provide a universal setting for evil and violence. (3) In stanza 2, the moon is associated with lunacy, thus symbolizing madness or depravity. The direction west, where the sun sets, traditionally symbolizes death. The raven symbolizes rapacity and greed. The horned gate is the entrance to the underworld through which true dreams emerge; hence this gate seems here to symbolize the reality of evil.

(4) Rachel in line 23 is animal like because Eliot conceives of her as living on an inhuman level, without morality or the capability for remorse. The selection of the name Sweeney, an obvious allusion to the Irish hero, seems intended as a disparagement of Irish traditions. (5) In lines 33-34, the host and the indistinct person are conversing about something undisclosed, but from the context we may conclude that they are making an agreement about robbing Sweeney and harming or killing him. (6) Nightingales are usually praised and admired because their songs symbolize the beauty of the universe. In lines 39-40, however, Eliot suggests that they turned their backsides and defecated upon the shroud of Agamemnon. This ironic reversal seems to be applicable to both modern life and to ancient. (7) Modern artifacts may not seem obvious as setting in the poem, but Eliot draws attention to a number of things which are uniquely modern. These are a cape imported from Spain, and coffee imported from South America. Oranges, bananas, and figs are all tropical, and the grapes are grown under artificial conditions. The symbolic value of these things is that life has been freed from daylong enslavement to necessity. This freedom should lead to a superior level of civilization, but the poem dramatically asserts that greed and brutality continue as before, as if no improvements in the quality of life have ever happened.

Writing topics: Sweeney as a symbol. Other symbols in the poem. Eliot's use of allusion. The poem as ironic commentary on ancient and modern life.

E.E. Cummings, In Just-, pages 805-806.

This poem is one of the more joyful that Cummings wrote, although students may be perplexed at first about the appearances of the balloonman. Sometimes they may need some prodding to see that the poem is about development and sexual growth, for the subject may superficially seem like a nostalgic memory of childhood. Here the change of the balloonman is important, for he alters from a colorful salesman to a symbolic figure representing spring and ritual fertility.

Study Questions: (1) As symbols, mud-luscious, puddle-wonderful, marbles, and hop-scotch all signify the excitement and joy of childhood. Spring symbolizes growth, and also incipient sexuality. The whistle, at first not more than a realistic sales-call of the balloonman, by the end of the poem symbolizes the urges and needs of sexuality. (2) At first the balloonman suggests the joy and color of childhood discovery. Once Cummings introduces the detail of the goat feet, however, the connection with Pan and natural sexuality is made plain. (3) Beyond the wee, or we, who may be an unidentified first-person plural group (it is, of course, a pun; the word leads the reader to we and wide), the four characters are Betty, Isbel (or Isabel), Eddie, and Bill. Cummings runs their names together to stress their close association and also their common identity as children, but also to symbolize their growth as sexual beings. (4) The concluding wee is not a subject in a predication as are the earlier two instances of wee. As a result, this last wee may be seen as an exclamation about the joy of living. At the same time, however, it also suggests the phrase far and wide, again indicating that these phenomena are universal. (5) The spacing and alignment definitely influence one's reading of the poem. Students may wish to experiment in spoken delivery. Interestingly, many students prefer the poem on the page, as a visual, seen artifact alone, rather than a poem to be read aloud or heard. Writing topics: the use of symbols. The relationship of spring to the topic of sexuality. The effect of the spacing, alignment, and lack of capitalization.

Isabella Gardner, Collage of Echoes, page 807.

In her lifetime, Gardner acted, edited Poetry magazine, taught, published four volumes of poems, and gave frequent poetry readings. This poem is from her final volume, which appeared two years before her death. Study Questions: (1) Granted the allusiveness, the poet clearly assumes that readers have sufficient knowledge to recognize the total context upon which she is drawing. (2) Gardner's many echoes make the lines resonate, for the poem would have little meaning without the lexical strength of the allusions. (3) The phrases in question suggest a sense of weariness, a feeling of having fulfilled obligations and borne many cares. The phrases might be considered as comic because they are usually seen only in the original sources. This collage (an assemblage of cuttings and pastings, often by children in the early grades), puts the echoes in an entirely new and original context. Witty is perhaps a better description of the allusions than comic. Writing topics: the integration of the echoes. The meaning and application of the allusions.

Carol Muske, Real Estate, pages 807-808.

"Real Estate" has a number of personal or private allusions, and for this reason students may find it difficult. Hence the reading must rely upon the suggestiveness and meaning of the references themselves, even though the exact applications may not be clear. It is not important, for example, to learn the identity of the paid escort, or to identify the family's real estate. Rather, what is needed is an understanding of how these things function in the poem. The key allusion is historical: the exhibition of the treasures from Tutankhamen's tomb that went on display in the Metropolitan Museum of Art in 1981. Study Questions: (1) The speaker is apparently a woman uneasy about her future, addressing herself as you in the second person. She is alert and knowledgeable, and thinks of her own need for power and self-determination. She apparently thinks that sex is used by people to attain status or to demonstrate acceptable and normal behavior. Her advice to herself is to gain security through buying land, which in its permanence offers the only security and power that she can have. (2) As a symbol, the teen-age pharaoh refers to the fact that death comes to everyone, powerful and weak alike. The modern set of objects suggests much the same thing: rich things or poor things, they all end up being useless for

167

a dead person, and they thus symbolize the futility of human acquisitions.
(3) The paid escort symbolizes the need of some single females always to
appear accompanied and desirable. The old trombone is a phallic symbol.
These symbols suggest the speaker's disaffection with conventional male-female
role-playing. (4) Lines 25-27 are ambiguous because they may refer either to
the control of land or to the stance of women with regard to men. The idea is
that a woman in an inferior position accepts a man (the river) out of
necessity, while with independence she is worthy of dignity and respect.
These lines must be considered symbolically because the specifics cannot be
exactly known. (5) Frost in "Build Soil" advises the entire nation to develop
its collective natural resources. In contrast, Muske's speaker's advice is
applicable to the role of women today.

Writing topics: Muske's use of symbols. The impact of the allusive
context (the exhibit of the treasures). Criticism of past assumptions about
the economic, social, and sexual roles of women, and suggestions for change.
Allusion as symbolism.

WRITING ABOUT SYMBOLISM AND ALLUSION IN POETRY, pages 809-813.

In teaching this section, you will probably need to stress the possible
developments described on pages 810-811. Questions that your students raise
about these patterns may be sufficient for your discussion. However, you
might additionally need to go over the material in detail. It is always best
to combine a discussion of essay forms with the reading and interpretation of
a specific poem that can be relevant to the forms. If you assign approach 2,
for example, you might wish to use Isabella Gardner's "Collage of Echoes"
(page 807) to illustrate how a poem may be shaped by allusion, or you might
find that Eliot's "Sweeney Among the Nightingales" (pages 803-805) can be
effective in illustration of the first approach, the meaning of symbols. In
your use of the sample essay (pages 811-813), it would be best also to teach
"The Second Coming" as a base from which to show students how they, too, may
apply an interpretaton of symbols and allusions to the task of writing.

CHAPTER 24

MYTH: SYSTEMS OF SYMBOLIC ALLUSION IN POETRY

This chapter has the double aim of giving students a quick introduction to mythology and a longer consideration of the ways in which poets employ myths as symbolic allusions that add layers of meaning and resonance to their poems. The introductory discussion of mythology (pages 814-816) seeks to establish the importance of myth to humanity and to emphasize the essentially symbolic nature of myth. "Mythology and Literature" (pages 816-817) takes up the essential differences between the two, and the ways they can intersect.

A problem that can come up in teaching myth in poetry is that students must recognize the mythic aspects of a poem at the outset of their reading. This process often idealistically assumes a high level of familiarity with a variety of mythic systems, including Buddhist, Hindu, American Indian, Norse, and Chinese myth. Often, the knowledge necessary for recognition isn't there. We have tried to avoid this problem by limiting the mythic systems evoked in the poetry here to the system most familiar and accessible to most students-- Greco-Roman myth. Even with this limitation, you may have to encourage students to do the minimal research necessary to understand the myths evoked. You can remind students that the process of reading and understanding mythic allusion in poetry explored in this chapter will work equally well with any poem that evokes any mythic system.

Besides the poems in this chapter, the text contains many others that lend themselves to an exploration of the impact of myth in poetry. These include Tennyson's "Tithonus" (page 497), Gardner's "At a Summer Hotel" (page 731), Keats's "La Belle Dame sans Merci" (page 797, folk mythology), Yeats's "The Second Coming" (page 800, Christian mythos and private mythology), T. S. Eliot's "Sweeney Among The Nightingales" (page 803), Cummings's "In Just" page 805), Behn's "Love Armed" (page 928), Crawford's "The Song of the Arrow" (page 939, American Indian myth), Plath's "Last Words" (page 984, Egyptian and Babylonian myth), and Silko's "Where Mountain Lion Lay Down with Deer" (page 1004, American Indian myth).

William Butler Yeats, Leda and the Swan, page 819.

The poem is explicated in the text (pages 819-821). For a look at earlier versions of the opening line, see page 539. In class discussion, you can begin with myth and meaning, but meter, rhyme, and form are also worth class time. Yeats employs iambic pentameter with substitute feet to stress important words and ideas (e.g., the spondee on great wings in line 1 that produces three heavy beats in a row). The Italian sonnet form organizes the poem's argument and ideas; rhymes present some elegant and suggestive connections (e.g., thighs-lies, up-drop).

Alfred, Lord Tennyson, Ulysses, pages 821-823.

Tennyson's "Ulysses" and Merwin's "Odysseus" (the same name in Latin and then Greek) allude to the mythic and literary hero of the Trojan War and Homer's Odyssey. Odysseus was the king of Ithaca, husband of Penelope, father of Telemachus. In myth, he is characterized as shrewd, intelligent, crafty, and eloquent. He spent 20 years away from Ithaca and family--10 at Troy and 10 trying to return home. He brought about the destruction of Troy and the end of the war by developing the strategy of the Trojan Horse, a giant hollow

169

figure crammed with armed men which the Trojans dragged into the city.
Odysseus's return home took an additional 10 years because he was opposed by
Poseidon (Neptune), god of the sea. Poseidon's hatred was born when Odysseus
blinded the cyclops Polyphemus, the god's son. Odysseus was driven from one
perilous (and amorous) adventure to another for 10 years before his return
home. These included confrontations with ghosts, sirens, monsters, and gods,
and amorous interludes with Circe and Calypso. When he finally arrived home,
he found his palace full of rapacious suitors seeking Penelope's hand and the
crown. With Telemachus's help, Odysseus destroyed all the suitors and
regained authority in Ithaca.

Tennyson's dramatic monologue (in blank verse) is spoken by Ulysses many
years after his return. In the poem, Ulysses represents a commitment to the
active life and the continual search for knowledge. The poem draws on the
mythic figure's intelligence and symbolic value as an adventurer and wanderer.
In teaching, you can get your students to establish quickly who the speaker
is, what his attitude is toward staying in Ithaca, and what he wants to do.
There may be debate about what Ulysses wants: adventure, knowledge, death,
escape. The key is found in lines 30-31.

The speaker establishes his attitude toward life in Ithaca (lines 1-5)
with phrases like little profit, idle, still hearth, and barren crags that are
images of uselessness, waste, and boredom. He has nothing in common with the
people he rules; they do not know him. At line 6, Ulysses takes up his attitudes toward life; he wants to live it to the fullest. One life is almost not
enough; he notes that it is dull to "pause . . . make an end . . . rust . . .
not to shine" (lines 22-23). His past adventures (lines 7-17) have become
part of his present (line 18) and this pushes him onward to "that untraveled
world whose margin fades / Forever and forever when I move." He contrasts his
need to move (explore, discover) with his son's complacency (lines 33-43).
Telemachus will be a good and happy king; Ulysses has other work (needs,
plans, desires). Ulysses's quest is for knowledge (line 31); his journey
westward (toward sunset, the western stars, Happy Isles, death, the unknown)
will be a new adventure and experience. The speaker admits that he and his
men are old and weak, yet he affirms that they are "strong in will / To
strive, to seek, to find, and not to yield" (lines 69-70). The poem thus
absorbs some of the features of the myth--Ulysses as adventurer--and expands
on them, turning the mythic figure into a symbolic affirmation of the active
and intellectual life that never yields to habit or decay. Writing topics:
good topics for essays can be developed from questions 5 and 6.

Dorothy Parker, Penelope, page 823.

This short lyric, the subject of the chapter's sample essay (pages
836-838), also gains resonance from its evocation of myths in the Iliad and
the Odyssey. Here, however, the focus is on Penelope, Odysseus's wife.

W. S. Merwin, Odysseus, page 824.

This poem draws on the mythic associations of Odysseus as a wanderer and
adventurer to suggest that such a life can become redundant and meaningless.
In teaching the poem, you can ask your students to begin by commenting on the
repetition of same in lines 1-2; this establishes the tone and central idea.
The repetition suggests monotony; the speaker (outside the poem, detached)
suggests that it is "As though he had got nowhere but older" (line 3).
Beginning at line 5, the speaker reviews Odysseus's adventures, blending them

through the use of unspecified allusions and Odysseus's own confusion into a repeated pattern of betrayal and abandonment. The identical reproaches may refer to women that Odysseus has abandoned, including Penelope, Circe, and Calypso. The unravelling patience and the one he kept sailing home to refer to Penelope. The last 6 lines suggest that Odysseus can no longer distinguish these women from one another or keep Penelope fixed in his mind. Odysseus's life becomes almost meaningless; "it was the same whether he stayed / Or went" (lines 11-12). The one who wished him Perils that he could never sail through may be Poseidon or any of the women; it really does not matter since Odysseus can no longer keep these figures straight. The first three poems thus form a triad based on the same mythic material; they demonstrate the ways that poets can evoke the same myth for different purposes. Merwin's Odysseus is much less admirable or positive than Tennyson's Ulysses. Penelope, a central figure in Parker's investigation of our attitudes toward women, fades to an improbable, remote and dim memory here. The possibilities for comparative paper topics are very rich. In addition, questions 1 and 3 can be developed into writing topics.

Margaret Atwood, Siren Song, page 825.

The Sirens were a trio of bird-women who lured sailors to their deaths with song. They appear in Greco-Roman mythology and in the Odyssey, where Odysseus saves his crew by filling their ears with wax; he has himself bound to the mast and listens to their song. The sirens' song was so seductive that sailors inevitably forgot their native land, lost their will to go on, and landed (or wrecked) on the island where they starved to death; the shores were covered with bleached bones.

In mythology, the sirens' song represents the combined seductive power of memory, rest from travel, and sexuality. Atwood focuses on the last of these: the sexually seductive power of the song and the male ego which undermines masculine resistance. The myth is moved into the present. The speaker is a contemporary siren; the colloquial language demythologizes the figure, as does her claim that she is trapped in a bird suit (line 12). In lines 1-9 the speaker defines her song; it is irresistable and unknown (to what extent is it this very poem?). This is the hook that the siren-speaker uses to get you (the reader, men) interested. In lines 10-18 the siren offers what appears to be a reasonable deal; she will reveal the secret/song if you will help her escape. The listener is drawn in deeper. Finally, the speaker appeals to the listener's (male) ego: "I will tell the secret to you, / . . . only to you" and "Help me! / Only you, only you can, / you are unique" (lines 19-24). But of course you are not unique because the song (poem, seduction) works every time. You can explore with your students the extent to which this poem is about men and women. It may suggest that males will always succumb because of their own egos. It also implies that women find the pattern of interaction boring, inevitable, predictable, and repetitious. Writing topics: the speaker or the listener, language, tone, or form. Questions 4 and 5 are also useful.

Olga Broumas, Circe, pages 826-827.

Circe is a sorceress in Greco-Roman mythology who has the power to turn humans into animals. Her most famous encounter is with Odysseus and his crew (Odyssey, Book 10). She turns half of Odysseus's crew into pigs, but Hermes helps Odysseus avoid her spells, and he forces her to change the men back into humans. Odysseus then spends a year with Circe on the island of Aeaes as her

lover. Like the Sirens, Circe's power ultimately symbolizes the power of
sexuality. And as in "Siren Song," Broumas uses the symbolic impact of the
mythic figure to comment on the relation of men and women.

The title identifies the speaker as Circe (or a Circe, it doesn't matter
since the poem suggests that all women can be Circe). The speaker's power
here, as in the myth, is sexual; it can turn "men into swine" (line 25). The
charm and the fire (lines 1-5) represent both Circe's power and her desire to
use the power. The Anticipation (lines 6-15) sets up the social and sexual
context in which Circe's power can work. They are men, society, and the
followers and enforcers of social custom; they court (weave, entrap, tie up)
the speaker (Circe, women) and, in doing so, create the situation (the spell)
that will undo them. The courting hands (limitations, customs, boundaries,
demands) of the men are balanced against Circe's spiderlike waiting and
knowledge that she has the power to change them. The Bite (lines 16-26)
presents anew the transformation myth. The speaker is confident, powerful,
self-satisfied, joyful, and divine. She becomes Circe and turns all men into
swine. The repetition of corner (lines 22-23) stresses the point of turning
or transformation that both the speaker and the men experience. Question 6
embodies the central writing topics. Other topics for discussion and writing
include the form, tone, language, and speaker.

Muriel Rukeyser, Myth, page 827.

For background on this poem, see the introduction to Oedipus The King
(pages 1130-1132) and the text of the play (pages 1132-1171). Briefly,
Oedipus's solving of the Sphinx's riddle--he answered "man"--freed Thebes from
the terror of the Sphinx. In return, he was rewarded with the throne and the
recently widowed queen, Jocasta. Class discussion can focus on the form of
the poem and on Rukeyser's tricky use of the word myth.

Rukeyser, like Atwood and Broumas, employs mythic material to comment on
a contemporary (and perhaps universal) aspect of the relationship/difference
between men and women. At one level, the word myth refers to the story of
Oedipus and the Sphinx. At another, however, it refers to Oedipus's assertion
that "When you say Man . . . you include women / too. Everyone knows that"
(lines 10-11). The Sphinx's response exposes the linguistic and sociological
problem with this myth; it suggests (but doesn't say) that exclusion rather
than inclusion has been the order of language and society for eons.

The "Icarus" Poems, pages 828-829.

In general, the mythic figure of Icarus symbolizes pride, ambition,
arrogance, striving, and daring as well as recklessness, foolishness, and
suffering. The myth presents the outline of a tragedy in microcosm; the
striving toward the sun is heroic, while the fall into the sea is tragic (or
at least pathetic--there is no explicit self-knowledge attained). The various
poets use the figure of Icarus to embody a series of different qualities and
ideas. As with the poems based on Odysseus and Penelope, these illustrate the
way the same mythic figure can be employed to very different ends by writers.

Stephen Spender, Icarus, page 829.

Stephen Spender (1909-1986) was a close friend of W. H. Auden's, and his
reputation as a poet reflects the tendency to compare the men's work. This

poem, published in <u>Poems</u> (1933), evokes both the daring flight and the tragic fall. It is often read as a description of the flight and crash of a World War One aviator; you can try this suggestion with your students and see if it changes their perception of the poem. The Icarus figure in the poem is proud and arrogant; he is described as <u>indifferent</u> to those beneath him (hawk, men, eagles), an <u>aristocrat, superb of all instinct</u>. The first ten lines focus on his flight and pride, his <u>War on the sun</u> (line 10). The last two focus on the fall; the figure is shattered into <u>Hands, wings</u>, an image that stresses the destruction and finality. Spender uses the whole myth (flight and fall) with most of its symbolic overtones intact; the focus remains on Icarus. Other things to consider in class: (1) the shift in verb tense (<u>will, had, are</u>); (2) the speaker (external, detached) and his attitude toward the Icarus figure; (3) the form (uneven iambic couplets) and its impact on meaning.

W. H. Auden, Musee des Beaux Arts, pages 829-830.

Auden's open-form poem uses the figure of Icarus (as presented in Breughel's painting) to explore ideas about suffering and the world's reaction to suffering. In teaching, you can focus on the way Auden moves from a general point to specific instances. In lines 1-13, the speaker asserts that the <u>Old Masters</u> (painters) were right about suffering; the victims always suffer alone while others remain indifferent and life goes on. He cites two unnamed paintings (one of the nativity and the other possibly of the crucifixion) as examples. Each presents a momentous event and (potential) victim surrounded by indifference: the children, dogs, horse. The last eight lines focus on the specific example of Breughel's "Icarus" (the painting is reproduced on page 830; you may need to point out to your students the legs entering the water at the right just below the ship). The myth of Icarus operates in this poem at second hand; Breughel's treatment of the myth (rather than the myth itself) becomes the focus. The painting ignores the heroic aspirations of the mythic figure and deals only with the fall. Auden, in turn, uses Breughel's placement of the figure (the legs) to underscore his point about suffering and indifference. The speaker observes the indifference of the plowman, the sun (nature), and the ship to the boy's fall. Writing topics: the ideas about suffering and the treatment of Icarus. The mythic figure is actually quite insignificant in the poem; Auden thus illustrates his own ideas. The effect only works, however, if the reader brings the whole symbolic impact of Icarus to the poem. We must assume the heroic and tragic stature, so that we can see how it is ignored by the figures in the painting, the painter, the speaker, and the poet.

Anne Sexton, To a Friend Whose Work Has Come to Triumph, page 831.

Sexton's "almost" sonnet (abab cdcd efgf hh, with many slant rhymes) focuses on the daring and heroic triumph of Icarus's flight. Icarus <u>acclaiming the sun</u> is contrasted with his <u>sensible daddy</u> (Daedalus) and with other creatures of earth (<u>trees</u>) and air (<u>starlings</u>). The fall, mentioned in line 12, is dismissed; it is secondary to the image and the fact of the flight. The tone--familiar, admiring, a bit condescending--undercuts the heroic presentation; it is established through diction and understatement. Note especially <u>sticky</u> (line 1), <u>little tug</u> (2), <u>quite well</u> (7), and <u>sensible daddy</u> (14). Writing topics: the figure of Icarus or Icarus contrasted to Daedalus. Diction and tone. Sexton's use of mythic material.

William Carlos Williams, Landscape with the Fall of Icarus, pages 831-832.

Like Auden's, Williams's treatment of the Icarus myth is once removed, filtered through the pictorial medium of Breughel's painting. Unlike Auden, however, Williams does not explore a separate issue such as human suffering; rather, he's interested in recreating the painting in verbal images. As in "Musee," the mythical Icarus is secondary but essential to this poem. We must bring all the mythic associations to the painting and the poem to appreciate the effect of displacing the figure from center stage to the lower right-hand corner. Williams recreates this effect in the poem by relegating Icarus to the opening (line 2) and the close (lines 14-20). The center of the poem, like the painting, focuses on the landscape rather than the fall. The speaker "pans" the painting from left to right, noting the farmer, the regeneration of nature, the edge of the sea and the sun before returning to the splash quite unnoticed of Icarus drowning. In lines 16-21, Williams focuses on Icarus drowning, only to note how unsignificant the event was to the world at large in the painting. Icarus's fall frames the poem, but most of the poem turns away from the event and the figure. Writing topics: the importance of the Icarus myth to the poem. The degree to which the poem recreates the effects of the painting. The ways that form contributes to this recreation.

Edward Field, Icarus, page 832.

In contrast to Auden and Williams, Field directs his attention squarely to the mythic figure of Icarus. Even here, however, there is a displacement; the heroic and tragic values in the myth make ironic the central figure's descent into the mundane and the quotidian world of suburban commuters. Like Atwood and Broumas, Field transports the mythic figure into the modern world and employs colloquial language to demythologize the myth. The poem explores the idea that the mythic, heroic, and tragic can be reduced to the ordinary, common, and pathetic in the modern world. Housman's "To An Athlete Dying Young" is an ideal poem for comparison, because Field illustrates what can happen to the hero/athlete/myth who goes on living too long past the moment of glory/tragedy. In the first stanza, the speaker reviews the disaster, reduces it to the usual drowning, and rewrites the end of the myth: Icarus had swum away and come to the city, where he rented a house and tended a garden (line 9). The remaining stanzas explore Icarus's feelings and his place (or lack of place) in this mundane existence. The mythic figure in the suburban world of neat front yards and commuter trains embodies alienation and despair. Writing topics: the way the mythic figure is used and undercut in the poem. The image of the modern suburban world. As an alienated figure who wishes he had drowned, Field's Icarus seems to illustrate that the modern world can accommodate neither heroic aspiration nor tragic fall.

WRITING ABOUT MYTH IN POETRY, pages 833-838.

The key point to emphasize to your students here is that myth must be explored and written about in connection with some other aspect of the poem, such as speaker, tone, or meaning. Your students will be tempted to write a merely descriptive essay, noting and explaining in series the mythic allusions in a poem. When you assign an essay about myth in poetry, warn them to avoid such an exercise in description. The sample essay on Parker's "Penelope" (pages 836-838) illustrates one way to write about mythic material in connection with character and meaning.

CHAPTER 25

THEME: THE IDEAS AND THE MEANING IN POETRY

This chapter takes up in detail a topic that runs throughout all the poetry chapters--the theme or meaning of a poem (the topic is also addressed in Chapter 10 in connection with fiction). In the introductory material, we make a distinction among three related terms defined in the text: subject, theme, and meaning. As you begin teaching, you may want to underscore these distinctions. In actual classroom practice, however, you will find that theme and meaning merge to indicate the same type of information. This is normal and reasonable; it is often difficult to filter out the emotional impact and the moment of experience from the ideas. Once you make the initial distinction, you can allow the concepts to flow back together. The section "Must a poem have a theme?" is important because students often assume that a poem must have a message, and if they cannot find one, they will invent one. If you push too hard in the other direction, however, students will give up on poems too easily. The ideal strategy is to steer a middle course between too much and too little emphasis on theme. The discussion of strategies for dealing with theme is also worth class time, since it pulls together all the ways of looking at poetry that we present in the text. The key idea to communicate in teaching is that every aspect (element) of a poem can contribute to its theme and meaning. In any given poem, however, not all the elements will be equally important or effective. One of your goals in teaching poetry (and this chapter) might be to develop your students' ability to focus quickly on the poetic elememts that do the most work in creating meaning.

Archibald MacLeish, Ars Poetica, pages 844-845.

The poem and explication (pages 845-848) tackle the question of meaning versus being raised earlier in the chapter (pages 840-841). Our reading of "Ars Poetica" asserts that poems and poets can have it both ways--that a poem can mean and be at the same time. This poem is part of a larger set concerned with poetry, including Shakespeare's "Sonnet 55" (page 486) and "18" (page 602), Spenser's "One Day I Wrote Her Name upon the Strand" (page 851), Moore's "Poetry" (page 852), and Housman's "Terence, This Is Stupid Stuff" (page 958).

Ben Jonson, To Celia, page 848.

This is the first of a set of three carpe diem poems in the chapter. In teaching this, you can show your students that meaning is a function of ideas, speaker, tone, and diction. The speaker is eager, cynical, and greedy; he wants to possess a woman who is not willing or available. He sees time as an enemy, love as a commodity, and Celia as an attractive object to be used. The first eight lines contain the traditional carpe diem argument; time is personified as an enemy who will sever lives. The speaker asserts that he and Celia should act while they still have time before perpetual night (death).

The speaker shifts his ground at line 9; he is no longer concerned with time, but rather with reputation and the ease with which he and Celia may get away with their theft. The speaker's cynicism comes through clearly here. He argues that reputation is unimportant (but toys) and that Celia's husband can easily be deceived. The central idea here also emphasizes the speaker's cynical amorality; he asserts that an act becomes a crime only if one is caught at it (lines 15-18). The diction also emphasizes the speaker's

175

demeaning and cynical tone; phrases like sports of love and sweet theft
trivialize love (sex) and demean Celia. The argument is thus undercut by the
cynical tone and amoral attitude. The theme of the poem is that one must act
now to get what one wants, and that any act is permissible so long as one
doesn't get caught. The total meaning combines these ideas with our emotional
and intellectual revulsion at the thoughts and the speaker. All the questions
(except 2) can be adapted to good writing topics. You might also look to
rhyme or form as topics for discussion and writing; the iambic tetrameter
rhymed couplets create discrete units of thought and a number of effective
rhymes that clinch ideas.

Andrew Marvell, To His Coy Mistress, pages 849-850.

This is one of the most famous carpe diem poems of persuasion ever
written. Your students may know it, but it will always yield new surprises in
class discussion. In teaching, you might focus on the connotations of coy,
and then consider the pseudo-logic of the poem, the hyperbole of the first
section, and the shifting imagery throughout. The poem is in iambic
tetrameter rhymed couplets, and it contains some very effective rhyming pairs
(e.g., dust-lust). The title identifies the characters; the speaker, a
would-be lover, addresses his coy (reluctant, playing hard-to-get) lady. Coy
is a loaded word here; it certainly does not suggest virtuous.
In lines 1-20, the speaker sets up a hypothetical situation (Had we) in
which there is vast space and time. References to the Ganges and Humber
rivers place the lovers on opposite sides of the earth (use a map or get your
students to imagine one). The allusions to Noah's flood and the conversion of
the Jews evoke a huge span of time (from Genesis to the Last Judgment). The
amatory arithmetic associated with the speaker's admiration of each part of
his mistress is delightfully exaggerated--an ideal example of hyperbole.
The hypothetical world enough and time are negated in lines 21-32; the
word But identifies and begins the refutation. Time is personified as an
ever-pursuing enemy (line 22). The lines are full of images of death and the
grave, all suggesting sterility, dryness, dust, and isolation (quaint honor in
line 29 is probably a bawdy pun). The third stage of the argument (lines 33-
46) offers the speaker's pseudo-logical conclusion: Now therefore we should
act with urgency and immediacy to "tear our pleasures with rough strife /
Thorough the iron gates of life." The imagery here suggests moist heat (dew,
fires) and violence, all pointing toward a sense of urgency. The image of
amorous birds of prey is both playful (in tone) and daring. By looking at
diction and tone in class, students can see the differences between this poem
and Jonson's "To Celia" (page 848). The speaker here is much more playful;
the lady is much less virtuous or determined. The tone is more humorous,
exaggerated, and joyful, less cynical and demeaning. Question 6 suggests a
number of possible writing topics; others include an analysis of meaning
through logic, speaker, imagery, or diction.

Robert Herrick, To the Virgins, to Make Much of Time, pages 850-851.

Herrick's lyric, the third carpe diem poem in the set, is the most moral
and least personal; the title indicates that it is addressed to a group rather
than an individual. In class discussion, you can focus on the public tone,
the symbolism of the rosebud and sun, and the implications of the speaker's
demand that the virgins go marry (the speaker doesn't want anything for
himself here). In stanza 1, the rosebuds symbolize life--here today and gone

tomorrow. The sun (stanza 2) serves a parallel function; one day becomes a lifetime. The carpe diem theme is stated explicitly in stanzas 3 and 4. The tone here is public, advisory, paternal, and hortatory; the speaker is concerned and moralistic. His advice that the virgins should marry emphasizes the distinctions between this poem and the two previous ones. Writing topics for all three carpe diem poems include analyses of speaker, tone, or theme. Comparison-contrast assignments might also be effective in dealing with these poems. Marvell's poem also lends itself well to an analysis of imagery, and Herrick's to an analysis of rhyme.

Edmund Spenser, One Day I Wrote Her Name upon the Strand, page 851.

This poem can be taught as part of the "poetry" group; it shares with Shakespeare's Sonnet 55 (page 486) the theme that poetry can be immortal and produce immortality for its subjects. Spenser employs a modified English sonnet form (Spenserian sonnet; iambic pentameter: abab bcbc cdcd ee) to organize the action and ideas. In teaching, a quatrain by quatrain approach can be effective; each one presents a distinct step in the poet's development of the idea, yet each is linked to the next through rhyme. In lines 1-4, the speaker explains that he and his mistress were on the beach; he wrote her name in the sand twice and each time the waves washed it away. In lines 5-8 the lady draws the obvious moral from these events; she sees the speaker's efforts to immortalize her as vain (arrogant, proud) and in vain (useless). She asserts that she will die and her name (person, memory) will be wiped out just as the writing is washed away. Lines 9-12 resolve the issue; the speaker says that the lady will live on forever in his verse. The couplet asserts that their "love shall live" beyond the end of the world. The theme here is that poetry can immortalize emotions and relationships. Writing topics: the ideas of the speaker or the lady. Setting, situation, and meaning.

Marianne Moore, Poetry, pages 852-853.

The title announces the subject; the poem can be considered with the "poetry" group. It argues that there is a place and a purpose for genuine poetry that deals with real experience in imaginative ways. The poem begins by dismissing poetry--a preemptive stance that is reversed by the however in line 2. The speaker claims to dislike . . . all this fiddle and assumes that the reader does too. The diction and stance here suggest that the tone initially is tongue-in-cheek. In lines 5-8, the speaker claims that poetry can be useful because of the emotional responses it can evoke. Here, Moore considers a series of things (animal and human) that we cannot understand and therefore do not admire: critic, baseball fan, statistician. All these things are important, but must be distinguished from genuine poetry. The remainder of the poem asserts that we will have it (genuine poetry) only if poets become literalists of the imagination and convey real emotion and experience through imaginative writing. The last five lines suggest that poetry is valuable and interesting if it embodies genuine and raw aspects of life. Like "Ars Poetica" (page 844), Moore's poem defines poetry by demonstration as well as explanation. It is full of the raw materials of life and poetry organized to create an emotional and intellectual response. In some ways, however, the poem may be too full to create a coherent experience; Moore's eventual cutting suggests such a decision on her part. Writing topics: the poem's ideas about poetry. An analysis of the speaker. A more ambitious assignment might ask the students to compare this poem to "Ars Poetica" in terms of theme.

William Wordsworth, Ode: Intimations of Immortality, pages 853-858.

The ode laments the loss of visionary power and celebrates the compensations of memory, sympathy, and philosophy. It is a difficult but useful poem for students because it demonstrates a poet's extended exploration of a few key ideas; it looks at the related problems of growing old and fading poetic vision. The ode is structured in two large movements; the first four stanzas present a problem, and the last seven provide two separate answers.
In stanzas 1-4, the speaker realizes that the <u>glory</u> that had transfigured all that he saw in his youth has faded away. There is a strong contrast here between the visionary past ("There was a time") and the mundane present ("It is not now as it hath been of yore"). Stanza 2 reveals that nature is fixed; it is the speaker's perception of nature that has changed. The nature imagery here defines the speaker's loss. In stanzas 3 and 4, the speaker attempts to return to his earlier visionary state (innocence, sense of wonder) and rejoice in nature; his demands for <u>shouts</u> and the clusters of sensual images suggest that the attempt is forced. At the close of stanza 4, the speaker realizes that his attempt has failed and that things (<u>tree</u>, <u>field</u>, <u>pansy</u>) still look different. He asks the poem's central question: "Whither is fled the visionary gleam? / Where is it now, the glory and the dream?" (lines 57-58).
The second movement (stanzas 5-11) provides two answers to this question. The first (stanzas 5-8) is based on the Platonic theory of preexistence; it explains the lost <u>visionary gleam</u> by describing its genesis. The soul pre-exists with God (stanza 5) and is born into the body <u>trailing clouds of glory</u>. As the individual grows older, however, the transfiguring light fades away and is replaced by the light of <u>common day</u> (stanza 6). Stanzas 7 and 8 focus on a single child as an example of this process; the six-year-old can still read <u>the eternal deep</u> (line 114), but he strives to imitate adults and to mature. The speaker asks (stanza 8) why the child seeks to grow up and accept the <u>inevitable yoke</u> of maturity. This explanation offers no hope for the speaker; there is no way to return to childhood. In stanzas 9-11, however, Wordsworth offers a second answer; the speaker claims that we can use the memory of this visionary power to compensate for the loss. The power is gone, but it is replaced by memory and a calmer and more philosophical contemplation of human suffering and sympathy. The ode is finally about the inevitability of growth and change, and the inheritance that the child leaves the adult. The child's visionary and transfiguring gleam may be nothing more than innocence or a sense of wonder. This power is lost to the adult, but it is replaced by memory, sympathy, and wisdom. Writing topics: meaning and its connection with speaker, statements, rhyme, form, or imagery. Wordsworth's use of nature imagery to illustrate the adult's loss of vision can be an especially fruitful area for writing.

John Keats, Ode on a Grecian Urn, pages 859-860.

This poem is about art, beauty, and truth; the imaginary urn is a work of art that evokes a response in the speaker's mind just as the poem evokes a response in us. The response, for the speaker, is the realization that truth and beauty are identical in an ideal and eternal state. The ode explores this idea by repeatedly contrasting the real world (change, decay, death) against an ideal world that is eternal and unchanging. These worlds are paradoxically and oxymoronically fused in the poem and the urn.
The ode suggests a dramatic situation; the speaker is contemplating the urn and the reader overhears the resulting meditation. The paradoxical nature of the urn is established immediately through phrases like <u>unravished bride</u>

and foster child of silence and slow time; the urn exists in real time but is little touched by it. Paradox continues in the description of the figures on the urn (gods or men, eternal or mortal) and in the contrast between the energy (passion) figured on the urn and the calm silence of the urn itself. The urn is a sylvan historian that can sing a better song than the poet (our rhyme). The reason why the urn's tale is sweeter is explained in stanza 2. Unheard melodies and "ditties of no tone" are heard in the mind (imagination) rather than through the sensual ear. In other words, the idea (Platonic ideal) of the song (poetry, art, beauty) is better than the reality. Three key sets of images are developed in stanzas 1-3 to illustrate this concept of the ideal: nature (leaf-fringed boarder, tree that will never lose its leaves), love (the pursuit, lovers who will never kiss), and music (pipes and timbrels, the youth who will never leave his song). All these images are frozen in time (on the urn), unchanging and eternal. These are contrasted (in stanza 3) to human passion that leaves us sick and sorrowful.

In the fourth stanza, the speaker sees a group of people leading a heifer to sacrifice. In lines 35-40 he wonders about the town this group has left, but the town is not on the urn; it only exists in the speaker's mind. It too is eternal and unchanging, but there is a new note of sadness and desolation here. To this point, Keats has developed a series of contradictory paradoxes that oppose real and ideal; these reach a climax in stanza 5. The urn is a silent form and a Cold Pastoral (both contradictory). It is also a "friend to man" because it tells us that "Beauty is truth, truth beauty" (line 49). Keats sustains the oxymora of the urn and the poem throughout; the poem makes us experience both the warmth and energy of passion figured on the urn and the cold stillness of the urn itself. The poem and the urn ask us to balance in our minds both the real (time, change) and the ideal (permanence, eternity) simultaneously. The urn and the poem, like eternity, tease us with an image of the ideal state that combines timeless permanence with the pleasures of life. It is in this state that truth and beauty are identical. This poem is quite difficult, and writing assignments should thus be as focused as possible. Students might be asked to write about meaning in connection with the speaker or symbolism (of the urn). Question 7 (page 860) is a good (though difficult) writing topic because it addresses theme and total meaning.

Philip Larkin, Next, Please, pages 860-861.

This poem, discussed at some length in the sample essay (pages 868-870) can be taught with the carpe diem group at the beginning of the chapter. Questions 3, 4, and 5 can be adapted into good writing topics.

Donald Justice, On the Death of Friends in Childhood, pages 861-862.

While the subject of this poem may be friends who died in childhood, the theme explores the degree to which we can recapture the past through memory. Time stops for the dead children; they will not grow beards or become bald. For the speaker and reader, however, time produces change; we no longer remember the names of the games we played. In the last line, the speaker points to (and personifies) memory as a way to recapture our dead friends and youth. Questions 2 and 3 (page 862) can be adapted to writing topics. Another topic for consideration: the way images of age and youth are contrasted to create meaning. The fourth question is worth class discussion; the instant of experience/understanding that the poem offers may depend on the reader's being a good distance from childhood.

179

Linda Pastan, Ethics, page 862.

The poem considers an ethical question from two perspectives (and in two settings), and finally asserts that nothing endures. In class discussion, you can focus on the two distinct situations (school, museum), and the shift of time and place at line 17. The speaker's response to the ethical question clearly changes, and the poem thus explores the shallowness of youth and the mature awareness that neither art nor life endures. In lines 1-16, the speaker recalls the ethics classes of her youth and the recurring question about the burning museum. The problem was irrelevant to the young people; they were caring little and chose one answer or the other half-heartedly. Even when the speaker attempted to personalized the issue by imagining that the old woman was her grandmother (lines 9-16), the matter was of little consequence. In the present (lines 17-25), the choice remains irrelevant because the speaker has come to realize that life, art, and time are almost one in that all are beyond saving by children (line 25). The poem does not advocate immediate action (carpe diem); nor does it champion the immortality of art. Instead, it suggests that there are no real choices in life and that nothing lasts. Writing topics: the meaning as conveyed through speaker, setting and situation, imagery, or diction. If you have taught carpe diem poems in class, you might ask your students to discuss the reasons why this is not such a poem (there is no urging of present action).

Sharon Olds, 35/10, page 863.

Olds employs a domestic context to explore the idea that life is cyclical and that humans replace themselves through children. The first sixteen lines make these points metaphorically through imagery and language; the last two lines state (overstate?) them directly. The total meaning grows out of the situation and setting, action and language, and the emotions evoked in us. The speaker, a 35-year-old mother, is brushing her 10-year-old daughter's hair at bedtime. The idea of youth's displacing and replacing age is conveyed in three sets of images related to hair (dark, gray), skin (fine, dry), and sexuality (images of ovaries as empty or bursting purses). Questions 2, 3, and 4 (page 864) will work well as writing topics, although the last can be difficult. As with Pastan's "Ethics" (page 862), emotional engagement with this poem may depend on the reader's ability to experience (or imagine) age.

WRITING ABOUT THEME AND MEANING IN POETRY, pages 864-871.

The discussion about prewriting and organization here is longer than usual because theme and meaning can be approached from so many different directions. These are all reviewed, and the movement from notes to a tentative central idea and first paragraph is carefully illustrated. If you assign an essay on theme, you can emphasize in class that the students should use the approaches (elements, topics) that are most significant and striking in the poem. It is often necessary to warn students that they cannot consider every element that contributes to meaning in a single essay. The sample essay on Larkin's "Next, Please" (pages 868-870) illustrates the way meaning can be explored through a single poetic divice. Your students can be encouraged to read this and the commentary (pages 870-871) before they begin to plan and write their own essays.

CHAPTER 26

POETIC CAREERS: THE WORK OF THREE POETS

JOHN DONNE, pages 872-875.

The Good Morrow, page 875.

1. What can you deduce about the speaker? Listener? Setting and situation?
2. What powers are attributed to love in the second and third stanzas?
3. How do the images of worlds (globes, spheres) emphasize the power of love?
4. What ideas about love and passion does the poem explore?

    The speaker (a lover) praises his beloved and their passion by comparing them favorably to all his previous romances; he sees their previous lives as sleep or infancy. The good morrow refers to the awakening of their love and the actual events--two lovers awakening in bed. The second stanza takes up the power of love--it controls emotion and perception--and begins an extended conceit on the image of worlds. The speaker creates a clear distinction between the public world (sea-discoverers, new worlds, maps), and the private world of the lovers that becomes an everywhere (see the sample essay, pages 914-918, for a discussion of this imagery). The one world of the lovers becomes two (line 14) and then the two hemispheres of eye-balls reflecting faces (lines 15-16), finally resolving back into a single world Without sharp North, without declining West (line 18). The tone is exaggerated and affirmative; love and passion are presented as valuable and powerful.

Song: Go and Catch a Falling Star, page 876.

1. What closed form is employed? What building blocks combine to form each stanza? How do rhyme and meter affect meaning and impact?
2. What does the speaker want the listener to do? What do all the actions in stanza 1 have in common?
3. What idea about women does this poem explore? What is the speaker's tone? How does tone contribute to meaning?

    The theme here is that no woman can be fair (beautiful) and true (loyal, honest) at the same time. The speaker lists a series of impossible tasks in stanza 1 to establish an aura of cynicism and difficulty; some of these (envy, the lack of advancement for honest minds) evoke social ills. The second stanza introduces the impossibility of the woman who is both true and fair. The third reinforces this cynical view by claiming that such a woman would become false before the speaker could meet her. The lyric is composed of 3 stanzas, each of which combines a quatrain, couplet, and triplet into a single sentence (iambic: 4a4b4a4b4c4c1d1d4d); the pattern of stanza 1 is repeated in 2 and 3. Rhyme (e.g., singing-stinging) and the short seventh and eighth lines of each stanza are especially effective in clinching meaning.

The Sun Rising, pages 876-877.

1. What can you deduce about the speaker? His companion? The setting and situation? To whom is the poem addressed?
2. What does the speaker tell the sun to do in stanza 1? What distinction is created between worlds? What is the connection of time to love?
3. What conceit is develped in stanzas 2 and 3?
4. What does the poem suggest about the power of love?

This lyric (abbacdcdee) is very similar to "The Good Morrow"; it asserts that love is all-powerful and consuming. The speaker and his beloved (in bed) have been awakened by the sun (busy old fool). The speaker tells the sun to go deal with the public world (school boys, prentices, huntsmen, farmers) since love creates a private world that is detached from time. The conceit of spatial manipulation developed in stanzas 2 and 3 (see the sample essay, pages 914-918) again suggests that love can control space, making the lovers and their bed an entire world. Donne pulls more and more of the cosmos into bed with the lovers: the Indies, all states, all princes, and the solar system.

The Canonization, pages 877-878.

1. What does canonization mean? Who is canonized in the poem? Why?
2. How does the speaker defend his love in the first two stanzas?
3. What mythic and religious mysteries are linked with love/sex in stanza 3?
4. What canonizes and immortalizes the lovers? What will future lovers ask of these saints of love? What does the poem finally imply about love?

This lyric is a defense of love and passion in which both are linked with mysteries of myth and religion. The poem explores the idea that love can transform lovers into saints who will become exemplars for future lovers. In stanzas 1-2, the speaker defends his love against the objections of an unnamed critic; he sends the critic out into the public world, claiming that his love has not injured anyone or anything. In stanza 3, Donne employs symbols (eagle and dove), allusion (the phoenix) and sexual puns (die = to achieve orgasm) to emphasize the mysterious powers of love. The reference to the phoenix and the phrase die and rise point toward both resurrection and the reawakening of sexual desire after orgasm. In the fourth stanza, the speaker claims that his and his lady's love will be chronicled in verse (this very poem) and the lovers will thus be canonized and immortalized. Future lovers (quoted in lines 37-45) will pray to these saints for a pattern of love. The poem thus explores both the power of love and the immortality of verse. "The Relic" (page 881) similarly joins love and religion.

A Fever, page 879.

1. To whom is the poem addressed? What is the relationship between speaker and listener? What's wrong with the listener?
2. What does the speaker claim that his lover's death would do to the world?
3. What is the tone of the poem? What point does the speaker finally make about his love? Does the tone emphasize or undercut this point?

The lyric (abab, cdcd, etc.) is addressed by a lover to his mistress who is sick with a fever. Donne uses outrageous overstatement in equating the fever with the fire that will end the world to show the power and passion of the speaker's love; the poem is an exercise in wit. Stanza 1 introduces the paradox of hating all women if the mistress dies. Stanzas 2-4 develop the idea of the lady's fever as the fire that will destroy the world. Stanzas 5 and 6 are based on the idea that fevers are fueled by impurities; since the lady is made of unchangeable firmament, the fever cannot last long. The situation would suggest a sorrowful and urgent tone, but the overstatement makes the poem ingenious and a bit amusing.

The Flea, pages 879-880.

1. Consider the poem as a play. Who are the characters? What action occurs?
2. What does the speaker want? How does he use the flea's bite and the flea metaphorically? What does the lady do to the flea before stanza 3? How does the speaker adjust his argument to reflect this event?
3. What is the poem's tone? How does form echo meaning? To what extent does rhyme unify the poem?

"The Flea" is a witty and ingenious song of seduction in which a young man (the speaker) attempts to convince a young lady (the listener) to make love. The poem is highly dramatic, the tone is tongue-in-cheek, and the argument is logical and bizarre. Before the first stanza, the flea bit the speaker and then jumped to the lady. The speaker claims that this mingling of blood (a metaphor here for sexual intercourse) is not a sin or loss. The flea enjoys before marriage (woo), but the lady denies such joy to herself and the speaker. The phrase pampered swells (line 8) is an oblique reference to pregnancy. Before the second stanza, the lady threatens to swat the flea. Now the speaker's logic and imagery become more bizarre. He claims that the flea has become three individuals (the lover, the lady, the flea), and he expands the image (flea) until the lovers are cloistered within the flea's black sides even though the lady and her parents reject (grudge) premarital sex. Between stanzas 2 and 3 the lady kills the flea. The speaker readjusts his argument and equates the flea's death with sex, claiming that giving in to his demands will be just as painless and insignificant as the flea's death. The tone is witty and ingenious; we sense no urgency or sincerity in this display of wit.

The Bait, pages 880-881.

1. How is this poem related to Marlowe's "The Passionate Shepherd" (page 484)?
2. What does the speaker invite his beloved to do? What effect will she have on the river? The fish? The sun?
3. How is the title relevant? What metaphorically becomes the bait? The fish? How do these odd comparisons work as praise for the lady?

This complex and sophisticated parody of Marlowe's "Passionate Shepherd" demonstrates Donne's ability to use bizarre imagery and situations to praise a lady's beauty. The alliteration and onomatopoeia throughout make the poem very sensuous. The speaker invites the lady to go fishing; she will warm the river and attract the enamored fish (the lady = bait; the fish = lovers). The lady's beauty will eclipse the sun and moon and thus conceal her nakedness from all but the lover. The last three stanzas make Donne's characteristic distinction between the public world (others) and the private world of the lovers. Have your students compare this poem to Raleigh's "Nymph's Reply" (page 486) and Lewis's "Song" (page 499).

The Relic, pages 881-882.

1. What future event does the speaker imagine in stanza 1? What is the significance of the bracelet of bright hair? What is the relic? What does the speaker imagine will happen to his and his mistress's bones?
2. What miracles did the lovers perform? What is the greatest miracle?
3. How does the poem link love and religion?

Like "The Canonization," this lyric links love with religion as miraculous, powerful, and mysterious. The relic is both the bracelet and the exhumed bones. In stanza 1, the speaker envisions future disinterrment and hopes that the grave digger will recognize the significance of the bracelet, letting the bones rest so that the lover and his mistress can meet on Judgment

Day. If the bones are removed, however, they will become saints' relics--the lady a <u>Mary</u> <u>Magdalen</u> and the speaker a <u>something</u> <u>else</u>. In that event, this paper (i.e., this poem) will reveal the miraculous power of love and the relics. Stanza 3 lists the miracles that the lovers wrought in their lives; their love was spiritual and transcended sexuality. The greatest miracle of all was the lady. The poem thus combines three themes: praise of one's mistress, the immortality of verse, and the power of love.

Holy Sonnet 6: This Is My Play's Last Scene, page 882.

1. List the metaphors for life and death that occur in the first 6 lines.
2. What distinction is made between the body and the soul?
3. What is the subject of this meditation? What does the speaker want?
     This sonnet (abba abba cdcd ee) is a meditation on death and salvation. The first two quatrains focus intensely on the moment of death, which is evoked by seven metaphors that imply the end of something. The body will become earth, but the soul will see God's face. The last six lines focus on salvation and the purging of sin. The form of the sonnet organizes the meditation and the ideas; the rhymes (e.g., <u>evil-devil</u>) emphasize the meaning.

Holy Sonnet 7: At The Round Earth's Imagined Corners, page 883.

1. How does the sonnet form organize the poem's movement and meaning?
2. What moment is imagined in lines 1-8? What is listed in the 2nd quatrain?
3. What does the speaker reveal about his own spiritual state in lines 9-14?
     Like most of Donne's Holy Sonnets, this one begins as a meditation on a specific moment--the apocalypse and Judgment Day. Lines 1-8 (abba abba) create a vivid and immediate image of bodies rising from their graves for judgment; lines 5-8 contain a catalogue of those who will rise from the dead or move directly to judgment from life. In lines 9-14 (cdcd ee), the speaker reflects on his own spiritual corruption; he prays for more time to repent his sins and to seek God's grace.

Good Friday, 1613. Riding Westward, pages 883-884.

1. What is the significance of <u>Good</u> <u>Friday</u>? Of <u>Westward</u>? What conceit is developed in lines 1-8? How does the speaker explain his movement <u>westward</u>?
2. What event does the speaker meditate on in lines 16-32? What specific images and references make this moment extremely vivid?
3. To what conclusions and requests does the meditation lead the speaker?
     The title is one way into the poem. On Good Friday (the crucifixion), the speaker is riding westward (toward death, sunset, away from the east, Jerusalem, sunrise, son-rise). The speaker explains this contrary movement in lines 1-8, where he metaphorically becomes a planet pulled out of its natural orbit (eastward) by the influence of <u>other</u> <u>spheres</u> and <u>foreign</u> <u>motions</u> (<u>Pleasure or business</u>). Lines 8-15 explain the paradox of this motion and of the crucifixion; The speaker is headed west when he wants to go east, toward the crucifixion and salvation. Christ (the sun-son) set (died) by rising on the cross and thus begot eternal life. The heart of the poem (lines 16-32) is a meditation on the crucifixion, made vivid by an accumulation of details. The meditation leads the speaker to consider his own spiritual failings; he asks God to provide correction and mercy. The image of God here is similar to the one in "Batter My Heart" (page 556), which also plays on the sun-son pun.

A Hymn to God the Father, pages 884-885.

1. To whom is the poem spoken? What does the speaker think about his own spiritual state? What are his sins? What does he want?
2. What puns do you find? How do they affect tone and meaning?

This poem, a prayer spoken to God the Father, is a confession of sins in which the speaker catalogues his own corruption and seeks divine grace. An important pun is the traditional one on sun-son (Thy sun = Son = Christ = redemption). The speaker's sins are listed in lines 1-14; the request for grace is voiced in lines 15-18. The central pun is on the word done (Donne). In stanzas 1-2, God's work is not done and God has not redeemed Donne ("Thou hast not done") because the speaker has more (sins). Some scholars suggest that more is also a pun on the name of Donne's wife (Anne More).

Hymn to God My God, in My Sickness, pages 885-886.

1. What is the speaker's condition? What does he want? Who is the listener?
2. What does the speaker metaphorically become in stanza 2? In what ways is the idea of a strait used in the poem?
3. How is the image of a flat map manipulated in stanzas 3-5 to make a point about geography, death, and salvation?

Here, the speaker meditates on his own death and salvation in a series of metaphysical conceits. In the 1st stanza, death is equated with joining God's choir and repentance with tuning the instrument (soul). The 2nd stanza begins the dominant conceit--a geographical or cartographic metaphor in which the speaker becomes a map and his fever a strait; the straits mentioned in the poem thus represent both the passage to death through fever and the road to salvation along the "straight and narrow." The map metaphor continues in stanzas 3-4, where the flat map becomes a globe to illustrate the confluence of west and east, sunset and sunrise, death and everlasting life. Stanza 4 offers a list of straits (straights) that lead to the Pacific (peace) and to salvation (the eastern riches). Donne uses the convergence of east and west to combine Eden and Adam with Calvary and Christ within the speaker, asking God to grant salvation to this Adam through Christ's blood.

EMILY DICKINSON, pages 886-889.

The Gentian Weaves Her Fringes, page 889.

1. Describe the structure of this poem. Lines 1-4 discuss the approach of fall with changes in flowers and leaves, and also the speaker's sense of her own departing blossoms. Lines 5-8 are logically linked to 1-4 because they describe illness and death. Lines 9-12 describe a short funeral procession of bird, bee, and bobolink, with a funeral address being given by the bee. Then there is a perplexing passage from 13-16 which may be the prayer mentioned in line 12. Here, the speaker expresses trust and the hope to go with the departed Summer, which is also a sister and a seraph. The concluding 3 lines are the invocative coda traditional in prayer, only here the Father, Son, and Holy Ghost are replaced by the Bee, the Butterfly, and the Breeze.

2. Explain the purpose of the spaces dividing the poem into 3 apparent stanzas. The first space separates the introductory section explaining the advent of autumn from the middle 12 lines describing the death in the house, the natural procession, and the prayer. The second space separates this middle section from the conclusion. It therefore points up the surprising,

daring invocation of the speaker's natural trinity.

3. How does the speaker connect herself in lines 1–4 with the flower and the tree? The connection is made between the changing <u>gentian</u>, the color of the maple changing from green to red, and the speaker's sense of losing the <u>blossoms</u> of youth. The speaker is unlike the flora, however, because there is no <u>parade</u> comparable in humans to the lovely fringes of the gentian or the blanket of leaves left on the ground by the maples. The human being is thus less showy than the flower and the tree, and also, perhaps, less important.

4. In what ways is this poem audacious and the tone irreverent? The mid section, describing the funeral procession, the song of the Bobolink and the address of the Bee, together with the concluding parody of the trinity, might be considered audacious and irreverent. If we understand, however, that the words of rituals sometimes become barriers rather than avenues to thought, then the <u>miracle</u> of the trinity can also be extended to the fusion of God with all living things both vegetab<u>le</u> and animal. Hence terms like <u>playful</u> and <u>challenging</u> would be more appropriate than <u>irreverent</u> to describe this poem.

I Never Lost as Much But Twice, pages 889–890.

1. To what degree is it necessary to know the specific occasions to which the speaker refers here? Biographers of Dickinson cite the deaths of two men and a woman as having had a profound effect on her. The departure of Charles Wadsworth for San Francisco also disturbed her significantly and may be the third loss mentioned (see pages 886–887). The poem is unspecific; regardless of the specific causes, the poem stands on its own not as an expression of grief but rather as an expression of the speaker's need for God's consolation.

2. What situation does the speaker propose for herself as a petitioner before God? The speaker envisages an idea of wealth and loss. Twice she has lost her substance and twice she has been a beggar asking God for help. She received it twice and now a new loss has occurred and she is again poor. The imagery intimating that God is a <u>Burglar</u> complicates the speaker's attitudes, however, for it calls into question the assumption that God is always and eternally good. Dickinson may be asking readers to recall the saying that "The Lord giveth, and the Lord taketh away," except that she is <u>not</u> asking us to add the usual "Blest be the name of the Lord."

3. What is the effect in this poem of Dickinson's use of internal rhyme? The <u>-ore</u> sound occurs five times in <u>Before</u>, <u>door</u>, <u>store</u>, <u>poor</u>, and <u>more</u>, even though it is a concluding rhyme only in lines 6 and 8. Because the poem is so short, the sound becomes a prominent internal rhyme, stressing the idea of the emotional poverty of the speaker and of her need for divine restoration.

Success is Counted Sweetest, page 890.

1. Describe the central idea of this poem. The main idea is stated in lines 1–2, namely that those who do not gain success are in the best position to appreciate it most, because human dissatisfaction always operates to cause people to want more. The poem fuses success, victory, and triumph.

2. What example is developed in lines 5–12? How does this example develop the idea of stanza 1? The example is drawn from a battle at which there has been victor and vanquished. The idea is that the dying soldier can define victory more accurately than those who have taken <u>the Flag today</u>. By extending the subject to the extremes of losing and dying, Dickinson stresses the fusion of regret, envy, and disappointment that makes the loser benefit from the loss by gaining vision and understanding even in defeat. For

comparison, see "My Triumph Lasted Till the Drums" (pages 897-898).

3. Describe Dickinson's use of metrical form. How does it operate in stanza 1? In stanzas 2 and 3? The pattern is a modified ballad measure, which should be 4a 3b 4c 3b in quatrains. Only line 5 contains four stresses; all others normally needing four contain three. The measure operates normally in stanza 1, where line 2 modifies the verb of line 1, and line 4 is the predicate of the subject in line 3. The last 8 lines, however, form a single continuous sentence. Thus the measure of stanzas 2 and 3 is almost incidental to the formal pattern. It is as though Dickinson, to stress the example of the defeated warrior, stretches out the grammar along with the anguish.

4. Is the diction of this poem mostly specific, general, concrete, abstract, or some combination? The diction is a combination of general and abstract, though the poem itself stays concrete because of the situations. Thus success is abstract, and those who ne'er succeed is general. Nectar is specific, but is a symbol of the sweet drink of the gods shared by triumphant mortals. Sorest need is applicable to anyone trying to find success, and therefore it is abstract. The flag is specific, and a metonym for those who have won. In short, Dickinson's language is broadly meaningful; the success of the poem is created by the accuracy and inclusiveness of her observations.

Just Lost, When I Was Saved, page 890.

1. What paradoxical situation is described in stanza 1? How does stanza 2 continue the narrative begun in the first? The paradox is that the speaker describes the recovery from an illness not as a rescue from death to life, but rather as a slippage from the surity of eternal life (in death) to being lost in life; the paradox is complementary to the Christian view that death is a release from earthly life. Stanza 2 continues the narrative, employing the metaphors of the sailor's returning from foreign shores and the reporter's coming back from the awful doors of Death. The speaker, in short, having approached the line between death and life, has acquired the wisdom that can make her a seer, and has returned to provide Odd secrets of the other side.

2. How is the synesthesia of stanza 3 comparable to and consistent with the initial paradox? The synesthesia is that the things to see have been unheard as yet by human ears. Here, the senses of sight and hearing are linked to the mysteries beyond the line of death. The idea of both the figure and the paradox is that death will provide answers in eternal life that life cannot provide to those now living.

3. Explain the poet's use of the infinitives (instead of complete sentences) in lines 12, 13, and 16. The infinitives complement the unfulfilled desire of the speaker. They mean, approximately, "O how good it would be, the next time I am seriously ill, to die and to stay and to see the things not yet heard and seen, and to tarry in eternity while the Ages, Centuries, and Cycles move ponderously upon earth." The infinitives also may be contrasted with the complete sentences of lines 17, 18, and 19. With this contrast, the infinitives mark points of permanence and certainty while the ages, centuries, and cycles on earth mark the relatively meaningless passage of time.

"Faith" Is a Fine Invention, page 891.

1. Why is Faith included within quotation marks; what do they add to meaning? They suggest that Dickinson is referring to a generally or popularly understood definition of the word. Here, it seems clear from the can see in line 2, Dickinson is alluding to the definition of faith in Hebrews 11:1, "Now

faith is the substance of things hoped for, the evidence of things not seen."
Without the quotation marks the usage might not be construed as an allusion.

2. What does microscopes (line 3) suggest or symbolize? What sort of
Emergency might arise in which microscopes would be better than faith?
Microscopes suggests the analysis and questioning of events of life. The
microscope is an instrument that gets beyond the obvious, and therefore it
symbolizes a questioning attitude, not the accepting one suggested by faith
alone. Thus the microscope marks a rejection of quiescence, and an acceptance
of inquiry. The Emergency could be a significant event, such as a departure
or death, that creates a crisis in the individual.

3. Explain the idea of the reference to "Gentlemen can see" (line 2).
The phrase is paradoxical. It may mean that Gentlemen can understand the
usual religious explanations for misfortune. The implication, however, is
that the gentlemen cannot see far enough and deeply enough to explain why
misfortune exists. In addition, Gentlemen suggests a sense of exclusion,
probably a hierarchical and sexist one. The gentlemen form the group who
interpret faith and provide comforting platitudes for those experiencing pain,
but their answers do not deal with the pain itself.

I Taste a Liquor Never Brewed, page 891.

1. What is the theme of this poem? It is the speaker's affirmation of
the ecstacy and exhilaration she feels with life. She bases the poem on the
analogy of being "drunk with the wine of life." She uses the phrase liquor
never brewed to explain the expansive mood she is describing, in line with
Keats's image (in "Grecian Urn") of ditties of no tone (an ideal).

2. In minimizing Dickinson's verse, Thomas Baily Aldrich in 1903 offered
a rewritten 1st stanza by "tossing a rhyme into it" as follows:
    I taste a liquor never brewed / In vats upon the Rhine;
    No tankard ever held a draught / Of alcohol like mine.
What is the principle on which Aldrich made his revision, and in what way is
it relevant to an evaluation of Dickinson's stanza? Aldrich's principle is
that the ballad stanza should be regular, with four stresses in lines 1 and 3,
and rhyming words ending lines 2 and 4. Aldrich concluded that Dickinson had
violated this principle and he "fixed" her verse. Modern readers are likely
to find such insistence on mechanical regularity irrelevant to the joyful
state of mind Dickinson presents in the poem.

3. Emily Dickinson composed an alternative last line which appears in the
manuscript of this poem: "Leaning against the -- Sun --." What improvement
does the alternative line provide? The image in the alternative suggests that
its speaker, in her ecstatic joy of life, is leaning drunkenly against the sun
as though it were a lamppost. The image is both ridiculous and joyful, and
seems to be an improvement over the image in the text which suggests that the
tippler has come from Manzanilla (i.e. drinking wine). Moreover, the last
word of the alternative (Sun) creates a perfect rhyme to end the poem.

Safe in Their Alabaster Chambers, page 891.

1. Who are the members of the Resurrection? Why are they meek? How are
they safe? They are the dead, so named here because epitaphs often read that
the dead person lies below, awaiting a joyful resurrection. The word meek
refers to Matthew 5:5, "Blessed are the meek, for they shall inherit the
earth." The dead in the grave are safe from any more worldly pain.

2. Contrast the subject matter of stanza 2 with that of stanza 1. Stanza

2 refers generally to the passage of time, to the eternal movement of heavenly bodies, and to the constant change in governments (in human society). The stanza suggests how long the dead must wait for their eventual resurrection.

3. How do the associations of the words <u>Crescent</u>, <u>Arcs</u>, <u>Firmaments</u>, <u>Diadems</u>, and <u>Doges</u> broaden the meaning of the poem? <u>Crescent</u>, in addition to its reference to the earth's curved surface, suggest the location in the mideast (the fertile crescent) where the Garden of Eden was located. <u>Arcs</u> suggests the Ark of the Covenant--the pact God made with the ancient Hebrews (Exodus 25:16-21; Numbers 10:33 and elsewhere). <u>Firmament</u> is also a Biblical word, signifying the heavens, in the shape of an arch. The word is also prominent in Joseph Addison's hymn "The Spacious Firmament on High." <u>Diadems</u> is Biblical (see Isiah 62:3) and is also an important and repeated word in the common hymn by Edward Perronet (1726-1792), "All Hail the Power of Jesus' Name." <u>Doges</u>, or <u>dukes</u>, suggests the Venetian Republic, which had lost its eminence early in the 19th century. All these words suggest the broad historical and religious milieu from which Dickinson is drawing her ideas.

4. In the last line, why is everything <u>soundless</u>? What does the word imply? <u>Soundless</u> suggests the insignificance of human activities in the context of eternity. Worldly power and the worlds which contain it shall pass, and they will be unimportant as compared with God's resurrective power.

Wild Nights -- Wild Nights, page 892.

1. Explain the meaning of the title. The title cannot be interpreted too literally because it is general. Night, however, signifies a time of love. The speaker is thus suggesting emotional and physical abandon and release.

2. What is the reading and interpretation of <u>done</u> in lines 7 and 8? Once a person knows the satisfaction of unity with a loved one, there is no further need for the controls (<u>chart</u>, <u>compass</u>) that keep a person seeking for love and tentatively establishing and then relinquishing unsatisfactory relationships. Hence, <u>chart</u> and <u>compass</u> may be <u>done</u> away with.

3. What is the metaphor of stanzas 2 and 3? How extensively is it developed? The metaphor is that of a ship going to port (line 6) and reaching a state of paradise (9). It is coextensive with lines 5-12, comparing the emotional identity (<u>Heart</u>, line 6) of an individual to a ship sailing to a secure port. In this poem, the port is the <u>thee</u> of lines 2 and 12.

4. In stanza 2 there are no complete sentences, and in stanza 3 the last 2 lines comprise a sentence in the subjunctive mode. Relate this relative incompleteness to the theme of the poem. The poem is about the yearning of the speaker for the <u>thee</u> to whom the poem is addressed. Because the relationship does not exist, the poignancy of the unfulfilled desire is underscored by the absence of declarative sentences.

There's a Certain Slant of Light, page 892.

1. What does the poem suggest about the relationship between a condition of light and human mood or character? The premise is that mood and character are not fixed but rather are being continuously created through momentary conditions in the environment. Here, the condition is a <u>certain slant of light</u> that unsettles the mind and leaves the perceiving individual depressed and hurt. The hurt is not temporary, like the slant of light, but a permanant <u>internal difference</u> that remains a part of life's conditions, literally an <u>imperial affliction</u> from the universe.

2. Describe the tone of stanza 1. The tone is built up out of the swift

movement from the reference to the slant of light to the weight (<u>Heft</u>) of
<u>Cathedral</u> <u>Tunes</u>. The shift from sight to weight and the sound of music
creates surprise and humor. Cathedral music is usually considered dignified,
but the word <u>Tunes</u> minimizes the sound, creating an anti-climax from the idea
of <u>Heft</u>. The reference to <u>Cathedral</u> is irreverent. These combinations create
a complex tone that is serious and comic.

    3. Explain <u>Where the Meanings, are</u> (line 8). The meanings of life, as
suggested in line 7, are all internalized, whether through the conscious
process characteristic of much of our learning, or through the unconscious
process suggested in this poem.

    4. What is the relationship of the last stanza's metaphors and simile to
the central idea of the poem? Lines 13 and 14 offer two personifications:
landscapes listen and shadows momentarily stop breathing. In lines 15 and 16
the simile is to the appearance of a dying person (the "Distance / On the look
of Death"). These figures, joining landscape and death to the slant of light,
are a climax to the main idea, suggesting both the universality and finality
of the mood and feelings created on <u>Winter Afternoons</u>.

The Soul Selects Her Own Society, pages 892-893.

    1. What condition of the soul or personality is described in this poem?
The soul as described here is independent of the will of a person because it
(<u>she</u>) dictates the associations that one has. The soul, after determining the
associates, closes the door to others (line 2) and remains unmoved even by
those with power and prestige (stanza 2). So firm is the soul that it closes
the person off from a personal relationship with anyone else, as though a
stone (gravestone?) has been put into place between the person and the world.

    2. What metaphor is used in reference to the soul? What meaning does the
metaphor lend to the concept of soul? Metaphorically, the soul becomes a
queen or goddess, living in a sanctuary that may be closed to prevent any
future communication with subjects (<u>her</u> <u>divine</u> <u>Majority</u>, line 3), with the
rest of the busy world (lines 5-6), and even with <u>an Emperor</u> (7). The soul
represents an entity of great worth; it is empowered to make a single choice
from all those within the possible sphere of acquaintance (line 9, 10). At
the end, the metaphor of <u>valves of her attention</u> suggests that the soul with
valves open is like a great organ that plays all pipes in expressiveness. The
valves may be closed, however, and then the soul becomes as silent as stone.

    3. How do the lengths of the second and fourth lines of the stanzas echo
the shutting down of communication described in the poem? In stanzas 1 and 2
these lines contain, respectively, 4 and then 3 words. In the last stanza,
however, the lines are reduced to 2 words each, being, metrically, a spondee
(line 10) and an iamb (12). Rhythmically, this reduction creates emphasis
upon the abruptness of the action and the simile with which the poem closes.

Some Keep the Sabbath Going to Church, page 893.

    1. What concept of worship is presented in this poem? The idea here is
built out of the contrast between the formal worship of a church service and
the spontaneous experience of witnessing Nature at home and in the orchard.
The theme is a recurring one in Dickinson's poems; see, for example, "The
Gentian" (page 889). The idea is that in the natural world one is closer to
God than in a worship service where the service itself, because it is the
focus of attention, interferes with one's relationship to God.

2. What is the tone of the lines (2, 6, 12) in which the speaker refers to I? The tone is one of cleverness and challenge--a certain degree of playful pride and mockery. In line 2 the speaker admits to keeping the Sabbath by staying away from church (remember that Exodus 20:8-11 commands the keeping of the Sabbath; also remember that this commandment was much more heeded in the 19th century than it is today). In line 6 the speaker endows herself with wings, and in the last line she indicates a belief that her way of keeping the Sabbath makes living a constant process of going to Heaven.

3. Who is the noted Clergyman? How does He preach? God preaches; the means is unclear, unless we assume that Dickinson is alluding to statements like that in Psalms 24:1, "The earth is the Lord's, and the fullness thereof, the world and those that dwell therein." If we accept the allusion, then all of nature--bobolink, orchard, singing sexton (a bird)--become the means by which God preaches. Given the pantheistic-like idea of the poem, any title attributed to God is an understatement. Hence the title noble Clergyman is designed as a rhetorical reminder of the intensity of God's power. There is also a strong note of defiance and unconventionality in the choice of phrase.

After Great Pain, a Formal Feeling Comes, page 893.

1. What is meant by formal in line 1? Ordinarily formal refers to appropriate and ritualized manners in social situations. That is partly its meaning here, but the word also suggests the images that follow in the poem. The feelings after great pain, in other words, are molded by forces into rigid patterns beyond the conscious control of the individual.

2. What do the images of the poem have in common? They have a common thread of stiffness, numbness, heaviness, and rigidity, as though the feelings with which they are compared are held in suspended animation and emotional isolation. Thus Tombs (line 2) force people into appropriate ceremoniousness, forbidding anything but solemnity. Wooden way (7) suggests a lack of spring and spontaneity. The Quartz contentment is hard and shiny, crystalizing the individual in passive acceptance and preventing any emotional interchanges. The Freezing image of lines 12 and 13 connects the ending of the poem with Tombs at the beginning. The response to great pain is a kind of death, even though the individual goes on living, because the emotional connections once possessed are now gone, and a link with life has been frozen or killed. For comparison, see "My Life Closed Twice" (page 898).

3. What is the connection of the poem's subject with the He of line 3? The He that bore is a reference to Christ's carrying of the cross. The connection with the poem is made at the end of the second line with Tombs, presumably an association with the tomb in which Jesus was laid (see Matthew 27:60) and therefore also prompting the third-line outcry about the passion. The reference underlies and explains the intensity of the great pain of line 1, for it makes the passion seem both comparable and immediate. Even though line 4 does not cohere grammatically with line 3, it nevertheless preserves the topical and thematic connection because it is a virtual reenactment of the disorientation about time that a person in great grief might experience. The line is therefore more dramatic and fragmentary than grammatical.

Much Madness Is Divinest Sense, page 894.

1. How may lines 1-3 be resolved gramatically? How does this resolution assist comprehension? Here Dickinson's use of the dash creates an immediate difficulty. This problem may be resolved, however, if the lines are under-

understood thus: "To a discerning eye, much madness is divinest sense [and] much sense [is] the starkest madness." This resolution reveals the lines to be an assessment of a topsy-turvy world in which things are seldom what they seem. The rhetorical arrangement of lines 1 and 3, a chiasmus or antimetabole on madness-sense and sense-madness, also suggests that the lines are to be read as a unit, with To a discerning Eye as the modifying phrase.

2. To what degree does the speaker suggest that the opening paradox is applicable to politics? The use of Majority . . . prevail in lines 4 and 5 indicates that the speaker is criticising the political decision-making process of democracy. The idea is a play on the idea of the proverb "vox populi, vox dei" ("the voice of the people is the voice of God"). If the people embody collective madness in their voting patterns, therefore, that madness is the divinest sense that will prevail. Similarly, the sensible person who dissents on reasonable grounds will be called mad. The concluding image of being handled with a Chain also suggests political associations.

I Heard a Fly Buzz -- When I Died, page 894.

1. What is the poem's situation? This is a deathbed scene. In the 19th century people died at home; family and friends maintained a bedside vigil. The witnesses would be tearful (line 5) and would constantly be preparing for the moment of death (7). The dying person would give personal effects and properties to those present, who were also witnesses of final wishes and wills (lines 9-11). Testimony and acknowledgement of the presence of God (the King, lines 7,8) also took place. Amid the speaker's description of such a scene, she notes the appearance of a buzzing fly, and this creature is the last connection she imagines having with the world before death. The personalized imagining of death or deathbed scenes was fairly common at Dickinson's time and before; several of Donne's poems offer a similar dramatic situation.

2. What is the effect of the fly upon the tone of the poem? The fly is an intrusion upon what should be seen as a serious occasion; it is uncertain, stumbling, and therefore it represents a comic element of the scene. With respect to the tone of the poem, the fly saves the imaginary situation from becoming sentimentalized because it represents reality and every-day life.

3. What are the effect and meaning of the last 2 lines? These lines constitute a powerful ending for the poem; they are connected to the sound and light represented by the fly because it interposes itself between the light and the speaker. Thus the phrase "the Windows failed" is logical because the speaker has been conscious of the fly outlined against the light. The use of Windows is a metonym--the substitution of one thing (Windows) for another with which it is closely associated (light)--which emphasizes the idea that death is a termination of the world externally and internally. In the last line, see to see is a way of describing death as a loss of capacity. The first see is the power to perceive; the second is the visual function of this power.

I Like to See It Lap the Miles, pages 894-895.

1. How does the poem create a sense of motion about a train? The poem begins with the construction "I like to see it . . ." and then includes ten one-syllable infinitives in this complementary position, of which it is the recurrent subject. Thus the speaker likes to see it lap, lick, stop, step, peer, pare, crawl, chase, neigh, and stop, with the present participle complaining in line 11. All the infinitive complements and the participle are verbs of action, thereby stressing the details of motion.

2. What is the dominant metaphor in the poem? How does Dickinson keep it from seeming ordinary? The major metaphor is the common one comparing a train with an iron horse. She keeps it frest by not ever mentioning that she is describing a train, by stressing the action of the train, and by withholding the verb most appropriate to a horse (neigh) until line 15. The metaphor thus does not become completely fixed until the poem is almost ended.

3. How is a comic, playful, light tone maintained throughout the poem? Overstatements create amusement. These are prodigious (line 4), supercilious (6), Boanerges (14), and omnipotent (16). In addition, the complaining in a horrid, hooting stanza (lines 11, 12), the chasing (line 12), and the neighing (line 14) are also comic. Another playful idea is that after all the hooting, the creature becomes docile once it stops (line 15). The metaphor stable for a railway roundhouse is also amusing.

I Cannot Live with You, pages 895-896.

1. What is the dramatic situation here? The speaker is responding to an invitation to live with you, presumably in marriage. She answers negatively and then explains the reasons for the denial. Those reasons, together with the concluding summary, form the poem, which is more like a written letter than an intimate, spoken speech. Once the poem is completed, there is no opportunity for response, and the concluding word, Despair, indicates the finality of the statement and the deep grief of the speaker. There is no way for us to identify the you as a specific person, although biographers indicate that the circumstances of the poem fit Charles Wadsworth (see page 887). The best we can do as modern readers is to consider the speaker and the you as two dramatic characters who must part permanantly, and the poem as the expression of the speaker's recognition and anguish.

2. What reasons does the speaker cite in support of the opening denial? How is the poem structured to embody these responses? Lines 1-12 form a negative denying the possibility of living together, citing a religious barrier (the Key kept by the Sexton, line 5). Lines 13-20 further deny living together because of the impossibility of the two dying together; neither could predecease the other. In lines 21-44, the denial extends to the impossibility of the two being resurrected together: [a] the speaker could not admire Jesus more than the you in Heaven because she admires you for shining nearer; [b] she would be ill judged for crowding out her vision of Paradise by filling her sight with you; [c] she could never bear to be anywhere in Heaven without the you, because being apart, even in Heaven, would be Hell to her. The conclusion, lines 45-50, summarizes the vastness between the two, who have only prayer for consolation and despair as a permanent condition.

Pain -- Has an Element of Blank, page 896.

1. What rhetorical figure does Dickinson use in referring to pain? What is the effect of this figure? The figure is personification; the speaker gives Pain the powers of possible recall and perception. The effect is to create a concept of emotional pain having superhuman and pervasive strength. The idea is that pain has a separate and independent existence enabling it to dominate the emotions and perceptions of the person experiencing it.

2. What is the effect of pain on the perception of time? How is the structure of time related to the poem's structure? The poem suggests that pain obliterates one's orientation to time. One cannot determine when the pain began, or when it will end. It becomes overwhelming, and, because of its

destructiveness of time, it almost literally thrusts one into a self-contained
enclosure, cut off from the identity that memory and future plans may provide.
The poem is structured so that the effect of pain upon the past is considered
in stanza 1 and the effect on the future in stanza 2.

3. How does diction convey the sense of the extreme power of pain? The
words are mainly abstract: Blank (1) conveys a sense of nothingness; recollect
(2) is an action of mind; begun, were (3), and time when it was not (4) are
all simple but abstract. The diction in stanza 2 is similar. Future, Past,
Infinite, Enlightenment, and Periods are all abstract. Dickinson also breaks
grammatical rules (with begun [3], contain [6]) of form and agreement to
complement the breakdowns that extreme pain creates in perception.

4. Why does Dickinson introduce the alliterative p sounds in lines 7-8?
The p sound, the first sound in the word pain, begins the key word in the
first half of line 7--Past. Because Dickinson has just used the word contain
in 6, a word rhyming with pain, in effect her subsequent use of the words
perceive and Periods puts the reader in mind of the word Pain with which the
poem closes. Thus the p sound is one of the means by which the poem, by sound
alone, insists on the phenomenon of pain.

One Need Not Be a Chamber -- To Be Haunted, pages 896-897.

How is the metaphor comparing a house to the mind developed in the poem
to demonstrate the frightening nature of identity? In stanza 1 the poem
asserts that the brain has its own corridors where a person may encounter
horrid fantasies. At the end the image is that of a single room in the mind
where a "superior spectre / Or More" is waiting, more deadly than a real-life
assassin (who can be shot). In between, the mind is compared to a cooler Host
(line 8), presumably ready to give a terrorizing party for the individual. In
line 12 the house metaphor is momentarily replaced by a lonesome Place. The
mind (one's self) is like a bandit waiting for the individual in a place of
concealment. Even here, however, in lines 9 and 10, the image of a room is
represented in the Abbey, where the stones might arise to chase the terrified
victim. The poem suggests that such a scare is less harmful than the horrors
lurking within the mind. These many separate representations of the mind as a
haunted house, five within five stanzas, create consistency and unity.

The Bustle in a House, page 897.

1. What specific setting does line 1 promise? How does stanza 2 indicate
that the setting is metaphorical? The first line suggests that the setting
is a household in which a family member has died the day before. The Bustle
is the hushed solemn preparations that need to be made before the funeral:
cleaning, preparing invitations, writing notices to friends. In stanza 2, the
Sweeping of the Heart (line 5) indicates a different setting--the interior one
of adjusting to life in view of the reality and permanence of death. The
appearance of the word Heart indicates the beginning of the metaphor.

2. A student once suggested that line 6 of this poem, And putting love
away, is cold and unfeeling. How do the central metaphor and lines 7-8
suggest an alternative reading? The thought of putting Love away might be
seen as cold and unfeeling if it means that the living can forget the dead.
Here, however, the metaphor of housework applies. Putting love away is like
storing something in a closet until a change of season makes it necessary
again. This analogy, together with the concluding reference to the reuniting

of the dead in Eternity, lends a strong note of poignancy and yearning to the poem. Stanza 2 thus expresses hope, resignation and acceptance.

My Triumph Lasted Till the Drums, pages 897-898.

1. Who or what is the speaker? What situation has prompted the poem? We can infer from the situation that the speaker is a member (or officer) of a newly victorious army. The victory has been celebrated by a series of drum rolls, and the speaker has been elated. After the noise, however, the speaker inspects the dead. Seeing their finished Faces (line 5), he feels so chastened (line 4) that he wishes to become one of the dead.
2. In what way are lines 9-16 a contrast to the first 8 lines, and in what way are they a reflection upon them? Lines 9-16 are a meditation on war and what people might learn from it if they were caring and sensible. Contrast occurs because the topic is abstracted from the specific situation of lines 1-8. Lines 9-16 consider how we might use the memory of past warfare to predict that future warfare would produce the same regret and guilt in the victors as that described in lines 1-8. If the future could contain something of this retrospective guilt, people would avoid warfare.
3. Does the image of the dead developed here stress the horror or the anguish of war? The image is neither immediate nor pictorial; the Dead have finished Faces and have turned their Conclusion on the speaker (lines 5, 6). Dickinson characteristically directs the topic inwardly to the responses of the speaker. The subject is therefore more about the anguish of war than physical horror and agony.

The Heart is the Capital of the Mind, page 898.

1. What is the central metaphor and what is its effect? The metaphor is that the individual is like a country (or continent) with the Mind being a single political unit that is coincidental with this country. The capital is the heart; the emotions are the primary source of strength and control, the recipient of the individual's mental and physical resources. The population of this country is one. The argument might seem solipsistic, but the poem is more about knowing one's self than about making the world over in one's image. The effect is to stress the importance of individual thought and identity.
2. Explain the grammatical structure and meaning of stanza 2. The punctuation and elliptical constructions make the stanza ambiguous. There are 2 possible readings: (1) the population [of this Continent] is One--numerous enough. Seek this ecstatic Nation: it is Yourself; (2) the population [of this Continent] is One. This ecstatic Nation [is] Numerous enough. Seek [it]; it is Yourself. Both stress the need to learn about one's self.

"Heavenly Father" -- Take to Thee, page 898.

1. Why are there quotation marks around Heavenly Father and We are Dust? Both are quoted from the Bible. Heavenly Father is used five times in Matthew and once in Luke. It is particularly appropriate here because it is first used in Matthew immediately after The Lord's Prayer. The sentence We are Dust is a reference to Genesis 3:19, in which God addresses Adam after the fall and describes human beings by saying "you are dust, and to dust you shall return."
2. In what way does this poem express a more complex attitude toward God than might normally be expected in a prayer? Normally one expects adoration,

gratitude, and petition in prayer. Here, the speaker is expressing criticism of God. The idea that humans are the <u>supreme iniquity</u> (line 2) is normal, but the idea that the <u>iniquity</u> was <u>fashioned</u> by God in a <u>contraband</u> moment is shocking, for it puts the burden of the evil on God. The request to be <u>More respectful</u> is not the usual petition for grace but a wish that God treat humans with more respect. The association of God with <u>Duplicity</u> ends the poem on a critical and surprising note. The poem thus embodies stances common to prayer, but adds the complexity of laying blame on God and humans. A well-known quandary about God may be operating as a basis for this complexity: "If God is completely good, why has evil been allowed in the world?"

My Life Closed Twice Before Its Close, page 898.

1. How does the structure of this poem work against the 2-stanza ballad measure? The sentences do not fall within the pattern of the stanzas. Line 1 is a complete sentence that features the use of <u>close</u> in both a figurative and literal sense of dying. Lines 2-6 form an extensive sentence that jumps the line and stanza patterns. The last 2 lines form a separate unit of statement.
2. What sorts of expectations does the speaker have about the <u>third event</u> (lines 2-6) that might occur? Because the 1st 2 events were figurative closings of the speaker's life, the implication here is that <u>Immortality</u> might have a 3rd event equally bad in store. But the language is ambiguous, for the description "So huge, so hopeless to conceive" may equally describe a positive as well as unfavorable event. The question of what <u>Immortality</u> might <u>unveil</u> is therefore still open, even though the previous experiences have been bad.
3. How are lines 7-8 connected to the ideas of the poem? The lines constitute a denial of the speculation about the magnitude of anything that immortality might offer the speaker. We usually regard going to heaven or hell as the major possibilities that death has in store for us. But, says the speaker, because her life has already been <u>closed</u> twice before her actual death, she has already experienced both heaven and hell. The poem therefore ends on a skeptical as well as a memorable note: Nothing that Immortality can provide--not heaven, and not hell--could be either better or worse than what she has known in life because of the partings she has experienced.

ROBERT FROST, pages 899-901.

The Tuft of Flowers, pages 901-902.

1. What is the setting and situation? What feelings about the human condition are expressed in lines 1-10?
2. What does the butterfly symbolize? To what does it lead the speaker?
3. What does the tuft of flowers represent for the speaker? How does it change his perspective on the human condition?
The poem (in iambic pentameter rhymed couplets) presents a process of discovery in which the speaker realizes that all humans are bound together in a spiritual unity with nature, beauty, and each other. The poem creates this meaning by narrating the process of discovery. In lines 1-10 the speaker feels isolated and <u>alone</u>; he cannot find the mower and he thinks that it is human destiny for <u>all</u> to be alone. In lines 11-20 a <u>bewildered butterfly</u> leads the speaker to a tuft of flowers spared by the mower; the butterfly represents both the speaker's questioning spirit (<u>tremulous wing</u>) and the tenuous bond between speaker, mower, and nature. Lines 21-40 describe the beauty and love embodied in the tuft of flowers. This single object awakens

the speaker to all of nature and the kinship among all humanity. He concludes
that "men work together . . . whether they work together or apart."

Mending Wall, pages 902-903.

1. What is the setting and situation? Who are the characters?
2. What is the neighbor's attitude toward walls? How did he get this
attitude? What is he like?
3. What is the speaker's attitude toward walls? How does Frost show that the
speaker is ambivalent? How is the speaker different from the neighbor?
     The poem (in blank verse) isn't really about walls. Instead, it employs
a specific action and situation to explore the differences between two types
of personalities. The two characters--speaker and neighbor--are repairing the
wall between their farms. The neighbor believes that "Good fences make good
neighbors" (lines 27, 45); his views are conservative and traditional,
inherited from his father (line 43). He is neither introspective nor
philosophical; he does not question inherited wisdom. The speaker is much
more philosophical, ironic, introspective, skeptical, and amused. He knows
that walls can be silly or worse--"Something there is that doesn't love a
wall"--but he is ambivalent about them; he calls the neighbor to start work
(line 12) and helps rebuild the wall. The speaker's tone and attitude combine
questioning with ironic humor and whimsey. These are reflected in the
speaker's assertions that a spell must be used to make some stones balance,
that wall-building is "just another kind of outdoor game," that his apple
trees will never invade his neighbor's pines, and that Elves knock walls down.
The speaker is thus uneasy and unsure about walls; he makes quiet fun of his
neighbor's attitude, but he recognizes the need for some walls and he helps
rebuild this one year after year.

After Apple-Picking, pages 903-904.

1. How is apple-picking employed metaphorically and symbolically here?
2. What is the setting and situation? How is winter linked with sleep?
3. What is the speaker's attitude toward apple-picking? Why does he refuse to
continue the endless labor?
4. What does the speaker expect to dream about? What does his dream suggest
about life? How does he respond to the dream?
     The speaker contemplates sleep (hibernation, death) as a withdrawal from
the ambitious struggles and achievements of life. This life of struggle and
accumulation is metaphorically expressed in apple-picking (apples are singular
and varied; as Biblical and mythic symbols they suggest conflict, knowledge,
awards for labor). After apple-picking comes sleep (death, perhaps heaven).
In lines 1-6 the speaker notes that his work is not done ("a barrel that I
didn't fill") but that he will not continue. He is drowsing off toward a
sleep (withdrawal, death) that is hastened by the odd vision through the "pane
of glass" (melting ice). The speaker knows that he will dream of further
apple-picking (more achievement, accumulation, lines 18-26) even though he
feels the weight of his labors ("the pressure of the ladder-round") even in
his sleep. He rejects this future (lines 27-36) even though he once desired
the great harvest because he now understands that all comes to nothing ("the
cider-apple heap"). At the close, he wonders if the approaching sleep will be
human rest (with dreams), hibernation, or death. The poem explores the idea
that human ambition and achievement are "of no worth."

Birches, pages 904-906.

1. What two ways of bending birches does the speaker discuss? Which way
permanently damages the trees? What does each way come to symbolize?
2. What kind of escape from earthly cares does the speaker want? Why is the
word toward (line 56) in italic?

Bowed birches remind the speaker of two ways that the trees can be bent:
ice storms and swinging boys. The ice-storms (lines 5-20) damage the trees
permanently; the birches "never right themselves." Such bending is harmful,
destructive, symbolic of death. A boy swinging on the birches (lines 21-40)
doesn't damage the trees; it takes "the stiffness out of them" (line 30).
Such bending is regenerative and healthful. The speaker was once a "swinger
of birches," and he dreams of returning to this pastime as a regenerative
process, to escape from the earth (drudgery) for a while and then "begin over"
(line 50). Birch swinging symbolizes a temporary escape that will not break
or damage the speaker permanently; he seeks escape and then return. The
italic toward indicates the denial of permanent removal from earth.

The Road Not Taken, page 906.

1. What do the two roads symbolize? What is the speaker's attitude toward
them? What must he decide?
2. How are the roads different? Which does the speaker choose? Why?
3. What does the speaker know about the unchosen road? What will be the
effect of his choice?
4. How do rhyme, meter, and form reinforce theme and meaning here?

This poem explores the idea that every choice we make determines the
ultimate direction our lives will take. The two roads symbolize choices of
direction in life. Stanza 1 sets up the circumstances of the choice; the
roads diverged and the speaker was sorry he could not choose both. Stanza 2
suggests that the two roads (choices) were almost equal, but there is a
difference. The speaker picked the one that wanted wear and was less traveled
(less conformist, traditional, normal, popular). Stanza 3 takes up the
inevitable closure produced by choice; the speaker saved the unchosen road
"for another day," but he knew that he would never "come back" (face the same
choice again) because "way leads on to way" (each choice leads on to
subsequent choices predicated on the first). All this is in the past; there
is no present in the poem. In the last stanza, the speaker considers the
impact of such choices on the future; although one choice may seem
insignificant, it will have made "all the difference." The fixed form of the
poem (abaab) reflects the speaker's attempt to order the past and future based
on choices. The speaker pauses (line 18) before announcing his conclusion.

"Out, Out--", pages 906-907.

1. To what does the title allude? How does the allusion help shape meaning?
2. What is the setting and situation? What types of imagery are employed
here? What is the boy doing? What happens?
3. Trace the poem's movement from accident to injury to death. How does the
speaker make each seem accidental, surprising, and relatively insignificant?

The title is an allusion to Shakespeare's Macbeth; it is quoted from the
usurper's speech about the emptiness of life:

Out, out, brief candle!
Life's but a walking shadow, a poor player

            That struts and frets his hour upon the stage
            And then is heard no more. It is a tale
            Told by an idiot, full of sound and fury,
            Signifying nothing. (5.5.23-28)
The title thus suggests that the poem will explore the uncertainty and
emptiness of life. Even without the allusion, this sense of unpredictability
and uncertainty comes across. The setting and situation are set up in lines
1-8 with images of sound (onomatopoetic snarled and rattled), smell (sweet-
scented stuff), and sight (dust, sticks, mountains). Our sense of the instant
is expanded in lines 9-14; we learn that the day has been uneventful, work is
over, and it's supper time. The boy's hand is severed by accident in one
moment of inattention. The poem moves by easy steps to death; each one is
unanticipated. The rueful laugh and the spoiled life are followed by fading
pulse (No one believed) and then death. No one understands what is happening;
the death, like the cut, is a product of chance. Those (we don't know who
they are) who turned to their affairs underscore the insignificance and ran-
domness of chance events.

Fire and Ice, page 907.

1. To what 2 types of cosmic destruction do the title and lines 1-2 refer?
2. With what emotions are fire and ice associated?
3. How do the word suffice and the closing rhyme affect the poem's meaning?
     The poem investigates the destructive power of human passion (desire and
hate) through the symbolism of cosmic destruction by fire or ice. The title
and lines 1-2 refer to two modes of ending the world: fire (war, apocalypse,
falling into the sun) and ice (ice age, cooling, flying out of orbit). Fire
is linked with desire; ice with hatred. The speaker knows both, and knows
that both are strong enough to end the world. The ironic understatement in
the word suffice suggests that hate (ice) is stronger than desire. The
concluding rhyme (ice-suffice) provides a clinching ironic tone.

Nothing Gold Can Stay, pages 907-908.

1. What do the leaf, human history, and a single day have in common? In what
sense do all begin in gold?
2. What does "gold" symbolize? What happens to everything that is gold?
     The poem explores the idea that happiness, perfection, bliss (all
symbolized by gold) cannot and will not endure for long. The apparent paradox
of line 1 is based on the fact that buds appear to be gold rather than green.
The speaker looks at the falling away from gold in nature, human history, and
time. The leaf, humanity, and the day all begin in gold (bud, Eden, dawn) and
decay quickly; perfection in any form lasts only for an hour.

Misgiving, page 908.

1. What do the leaves promise in spring? How are they changed by the fall?
2. What do the leaves symbolize? The spring and fall? The wind?
3. In what ways does the speaker hope to be different from the leaves?
     The poem investigates the human fear of the unknown (adventure, death)
through the metaphor of leaves driven by the wind. Stanzas 1-3 develop the
metaphor and the leaves as a symbol for aging humanity. In spring (youth),
the leaves promise to travel with the wind. In fall (age), however, the

199

leaves become oppressed by sleep (fear, reluctance) and they ask the wind to stay with them. Early promises of flight give way to a vaguer and vaguer stir or a reluctant whirl that does not change or move the leaves. In the last stanza, the speaker hopes he will be different and have the courage to move beyond the bounds of life in quest of knowledge when he is free.

Acquainted with the Night, page 908.

1. What is the speaker like? What does he know? What has he done?
2. What are the central symbols in the poem? How do they create meaning?
3. What aspects of human existence does the poem reveal?
     The poem, in iambic pentameter terza rima (aba, bcb, cdc, dad, aa), investigates the human dilemma of loneliness and isolation. Night is the central symbol for sadness, loneliness, and all the negative aspects of life. The speaker's acquaintance with the night suggests that he has experienced life's bitterness; acquaintance also implies cold knowledge rather than warm familiarity. Subsequent images (rain, furthest city light, saddest city lane) reinforce the initial symbol of night as sadness, misery, isolation. The watchman that the speaker passes suggests a denial of human contact and perhaps suspicion and guilt; the silence and interrupted cry (stanza 3) hint at isolation and violence. The luminary clock (a lighted clock on a post or perhaps the moon) is detached and non-judgmental; it indicates that time is neither wrong nor right. The repetition of I have seven times, the repeated end rhyme, and the interlocking terza rima all pull the poem together. The rhymes (e.g., beat-feet-street) clinch ideas. The high number of end-stopped lines combined with the repetition suggests compression and sparseness.

Design, Page 909.

1. What three white objects are described in lines 1-8? What do they symbolize? What design do they suggest?
2. What question does the speaker consider in lines 9-12? What answer does the closing couplet suggest? What does the answer imply about the cosmos?
     The speaker uses the coincidence of three white things coming together in nature to imply that the universe is controlled either by evil designs or no intelligent plan at all. Frost employs a modified sonnet form (abba, abba, acaa, cc) to organize these ideas and to create a tight network of rhyme sounds that clinch ideas throughout. In lines 1-8, the speaker observes the deadly convergence of white flower, spider, and moth; all three ironically (because white) symbolize death and blight and evil (witches' broth). The third quatrain asks what brought these three things together; the idea of design is emphasized in the unnatural whiteness of a normally blue flower. The couplet answers the question: either malevolent intelligence (design of darkness to appall) or pure chaotic chance (if design govern).

The Gift Outright, page 909.

1. What circumstances of U.S. history are considered in lines 1-7? In lines 8-16? What caused the change in the relationship between land and people?
2. What ideas about the relationship between a nation and its people does the poem express?
     Frost examines the relationship between a nation and the land; the poem suggests that nationhood demands "surrender" from the land and the people.

Lines 1-7 look at the one-sided relationship between the land and people who have made no commitment in blood; the land gave itself first. In lines 8-16, the speaker considers the ways in which the people gave of themselves (in war, exploration, labor) to form a nation.

A Considerable Speck (Microscopic), pages 909-910.

1. What is the setting and situation? What does the speaker find on his paper? How does he deal with it? Why?
2. To what extent do rhyme, meter, and diction contribute to tone and theme?
3. How is "on any sheet the least display of mind" used with a double meaning?
    The tone here is playful, ironic, and wry; Frost uses an insignificant insect and event to comment on the general dearth of intelligence. Tone is established in part by the iambic meter, the rhymes (e.g., ink-think, feet-complete), and the colloquial diction. The speaker finds a microscopic insect on his paper and eventually recognizes it as "an intelligence" (line 15). He spares the mite partly because it is innocent and partly because the speaker is glad to find "On any sheet the least display of mind." The implication is that most things (written) on paper are mindless.

Choose Something Like a Star, pages 910-911.

1. How is the star described? Characterized? What qualities does it embody?
2. What differences between the star and humanity does the poem detail?
3. What does the star provide for humanity?
    This poem contrasts the silence and steadfastness of a star with the changeable and questioning nature of humanity (us). The star is character-ized as fair, lofty, mysterious, proud, and taciturn. It answers our demands for measurement, scientific fact, and specificity with only the fact of its fire (I burn). More important, it provides a touchstone or standard against which humanity (the mob) can measure and balance its own excesses.

U.S. 1946 King's X, page 911.

1. What historical moment does the poem evoke? What is the new Holocaust?
2. What do the phrases fingers crossed, King's X, and no fairs suggest about the U.S. and its attitude toward nuclear weapons in 1946?
    The phrases in question 2, all related to children's games and going outside the rules, suggest that the U.S. is acting childishly in its demand that all nations follow its rules in dealing with atomic weapons.

WRITING ABOUT A POET'S WORK, pages 911-918.

    This section discusses biographical, developmental, and comparative approaches to a number of poems by a single author. The most accessible type of essay for students is the comparative one in which students can write about a common element or technique in a number of poems. The sample essay (pages 914-917) illustrates such an approach to Donne's love poetry.

ADDITIONAL POEMS

Leonard Adame, My Grandmother Would Rock Quietly and Hum, pages 919-920.

The speaker evokes memories of his grandmother, his Hispanic background, and his happy childhood. The grandmother represents a period of peace and joy, calm acceptance, and the speaker's Mexican heritage. Lines 1-45 focus on memory and past; the speaker's childhood is contrasted with the poverty and turmoil of the Grandmother's girlhood in Mexico (lines 34-45). Specific images (braids, papas, cafe) make the speaker's childhood vivid and immediate. In the present (lines 46-56), the grandmother's empty house can still evoke images of Mexico and childhood for the speaker.

A. R. Ammons, Dunes, pages 920-921.

Ammons employs careful observation of a natural landscape to comment on the difficulty and the tenacity of life. The dunes (windy sand, loose world) are a difficult place to live and grow, but they represent the only available ground. Life must generate and endure (something can be started) in this marginal territory because Firm ground is not available ground. These observations about growth and survival are obliquely related to the human condition.

Maya Angelou, My Arkansas, page 921.

Angelou, a black writer known more for her fiction than poetry, explores her own reactions (My Arkansas rather than simply Arkansas) to a state deeply scarred by racial strife. Arkansas' history of violence against blacks affects the speaker's perception of the land and nature. The old crimes that pend from poplar trees imply lynchings; the sullen earth is red with clay and blood. In stanza 2, the speaker's awareness affects her view of sun and shadow. In stanza 3, she suggests that the racial hatreds and attitudes (ante-bellum lace) of the past are still very much alive. Indeed, the past is still very much present for the speaker.

Anonymous, Edward, pages 922-923.

Anonymous, Lord Randal, pages 923-924.

These popular ballads tell of horrendous murders; Edward killed his father and Lord Randal was poisoned by his true love. In both, most of the story is omitted; only the climactic dialogues between mothers and sons are presented. In each case, the mother asks questions and the son answers; this repetitious pattern slows the ballads down and creates progressively more tension. Edward tells various lies (the blood is from his hawk, then his steed) before admitting to patricide. The progress in "Lord Randal" is equally delayed. The repetitious patterns of Edward's and Randal's testaments lead to the assignment of guilt and the climax in each poem. In "Edward," the closing lines indicates that the son murdered his father at the mother's urging. Randal's will places guilt squarely on the young man's true love.

Anonymous, The Three Ravens, pages 924-925.

This gruesome ballad makes a point about loyalty and love. The ravens (carrion eaters, attackers, death) plan to dine on the knight's body. They are opposed by the hounds, hawk, and doe (doe = leman, mistress, wife), which embody loyalty and protection. The doe's love and loyalty are illustrated by the kiss, the burial, and her subsequent death (is the doe a symbol for the knight's beloved or a transformed woman?). The repeated refrain (down a down, etc.) clashes ironically with the verses of the ballad; it slows the ballad, creates tension, and provides continuity.

John Ashbury, Illustration, pages 925-926.

Ashbury presents a specific instance and then offers a generalization about human existence. The illustration (1-22) offers the the self-fulfilling suicide of the novice. She wants monuments that fulfill her own self-image. In part 2, the speaker notes that humans act to resemble a taller impression of themselves. The catch is that no one's actions affect anyone else; the whole process is focused on the individual's consciousness of him or herself. Hence, the novice was only an effigy of indifference and Not meant for us.

W. H. Auden, The Unknown Citizen, pages 926-927.

Auden employs an ironic tone and sociological jargon to satirize the loss of identity and individuality in modern society. The epitaph and the poem are spoken by a representative of the state, who identifies the citizen by number rather than name. The speaker knows the citizen's statistics thoroughly, and he praises the citizen's tendency to conform in all matters. The citizen's work habits, social behavior, consumption, and ideology were all known and normal; he had the right appliances (everything necessary to the Modern Man), opinions, and number of children. In most respects, the citizen is certainly not unknown in the sense of the "unknown soldier." But the state cares nothing about the inner man (Was he free? Was he happy?); in this sense, the citizen is unknown. While the speaker's tone is smug and admiring, the tone of the poem is ironic and contemptuous; the poet deplores the modern impulse toward dehumanization and conformity. Auden also uses the rhyme to create the tone and clinch ideas; note that even the epitaph rhymes.

Margaret Avison, Tennis, page 927.

Avison, a Canadian poet, usually writes in closed forms and metaphysical conceits. This Shakespearean sonnet describes a game of tennis in conceits of music (viol, musicked gravity), writing (foolscaps), dancing (galliards) and geometry (ellipse, liquid Euclids). The tennis jargon employed throughout also suggests other contexts and implications. Compare Heather McHugh's "Language Lesson, 1976" (page 549).

Imamu Amiri Baraka, Ka 'Ba, page 928.

The poem contrasts the beauty of black lives and the glory of black heritage with the enslavement and degradation encountered by blacks in the society of the United States. Blacks defy the chains and limitations of their world (dirty courtyards, physics, "grey chains in a place full of winters") through "the stream of their will." Although they suffer, kill, and fail, their world is vital and lovely. The heritage is one of freedom, sunlight, and Africa. At the close, the speaker wonders what <u>magic spells</u> or <u>sacred words</u> will restore blacks to themselves and their <u>ancient image</u>. Compare this poem to Gwendolyn Brooks's "Primer for Blacks" (page 933), which also deals with the problem of black self-images.

Aphra Behn, Love Armed, pages 928-929.

Behn's lyric personifies love (as Cupid, the god of love) to suggest that the relationship between the speaker and his or her beloved is unequal and agonizing. The poem describes the arming of love with weapons drawn from the speaker and the beloved. The speaker supplies desire, but also all the agony of love: "sighs and tears" and "Languishments and Fears." The beloved supplies all the weapons of scorn: "Pride and Cruelty" and "every killing dart." Between them, the two arm Cupid with all the pleasures and pains of love. In the process and the relationship, however, the speaker suffers while the lover is <u>free</u>. The poem is thus an allegory of unrequited love.

Marvin Bell, Things We Dreamt We Died For, page 929.

Bell uses metaphors for patriotism (<u>Flags of all sorts</u>) and scholarship to imply that the academic opposition to war and the defense of learning is something of a fraud. The <u>causes</u> put away <u>in closets full of bones</u> may imply earlier or youthful periods of radicalism (perhaps the 1930s). These <u>plunderers</u> have gained fame and fortune through such activity. The term <u>dreamt</u> suggests that the whole process has been a sham and an illusion for those <u>saviours</u> of literature and the young.

Earle Birney, Can. Lit., pages 929-930.

The speaker blames Canadian history and habits for the relative dearth of great Canadian Literature. The first stanza establishes a metaphor based on birds that fly away. The vast spaces of Canada and the ongoing <u>civil war</u> between the French and the English have subverted the impulse to develop great national poets such as Emily Dickinson or Walt Whitman (both alluded to in the poem); energy has gone into conflict and control instead of literature.

William Blake, The Sick Rose, page 930.

William Blake, Ah Sun-Flower, page 930.

The <u>Rose</u> (beauty, a girl's name, innocent sexuality) in a <u>bed</u> of <u>crimson joy</u> (brilliant beauty, passionate love) is destroyed by the <u>invisible worm</u>, which may represent time as a destroyer of beauty or repression as the source of internal corruption. The word <u>worm</u> is also linked historically with <u>snake</u> or <u>serpent</u>. Thus good (the Rose) is destroyed by a hidden and secret evil. The sun-flower can be a symbol of youth, innocence, or repressed sexuality. It is weary of tracing out the movement of the sun across the heavens (<u>steps of the sun</u>) and seeks that <u>sweet golden clime</u> where the <u>journey is done</u> (death, peace, freedom). Stanza 2 offers two parallel symbols of repression: the <u>youth</u> who <u>pined away with desire</u> and the <u>pale Virgin</u>. These figures, like the sun-flower, seek to escape repression (of society, morality) and be free.

Robert Bly, Snowfall in the Afternoon, page 931.

Bly uses common, familiar images in unexpected ways to create an external
landscape and an internal mindscape. The snow is dark and heavy; it changes
the earth, but it also changes the speaker's perceptions (e.g., the barn moves
nearer to the house). The concluding metaphor of a ship in a storm suggests a
complete shift in perspective as well as universal blindness.

Louise Bogan, Women, pages 931-932.

The poem explores the idea that women are self-limiting and improvident
through their careful providence. Women withdraw into the tight hot cell of
themselves; they do not experience (see, hear) life fully. They are passive
(wait) and lack flexibility or moderation (stiffen, too tense, or too lax).
Provident decisions thus become unwise and repressive for women.

Arna Bontemps, A Black Man Talks of Reaping, page 932.

This lyric is a truncated sonnet (abab, cdcd, efef); the quatrains
organize the speaker's thoughts and feelings. The poem expresses the sorrow
and bitterness of black existence; the central metaphors are sowing (labor of
any sort) and reaping (wealth, happiness, reward, advancement). The speaker
observes the vast extent of his own sowing (lines 1-6), the meagerness of his
harvest (7-8), and the fact that others harvest the fruits of his labor (9-10)
while his own children (people, blacks) collect the leavings in fields "they
have not sown, and feed on bitter fruit." The poem thus implies that blacks
labor in vain, since they are excluded from reward or advancement of any kind.

Anne Bradstreet, To My Dear and Loving Husband, page 932.

The poem praises the speaker's husband and the happiness of married love
in six rhymed couplets. The speaker notes the closeness, passion, and value
of their love. The poem ends with the hope that salvation will allow husband
and wife to live ever in love. Compare E. B. Browning's "Sonnet 43" (page
934), which also ends on a note of mutual salvation and eternal love.

Robert Bridges, Nightingales, pages 932-933.

Bridges's poem contrasts expectation with reality or the ideal with the
real by evoking and then reversing traditional associations with nightingales.
In lines 1-6 the speaker addresses the nightingales, calling forth traditional
associations of beauty and immortality with the birds' song (compare Keats's
"Ode to a Nightingale," page 761). The nightingales reply in lines 7-18.
Their world is neither beautiful nor ideal, and their song embodies the voice
of desire and a dark nocturnal secret. Their art cannot communicate the
forbidden hopes profound. The nightingales thus live in frustration during
the night and dream during the day, while humans experience beauty (sweet-
springing meads) and regeneration (bursting boughs of May, dawn).

Gwendolyn Brooks, Primer for Blacks, pages 933-934.

205

Brooks is a black poet whose first audiences were mostly white; in 1967 she began directing her work toward black readers. This poem reflects that shift in orientation; it attacks blacks for self-denegration and low self-esteem (<u>self-shriveled</u>), and asserts that blackness is power and glory. The speaker castigates the <u>slack in Black</u> who believe that <u>It's great to be White</u>. The speaker argues that blacks have geographic power, and concludes that all blacks must learn to find value and strength in their blackness.

Elizabeth Barrett Browning, Sonnets from the Portuguese, pages 934-935.

In this Italian sonnet (abba abba cdc ece), the speaker describes the abundance of her love with reference to infinite spaces and abstract ideas (<u>the ends of Being</u>). In the second quatrain, the love is measured against daily necessities (<u>quiet need</u>) and ideals of freedom and purity. In 9-12, the speaker asserts that her entire life expresses her love; she loves with a child's faith and with all her <u>breath</u>. Lines 13-14 suggest that the love will continue after death. Compare this poem to "To My Dear and Loving Husband" (page 932); both end on a note of mutual salvation and eternal love.

Robert Burns, To a Mouse, pages 935-936.

Burns employs a specific incident--the plowing up of a mouse's nest--to consider and compare the conditions of mice and men. The speaker regrets that he has caused the mouse to fear <u>man's dominion</u> and that he has destroyed the mouse's <u>cozie</u> home. These considerations lead the speaker to the basic similarity between mice and humanity; their <u>best-laid schemes</u> often go awry. This similarity, however, is overshadowed by the mouse's advantage of living only in the present. People are cursed with both the ongoing knowledge of their past mistakes and their fears of the future.

Lucille Clifton, My Mama Moved Among the Days, page 936.

The poem comments on black existence and motherhood. The speaker's mother led a dreamlike existence in which she was relatively untouched by the world but could affect everything she touched. She led (raised, nurtured) her children through the <u>high grass</u> (life) and then <u>ran right back in</u>.

Leonard Cohen, Suzanne Takes You Down, pages 936-938.

This lyric, predominantly in iambic tetrameter, is unified by repetition and imagery. The major strands of imagery--water, love, bodies, and regeneration--link Suzanne ("our lady of the harbour") with Jesus as a mystical and exotic force of interaction, regeneration, and salvation.

Stephen Crane, Do Not Weep, Maiden, for War is Kind, page 938.

The poem is a very strong and ironic anti-war statement. Stanzas 1, 3, and 5 focus on the losses and deaths produced through war: a maiden loses her lover (lines 1-5), a baby loses her father (12-16), and a mother loses her son (23-26). There is nothing <u>kind</u> about the losses or war. Stanzas 2 and 4 mock the symbols and passions that drive men to war: booming drums, unexplained glory, the blazing flag of the regiment, the eagle on the flag. Both stanzas close with the same image of the reality of war: "A field where a thousand corpses lie." The realities of carnage and loss are thus contrasted with the illusions of ideals. Compare Owens's "Dulce et Decorum Est" (page 644) and Cummings's "next to of course god america i" (page 940).

Stephen Crane, The Impact of a Dollar Upon the Heart, pages 938-939.

Crane explores the differences between moderate domestic wealth and great masses of wealth that corrupt nations and lead to war and degradation. The speaker contrasts the impact of a dollar with the impact of a million dollars (line 6). In the first case, all the associated images are positive and domestic: smiles, warm, hearth, white table, cool velvet shadows. The million dollars, however, is linked with images of international chaos and war.

Isabella Valency Crawford, The Song of the Arrow, pages 939-940.

Crawford's characteristic vigor and violence both come across in this poem. The speaker in stanzas 1-4 is the arrow; it rejoices in its own vitality, speed, and sharp zest. Its whole world is expressed in images of life and death; even the sky is alive ("blue veins of the throbbing sky"). The arrow's existence is motiveless action; it knows nothing of the will that directs its flight. Stanzas 5-6 offer a symbol of union in the coincidental meeting of arrows from different bows in the breast of the eagle.

Countee Cullen, Yet Do I Marvel, page 940.

Cullen was a black poet very much involved in the Harlem Renaissance. Each of the quatrains in this Shakespearean sonnet takes up a different aspect of the mysteries of God's ways. In the 1st, the speaker questions the necessity of death; good and kind are ironic here, and well-meaning suggests less than ideal results. The allusions to the myths of Tantalus and Sisyphus (lines 5-8) emphasize the futility of existence; these men are unable to achieve what they are fated to perform. The 3rd quatrain explores humanity's inability to understand any of God's purposes. The couplet offers the most mysterious and paradoxical problem--a black poet asked to sing (write poetry) out of the bleak wretchedness of black existence; this is the mystery of God's demands that the speaker finds most remarkable.

E. E. Cummings, next to of course god america i, page 940.

The poem satirizes the cliches and banalities of super-patriotism. The quoted material (lines 1-13) is spoken by an impassioned yet ignorant traditionalist who sees death in war as heroic and admirable (compare Owens's "Dulce et Decorum Est," page 644). His monologue is full of half-digested and fragmented phrases from patriotic songs. The alliteration and repetition (especially in lines 7-8) underscore the foolishness. Line 14, spoken by a detached observer, puts the preceding diatribe into perspective and also indicates that this particular voice of liberty has become ironically mute.

E. E. Cummings, if there are any heavens, page 941.

The open form here makes the poem itself fragile; it keeps breaking up. What is the speaker's attitude toward his mother? She has a heaven "all by herself"; her heaven will will be tough and vivid, not fragile (pansy, lilico-of-the-valley). The poem contradicts itself by placing the father (as a subservient rose) in the mother's heaven. Notice that the word mother is omitted where it would logically occur in lines 7 and 15. The poet-speaker-son is linked with the adorer-rose-father in opposition to the mother.

James Dickey, The Lifeguard, pages 941-942.

In this poem about death and resurrection, the speaker-lifeguard becomes a Christ figure in his own dream vision. Stanza 1 establishes setting and situation. The children (probably at summer camp) are asleep at night; the lifeguard in alone, lying in a boat tied up in a boathouse. In stanza 2, he walks on the water in quest of the miracle of resurrection. Stanzas 3-6 are flashback to an earlier failure at salvation (saving a drowning child that afternoon). Although the children had faith (believed), the speaker failed to save the "one who had sunk from my sight." Stanza 4 is full of images of cold, water, dark, and death, while stanza 5 conveys the speaker's defeat and the children's disappointment. In stanza 6, the speaker hides in the boathouse awaiting night and the moon reflected on the water. Stanzas 7-10 embody the present dream (or reality) of resurrection; the lifeguard walks to the center of the lake to be the "savior of one who has already died in my care." He calls out; the child answers and rises from the depths. The child of water can represent either rebirth (and baptism) or illusion (and death).

H. D. (Hilda Doolittle), Pear Tree, page 943.

The images are all important here; the speaker sees the fertility and beauty of the pear tree in linked central images of silver and strength. In lines 1-7, the tree is imagined as silver dust; the strength is conveyed in verbs (lift, mount, reach, front) and in images of height and mass. The flower and leaf also combine images of silver and strength. The thick flowers will bring summer and ripe fruits in their purple hearts.

Alan Dugan, Love Song: I and Thou, pages 943-944.

The title is an allusion to I and Thou by Martin Buber, a Jewish mystic and philosopher who believed that the suffering inherent in the human condition could be mitigated through the formation of "I-thou" relationships. The speaker's self-made house, shaky by nature, is a symbol of his life of suffering, an ongoing crucifixion. The references to Christ (line 7) and carpenter (8) pull together the house and crucifixion motifs. The dance with a purple thumb (careless hammering), the instant of prime whiskey, and that great moment can all refer to birth or infancy (the completion of the house). The house (life) is a hell of suffering that must be endured until death. The speaker needs help (love, a wife) to endure, even though such help will also augment his suffering (help him complete the crucifixion). The double implication of this wifely help (to suffer and to endure) makes the poem's ending both bitterly ironic and tenderly loving.

Paul Laurence Dunbar, Sympathy, page 944.

This lyric voices the emotions and desires of blacks in general and of a black poet in particular. The caged bird is a symbol for blacks and the black poet; the bird's imprisonment metaphorically captures the essence of black status. Stanza 1 contrasts the bird's cage (imposed limitations) with natural freedom and beauty. Stanza 2 expresses the bird's driving desire to be free. Stanza 3 identifies the bird's song (a traditional symbol for poetry) as a plea for freedom. Compare Cullen's "Yet Do I Marvel" (page 940).

Sir Edward Dyer, My Mind To Me a Kingdom Is, pages 944-945.

This Elizabethan lyric puts forth the ideal of a contented life and mind, based on health and moderation. By describing those human excesses that are lacking from his kingdom, the speaker catalogues the social and spiritual ills that plague humanity, including pomp, wealth, force, deceit, treachery, greed, and envy. For each of these, the speaker substitutes the contentments of "a quiet mind." The poem thus satirizes society and advocates an inwardly focused life of quiet satisfaction. The tone of smug didacticism, however, makes the poetic experience a bit off-setting.

Richard Eberhart, The Groundhog, page 946.

The poem embodies an intellectual and emotional process of discovery and renewal based on four separate observations of the decay of a dead groundhog. The groundhog itself is a symbol of natural process and rebirth (consider Groundhog Day). At the first observation in June (lines 1-25), the speaker is shocked by the ferocious vitality and vigour of nature; he reacts with love and loathing, passion and prayer. In the second stage (Autumn, lines 25-32), the ferocious activity of nature in decay yields a "bony sodden hulk" and the initial emotions modulate to consideration and wisdom. On third viewing (Another Summer, lines 33-40), the vitality of nature and the decay of the groundhog (now only hair and "bones bleaching") is further humanized and intellectualized through images of architecture and geometry. In the final scene (after three years, lines 41-48), the lesson of the groundhog--the ferocious vitality of nature--is applied directly to humanity. The speaker understands and accepts ferocious nature in the human spirit as well as the inevitable cycle of life and death. The three figures cited in lines 46-48 thus represent this vitality, intellect, and cycle from life to death through various endeavors in different historical periods.

T. S. Eliot, The Love Song of J. Alfred Prufrock, pages 947-950.

This poem is difficult but rewarding; it offers a splendid opportunity to examine speaker, setting and situation, imagery, metaphor, allusion, and theme. The dramatic monologue is spoken by Prufrock (the name is both a pun and a parody), a man who feels trapped in the hell of his own inadequate character (hence the epigraph from Dante's Inferno). Prufrock, a cultured man going to an afternoon tea, is consumed with an overwhelming question of whether or not to declare his love to one of the cultured women ("speaking of Michaelangelo") taking toast and tea. This indecision dominates lines 1-83. The you and I in line 1 have been variously identified as Prufrock and a friend, Prufrock and the reader, or Prufrock and himself (perhaps even Prufrock's ego and superego or desires and self-consciousness). The metaphor of evening as an etherized patient (lines 2-3) suggests Prufrock's difficulty

with feelings. This is contrasted throughout the poem with the sexual
vitality of the lower classes (cheap hotels), almost always linked with water
images (oyster shells) that suggest sexual vitality. The impending visit and
the overwhelming question, combined with Prufrock's ongoing impulse to revise,
rethink, and retreat, recur as the central motif of the first section of the
poem in lines 10-14, 25-41, 46-49, and 79-83. These are matched with
Prufrock's constant meditation on his own inadequacy, expressed in baldness,
thinness, and images of him mounted like a dead butterfly (lines 55-61).

Failure, the crisis of the poem, occurs in lines 84-86; Prufrock was
afraid. He rationalizes and justifies his total failure in lines 87-111,
assuming that his approach would have been out of place, badly done,
misunderstood, and rejected; he imagines that the woman would have told him
that "That is not what I meant at all." In the last 20 lines, Prufrock offers
an accurate assessment of his own present and future. The Hamlet metaphor
(lines 111-119) identifies him as an insignificant and foolish character, far
removed from the center of activity. He realizes that life and time have
passed him by. The mermaids (sea imagery, sexuality) represent a fulfillment
that Prufrock will never have ("I do not think that they will sing to me").
Prufrock can experience such vision in his dreams (lines 125-130), but human
voices (life, reality, society) awaken him to failure and inadequacy.

John Engels, Naming the Animals, pages 950-951.

The title is probably an allusion to Adam's "naming the animals" in Eden
(in Genesis). The two deer represent the contrast of life and death, natural
cycles and necessities, in reference to humanity (poet, speaker, Adam). The
deer that the speaker names (counts, describes) embody cycle and opposition
(death and life, eating and dying) more fully than the three mildly alert
does. The contrast is focused and recapitulated in the images of the antlers
"still in velvet" and the "tongue frozen to the rusty hood." Xompare Harper's
"Called" (page 953) and Kinnell's "The Fly" (page 963).

Mari Evans, I Am A Black Woman, pages 951-952.

Evans's open-form poem celebrates the power and renewing strength of the
black woman in the context of centuries of racial hatred, poverty, and war.
The bitterness of life is implied in the image of a song written in a minor
key. The long history of poverty and destruction is evoked by the images of
death and birth (lines 10-12) and the four allusions to lynching and war (13-
20). The last 14 lines express the power and renewing force of the black
woman; key terms are tall, strong, defying, impervious, and indestructible.

Carolyn Forche, The Visitor, page 952.

The poem explores the inhumanity that humans can inflict on each other
through a momentary vision of a prisoner (perhaps in El Salvador). The
"visitor" is either the speaker or the prisoner's dreams of his wife's visits
(or both). The images create a sensual web of lonely isolation, desperation,
futility, and impending death (no time, arching scythes).

Nikki Giovanni, Woman, pages 952-953.

The speaker asserts that men have failed to support the aspirations (needs, dreams, desires) of women, couching the argument in five metaphors: blade, robin, web, book, and bulb. Each metaphor suggests growth, creation, and order; in each, he refused to cooperate in the process of fulfillment. The final stanza suggests that women must seek such fulfillment, definition, and value within themselves, without reference to men.

Frances E. W. Harper, She's Free!, page 953.

The poem tells the story of an escape, and condemns the society that made escape necessary. Lines 1-8 condemn the society based on slavery and racial bigotry, and tell of the woman's escape north (her step on the ice). Stanza 2 follows the same pattern. The poem, in iambic pentameter rhymed couplets, repeats the c and d rhymes in both stanzas.

Michael S. Harper, Called, pages 953-954.

The poem offers a series of images that contrast life and death, heat and coolness, light and dark, movement and stillness. The grave, black dirt, the body, and the image of "the bed" and "earth and rock / which will hold her," the sunset, and the past tense of called all embody half of this contrast. The opposition is established in the heat, the brother, the three questions that end the poem, and the present tense of calls. The act of burial brings the speaker and his companion into direct contact with these two opposed aspects of natural cycle. Compare Engels's "Naming the Animals" (page 950).

Robert Hayden, Those Winter Sundays, page 954.

Hayden writes of the love that is always expressed through mundane acts, and a child's inability to understand or appreciate that love. The speaker recollects his childhood and his father's habitual Sunday morning labors. The poor and hard life is vividly expressed in images like blueblack cold and cracked hands. Life was bitter for both father and son; the father always got up early (even on Sunday) and the son feared the chronic angers of that house. The adult speaker understands, in retrospect, that driving out the cold and polishing my good shoes were acts of love; he calls them "love's austere and lonely offices." But the child never realized this; he spoke indifferently to his father and no one in the family never thanked him.

Robert Herrick, Corrina's Going A-Maying, pages 955-956.

In this carpe diem lyric, Herrick combines religious and nature imagery to suggest that all life passes as if it were a single day and that living must be siezed with energy and reverence. May day becomes a lifetime; Corinna is encouraged to rise and gather the flowers of love and marriage. The speaker-lover wants Corinna to get up; the world outside is young and fresh. Words like matins, hymns, and profanation link nature and love with religion. The speaker (stanza 2) wants Corinna to dress and pray quickly since their rituals of love will provide both sanctity and gems in abundance. In stanza 3, the speaker describes the outside world, fusing nature, religion, and society; "each field turns a street" and "each door" becomes a "tabernacle." He populates this world in stanza 4. Every other boy and girl has already

211

celebrated May Day; many have already returned home, eaten "cakes and cream," "plighted troth," and "chose their priest." Stanza 5 advances the traditional <u>carpe diem</u> argument with Herrick's typically moral focus on marriage. The shortness of life is equated to a single day, and the speaker encourages Corinna to <u>take the harmless folly of the time</u>.

Roberta Hill, Dream of Rebirth, pages 956-957.

Hill, an Oneida Indian, presents a vision of despair and starvation (lines 1-7) based on historical oppression (8-11). This vision is modified by dreams of rebirth and revitalization (lines 12-16).

A. D. Hope, Coup de Grace, page 957.

This amusing revision of the "Little Red Riding Hood" myth is made humorous by its tone (mocking and admiring), meter (a mixture of dactylic and iambic feet), and rhymes (each stanza is abcabc). The characterization of the wolf is traditional until line 9 (<u>seduce and beguile</u>). Here, the poet shifts into a contemporary sexual myth. Red Riding Hood considers the wolf a <u>handsome beast</u>. She is described (in stanzas 2-3) with images and terms that hint at a bit too much innocence and daintiness, with just a touch of sexuality ("Velvet red of the rose"). The hint is expanded in lines 17-24 when Riding Hood devours the wolf to great applause. The revision implies a parallel shift in the relationship between men and women. The title, which loosely translates as "the finishing blow," also suggests an end to traditional myths and modes of male-female interaction.

Gerard Manley Hopkins, The Windhover, pages 957-958.

This song of praise to Christ gains much of its impact from Hopkins's irregular rhythms and vibrant alliteration. The rhymes are also powerful; the scheme is that of an Italian sonnet (abba abba cdc dcd). Lines 1-8 describe the glorious energy and valor of the falcon that the speaker <u>caught</u> sight of <u>this morning</u>. This glory is conveyed in the image of the noble (<u>dauphine</u>) bird <u>riding</u> the wind. The first triplet (lines 9-11) produces the transition from falcon to Christ. The falcon combines beauty, valor, pride, strength, and action, but the glory (<u>fire</u>) of Christ (<u>thee, O my chevalier</u>) is "a billion times" more lovely and dangerous (significant). Christ's glory (lines 12-14) transfigures the earth and makes <u>embers</u> (coals, sparks) <u>gold vermilion</u>. Students may see the falcon as a symbol for Christ; this is a common reading, but the poem finally asserts a contrast rather than a parallel.

Gerard Manley Hopkins, Pied Beauty, page 958.

The lyric praises God by enumerating a marvellous assortment of <u>pied</u> (dappled, multicolored, varied) aspects of creation. The <u>skies</u>, <u>cow</u>, <u>trout</u>, <u>chestnut-falls</u>, <u>finches' wings</u>, and <u>Landscapes</u> are all streaked, spotted, or multicolored. The tools (<u>gear</u>, <u>tackle</u>, <u>trim</u>) of trades are <u>pied</u> in their overwhelming variety. In lines 7-9, the speaker moves to images of variety in movement, behavior, and taste. Lines 10-11 gather all the images to their focus; God <u>fathers-forth</u> all the infinite variety of creation. All this variety praises God, and the speaker encourages us to do likewise.

A. E. Housman, Terence, This Is Stupid Stuff, pages 958-960.

Housman defends serious or depressing poetry by asserting that it is good preparation for the realities of life. In teaching, the poem can be divided into 4 parts. In part 1 (lines 1-14), Terence's friends criticize him for writing unhappy poetry that "gives a chap the belly-ache" and "killed the cow"; they want a tune to dance to (happy poetry). In part 2 (lines 15-42), Terence recommends tunes other than poetry for dancing and ale for those who do not want to think about the world. He adds that beer is only a temporary solution, because one always awakens the next morning in the muck and must begin the game anew. Part 3 (43-58) conveys the core of Terence's argument. Since the world is less good than ill and since trouble's sure, it is wiser to prepare for ill and not for good. This is the useful service that sour poetry provides--preparation for the embittered hour. Part 4 (59-76) repeats the same idea through the parable of Mithridates, a king who sampled poisons (troubles, bitterness) every day until he was immune to them.

Langston Hughes, Negro, pages 960-961.

Hughes looks at the plight of blacks through a series of images that encompass wide expanses of time and space. The identical first and sixth stanzas frame and unify the poem, defining the speaker as a symbol for all blacks and linking him with night and Africa. The repetition of I at the opening of 10 lines maintains this clear focus on speaker and symbol. The speaker identifies himself as a slave, worker, singer, and victim; in each case, the following lines create a historical or geographical context suggesting that the suffering of bondage and enforced labor has continued throughout time (Caesar to Washington, the pyramids to the Woolworth Building) and all over the world (Africa to Georgia, the Congo to Mississippi).

Randall Jarrell, Next Day, pages 961-962.

This dramatic monologue is spoken by a middle-class housewife who hates growing old and despairs over her "commonplace and solitary" life. The immediate setting is the supermarket (a symbol of modern life?); the speaker does her symbolic shopping and reflects on the difference between past and present. The names of the detergents are loaded; cheer, joy, and all (other pleasures) are reduced to packages on shelves. In the past, she was "young and miserable and pretty and poor"; she was "good enough to eat" (a parallel with the groceries) and men's eyes undressed her. Now she is old, ignored (she wants the grocery boy to look at her), and alone (children "away at school, husband away at work). Her life has become sure unvarying days of boredom, isolation, and fear. She hates growing old and the evidence of such aging in her body. In the last two stanzas, a friend's funeral becomes a symbol of the speaker's existence; her life has become a grave. An excellent companion piece to this poem is Jarrell's "The Woman at the Washington Zoo" (page 501). The two female speakers share age, isolation, and desire.

Robinson Jeffers, The Answer, pages 962-963.

This poem, like "The Purse-Seine" (page 802) reflects Jeffers's conviction that humanity is much less than admirable. The question, unstated here, is how to endure the human condition without sinking into confusion and despair. The speaker offers a series of answers, each of which catalogues aspects of human suffering. He suggests that we not be <u>deluded</u> by false dreams of <u>universal justice or happiness</u> and that we look to history for a pattern of survival. He also suggests that we avoid violence, keep our integrity, and <u>not wish for evil</u>. Integrity represents the best solution. This integrity requires putting humanity into the context of the <u>wholeness of life</u> and <u>the divine beauty of the universe</u> (line 9). Only if we <u>love</u> the whole cosmos, including humanity, can we avoid despair.

Galway Kinnell, The Fly, page 963.

Kinnell employs the bee and the fly as contrasting symbols that juxtapose beginnings and endings, life and death, birth and decay. The bee is described (lines 10-17) in terms of beauty, regeneration, and sexuality; she is linked with fulfillment, flowers, and <u>opening</u>. Even here, however, death (<u>stings and dies</u>) is present. The fly (lines 1-9, 18-22) is linked with death and corpses (<u>flesheater</u>, <u>starved for the soul</u>). <u>His burnt singing</u> implies consumption and cremation. The terms <u>goodbye</u> and <u>last</u> (repeated 5 times) emphasize the finality of death. The <u>naked dirty reality</u> of the fly is death, and it is what all come to eventually. Compare "Naming of Animals" (950) and "Called" (954).

Carolyn Kizer, Night Sounds, page 964.

The poem fuses images of the nightscape with the speaker's feelings to portray the loneliness of failed love. The central images are visual and auditory. The moonlight is cold, disturbing, and a <u>map of personal desolation</u>. The night sounds (lines 2-6, <u>voices</u>, <u>weeping</u>, <u>love-cries</u>) stress the speaker's isolation. She alters the <u>history</u> of the relationship (lines 10 -17), seeking comfort in the lover's restlessness and abstraction, but the attempt fails in the memory of joyous sexuality (lines 18-19). The speaker is left with only the night sounds of others, <u>distant voices</u> and <u>a dog's hollow cadence</u>. <u>Distant</u> and <u>hollow</u> convey the present emptiness.

Etheridge Knight, Haiku, pages 964-965.

These haiku from Knight's first book, <u>Poems from Prison</u>, reflect the black poet's experiences when he spent six years in prison for robbery (1960-1966). The sequence begins by presenting 3 images of prison life, and then moves through black existence and nature to poetry. Images are central here; they define the world and evoke overtones. Convicts like lizards, for example, suggests both little movement and wary intelligence. Stanzas 4 and 9 focus on the discipline and the power of art. The <u>blues song</u> and the <u>jazz</u> are both ways for Knight to talk about his own poetry. Indeed, the concluding haiku focuses on Knight's poetic skill; he identifies his craft as <u>jazz</u> and claims that there is nothing <u>square</u> about it.

Maxine Kumin, Woodchucks, pages 965-966.

The speaker of this poem comes to painful realizations about herself (and humanity) while trying to destroy the woodchucks. Her <u>case</u> against them is <u>airtight</u>, like the gas chambers alluded to in the last two lines, and she plans to use a <u>knockout bomb</u>. The gas fails (stanza 2), and the woodchucks

214

continue to devour the garden. The speaker's <u>Darwinian pieties</u> (survival of the fittest) lead her to employ a more immediate form of execution. The poem expresses the beginnings of pity and regret in the image of the <u>littlest woodchuck's face</u> and the body in the <u>everbearing roses</u>. At the same time, the speaker experiences the rise of the <u>murderer inside</u> her and the <u>hawkeye killer</u>. Killing the last woodchuck becomes a contest of extermination, and the last two lines suggest a link between the speaker and the Nazis. The poem finally suggests that all killing is dehumanizing and destructive for both killer and victim. The speaker is horrified and fascinated at the same time; she moves from a state of innocence to one of experience in which she has learned some very unpleasant things about herself. Kumin combines a closed form (abcabc) with run-on lines to create a narrative in which rhyme works almost subconsciously to reinforce meaning.

Philip Larkin, Church Going, pages 966-968.

    The speaker begins by dismissing churches as unimportant and ends with the realization that they will always be meaningful for humanity even if religion and belief disappear. The poem can be taught in 3 sections: visit, meditation, and conclusion. In part 1 (lines 1-18), the speaker visits an empty church and decides <u>it was not worth stopping for</u> (line 18). The diction (<u>thud</u>, <u>stuff</u>, <u>holy end</u>, <u>snigger</u>) and imagery (<u>brownish flowers</u>) produce an irreverent and flippant tone. In part 2 (19-54), the speaker meditates on the future of churches. He imagines them as museums, unlucky places (stanza 3), centers of witchcraft, and empty buildings (stanza 4). He also considers what will draw the last visitor to a church (stanzas 5-6): architecture, nostalga, archeology, or <u>uninformed</u> interest in the silent aura. The countermovement of thought begins here, as the speaker realizes that "power . . . will go on" and that the church provides a special kind of silence. In the last section (55-63), the speaker concludes that churches will always be valuable as places that ritualize and codify human <u>compulsions</u>. The iambic pentameter and loose rhyme scheme add a sense of control.

Irving Layton, Rhine Boat Trip, page 968.

    Layton draws together two strands of imagery related to German history and myth to suggest that modern atrocities of death have blotted out all that went before. Each image of the mythic past (<u>castles</u>, <u>grapes</u>, <u>Lorelei</u>, sweet singing) is cancelled and displaced by an image of carnage and death (<u>ghosts</u>, <u>blinded eyes</u>, <u>crimson beards of murdered rabbis</u>, <u>wailing of cattle-cars</u>).

Don L. Lee, Change is Not Always Progress, pages 968-969.

    The poem announces its theme in the title and makes the point again in the text. The speaker associates <u>faces</u>, <u>circles</u>, and <u>bodies</u> with harmony, nature, and Africa; he associates <u>squares</u>, <u>concrete</u>, and arrogance with westernized (white) attitudes and architecture.

Philip Levine, They Feed They Lion, pages 969-970.

    Draw the student's attention to the way alliteration, repetition, and imagery build a portrait of growing rage and reaction to poverty and repression. The word <u>lion</u> is worth investigation; it works as a noun, a verb, and an image of ferocious rebellion. The massive amount of repetition in the poem creates a sense of prayer, chant, or incantation.

Richard Lovelace, To Lucasta, Going to the Wars, page 970.

This lyric explores an apparent conflict between love and honor, and asserts that love cannot exist without honor. Although the tone is light and witty (created through rhyme, meter, and diction), the poem is serious. The speaker is leaving Lucasta because his honor demands that he go off to war (serve country or king). Lucasta is <u>chaste</u> and <u>quiet</u>; war is personified as a "new mistress" with greater vitality, and the speaker humorously calls his departure an instance of <u>inconstancy</u>. Finally, the speaker asserts that his love for Lucasta is based on a greater love of honor, a driving force in life.

Amy Lowell, Patterns, pages 970-972.

Lowell's anti-war poem protests against rigid <u>patterns</u> of thinking and behavior that constrict life and lead to war. The speaker, an aristocratic woman walking in her garden and mourning the death of her fiance in battle, grounds her protest in images that evoke four distinct patterns: formal gardens, stiff clothing, social and sexual decorum, and warfare. Stanzas 1 and 2 combine the patterns of garden and clothing; the speaker's <u>whalebone and brocade</u> make her <u>a rare pattern</u> like the formal garden. Her <u>passion</u> fights against both patterns. Stanzas 3-4 add the pattern of social and sexual restraint. Again the speaker notes that her <u>stiffened gown</u> conflicts with the <u>softness of a woman</u>. The stanzas present an erotic dream (and an escape from patterns) in which the speaker discards her rigid dress, bathes in a fountain, and is discovered and embraced by her lover. The dream conflicts with the reality of patterns (dress, behavior). Stanzas 5-6 introduce two further aspects of pattern--war and the proper behavior for grief. The news of her lover's death <u>squirmed like snakes</u>, but the speaker stiffly <u>stood upright</u> and returned <u>no answer</u>; her desire to mourn is held in check by patterns of social restraint. Here, patterns of dress, behavior, and the garden fuse into a single repressive system. In stanza 7, the speaker has a vision of what might have been--an escape from patterns through marriage. This is cancelled in stanza 8, which reveals the speaker's future. She is condemned to rigid and unchanging patterns of dress, behavior, chastity, and loneliness. In the last lines the speaker breaks decorum--the pattern of appropriate language--and rages against all these patterns (especially war).

Robert Lowell, For the Union Dead, pages 973-974.

Lowell condemns the lack of public service and human values in the present by contrasting it with aspects of the past that symbolize service and honor. The past of heroic service and honor is symbolized first by the deserted aquarium. This contrasts with the present of <u>dinosaur steamshovels</u> and <u>parking spaces</u> (stanzas 1-5). The central symbol of service, values, and self-sacrifice is Colonel Shaw and his black infantry (stanzas 9-13). These figures (in history and bronze) are linked with <u>old white churches</u> and other <u>stone statues</u> to embody the values of the past. These are contrasted with the <u>savage servility</u> of the modern world: nuclear war, advertising, racial strife, and the parking garage that has displaced the aquarium.

Ben Luna, In Days of Wine, page 975.

The poem explores racism from a Hispanic perspective and suggests that it is universal. Lines 1-5 deal with the emptiness of violence, mindless patriotism, and broken promises (for progress, equality). In this place (perhaps Mexico, perhaps the United States), there is no voice of reason: <u>no one to speak above the screaming of idiots waving their country's flag</u>. Lines 6-10 address the problem of racism directed against Hispanics, while lines 11-13 turn the problem around and look at Hispanic racism against others. Generally, the speaker condemns American society because it gives rise to such racism. Although clearly written in an open form, the function or effect of the linear arrangement of the text is not readily clear.

Cynthia MacDonald, The Lobster, pages 975-976.

The poem begins as a detailed study of an object (the lobster), but evolves into an exploration of love; the lobster becomes a symbol of the dying and then renewed relationship between the speaker and her lover. The lobster initially suggests decay and corruption; the images are strongly visual. In stanza 2, the lobster's corruption pervades the speaker's life (<u>bureau drawer</u>, <u>private places</u>) and the imagery focuses on the smell of decay. In the 3rd stanza the relationship revives; the lobster becomes healthy and whole (<u>smooth and green</u>). Finally, the lobster becomes a feast for the lovers; the imagery here is both culinary and sexual. The complete repast--eating the lobster--is also sexual and emotional rapprochement.

Claude McKay, The White City, page 976.

This sonnet utilizes elements of the Petrarchan sonnet in its paradoxes, irony, and capitalized personification. McKay uses this tradition to express his simultaneous acknowledgement of the material grandeur and appeal of white society, and of the rage and resentment it can elicit from a black who both is and is not part of it. The speaker is obviously highly educated in the traditions of white European culture. But he does not belong, and uses one of that culture's most complex literary achievements to declare both his mastery and his rejection of the white world and the city which is its symbol.

Josephine Miles, Belief, pages 976-977.

This poem is an ironic and semi-humorous commentary both on the inexplicable causes of good and evil (or success and failure), and on the tendency of mothers to feel responsible for their children, and also, perhaps, for the condition of humanity. Thus, while aware that <u>Causation is sequence</u> (a logical statement mocked by the more mundane observation offered almost in opposition that <u>everything is one thing after another</u>), the speaker also observes that much of life is a matter of chance. Knowing the mother, the adult children keep bad news from her in her illness. That she should have felt fortunate is a touching surprise in the poem, and a compliment to her children that is rendered all the more ironic (and perhaps tragic) by the fate of the son who was arrested. The poem's title thus covers the apparent philosophy by which the mother lived (chance), her real beliefs (<u>noblesse oblige</u>) and the actuality (that the children, because of love, allowed her to die in ignorance of reality).

Edna St. Vincent Millay, What Lips My Lips Have Kissed, page 977.

This sonnet explores the traditional subject matter of love, but there are several surprises. The speaker is female; the love is remembered, not actual, and thus the tone is nostalgic. Finally, the female speaker is reflecting upon a series of past lovers--so many that she has forgotten them as individuals. Such a confession has traditionally been unusual for a woman, since it opens her to charges of promiscuity. The speaker keeps that judgment in abeyance, however, by turning the subject, in the sestet, to her present state. Now, she asserts, she is old and alone, and her summer has gone.

Vassar Miller, Loneliness, page 977.

The structure of the poem is unusual: six-line stanzas held together by rhythm and verbal repetitions rather than rhyme. The subject matter is a decription of an apparently self-imposed discipline of silence and meditation. But the speaker, aware of the dangers of deliberate alienation from human contact, cries out to God for help. The danger is that the speaker will become so satisfied with this state of sensory deprivation that he or she may be unable or unwilling to return to life. Thus loneliness, to many a dreadful state, is here asserted to be satisfying and alluring. By crying out to God for rescue, however, the speaker shows that he or she is not totally alone.

John Milton, How Soon Hath Time, page 978.

This sonnet expresses the speaker's impatience with his life. At the age of twenty-three, he believes that he should have achieved more, and that time is passing while he produces no bud or blossom (i.e., not even the beginnings of any great accomplishment). Whereas in the octave the speaker lays out his impatience and disappointment, in the sestet he consoles himself with the awareness that God governs all, and that the will of Heaven is involved in his career. His own role, however, is not to be passive, for the Taskmaster (God) has a plan for him which he must fulfill. The final tone is one of hopeful acceptance, based on the speaker's confident religious faith.

John Milton, O Nightingale! page 978.

In this love sonnet, addressed to the nightingale, the speaker asks for success in love. For years the bird (the traditional aid to lovers) has failed to assist him for no reason that he can tell (line 12). Now he asks, on the condition that Jove's will is linked to the bird's song (lines 7-8), that the nightingale aid him because he, as a poet, serves both poetry and love. The poem is noteworthy, partly because it gives a seldom seen aspect of Milton's work, and partly because of the sense it gives of humankind as part of the created world, living with and subject to the powers of Nature, shown as birds, flowers, woods and groves, and even the seasons in their passing.

Ogden Nash, The Camel, page 978.

Ogden Nash, The Lama, page 979.

Both poems aim primarily at amusement. "The Camel" demonstrates how, out of prose, the rhythms and rhymes of poetry may spring. In terms of content, it reminds us of the inexactness of our knowledge about the animal world. In

"The Lama," we see Nash's joy in sound and cleverness in playing with spelling
and rhythm. But his delightful eight lines also tell us how powerful single
letters are, containing as they do the capacity to change meanings totally.

Thomas Nashe, A Litany in Time of Plague, pages 979-980.

The effect of this poem's tight structure--seven line stanzas with lines
6 and 7 being repeated in each stanza--is to emphasize the form of the poem as
a litany, and to stress the repeated appeal to God. The words Lord, have
mercy on us are basic to Christian services, in Greek (Kyrie Eleison) or English. Thus the formal seriousness of the poem assumes prominence over the
relatively traditional recitation about the evanescence of all things human
(wealth, beauty, power, strength). With the switch at line 5 of each stanza
from general to personal (I am sick, I must die) the speaker emphasizes the
force of religious belief; in the final stanza he or she deplores the
unreality of worldly life and looks forward to the promise of eternal life.

Howard Nemerov, The Goose Fish, pages 980-981.

This poem shifts mood and tone, as the same object changes in value and
meaning in the eyes of the lovers. With the discovery of the dead fish, the
lovers reassess their passion even though, just before, their love has made
the world their own (line 27). The bizarre grin on the fish calls into
question the lovers' conclusion that the dead creature is a rigid optimist
(line 36). As they wonder, the moon, originally seeming so hospitable to
their lovemaking, becomes a distant, disappearing part of a celestial system
that exists with its own interrelationships. This ironic cosmic setting makes
plain that little can be understood about a universe in which passion and
death may be found in the same space at almost the same time.

Frank O'Hara, Poem, page 981.

"Poem" is built on a bizarre reversal of expectations and their tragic
and ironic outcome. There seem to be two time schemes in simultaneous
operation: the speaker's receipt of the eager and apparently happy note,
prompting him to pack quickly and head straight for the door, is played
against the mystery of the statement "It was autumn / by the time I got around
the corner" (lines 5-6) and the concluding statement that the invitation had
been issued several months ago (line 16, what does this say about the subjec-
tivity of time?). The speaker's understated words--I did appreciate it (i.e.,
the death)--and his effort to pretend that the death is part of a host's
careful preparation for a guest, all suggest a considerable depth of emotion
beneath this deliberately commonplace description of a macabre experience.

Americo Paredes, Guitarreros, page 982.

The scene could well be the American southwest, where two guitarists,
"One leaning on the trunk, one facing" (line 8), are engaged in a duelling
duet. (Students who have seen the film "Deliverance" may remember the scene
of the duelling banjos.) The poem describes the images the music evokes,
images of stallions and a bull from the mountains, images created and
recreated by the music, which seems to be Thrown, not sung (line 14). The old

man's response, "It was so . . . / In the old days it was so" (lines 18-19)
complements a condition of life not of beauty or lyricism but rather of labor
and struggle, and yet a life valued because it has been fully lived.

Dorothy Parker, Resume, page 982.

This ironic and funny poem is based on the startling idea that one <u>might</u>
<u>as well live</u> simply because all the ways of committing suicide are either
uncomfortable or unreliable. Virtually each statement is inaccurate in some
way: for example, razors don't just <u>pain you</u>, and rivers are far deeper and
wetter than <u>damp</u>. The speaker's tone of sophisticated ennui suggests that one
lives because doing otherwise is just too much trouble. The title "Resume"
(suggesting both a summary and also the vita that one presents as part of a
job application) is an understated, whimsical, offhand defense of life, with
the implication that there are many strong reasons for living--including
enjoying the laughter from a poem like this one.

Katherine Philips, To My Excellent Lucasia, on Our Friendship, page 982.

The poem is a serious tribute to the power of deep friendship to create
in two separate individuals a sense of oneness. Women have traditionally been
freer than men to have and express close friendships. Thus, <u>Orinda</u>, the
speaker, is free to compare her sense of expanded and vibrant life to that of
a <u>bridegroom</u> or a <u>crown-conqueror</u>, and, more over, to assert that her love
gives an even greater experience of joy.

Marge Piercy, The Secretary Chant, pages 983-984.

The subject of this poem is the dehumanization of women secretaries,
since this is <u>the</u>, not <u>a</u> secretary's chant. The first person speaker (all
secretaries) describes how her character is submerged by the functions and
sounds of her work, for in the business world she is considered to be little
better than the machines she uses. The parts of her body described and many
of the activities in which she engages are quintessentially female (such as
hips, breasts, navel, delivery of a baby), but here they perform mechanical
rather than human functions. The tone conveys a sense of rage rather than
resignation. The striking alliteration at the close (and the bizarre spelling
of <u>wonce</u>) hammers home the idea of dehumanization.

Sylvia Plath, Last Words, page 984.

The poem juxtaposes images drawn from ancient Egyptian practices of
mummification and from a housewife's daily life in the kitchen. The speaker
sees herself losing life slowly, to the point where a mirror held against her
lips (to mist over with breath) will soon show nothing. Yet oddly enough, the
speaker demonstrates a macabre rejoicing in the household things which are
part of her burial, because they are lustrous and <u>warmed by much handling</u>
(line 18), and can therefore become a comfort in the grave. Indeed, line 23
describes an almost ecstatic joy at the virtual loss of personality (<u>I shall</u>
<u>hardly know myself</u>) in the dark sarcophagus. It is as though, finding
motherhood and housekeeping to be destructive, this speaker has determined to
love the things killing her rather than to escape from them.

Sylvia Plath, Mirror, pages 984-985.

The personified mirror speaks of its life, in which it reflects and has come to love the wall opposite itself. Yet it also reflects the woman who sees herself aging daily, changing from a young girl into an old woman resembling a terrible fish (lines 17, 18). The fish is clearly a symbol of a horrible and inevitable transformation from loveliness to ugliness. The truthful mirror (line 4) reminds its owner that her days are running out, and that once her beauty is gone she will be considered something less than human.

Ezra Pound, The River-Merchant's Wife: A Letter, pages 985-986.

The poem tenderly reflects a happy marriage, albeit one very different from modern assumptions about marriages of choice. The speaker is the young wife, who may well be subservient by our standards (see her reference to her husband as My Lord you [line 7]). Clearly, however, their love is mutually deep and fulfilling. The details of Chinese village life in the eighth century (suggested by the children's occupations, the monkeys overhead, and the young wife's description of her decorous bashfulness) are vivid and compelling. The speaker's unexpected declaration of transcendent love (lines 12-13), her sorrow at their separation (line 18), and her eagerness to rejoin her young husband (lines 26-29) are affectingly rendered, and in this way the poem transforms an alien time and place through the deeply moving recognition of commonly shared experiences.

E.J. Pratt, The Shark, page 986.

The poem is descriptive, sketching the unexpected appearance of a shark in the harbor and its equally unexpected departure. Everything about the shark is ominous, but it is fully in control and completely without fear, and it is the strangeness and alien quality of this life, so different from and so potentially menacing to human beings, that the poem captures.

Thomas Rabbit, Gargoyle, page 987.

The poem uses the gargoyle as a symbol of the human need for reminders of ugliness as well as beauty. The speaker suggests that human beings have enough lovely things--lovers, cherry blossoms, singing birds. What they need in addition is something so incapable of joy or comprehension that it acts almost as a barrier against evil, a focus for malign powers. Thus, though the lovers do not notice this ugly creation perched above the river, its stony presence is nevertheless protective and therefore essential to life.

John Crowe Ransom, Bells for John Whiteside's Daughter, page 987.

This poem avoids sentimentality, despite its painful subject matter, by describing the child's death as a brown study (line 3), as though she could awaken from a meditative moment, shake it off, and return to her usual rushing life. Similarly, the grief of those who knew her is not tears but astonishment or vexation (line 19). The contrast between the child alive and dead, now lying so primly propped (line 20) is sharply drawn, since her life is described in the past images of sound and joy, color, and motion. The

221

speaker's tribute about her, that the geese themselves cried in goose, Alas line 12), is expressive of the poem's mixture of fond memory and deep sorrow.

Adrienne Rich, Diving into the Wreck, pages 988-990.

The master metaphor of this poem (deep sea diving) describes and defines the search of modern women through the symbolic history and myths of patriarchal culture (the wreck, short for record) to recover their own identity. That reality is buried beneath the accretions of story (the book of myths [line 92]) written by others whose point of view excluded female experience. The way down into this wreck (the ladder) is always there; the material is always available to women who know what it is for. To achieve freedom and knowledge, the poem implies, women must take direct possession of their own experience (that is, dive into the wreck), not as that experience is mediated through males, but through themselves. The symbolic equipment needed by women diving into the wreck of history includes a knife to cut away appearance from reality (line 3); a camera, to record that reality (line 2); and diving equipment, to keep them alive during the dangerous search and discovery (line 5).

Edward Arlington Robinson, Mr. Flood's Party, pages 990-991.

The poem captures the pathos of someone so alone that he can have a party only by talking to himself while drunk. There is charm in Flood's courteous dialogues with himself, sadness in the almost maternal care he takes of his jug, and comedy in the fact that by the poem's end he is so drunk that he sees two moons above him. The poem reminds us that many persons drink to escape the loss of status and friends, and that disappointment and an empty future are sufficient cause for Flood's actions.

Theodore Roethke, I Knew a Woman, pages 991-992.

The poem recounts the memories of love, in which the male, the speaker, has been student, and the female has been teacher. (It is not clear whether the relationship is continuing or whether it has ended for some undisclosed reason.) Through imagery and metaphor, the speaker describes fully the deep satisfaction and happiness that the passion of the experience has given, and then, in the final stanza, suggests that his love has transcended both the physical and the temporal. The full and joyous physicality of the relationship is underlined by all the references to parts of the body.

Theodore Roethke, The Waking, page 992.

The immensely demanding villanelle form used here (based on terza rima and lines repeated in a required sequence in whole or in part) creates a complex and incantative concentration of rhyme and verbal repetition. The poem deals with the closeness of death (sleep), and the truth that life (wakefulness) leads us inevitably toward death. Thus, wisdom suggests that we take that waking slow, savoring life while we have it. Here the carpe diem theme of the poem comes through fully, but it is clear that the speaker is not just writing a poem of seduction, but is fully aware that all things are subject to what falls away.

Dante Gabriel Rossetti, The Blessed Damozel, pages 993-996.

The influence of Rossetti's involvement in the Pre-Raphaelite Brotherhood may be seen in the pictorial quality of this poem: its description of the damsel could be considered as instructions for a painter. The influence may be seen also in the semi-medieval quality of words like <u>Herseemed</u> (line 13) and <u>ungirt</u> (line 7), not to mention <u>damozel</u> itself, and in the self-conscious Catholicism of the emphasis on Mary. Like a ballad, the poem tells a story about separated and pining lovers. Here the power of human love is demonstrated both in the earthly lover's fidelity and the obvious preference of the damsel for that love even over the joys of heaven. The speaker is the damozel in heaven (the <u>gold bar</u> suggests a kind of gloroius imprisonment). Time is treated in an interesting fashion: the speaker feels that she has been dead <u>scarce a day</u> (line 13); she has actually been dead <u>ten years</u> (18), and her lover feels as though it has been <u>ten years of years</u> (19). In the course of the poem, the damozel watches lovers, <u>newly met</u> in heaven (37) become reacquainted. Beginning at line 67, she imagines what it will be like when her lover arrives in heaven and they are reunited. Note that all lines in parentheses reflect the words or thoughts of this earthly lover.

Luis Omar Salinas, In a Farmhouse, page 996.

The speaker is an eight-year old migrant worker child, forced like so many to work in the fields with all other members of the family so that they can earn enough to live through the year. The ironic musing of stanza 2 points out the disparity between Christian promise of happiness in a life to come and the reality of the child's earthly life. The irony is signaled by words that are oddly incompatible with the expected vocabulary of the speaker: "profoundly, / animated by the day's work / in the cottonfields" (lines 5-8). The poem thus questions the moral basis of our national economic well-being, and our society's professed concern for children.

Sonia Sanchez, right on; white america, page 997.

The striking thing about this poem initially is its disjointed presentation on the printed page, a graphic reminder that the world is disordered, a threat to stability and harmony. The speaker refers to two significant moments in American history: Custer's last stand, and the daily shootouts which popular history tells us were real parts of our past. Although native Americans lost most of their land and their culture, they literally blew "custer's mind / with a different / image of america" (lines 8-10), a point made with savage humor. The prophetic assertion is that the past persecution of minorities has not stopped, but is an ongoing condition in white America.

Carl Sandburg, Chicago, pages 997-998.

The speaker's recitation of the attributes of this raucous city, repeated with pride in the last section, gives the poem a far tighter organization than one may recognize on first examination. The images are pictorial, a series of action vignettes out of which the young, strong, vitally male city emerges with brashness. The speaker's descriptions of the city in its vital processes of <u>Building</u>, <u>breaking</u>, <u>rebuilding</u>, parallel the attributes for which poets have praised the earth: fecundity and the capacity to live and grow.

Siegfried Sassoon, Dreamers, page 998.

That the poem is a sonnet reminds us of the customary amorous and/or meditative content of that form, here used ironically to contrast the ugliness, pain, and suffering of the soldier and the ordinary pleasures of civilized life. Sassoon based the poem on his own experiences in the trenches during World War I. Even the daily grind of going to the office in the train (line 14) is part of the hopeless longing (line 12) of these citizens of death's grey land (line 1). The first World War is far different from what world wars would be like today, but the suffering and waste are unchanged.

Delmore Schwartz, The Heavy Bear Who Goes With Me, page 999.

The bear symbolizes not only the animal or sexual, and therefore mortal aspect of human nature, but also the infantile and the inarticulate. In this framework, the speaker berates his own physical and spiritual inadequacies, which he perceives to be gross and unattractive, bearlike. It is interesting to reflect on the nature of the speaker's very dear (line 28); she, clearly, is seen to be without a bear of her own. In that sense she is pedestalized, and and as such she is a figment of the speaker's imagination, not to be permitted her own humanity with all its contradictory complexity.

Alan Seeger, I Have a Rendezvous with Death, pages 999-1000.

The poem turns on the double paradox of (a) springtime as a time of death, not life and growth, and (b) the speaker's acceptance of this fact as a rendezvous (i.e., a destined love meeting) to which he has given his pledged word (line 23). It is the ironic situation, in which soldiers are nothing but helpless pawns, that creates the argument of the poem. Implicitly, Seeger deplores the institution of warfare in light of the earth's cyclic fecundity and the attractions of human love.

Anne Sexton, Three Green Windows, pages 1000-1001.

The windows are metaphorically green because they look out onto the leafy trees, blocking out all other vistas. Looking at them, the speaker is stirred by childhood memories and present fantasies. In this half-humorous and sensuous moment, she muses about losing all physical and social concerns, and she regresses to restful comfort amid images of natural beauty.

William Shakespeare, Fear No More the Heat o' the Sun, pages 1001-1002.

This song blends two themes: the first is that death is the great leveler, the end to which all persons, however powerful or powerless, must come. The second is that death is a restful and safe haven, where one is free from injustice, discomfort (like the sun's heat), slander, and censure. The first stanza enumerates natural adversity (heat o' the sun, winter's rages). There is, of course, a striking pun in the use of chimney-sweepers and dust; the dust is (a) the soot that clogs chimneys and (b) the body returned to earth. Stanza 2 enumerates social ills, and stanza 3 combines both types. Stanza 4 offers a blessing, a kind of magic spell over the grave, to keep it safe from predators or spirits, so that the lost one may rest in peace.

William Shakespeare, Sonnet 146: Poor Soul . . . Sinful Earth, page 1002.

This sonnet attempts to put into perspective the things that are valuable and important in life. The speaker laments the over-attention that he or she has paid to physical needs, the metaphorical outward walls (line 4) of the fading mansion (line 6) of the body, which, we are reminded, is made up of nothing more than sinful earth (line 1). Concluding that the metaphorical lease on life is short (line 5), and that flesh will decay, the speaker exhorts his or her soul to concentrate on things divine, to cultivate the spiritual rather than the physical, so that eternal life will overcome death.

Karl Shapiro, Auto Wreck, pages 1002-1003.

This poem could not have been written except in our age of cars. As witness to a terrible automobile accident, the speaker confronts the horror of accidental mutilation and death, pointing out that, while many deaths are explicable or at least understandable, the carnage of collision is especially terrible because it is also especially illogical. The vivid decription, and the uses of color, sound, light, and darkness, all contribute to the poem's impact. The survivors, in a state of shock (line 14), confront unanswerable questions which in their mystery can only be dealt with by the occult mind (line 36), for accidental death makes logic and reason inappropriate.

Sir Philip Sidney, Astrophel and Stella, Number 71, page 1003.

In this sonnet series, Astrophel means star lover and Stella means star. The speaker, after paying his lady a series of compliments (such as that she is is all goodness, all virtue, the possessor of an inward sun, and so on), ends with a sudden and dramatic shift of tone and meaning. Despite the catalogue of spiritual virtues, we find that his desire breaks into his thought, demanding to be fed. Thus the poem demonstrates that spiritual love is not enough, for the body has needs too.

Jon Silkin, Worm, page 1004.

Concentrating on a lowly and unattractive subject, the speaker describes in lines more like prose than poetry the life of a worm. Unlike human beings, told to be self-centered (line 1), this little fellow makes the rich soil needed for human food, and yet to most of us it is at best insignificant, at worst, repulsive. The unspoken disparity between these responses and the reality of the worm (useful, virtuous [lines 15, 20]) lead us to reassess our easy assumptions about what makes the world a viable pace for human beings.

Leslie Marmon Silko, Where Mountain Lion Lay Down with Deer, pages 1004-1005.

The poem (based on native American Indian myth) is cast visually in the form of a physical journey (see pages 753-755) up a mountain to a high point, which is paralleled by a journey through time, back almost into a racial memory to the beginning of time. In a sense the speaker (if he or she is meant to be a literal person) is telling a Creation myth and at the same time lamenting the changes that have occurred in recent history. The tragedy is that past people, tribes, cultures, ways of life, are now forgotten, along with the <u>old</u> <u>songs</u> that told the stories (line 17); by implication, no one now cares, except those who are affected by the poem.

Charles Simic, Fork, page 1005.

In this poem, the speaker imagines being so alienated from one's own body and from the ordinary actions of life involved in eating, that he or she sees a fork as a bird claw and the hand holding the fork as the head of a predatory bird. The action by which we remain alive thus seems to be nothing more than an act of mindless appetite. The poem's images are dramatic and shocking.

Louis Simpson, The Pawnshop, page 1005.

The universe itself here is compared to a pawnshop, the individuals in it to items placed in pawn. At first the pawnshop, and by analogy the universe, appears meaningless (line 2), but the speaker insists, perhaps with some irony, that there is in fact <u>a</u> <u>reason</u> <u>for</u> <u>everything</u> (line 5). Three kinds of human vocations—artistic, religious, commercial—are like pawnshop items; that is, they are arranged like desirable forms or patterns so that someone will select them (or be born into them) as a way of life.

Dave Smith, Bluejays, page 1006.

The situation is the interplay between a girl and a flock of bluejays. These birds are notoriously noisy and raucous, and they respond only with more noise to the girl's efforts to get them to come down from the trees. But they do not fly away, and thus the speaker compares them to boys, afraid of beauty but fascinated by it. In that sense the poem is a paradigm of a pre-adult sexuality, in which the female attracts males, and they hover about her, unable to leave but unable quite to approach her except in groups and even then at a distance.

Stevie Smith, Not Waving But Drowning, page 1006.

Stevie (Florence Margaret) Smith was born in Hull and spent most of her life in London; she wrote poetry and novels. This poem uses the image of a drowning man waving frantically to those ashore, who mistake his gestures for greetings. The symbolic parallel is the frequency of human misunderstandings in communication, sometimes with tragic results. The situation becomes poignantly moving when we realize that this failure to be understood has been typical of the dying man's entire life.

W.D. Snodgrass, Lobsters in the Window, pages 1006-1007.

The speaker describes the present-tense action of a lobster, lying with a heap of others on a bed of crushed ice, momentarily lifting his <u>one</u> <u>great</u> <u>claw</u> (line 6) <u>over</u> <u>his</u> <u>head</u>. The poem thus conveys the rarity of individuality, for mostly life seems <u>ice</u> <u>slow</u>. Most people, with their emotions and actions frozen, accept things without protest. The moments of individuality pass, like the lobster falling back into the <u>mass</u> in the <u>common</u> <u>trench</u>, and the mass thus continues in its unexceptional, unhearing, and unaware condition.

Cathy Song, Lost Sister, pages 1007–1009.

The poem details the repressed and restrained life of a Chinese woman, with her feet traditionally bound (line 16), and contrasts her life with the physically freer life of a woman who emigrated to the United States. But the speaker finds a good deal to admire in those women who remained in China (line 22). By contrast, the expatriate finds the loneliness of unfamiliar and threatening surroundings. None of the women leaves any <u>footprints</u> (line 61), i.e., no special marks of identity, whether in the homeland or in the new land, but the traditional woman at least has the identity of being part of a long line of women upheld by well-understood and honored traditions.

Anne Spencer, At the Carnival, pages 1009–1010.

Abne Spencer, a black woman born in West Virginia, wrote very little poetry. The scene imagined here is a carnival, a symbolic world in little, complete with olfactory and visual images like cooking sausages, a honky-tonk dancer, and game booths. For the speaker, the girl of the diving tank seems <u>pure and free</u> (line 32), clean and brave, a <u>Naiad of the Carnival-Tank</u> (line 46), although this girl's special qualities are not demonstrated by any actions in the poem. Thinking that the future may destroy the girl's special qualities, he or she asks <u>Neptune to claim his child to-day</u> (line 50); that is, to let her die rather than face the inevitable sullying which life brings. For comparison, see A.E. Housman's "To an Athlete Dying Young" (page 727).

Edmund Spenser, Of This World's Theater in Which We Stay, pages 1010–1011.

This sonnet is in the tradition of the lover's complaint. The speaker laments his being able to do nothing to induce his beloved to respond to him with kindness, and he concludes that her insensitivity and unkindness to him renders her something less than human (line 14). The tone is both angry and frustrated. The master metaphor is the theater of the world (the <u>theatrum mundi</u>, a common medieval and Renaissance topos; recall Jaques's assertion in <u>As You Like It</u> that "all the world's a stage"). In this extended conceit, the lover-speaker becomes the actor playing comic and tragic roles in a fruitless attempt to interest or attract the lady. The lady is metaphorically cast in the role of the spectator. She either reacts perversely (criticising his <u>comedy</u> and laughing at his <u>tragedy</u>) or fails to react at all (<u>hardens evermore her heart</u>) to these <u>pageants</u>.

William Stafford, Traveling Through the Dark, page 1011.

The subject of this poem is derived from the killing of wildlife on our highways. A pregnant doe has been killed, and the speaker, coming upon it in the dark, describes his thoughts about saving the living but unborn fawn. The pathos is intensified by the fawn's being pictured as <u>alive, still</u> (unmoving and always), <u>never to be born</u> (line 11). As the speaker decides what to do, it is as if the whole landscape listens. But his decision is virtually fixed by his participation in mechanized society; the lights of his car are focused forward, and he examines the doe <u>by the glow of the tail light</u> (line 5), as if Nature is being lost and forgotten. At the close of the poem, the death of the deer and the <u>swerving</u> (in driving and in thinking) bring the speaker to a momentary consideration of his (and our) mortality.

Gerald Stern, Burying an Animal on the Way to New York, page 1011.

This makes a nice companion piece to Stafford's poem. In both, the
subject is the killing of animals on highways. Here the speaker addresses a
generalized listener-driver who feels regret at the sight of a dead animal
being powdered and vaporized by the many passing cars. The speaker suggests
that the cars passing over the body, and carrying traces of it along the
highway, are in fact burying it. Consequently, not only the body but the
animal's ghost is being spread along, and the driver is asked both to imagine
the death and be alert to the twittering of the passing spirit.

Wallace Stevens, The Emperor of Ice-Cream, page 1012.

This poem dresses the classical carpe diem tradition in modern garb. It
proceeds in images, which initially suggest sensual enjoyment: big cigars,
muscularity, girl/boy flirtation, ice-cream, and concoctions made of
concupiscent curds (lines 1-8). The contrast beginning with line 9 focuses on
the impoverished life and death of a woman and the grotesque reality of her
corpse. Thus, if be is the finale of seem (i.e., an honest attempt to
understand life's realities as opposed to illusion), we recognize that death
is the reality that none can avoid. In this circumstance, what can human
beings do? The speaker's answer is perhaps an avoidance: live for the moment,
even though we know that the moment is fleeting and brief; follow the pleasure
and sweetness of the emperor of ice cream. This leader's empire may melt
away, but it gives pleasure while it exists.

Jonathan Swift, A Description of a City Shower, pages 1012-1014.

This poem, a companion to Swift's "Description of the Morning" (page
698), is a vivid and zestful depiction of a world now gone, yet the images are
still real. The refuse-filled gutters, the brisk maid taking in the wash, the
poor and bedraggled poet, the cluster of women pretending to shop while really
taking refuge from the rain, the strangers who gather in unexpected
camaraderie in a shed, and all the rest, all evoke a world brimful of life as
it is (or was) in reality, not in ideal dreams. If the impatient beau in his
enclosed sedan chair is a sharply contasting and comic analogue to the Greek
heroes in the Trojan horse, so the refuse exuded by human life and animal
death is also meant to contrast with the vitality of that life. The poem ends
on an ironic note, for the streets carrying the floods of garbage are just
those streets along which condemned criminals began their last journey from
Newgate Prison to Tyburn, where they were were to be hanged.

James Tate, The Blue Booby, pages 1014-1015.

On one level, the poem describes the mating ritual of the booby, whose
silly name makes it easy for the reader to become relaxed and positive. The
male booby, a simple, undemanding fellow, has found the courting behavior
which has the perfect magical effect (line 31) on his mate. Thus the reader
is prepared, at line 37, to understand their mating not as copulation but as
lovemaking, and to perceive how distant stars are reflected in the foil lining
their nest like the eyes of a mild savior (line 41). Their behavior becomes
part of the scheme of things in the universe, which for this reason seems
gentle, benevolent, and loving. The poem thus is an idyll, a kind of Edenic
vision of a desirable and enviably unfallen world.

Edward Taylor, Upon a Spider Catching a Fly, pages 1015-1016.

Here the speaker introduces a spider, who adapts his killing methods to the special qualities of his prey. The spider is a symbol of the Devil, the predator of humankind, and the web symbolizes human sinfulness. Pursuing the symbolism, the speaker points out that God's grace breaks the cord or web of sin, freeing the human soul to sail like a nightingale to Glories Cage, or heaven (line 48), and sing joyfully in gratitude to God.

Dylan Thomas, Fern Hill, pages 1016-1017.

This poem celebrates youth as a time of Edenic joy and innocence. The world itself has seemed sacred to the speaker. Words like green, golden, white, blue, as well as the colors suggested by the objects described (daisies, hay, etc.), combine with the auditory and other visual imagery, and the richly repetitive exuberance of the language, to reawaken youthful joy and expansiveness. The colors are symbolic of youth, growth, and weatht. Youth's enthusiasm is illusory, however, since a person is in chains (line 54) from the beginning. Yet the delight of the speaker's recollection is beautifully realized; its sounds and slant rhyme schemes are complex and fully supportive of the idyllic experiences that Thomas renders in the poem.

Dylan Thomas, A Refusal to Mourn . . . in London, pages 1017-1018.

The language here calls deeply upon Biblical and theological traditions: mankind making (line 1), Fathering (line 3), Zion (line 8), and synagogue (line 9) all elevate the event of a dying child to a dignified and serious level. The initial statement about the refusal to mourn is perplexing and startling: how could a person not mourn so terrible a death, especially that of a child? But the speaker widens this individual case into a universal one, and determines that it is all death, any death, which is the issue, in all its stark tragedy. As is typical of Thomas, the poem is highly musical, with complex rhythms and rhymes which undergird its content fully. The announced refusal to mourn beomes a stately elegy, itself a form of mourning.

Leslie Ullman, Why There Are Children, pages 1018-1019.

Here the speaker deals with the concept that each woman (and indeed each person) is always not only herself but is also her immediate past, her ancestors, and the race itself. Needing, or being unable to avoid, that history and its insistent demands, the woman inside every woman (line 1) reaches out to the activities of that traditional life, such as childbearing, lighting the Sabbath (or other observant) candles, tending to the lace on the dresser, preserving lockets of hair, and shivering on the porch while waiting for loved ones to return home.

Mona Van Duyn, Advice to a God, pages 1019-1020.

The Greek God Zeus, who wooed many a mortal woman, could not appear to mortals in godly form because his awesome power would kill them. As a result, he came to them in other guises. Thus his union with Danae, the situation which presumably has just happened as the occasion of this poem, is presented in myth as a shower of gold which fell upon her. In the poem (written in slant rhyme triplets), the speaker calls upon Zeus to explain his departure, and asks him to warn her against love, which ultimately brings helplessness. At line 26, the speaker asks Zeus to reveal the weakness in his strength: were he to allow himself to be compassionate, he would be unable to bear the pain of humanity. His indifference is thus his protection. Underlining the poem's irony is the detail that the shower of gold consists of golden coins, together with other images suggesting the coldness of money and commerce.

Tito Villanueva, Day-Long Day, pages 1020-1021.

This poem may be seen as social protest. It describes the long, hot, arduous labor of picking cotton for migrant workers, and the unbending dreams (line 14) of a mother who wants her child freed from this misery. The mingling of Spanish and English presents the mixture of two cultures and two peoples. The demands of the harvest turn the family into sinews and backs (line 8), and their exhaustion at day's end and their powerlessness combine to damn the child to become part of the world they have never been able to escape. For comparison, see "In a Farmhouse," by Luis Omar Salinas (page 996).

Diane Wakoski, The Ring, page 1021.

The ring is a remnant of the speaker's ended marriage. Worn on her key chain, it symbolizes for her not love but possession, power (line 12). It also reminds her of the past, of her now lost beauty, and of the failure of her search for love (line 16). The divorced husband's search for love has also been unsuccessful, since the speaker observes that he has gone to other wives (line 10). But the poem's concentration is on the speaker, and the final stanza introduces powerful images of fragile illusion, brokenness, pain, and utter loneliness.

Alice Walker, Revolutionary Petunias, pages 1021-1022.

The poem presents a vivid picture of the black underclass in American society. Touched with a smattering of traditional culture (note the names of the woman's five children (lines 18- 20), and probably unable to get justice from the white legal system, Sammy Lou of Rue revenges her husband's death with the tool at hand, a farmer's hoe. White society, by contrast, has more efficient machinery, and will dispatch her by electric chair (line 23). Her final words give the dimensions of her world--the word of God and the demands of her garden (lines 21-26).

Margaret Walker, Iowa Farmer, page 1022.

This is a poem where a certain amount of biographical information can be very helpful in reading and understanding. Margaret Walker (Alexander), a black poet and teacher living in Mississippi, won the Yale Poetry Prize in 1942 for her first book, For My People, from which this modified sonnet is taken. The poem appears to celebrate an idyllic vision of a land of peace, plenty, and contentment. Yet the unexpected and enigmatic final line calls all that into question. The speaker does not tell us what the more familiar sights (line 14) are that fill his or her memory, but the poem's date (1942) may be helpful: in 1942 America was at war, and the terrible dustbowls of the 1930's were still recent. The poem may therefore be an ironic suggestion that the security of the Iowa farm was without foundation, for beyond America's shores there was turmoil, and even in America there was grinding poverty. Our knowledge that the poet is black opens the poem up to another broad spectrum of more familiar sights, reflecting the degradation of segregation. On second reading, it is clear that the speaker constantly distinguishes between himself or herself and the farmer in the poem, suggesting different perspectives and attitudes on the farm, the land, and the country.

Plyllis Wheatley, On Being Brought from Africa to America, page 1023.

The speaker of this poem, who is visualized as a person displaced from his or her native Africa in the eighteenth century, accepts the supremacy of Colonial America and the Christian religion. In the speaker's white/black imagery, white equals the angelic and the saved, black the sable race (line 5), the benighted soul (because non-Christian), and God's judgment on Cain (line 7). Although the concluding lines exhort Christians not to condemn blacks, they do so only in the belief that blacks, once converted, become spiritually (or theologically) equal to whites.

Richard Wilbur, In a Bird Sanctuary, pages 1023-1024.

Here the speaker deals delicately with a difficult topic: those who love nature but who do not quite understand it. Their beliefs lead to the action of creating a bird sanctuary, but, with the best of intentions, they also sap-headedly put statues of famous persons within the sanctuary, and therefore are compelled to clean bird dung out of granite hair (line 24). The speaker connects the liberty of one order of beings--birds--with that of all orders-- including the routine visions (line 35) of human beings, and declares that the essentially human task is to attempt to understand the world: "we must figure out / what all's about" (line 36).

William Carlos Williams, The Red Wheelbarrow, page 1024.

The red/white contrast of the mentioned objects bears the weight of the poem's only assertion, "so much depends . . ." The wheelbarrow, the rain, and the white chickens are simple but essential to the life of the farmer and therefore to all life.

William Carlos Williams, The Yachts, pages 1024-1025.

Although supremely maneuverable in a protected body of water, yachts are less seaworthy than other less rare and more utilitarian ships. Although in the opening stanzas the speaker celebrates their uniqueness, he or she points out their short comings in the description of the yacht race. Those piloting the yachts ignore the bodies (are they real, or are they imagined?) grasping for help in the water. The horror of the race is thus the symbol of how a privileged and beautiful few keep their preeminence only by ignoring the needs of the many. The abrupt break at line 25, from objective description to the surreal insensitivity of the racing yachts, jars readers into a reflection about the contrasts on which the poem is built.

William Wordsworth, Lines Written in Early Spring, pages 1025-1026.

The poem contrasts the beauty of the natural world with the horrors of
injustice and persecution that humankind (here called <u>man</u>) has perpetrated.
Wordsworth's speaker, observing the loveliness of a natural scene in spring,
finds there the basis for the conclusion that living things enjoy the beauty
in which they live. The speaker then posits the argument that if this belief
is correct and is both God given and God intended, then there is ample "reason
to lament / What man has made of man" (line 24). The simple stanzaic form of
the poem underlines its elementary but also emphatic assertion. The speaker
sees nature not just as a pleasant respite for human beings but also as the
source of divine truth and philosophical reflection.

William Wordsworth, The Solitary Reaper, pages 1026-1027.

The intitial situation visualized in the poem is simple and compelling.
The speaker, walking in the Scottish Highlands, comes upon a young woman who
is cutting and binding grain, and who is singing as she works. Because he
cannot understand her language, he speculates upon the meaning of her song.
In doing so, his thoughts take the experience far beyond the specific time
and place, making of it a universal moment, one which remains in memory long
afterwards. The solitary singer is emplematic of the mystery of the sources
of art, her song the symbol of the wide ranges of human experience.

Eleanor Wylie, The Eagle and the Mole, page 1027.

"The Eagle and the Mole" is in the imperative voice, offering the reader
words to live by. In a strange way, the poem takes up the age-old question of
whether a life of isolated contemplation is better than a life of passionate
involvement with humanity, and answers in the affirmative. Whether soaring
above the world like the eagle, or burrowing underground like the mole, the
reader is advised to live alone (away from the <u>reeking herd</u>, <u>polluted flock</u>,
<u>huddled warmth of crowds</u>) in order to keep an unspotted soul. Such withdrawal
will affort the opportunity for the individual soul to delve into (<u>hold</u>
<u>intercourse with</u>) the beginnings (<u>roots</u>, the <u>source</u> of rivers) and the ends
(<u>disembodied bones</u>) of all things. Rhyme is used well to clinch ideas and to
place opposed ideas/concepts in apposition.

William Butler Yeats, Sailing to Byzantium, pages 1027-1028.

From the vantage point of age, the speaker reflects upon life. In youth
we are caught up in <u>sensual music</u> (line 7) and ignore the more permanent
things of the intellect. In stanza 2 the speaker compares the aged man to a
scarecrow, <u>paltry</u> (line 9) unless his soul sings a song of intellectual and
spiritual achievement. Then swiftly, the speaker calls upon the memory of
Byzantium, to Yeats the primary symbol of civilized achievement, in order to
learn from its sages how to become part of <u>the artifice of eternity</u> (line 24).
Dreaming in stanza 4 of this post-physical state, the speaker sees himself as
an intricate and beautiful work of art embodying creative wisdom. Thus in
this poem Yeats stresses that art (which is as intellectual as philosophy or
science) is the only means by which time-bound human beings can gain the
eternity which many religions have promised.

William Butler Yeats, Byzantium, pages 1028-1029.

Convinced that pre-Christian and Christian imagery was ineffective for his purposes, Yeats sought meaningful symbols in Irish mythology and in a private symbol system. In "Byzantium" he draws upon these images. Thus at midnight (in Celtic thought, moments of transition like midnight or dawn were particularly open to the interpenetration of things spiritual), a passage from human and physical complexity to intellectual and spiritual eternity of art occurs. While praising this transformation, the speaker describes only the belief that this change occurs (the dance, the flickering of purifying flame) and its purpose (the transition into the condition of artifice). He or she does not describe what happens afterward, or even if the transition can be successful. Readers are left with the speaker's passionate and agonized longing, out of which these vivid and mysterious pronouncements were created.

Paul Zimmer, The Day Zimmer Lost Religion, page 1030.

The title is ironic. It should be "Zimmer's Coming of Age," for the poem describes the thoughts and feelings of a young speaker who, raised as an observant Catholic, chooses to miss Sunday mass. As a result, he speculates that a pugnacious and agressive Jesus will <u>wade into</u> his <u>blasphemous gut</u> and knock him out, as though he is in a boxing match cheered by the devil in a <u>reserved</u> seat (stanza 1). The imagery of the poem abounds with the holy objects of Catholic worship together with the symbolism of the boxing ring. The principal mode of description is overstatement, producing the poem's irony and also its comedy (the similes are fresh, clever, and funny). The poem offers a comic parallel to St. Paul's famous assertion that when he was a child he thought like a child, but when he became a man he put away childish things (I Corinthians, 13:11).

DRAMA

COVERAGE OF THE MANUAL

The 12 plays included in the text feature introductions, explanatory glosses and notes, study questions, and writing topics. Because this material is relatively extensive, we have limited coverage in the manual to discussions of some of the more vexing study questions and suggestions about teaching. We will also direct you, where possible, to filmed or videotaped versions of the plays that you might use to supplement your students' reading.

ORGANIZATION OF THE DRAMA SECTION

Unlike the other major sections of the text, the drama section is not organized with reference to a series of discrete elements. Rather, the elements of drama are introduced and discussed in Chapter 27. This material is followed by five short plays, any one of which can be used in class to illustrate the elements. Chapters that focus on tragedy, comedy, and realism in drama follow this introductory chapter. While the elements of drama remain important considerations throughout the drama section, these latter chapters focus on the distinctive qualities of the mode (i.e., tragedy, comedy, realism, nonrealism) rather than on the traditional elements.

ORGANIZATION OF EACH DRAMA CHAPTER

Each chapter follows the same general plan; it begins with introductory material and then moves on to a selection of plays. The plays are accompanied by extensive apparatus, including introductions, notes, glosses, questions for study and classroom use, and topics for writing and further discussion. Each chapter concludes with a discussion of writing geared to the topics taken up and plays in the chapter. These include discussions of strategies for writing about specific aspects of drama, sample essays, and commentary on the essays. The sample essays always take up elements or aspects of one of the plays included in the chapter; they can be used in connection with your own writing assignments or assigned as supplementary reading.

SUGGESTIONS FOR TEACHING DRAMA

We do not expect that most instructors will use all or even most of the plays in this text during an introductory course (unless the course focuses primarily on drama); the broad scope of the selections provides for variation and flexibility in setting up your classes. We do recommend that you begin with Chapter 27 and have your students read the introduction to the elements. Any one of the plays in this chapter can be taught to illustrate the elements. Some plays are clearly more effective than others in looking at specific elements; Before Breakfast is ideal for examining perspective, while The Sandbox is especially good for a close look at language. For the most part, however, all the plays provide an opportunity to discuss most of the elements.

For the remainder of your course, you can pick and choose as your interests dictate. You might concentrate on a specific mode of drama, or offer your students a wide variety, combining, for example, tragedy with comedy. You might also explore the possibility of a thematic orientation here, focusing on plays that deal with marriage, the family, death, society, or the like. A good combination along these lines might be Trifles and A Doll's House or The Happy Journey, The Sandbox, and Death of a Salesman.

In teaching dramatic literature to students with little or no background in the field, you will have to make sure that they understand how plays work on the stage so that they can build imaginative theaters in their minds. To this end, we have discussed aspects of production at some length in the text. We recommend that you encourage students to go to whatever live theater is available during this segment of the course. We also suggest that you screen a film or videotape of at least one play you are teaching, if time permits. These can be shown to students in the evening, outside of class time, after they have read the play(s) at least once.

Many other strategies can be used in the classroom to make plays come alive for students and to give them a sense of the power that drama can convey. One of these is an on-book reading of an entire short play in class by your students. A short play, like The Sandbox or Before Breakfast, can be read aloud by student readers in about ten minutes. While you cannot expect polished readings from your students, the spoken words will often carry more impact than the words on the page. Another possible approach involves having a group of students stage specific and crucial scenes. This sort of scene work takes a bit more time and involves a good deal of out-of-class preparation, but the resuls can be quite impressive. This technique can be highly effective in highlighting specific scenes such as crises or catastrophes. Two examples that come immediately to mind are the fencing match that closes Hamlet and the final confrontation between Nora and Torvald in A Doll's House.

If you teach at a school that has a drama department, you might look into the possibility of using some of the expertise of those people to bring theater alive for your students. Given this situation, another broad range of options becomes available to you. You might, for example, arrange for a group of acting students to stage one of the short plays in the book for your class. At some larger schools, a significant number of literature classes might study the same play at the same time. In this situation, a drama department, given enough lead time, might be willing to plan a full-scale production of one of the plays in the text. Keep in mind that theater students are often eagerly looking for audiences; such projects can be mutually constructive.

In teaching an individual play, your approach will be determined by the available time and the level of preparation you find in the students. Given the worst possible combination--little time and no preparation--you can aim to deal with only the major features of the text: what happens, why it happens, the major characters, the subjects, and some of the themes. Even this sort of overview can teach students a great deal about reading plays. If you have a bit more time, you can have your students examine conflicts, structure, irony, and language. A close look at these elements will help them significantly in becoming better readers of drama. In any event, your approach should always be geared to the students' needs and abilities. A close analysis of the flower imagery in Hamlet or the Ovidian elements in A Midsummer Night's Dream, for example, is almost never useful for beginning students.

235

CHAPTER 27

THE ELEMENTS OF DRAMA

The introductory material in the text provides a definition of drama (page 1033), a discussion of the differences between texts and productions (1034), a survey of types of drama (1035), and a discussion of the elements of drama (1037-1046). Most of this can be assigned as outside reading; only the discussion of the elements should require class review, and this can be combined with consideration of a specific play. The section on "How to Read a Play" (1046-1048) may help students come to grips with this experience.

Thornton Wilder, The Happy Journey to Trenton and Camden, pages 1048-1059.

This play explores family dynamics and individual strength in the face of relative poverty and personal loss. Ma is the cement holding the family together and on course; she provides the resources for coping with life.

Discussion of Questions

1. The opening stage direction stresses the theatricality of the play and the role of the stage manager. It suggests the social class of the Kirby family and that something is about to happen (anxiously). During the preparation for the journey, we learn that the family lives in a lower class neighborhood in Newark, and that they are going to Trenton to visit a daughter.
2. Ma's reaction to the missing hat and red cheeks (suspected make-up) suggests her sense of values and commitment to traditionally appropriate behavior. Her warm relationship with the neighbors helps characterize her.
3. We learn that Beulah (the name means married, see Isaiah 62:4) has been sick (page 1050). We also have a reference to Mrs. Schwartz's sick baby. During the journey, we have the funeral and Ma's reminder of Harold's death.
4. Arthur and Caroline are loving but a bit rebellious; Arthur is the more independent and occasionally mocking towards Ma. The argument about God during the trip reinforces this initial image of Arthur.
5. Elmer is passive, compliant, quiet, and competent. Key adjectives are even-voiced and anxious (page 1050). Most of his statements to Ma are a bit tentative, as though he were seeking confirmation.
6. The advertisements provide a light satirical touch; Wilder is making fun of society. They also provide more information about the family.
7. Ma reacts to the funeral with solemn respect, personal recollection, and meditation. She forces Arthur to remove his hat and recalls "our good Harold." She also contemplates her own death, announcing that she is ready and wants to go first. Ma is outraged by Arthur's remarks about God. The remark and Ma's response suggest that Ma is religious and firm in her faith. Both the funeral and this exchange bring out Ma's ability to deal with concepts such as God and death with absolute faith.
8-10. All three episodes stress Ma's goodness and commitment to humanity. Her exchange with the attendant illustrates her open friendliness and her conviction that "the world is full of nice people" (page 1054). Ma accepts Arthur's apology, comforts him, and moves on to more immediate concerns (food); there is no residual resentment. She admires Washington's honesty and implicitly sets it up as an example for her children.
11-12. Ma's wishes are selfless, traditional, and idealistic; she wants Caroline to "be a good girl" and "Arthur to be honest-in-word-and-deed." Her spotting the sign (page 1056) symbolizes her function as guide and manager.

13. Ma's reaction to Caroline's observation reveals that goodness (<u>nice</u>) and family are much more important to her than wealth or property.

14-15. Beulah has lost a child at birth. Ma deals with this by invoking God's mysterious ways and then moving to immediate concerns (food). The hymn fragment, like Ma's references to God's thoughts, stresses her firm faith.

Discussion of Topics for Writing

1. The stage manager, like the minimalist set, provides a constant reminder that we are dealing with a play (imitation, art, illusion) rather than reality. He does not function as a narrator at all; he provides no connective narration and never speaks directly to us. His constant presence, however, creates a pervasive perspective; we are always aware that the characters are fictive and we are constantly alienated (distanced) from the stage action. Such distance normally produces objectivity.

2. While the 5 stages of structure are not clearly delineated here, all are present. Exposition occurs during the preparation; complication (in the family dynamics) consumes most of the journey. Crisis and catastrophe occur simultaneously when Ma confronts and deals with her own and Beulah's grief. The play resolves with an affirmation of faith and family.

3-6. As protagonist, Ma faces conflicts with her children, society, and the cosmos (especially death). The central conflict is Ma's confrontation with the inevitability of death; she resolves this through faith. Ma is a flat and static character with some stereotypical characteristics, such as her interest in food and appearances. This does not make her any less central or important. She is the foundation and strength of the family; she keeps them literally and figuratively on the right road (toward Trenton and in life). Spotting the signpost is the key symbol of this function. Ma's guiding values are faith, love, honesty, and openness; these shape her attitude toward everything. The journey can be considered <u>happy</u> because it embodies the cohesion of the family. More important, it is a journey toward faith and the acceptance of God's will.

Eugene O'Neill, <u>Before Breakfast</u>, pages 1060-1067.

O'Neill's play is a study in character and perspective that makes a point about what marriage can become. Mrs. Rowland is a greedy and small-minded person who drives her husband to suicide through vindictive and vicious taunting. Alfred is certainly weak and culpable here, but the burden of the play's opprobrium falls on the wife. She leaves Alfred no hope and no means of escape but death.

Discussion of Questions

1. The setting implies that the Rowlands are poor, bohemian, and careless (perhaps alienated). The plants <u>dying of neglect</u> are symbolic of Mrs. Rowland's nature and the couple's relationship. See questions 1-2 below in the discussion of Topics for Writing.

2-3. Mrs. Rowland comes across initially as careless and coarse. O'Neill uses negative adjectives to convey this image: <u>slovenly</u>, <u>drab</u>, <u>formless</u>, <u>shapeless</u>, <u>shabby</u>, <u>worn</u>, <u>characterless</u>, <u>nondescript</u>, <u>pinched</u>, <u>weak</u>, and <u>spiteful</u>. Her initial actions--putting on the apron, coffee, getting a drink--are equally definitive; she moves <u>slowly</u>, <u>wearily</u>, and acts with <u>clumsy fingers</u>. There is also a sneaky and <u>vindictive</u> aspect to Mrs. Rowland; she <u>hastily</u> sneaks a drink and then <u>stealthily</u> finds and reads Alfred's letter from Helen.

These initial impressions are sustained and expanded throughout the play.

4. Throughout the play, Mrs. Rowland treats Alfred with scorn, derision, viciousness, and gloating condescension. She accuses him of being lazy, good-for-nothing, silly (page 1062), and a coward. Her taunts become especially nasty when she speaks about Helen (pages 1064-1066).

5. Apparently, Mrs. Rowland got (managed to get?) pregnant during her affair with Alfred. We can infer that she didn't let Alfred's millionaire father "buy her off" because she assumed that Alfred would inherit a great deal of money. While the play does not make this point clear, such conclusions arte consistent with Mrs. Rowland's character and nature.

6. Mrs. Rowland is truly vicious in her attitude toward Helen and her treatment of Alfred's feelings. She gloats over Helen's pregnancy and Alfred's entrapment; she calls Helen a common street-walker (page 1066).

7-8. The crisis occurs after Alfred cuts himself (page 1065), when he begins to stare at himself and Mrs. Rowland. Here, he probably begins to contemplate suicide. Other signs of crisis include Alfred's growing pale and shaking dreadfully. Mrs. Rowland's vicious chatter about Helen's pregnancy pushes Alfred to suicide and the play to catastrophe; the catastrophe is Alfred's slitting his throat and Mrs. Rowland's discovery of the body.

Discussion of Topics for Writing

1-2. The setting defines the characters as poor, careless, and arty. Significant details include the size and location of the apartment, the dying plants, the clothing hung on pegs (no closets), and the clothes line. The setting reflects the circumstances and life styles of O'Neill's original Greenwich Village audience. This convergence suggests an attempt at realism and verisimilitude. It also suggests that O'Neill expected his audience to understand the implications of the setting immediately.

3. Alfred, although obviously weak and culpable, is the protagonist; O'Neill forces us to sympathize with him by making Mrs. Rowland (the antagonist) a monster of greed and vindictiveness. The central conflict exists between these two characters; it probably started before the marriage. Alfred sees no end to the torture; his wife is relentless and will not divorce him. Hence, he ends the conflict with his own suicide.

4. Mrs. Rowland is flat, static, and stereotyped. These choices, and the missing first name, suggest that she is designed to represent a type.

5-6. By keeping Alfred off-stage (except for his hand), O'Neill is able to present the conflict completely from the wife's perspective. In this respect, the play is very much like Browning's "My Last Duchess" (page 488). O'Neill gives Mrs. Rowland enough rope (and time) to hang herself. Had Alfred been brought on stage to respond to the attacks, the focus and impact of Mrs. Rowland's malevolent personality would have been diffused. In addition, we would have had to deal with the real problems of Alfred's weaknesses, vices, and guilt. Mrs. Rowland's portrait of Alfred is distorted by her crudeness, greed, insensitivity, and limited mentality. She puts absolutely no value on art, education, or sensitivity, calling poetry silly. Since she values none of the things Alfred does, she cannot offer us an accurate portrait.

7. By presenting the background (exposition) out of order and in fragments, O'Neill creates tension and prolongs the revelation of Mrs. Rowland's character. Chronologically, Alfred graduated from Harvard (why Harvard?), began to write poetry (why poetry?), and became involved with his future wife (why does O'Neill make her father a grocer?). The couple became pregnant, his father tried to buy the woman off, she refused, they married, and the father died, owing all his fortune. Once this information is put back in order, Mrs. Rowland's interest in the Rowland money becomes clearer.

8. Both. The play is clearly a study in conflicting values and personalities. At the same time, it suggests that an unhappy (or badly matched)
marriage can become an insufferable prison.

Edward Albee, The Sandbox, pages 1067-1074.

Albee's absurdist play is a satire on the middle class, our treatment of
old people, and the American way of death. Language and character are
especially effective in building the play's satirical thrust. Many of the
absurdist techniques are designed to reveal the inane emptiness of Mommy and
Daddy by stripping them down to caricatures. Other techniques, like giving
cues to technicians and speaking to the audience, have the effect of reminding
us that we are dealing with illusion rather than reality.

Discussion of Questions

1-2. The bare stage and minimal props reinforce the sense of
theatricality and illusion. The sandbox turns out to represent the beach and
to symbolize the grave. The opening notes imply that the characters are
symbolic and representative. Mommy and Daddy are introduced as universals
without regional identity; the Young Man is identified as the Angel of Death.
3. Mommy identifies the beach to establish setting; the minimal set does
not do this. The family has come to the beach to watch Grandma die and to
bury her; death and funeral are conflated into a single, hurried, and cliche-
ridden process. Mommy and Daddy await the off-stage rumble (death, pages
1071-1072) so that they can be rid of Grandma.
4. Daddy's whining, along with his repeated deferrals to Mommy, his
vagueness, and his questions, defines him as passive and dominated. He is
clearly the weaker character. See questions 4-6 in topics for writing.
5. The cue breaks the integrity of theatrical illusion and reminds us
that we are dealing with a play. See question 3 in topics for writing.
6. Mommy treats Daddy with firmness, scorn, and condescension; he treats
her with fawning admiration, deference, and fear. They both talk about
Grandma with respect, but treat her as though she were garbage. They dump her
into the sandbox and then ignore her until the off-stage rumble.
7. Grandma's two modes of language--howling nonsense to Mommy and Daddy
and speaking quite articulately to us and the Young Man--embody an absurdist
technique that allows language to reflect attitude. The howls that Mommy and
Daddy get are what they expect of old people; the implication is that they
would not hear sense in any event. The 2nd mode has the effect of placing the
reader (audience) in parallel with the Young Man (Angel of Death).
8. Grandma suggests, through diction and exaggeration, that the relationship was horrid. She tells us that they "fixed a nice place for me under the
stove . . . gave me an army blanket . . . and my own dish" (page 1071), thus
implying that she was treated like a dog. She refers to Mommy as that big cow
and that over there, suggesting scorn and disgust.
9-10. The Young Man also symbolizes youth and the younger generation (see
question 9 below in the discussion of Topics for Writing). As a Hollywood
actor who has not yet been given a name by the studio, he also represents
superficiality and loss of identity. His pursuit of physical health and the
body beautiful (the calesthenics) is perhaps more apt today than it was in
1960; it is another comment on superficiality and ego orientation. The
off-stage rumble is a traditional and trite way (on stage and in films) of
signifying trouble or danger; it is treated exactly that way in the play. The
characters recognize it as a trite convention, but they also recognize it as
the harbinger of Grandma's death.

11-12. Mommy and Daddy react to Grandma's death with conventional and
formulaic cliches about how <u>happy</u> Grandma looks, how <u>brave</u> they must be, and
how they must now <u>face the</u> future (page 1072, see question 6 below in the
discussion of Topics for Writing). Grandma recognizes their response as
empty, conventional, and trite; she reveals how completely self-centered Mommy
and Daddy are by mimicking and mocking them.

13. The catastrophe occurs when Grandma realizes that she really is dying
(page 1073). The play resolves on a note of acceptance and forgiveness;
Grandma praises the <u>actor</u> who played the Angel of Death, and welcomes her own
death by forgiving the Angel.

Discussion of Topics for Writing

1-2. All the characters are flat, static, representative, and symbolic;
the absence of names underscores this representation. Mommy and Daddy
symbolize the sterility of marriage and the vacuity of the middle class.
Grandma symbolizes old age and traditional values; her treatment symbolizes
the discarding of values and contemporary attitudes toward the old. Albee
seems to view middle class marriage and the family as destructive institutions
that force people into dehumanizing molds. He also suggests that wives become
dominant and pushy while husbands are rendered passive and useless.

3. All these blatantly theatrical moments serve to destroy any shreds of
realism or verisimilitude in the play and remind us that we are dealing with
dramatic illusion. These are alienating or distancing devices, designed to
push us away from the play and to create objectivity (aesthetic distance).

4-6. Language is one of the play's key devices. Albee uses repetition
to emphasize the formulaic and vacuous lives of Mommy, Daddy, and the Young
Man. Daddy's repetition of questions and complaints underscores his inanity
and subservience to Mommy. Mommy and Daddy's language is fairly neutral, but
Grandma's lines are full of dialect, idiom, and connotative words (<u>fat cow</u>,
<u>figgers</u>, <u>lordy</u>) that help us define her and help her define her family. Mommy
and Daddy speak in cliches, especially when talking about Grandma's death.
Like repetition, the cliches underscore the conventionalized and meaningless
pattern that life has become for these characters. There is no sincerity or
feeling--just a collection of conventional responses.

7-8. The settings are similar in their nonrealism and minimalism; the
difference resides in Albee's investment of symbolic power in the sandbox (the
grave, 2nd childhood). The two married couples are similar in their flatness
and representation; in both cases the wife dominates. Ma and Elmer Kirby
embody much that is good and strong in the American family, but Mommy and
Daddy illustrate Albee's view of the vacuous sterility of family life.

9. The play presents 3 generations in Grandma (old, grandparents), Mommy
and Daddy (middle aged, parents), and the Young Man (youth, the child).
Grandma embodies the values and standards of the past, especially the solid
self-sufficiency of the 19th century and an agricultural nation. Mommy and
Daddy represent the dehumanizing urbanization of the 20th century and the
vacuous sterility of the present (1960). The Young Man embodies the innocent
and mindless focus on ego and "body beautiful" that Albee saw in the future.

Anonymous, Everyman, pages 1075-1099.

In teaching this play, you can stress the elements of symbolism,
allegory, plot structure, and theme. It is especially easy for students to
see theme at work here because the play is so blatantly didactic, establishing
its message in both the prologue and the epilogue as well as the action and

language of the play proper. The allegory is rigidly consistent and sustained; characters in the 1st half of the play represent social types or worldly concerns, while those in the 2nd half symbolize human or religious values or processes. Every character operates on an individual and universal level at the same time.

Discussion of Questions

1. The messenger provides a prologue (or introduction), announcing the title and subject of the play. Although he does not reveal the resolution, he does introduce the pattern of abandonment that Everyman will experience. Most important, he provides the 1st of 3 statements of the play's central idea: worldly life is transitory and only good deeds and Grace matter for salvation.

2. God decides on judgment because Everyman has forget clean God's laws and sacrifice and has pursued the 7 deadly sins with enthusiasm (lines 22-63).

3-4. Everyman resists going to judgment; he claims that he is not ready, begs for more time, and tries to bribe Death with a thousand pound (lines 121-123). His pleading and attempts at bribery suggest his degree of sinfulness. Death is unmoved; he is uncorruptible, implacable, and absolutely egalitarian in his treatment of humans. He is not interested in wealth, and he gives Everyman his first lesson in the true nature of goods (lines 161-170).

5. Fellowship appears at first to be loyal and helpful; he promises to die for Everyman (line 219) and to go to hell for him (233). When he understands the true nature of the pilgrimage, however, he retracts his promises. He is more than willing to indulge in life's sinful pleasures and even commit crimes with Everyman (lines 272-282), but he will have nothing to do with judgment. In soliloquy, Everyman draws the obvious moral about Fellowship.

6. Kindred and Cousin promise to live and die together with Everyman (line 324) before they know about his problem. When they find out about judgment, however, they both leave as fast as they can. Again, Everyman draws the moral in soliloquy; family is no more to be trusted than friends.

7. Everyman has loved Goods (worldly wealth) and assumes he will help him do anything. Goods explains that he can help in this world but not the next (line 401). He teaches Everyman that the excessive love of wealth is damnable (413-450) and he gloats and laughs over Everyman's situation, pointing out that it is his job to deceive and ensnare humanity (lines 455-56).

8-10. Good Deeds is pressed to the ground with the weight of Everyman's sins; she cannot stand or walk until Everyman goes to Confession in the House of Salvation and is cleansed of his sins by Grace. This course of action is advised by Knowledge, who represents not only knowledge of sin but also of the religious and spiritual process through which one may be redeemed. This process, which is spread throughout much of the 2nd half of the play, involves confession, contrition, penance (scourging), and the holy sacrament (communion and extreme unction). The play reflects Catholic (rather than Protestant) ritual and theology in that salvation is achieved through Grace and good work.

11. These characters represent good but earthly human characteristics. They promise to bring him all thither (line 675) on his pilgrimage, but they all abandon Everyman (are lost) when he goes into the grave. Good Deeds makes the moral of these events clear (870-873): "All earthly things is but vanity."

12. Everyman is saved (the play is thus a comedy). We know this because Good Deeds hears the angels singing and because the Angel welcomes Everyman Here above as the excellent elect spouse to Jesu (lines 894-901).

Discussion of Topics for Writing

1-2. The allegory is rigorous, consistent, and effective; each character works on an individual and symbolic (universal) level. Everyman's encounters, actions, and conclusions can be universalized to illustrate the way in which every human must live to achieve salvation. Although the characters are allegorical, the playwright individualizes some of them with little touches to add to the play's impact. We can see this in Kindred and Cousin, especially when one claims a cramp in his toe (line 356) and the other offers to let his maid go on the pilgrimage (line 360) because she likes parties.

3-5. The play can be thought of as "The Education of Everyman" because he learns the emptiness (vanity) of earthly things and the way to salvation. In this process he changes significantly. At first, he values worldly things (money, family, friends) and does not consider spiritual matters. Each soliloquy in the 1st half of the play signifies another stage in Everyman's education as he learns the truth about another aspect of the world. The soliloquies reinforce the lesson of each encounter for the audience (reader). Once Everyman rejects the world and turns to Good Deeds, the soliloquies stop; now the lessons focus on spiritual matters. In addition, Everyman is never alone once he makes this correct decision; Good Deeds never abandons him.

6. The plot offers a repetitive pattern of rejection; it exists only to convey the play's thematic material. In one sense, the entire play is an extended catastrophe following the crisis of Death's visit and summons. In another sense, however, traditional stages can be located throughout. The prologue and God's speeches make up the exposition; the pattern of abandonment in the first half of the play embodies complication. Crisis occurs when Everyman decides to turn to Good Deeds; this fixes the outcome. Catastrophe occurs at the grave, and resolution is salvation.

7. Please see the first sample essay (pages 1116-18) for an extended discussion of this point.

8. Everyman is in conflict with God (God's law) and himself (his own mis- understanding of the world and his failure to live up to God's law). This second conflict is divided, in the play, into a series of confrontations with various figures who represent aspects of worldliness and sin. Both conflicts are resolved when Everyman achieves salvation.

9-10. Please see the second sample essay (1118-21) on these issues.

Susan Glaspell, Trifles, pages 1100-1112.

This play examines the agony and desperation that can occur in marriage (good companion pieces are Before Breakfast and A Doll's House). More important, it explores traditional male attitudes toward women and the ways in which society systematically keeps women suppressed (caged, quiet, married). The key irony, of course, is that the women do what the men cannot do; they solve the problem of motive based on the evidence of "trifles" and they pass judgment on the murderer based on both the crime and the context.

Discussion of Questions

1. The kitchen is abandoned and gloomy; nothing has been put in order (the bread is left out) and there are many signs of incompleted work. All this suggests a recent and sudden interruption of daily life.

2. The men enter first in a group and move directly across the stage (room) to the stove. The two women follow; they move slowly, look fearfully about, and remain near the door (in the cold). The two groupings and the differences in movement establish traditional hierarchies and suggest very different attitudes toward the present moment.

3. Hale reports finding Mrs. Wright in the kitchen, rocking back and forth and pleating her apron, and Mr. Wright upstairs, strangled in bed. He is relatively observant, and his testimony is accurate as far as it goes. He doesn't notice signs of disturbance in the kitchen, and he doesn't make much of Mrs. Wright's _laugh_ or her _scared look_.

4. The authorities (men) need a motive. The sheriff is convinced that there is _nothing_ in the kitchen that will help establish motive--"nothing here but kitchen things" (page 1103). Because the women figure out the motive and the moment of rage based on _kitchen things_, we can conclude that the men are blinded by narrow minds and traditional patterns of thinking. We can also conclude that the women understand the psychology of marriage better than men.

5. The preserves froze and the jars broke. Mrs. Wright (in jail) and the two women are concerned about this; the men ridicule this concern, claiming that "women are used to worrying over trifles." Trifles (food in this case) are not unimportant; they prove to be the key to the crime and understanding.

6. The badly stitched square (page 1106) suggests to the women that Mrs. Wright was confused or upset ("didn't know what she was about"). Mrs. Hale resews the square; she may suspect Mrs. Wright at this point, but her action is presented as instinctive rather than a conscious suppression of evidence.

7. Mrs. Hale reveals that Minnie Foster had been a pretty but frail young woman who liked to sing in the choir (like a bird). Her childless marriage removed her from social contact and isolated her on the farm with Mr. Wright, a dour and _hard_ man "like a raw wind that gets to the bone" (page 1108). This background, scattered throughout, lays the groundwork for motive, but it also begins the justification of Mrs. Wright's actions.

8-9. The broken cage and the strangled bird provide evidence of the motive or trigger for the murder. The women look at each other with _growing comprehension_ and _horror_ at this point (page 1108). This is the crisis; the women have proof of a motive and must decide what to do with it. The cage symbolizes the Wright's marriage or Mrs. Wright's status in it (it also parallels the jail). The fact that the cage is broken reflects the current status of the marriage and Mrs. Wright's desperate act to escape. The bird with its _neck wrung_ is a visual parallel to the strangulation of Mr. Wright, but symbolizes Mrs. Wright. Mrs. Hale says that Mrs. Wright was "kind of like a bird herself" in her youth (page 1108).

10. At first, the women have different reactions to the evidence and their knowledge. Mrs. Peters is torn; she understands the situation, but she is conventionally fixed on the idea that "the law has got to punish crime." Mrs. Hale blames herself for not helping Minnie and feels that the murder was justified. Finally, however, they tacitly agree to supress the evidence; both try to hide the box containing the dead bird. Mrs. Peters cannot do it, so Mrs. Hale puts it in the pocket of her coat (page 1110).

11. Mrs. Hale feels partly responsible because she did not provide human contact and support for Mrs. Wright: "Oh, I wish I'd come over here once in a while! That was a crime!" (page 1109). She knew how wretched the Wrights' marriage was, but she didn't visit. Her guilt is justified only in so far as society as a whole is responsible for the conditions and conventions that led to Mrs. Wright's desperation and isolation. Nevertheless, Mrs. Hale feels personally at fault, and this contributes to her final decision.

Discussion of Topics for Writing

1. The title and the word _trifles_ (used on page 1103) refer to domestic matters or concerns that the men consider insignificant and laughable. Ironically, these trifles have a profound impact on life, death, and judgment in the play. They revealed the shape of the Wright's pathetic life and the

events leading up to the murder. The men's mocking attitude and the women's sensitivity to trifles underscore the basic distinctions in the play.

2-4. The characters are flat, static, and representative; the result is that they are universalized. Rather than dramatize a single murder, the play presents conflicts and problems that Glaspell considers relevant to the world at large. The men in the play, representative of male attitudes throughout society, are puffed up with their own importance and condescendingly tolerant of the women who worry about <u>kitchen things</u>. Their minds work in narrow and conventional patterns. Thus, they miss the significance of the trifles or the women's agitation. Mrs. Hale is strong, assertive, and sympathetic. She quietly makes light fun of the men and their work, wishing they would be quick about getting evidence. She picks up on the significance of the trifles and understands the crime without difficulty. She feels a sisterly responsibility for Mrs. Wright and thus blames herself for much of Minnie's bitter isolation.

5. A case may be made either way for the importance of Mrs. Wright. On the one hand, she is the center of the play--the character most talked about. Her life and marriage are slowly revealed to us. On the other hand, she functions almost as an abstract symbol; the play implies that she could be any woman (note that Mrs. Hale and Mrs. Peters both understand her situation completely). Glaspell keeps her off-stage so as not to prejudice the case; we must decide about justice without seeing the victim/criminal. In addition, keeping her off-stage helps to universalize her as an everywoman figure.

6-7. Although the play is set on a farm and concerns a murder, it is about neither. Rather, it focuses on marriage, society, and the relationship between men and women. These thematic concerns are repeated on three levels: the history of Wright's marriage, the social repression of women in general, and the conflict between the men and women at the farm. In each case (and in general), woman is protagonist and man (society, convention) antagonist. The conflict is not resolved. In an immediate sense, we find resolution in the women's decision to suppress the evidence; they find Mrs. Wright "not guilty." In the larger sense, however, the conflict remains unresolved in society.

8. The symbolism of the cage and bird is discussed above (questions 8-9 in the discussion of the study questions). The word <u>knot</u> links the quilting (a "womanly" occupation and thus an amusing trifle as far as the men are concerned) to the rope which was knotted about Mr. Wright's neck.

WRITING ABOUT THE ELEMENTS OF DRAMA, pages 1112-1121.

The aim of this discussion is to help students formulate ideas and write essays about the ways in which significant elements work toward meaning and impact in a given play. The review of elements (pages 1112-5) discusses ways to begin forming central ideas about specific aspects of a play. It also refers students to relevant sections earlier in the text. The section goes on to discuss organization and to provide two sample essays, one on plot and structure (pages 1116-7) and the other on theme (pages 1118-20) in <u>Everyman</u>. All this material can be assigned in conjunction with any play in the text; it is as relevant to tragedy or comedy as it is to the five plays in this chapter. Students can be directed back to this discussion and the relevant cross references whenever they are asked to write about a traditional element. Perhaps the most important point to stress in teaching this material is selectivity. In an effort to fill the pages as quickly and painlessly as possible, students often reach out in every direction, and fill their essays with disconnected observations about as many elements as possible. These observations are often regurgitated from class. The solution: encourage selectivity; make the students think about and deal with only one or two topics.

CHAPTER 28

TRAGEDY

The goal of this chapter is to introduce students to the concept of tragedy and the special considerations that come into play in dealing with tragic drama. The chapter contains extensive introductory material on tragedy and on each of the three superb tragedies. The opening discussion takes up the nature and scope of tragedy (pages 1122-27). If you have students read a tragedy (or all three), you can begin with a general discussion of the mode (i.e., tragedy) or you can develop a working definition based on the introductory material in conjunction with the play under consideration. In any event, some class discussion of the mode will be helpful for students, especially since the term tragedy is loosely applied to any unhappy or unfortunate event in modern usage.

Sophocles, Oedipus the King, pages 1130-1173.

If you assign Oedipus, you should have the students read the introduction to Greek theater (pages 1127-30) and the introduction to the play (1130-32). Both explain many of the conventions of Greek drama that students may find odd or intrusive. In teaching the play, you will have to guard against the students' tendency to see Oedipus as either a fool (why couldn't he see what we saw) or a symbolic figure representing all humanity (we are all controlled by fate or whatever). Neither is an accurate assessment of Oedipus. His circumstances are quite singular, and he is no fool--he solved the riddle of the Sphinx and ruled Thebes successfully for twenty years.

Oedipus is like a murder mystery in which the reader (or viewer) already knows who did it; the pleasure and agony are produced as we follow the slow process of discovery. But Oedipus offers a new (or very old) twist: the detective discovers finally that he is the murderer. One of the play's central problems is stated at the close of the introduction (page 1132) and raised again in the last two writing topics: the question of fate or character as the mainspring of tragedy. A good teaching approach is to balance these two alternatives and present each side of the argument with equal force.

At least two productions of Oedipus are available for classroom use. A 45 minute film or videotape of a production done in masks in an ancient Greek theater is available from Films for the Humanities (Box 2053, Princeton, NJ 08540). A film of a production directed by Tyrone Guthrie (1957) is available from Contemporary/McGraw Hill Films (1221 Avenue of the Americas, New York, NY 10020). Either would be a useful supplement in teaching this play.

The following questions, answers, and comments can serve as a programatic teaching guide to Oedipus; the material may be used to organize either class discussion or lectures. Discussions of the basic study questions (pages 1171-1172) are incorporated into the guide. Questions are indicated by the letter "Q" while answers or line citations are in brackets.

I. PROLOGUE (lines 1-150). 1. The first stage direction (s.d.) and Oedipus's opening speech (lines 1-13) provide exposition about the state. Q: What does the first s.d. tell you about the city? About Oedipus? [Since the people are suppliants--praying to Oedipus for help--we know that something is seriously wrong. Since the prayers are addressed directly to Oedipus, he is identified as a significant power.] Q: What do we learn about Thebes in Oedipus's 1st speech? [Prayers to Apollo and the cries of mourners weigh the city down; there is death and mourning.]

245

Q: What is Oedipus's attitude toward the people? Toward himself? [He calls the people My Children, suggesting dominance. He refers to himself as "I, Oedipus, a name that all men know." His greatness is based on defeating the Sphinx and on his own success as ruler for twenty years.]

2. The priest's answer (lines 14-57) is expositional.
Q: What does the priest tell us about the city's current problem? About Oedipus? [Thebes is facing plague, sterility, famine, divine fire, and death. Oedipus once saved the city from the Sphinx; he holds the power here.]
Q: What attitude toward Oedipus is reflected in the Priest's speech? [Respect, awe, the expectation that he will make everything right.]
Q: How do the people (chorus) put pressure on Oedipus throughout the play? [Their expectations; they assume he can fix whatever is wrong.]
Q: How are these expectations ironically right? [They are ironic because Oedipus unwittingly caused the problem in the first place. They are also ironic because making things better will require self-banishment.]

3. In answering the priest and suppliants (lines 58-78), Oedipus claims that he is well aware of the suffering; he says that "not one of you [is] so sick as I" (line 61). How is this claim an instance of foreshadowing and irony? [It is ironic because he will turn out to be sickened by his own life and he is the source of the plague that is destroying Thebes; in addition, Oedipus's assertion here ironically foreshadows the catastrophe and resolution.]
Q: What steps has Oedipus already taken to correct the situation? [He has previously sent Creon, his brother-in-law, to the Oracle at Delphi to find out what must be done. NOTE: At this point you might want to take a minute to explain what the Oracle at Delphi was. You might also diccuss here the symbolic value of the oracle (the voice of Apollo, it represents divine will) and the frequency with which this oracle impacts on the course of the play.]

4. No sooner mentioned, than Creon arrives from Delphi (84 s.d.). This is an example of the compression of time in drama and of the kind of coincidences that often occur in this play. Creon returns and reports Apollo's message; we learn more background about Thebes and Oedipus.
Q: What happened long ago to Laius, the former king? [Killed by bandits.]
Q: Why weren't the murderers tracked down at the time? [The Sphinx problem.]
Q: What must be done now? [Thebes must be purged, cleansed, purified. The murderer(s) of Laius must be punished by death or banishment.]
Q: What does Oedipus promise to do? [He will begin the search for the murderers again; "make it plain" for all to see.]
Q: What personal reason does Oedipus give for finding the killers? ["Whoever murdered him may also wish to punish me" (139); self-preservation.]
Q: How is this entire speech ironic given what we know about events? [His quest for justice and vengeance will lead him to himself. Laius's murderer could only kill Oedipus if he committed suicide.]
Q: How is Oedipus's promise to make everything plain consistent with his personality? [Reflects his driving need to know or discover hidden things.]

II. PARADOS (lines 151-220). This is chanted by the chorus when they first enter. It is usually accompanied by dance movements in which the chorus moved back and forth across the playing area. The chorus represents the voice of the people, reflecting standard values and attitudes. The entire parados is basically a prayer to the gods interrupted (lines 173-190) by a vivid description of the plague. Thus, the plague is linked directly to the power of the gods very early in the play.

Q: On which gods does the chorus call? What do they want the gods to do?
What is the chorus's attitude toward the gods and prophecy? [Zeus, Apollo,
Athena, Artemis, and Bacchus. They want the gods to cure the city and destroy
the murderer. Their attitude is respectful, awestruck, believing, reverent;
this is the social and ethical standard--the public and traditional position.]

III. EPISODE 1 (lines 221-467). Initially, Oedipus responds to the
prayers of the chorus and claims that they will have relief if they obey him.
He demands any information about the murderer of Laius that the chorus might
have (lines 221-228). Oedipus places a curse on both the murderer and anyone
who knows about the murder and does not reveal the information.
Q: What kind of curse is placed on the murderer and those who have knowledge
of him? [Ostracism and a prohibition from religious rites.]
Q: How does Oedipus ironically turn this curse on himself? [Calls the curse on
himself if he has knowledge of the murderer (lines 254-6).]
Q: Why is Oedipus's claim that he will fight for Laius "as if for my own
father" (269) ironic? [Laius is his father; we know it and he does not.]
Q: What second way of getting information about the murder does the Choragos
suggest? [The prophet and seer, Tiresias.]
Q: What is the significance of Tiresias's blindness? [Ironic reversal;
Tiresias is blind but can see the truth; Oedipus has sight but is blind. The
blindness also foreshadows Oedipus's blinding of himself at the catastrophe.]

2. Tiresias arrives on stage at line 301 s.d. Oedipus explains the whole
problem--the plague and the defilement--and asks for help (lines 305-20).
This is, of course, a method of review for the audience.
Q: What is Tiresias's 1st response? Why does he react this way? [He does not
want to say anything; he wants to leave: "Let me go home" (434). He reacts
this way because he knows the truth and he anticipates the overwhelming agony
that revelation will produce.]
2. Q: How does Oedipus respond to Tiresias's refusal to speak? What does this
show us about Oedipus? [He flies into a rage, becomes abusive, and accuses
Tiresias of being a traitor. Oedipus has the tendency to reach quick
conclusions and suspicions; he flies into a rage very rapidly.]
2 Q: What other instances of rage are significant in Oedipus's life? [His rage
takes over at the feast in Corinth, at Delphi, at the place where three roads
meet, in conversation with Creon, and at the catastrophe.]

3. Tiresias tells Oedipus the whole truth: "you are the vile polluter"(358);
"You are the murderer"(367); "You live . . . in the greatest shame"(372).
Because we know that this is true, our interest is not in the revelation, but
rather in Oedipus's reaction to it. Again we see blind rage.
Q: How does Oedipus respond? [He calls Tiresias blind and a liar, accusing
him of plotting usurpation with Creon; he belittles seers and prophecy.]
Q: How does the Choragos react? [The Choragos suggests that both men have
spoken in anger (line 410). The chorus embodies moderation and calmness.]
Q: What do Oedipus's rage and accusations drive Tiresias to do? [Deliver a
prophecy (lines 417-433) and tell truth in an indirect riddle (454-467).]
Q: What does Tiresias prophesy for Oedipus? [Blindness and wretchedness.]
Q: What does Tiresias imply will be revealed? [Truth about Oedipus's birth.]
Q: On what aspects of Oedipus's life does the riddle touch? [His birth in
Thebes, future blindness, incestuous marriage, and the murder of his father.]
Q: Why doesn't Oedipus recognize the truth here? [(1) His thinking is clouded
with rage. (2) He thinks that Polybus and Merope are his parents, and he sees
no connection between the bandits who murdered Laius and his own life.]

IV. STASIMON 1 (lines 468-517). This embodies the choral reaction; each stanza takes up a different aspect of the chorus's feelings and responses to what has just happened between Oedipus and Tiresias.

Q: What is discussed in each stanza? [Strophe 1 considers the power of Apollo over the murderer. Antistrophe 1 discusses the killer's attempt to escape and his inevitable doom. Strophe 2 expresses the fear and confusion the chorus feels over Tiresias's accusations. Oedipus's failure to see the truth is at least partly justified by the confusion that the chorus evidences. In Antistrophe 2, the chorus admits that the gods know about mortals, but they are unwilling to accept Tiresias's accusations; they also reaffirm their faith in Oedipus and in his power to solve the problem.]

V. EPISODE 2 (lines 518-867). 1. The debate between Oedipus and Creon.

Q: About what is Creon upset? [Oedipus's charge of treason & usurpation.]

Q: How does the Choragos explain Oedipus's words? [Spoken in _anger_.]

Q: Of what crimes does Oedipus accuse Creon? What proof does he have? [Murdering Laius, stealing the throne, plotting treason with Tiresias. He has absolutely no proof at all; Creon calls it _unsupported thought_ (line 613).]

Q: What emotion(s) dominate Oedipus during this debate? Does he ever really hear Creon? [Rage or _mindless willfulness_ prevents Oedipus from hearing. This rage is an extremely important factor in Oedipus's personality.]

Q: How does Creon defend himself and refute the charges? [Creon bases his defense on reason and religion. In terms of reason, he correctly points out that he has all the power and influence of kingship without the anxieties (lines 584-607). In terms of religion, he tells Oedipus to check with the Oracle; he condemns (curses) himself to death if he has misreported.]

Q: Characterize Creon. How is he different from Oedipus? [Rational, calm, careful, prudent, not hasty: "I never talk when I am ignorant" (574); "think about this rationally, as I do" (588); "a prudent man is never traitorous."]

2. Jocasta appears for the first time at line 638 s.d.; she is upset with Oedipus and Creon for stirring up _private troubles_ during Thebes's sickness.

Q: What does Jocasta want the men to do? [Stop arguing; go inside.]

Q: How does the chorus echo Jocasta? [They want Oedipus to defer to Creon.]

Q: Why does Oedipus view this as a _him_ or _me_ situation? [Absolving Creon implies that Tiresias was right and that Oedipus will face exile or death.]

Q. What is Creon's view of Oedipus's character? [Sees him as _sullen_, angry, and _unreasonable_; "Natures like yours are hardest on themselves" (679).]

3. The conversation between Jocasta and Oedipus (lines 682-867). Jocasta's questions about the argument provide an opportunity for more background. Oedipus explains Tiresias's accusations and discusses his own history.

Q: What is Jocasta's attitude toward prophecies? What accounts for this attitude? What proof does she offer? [She rejects them: "no mortal is ever given skill in prophecy" (713-4); she tells Oedipus to _forget prophetic words_ (728-9). Proof: the prophecy that her child would kill Laius could not have come true since the child was dead and Laius was killed by _foreign robbers_.]

Q: How is this proof ironic? [Oedipus is the child; neither knows it.]

Q: Why does Oedipus begin to suspect that he may have killed Laius? [He remembers killing some men at Phocis, the place where three roads meet.]

Q: How does Oedipus push for additional information at this point? Why? [He asks about Laius's _appearance_ and the _size of the travelling party_. He wants the _one survivor called so that he can be questioned_. Oedipus's drive toward truth here is partly a function of his character and partly the result of his initial vow. It parallels his quest for information about his parents.]

248

Q: What occurred at the feast? ["A man denied I was my father's son."]
Q; How did Oedipus react? [He could barely control his depression, and he was driven to find out the truth: "it kept grinding into me" (790).]
Q: Where did Oedipus go to discover the truth about his parents? [Delphi.]
Q: What prophecy was delivered? [Murder father, marry mother, lines 796-8.]
Q: How did Oedipus react to the prophecy? How is the reaction characteristic? [He fled; the reaction is characteristically hasty and irrational because he gained no real information about his parents.]
Q: What happened at the place where three roads meet? [Oedipus killed men.]
Q: What was the psychic trigger of Laius's death? [Oedipus's rage at being struck. The past is parallel to the present; Oedipus has not changed.]
Q: What is Oedipus on the verge of knowing? [That he killed Laius, not that he killed his father; he does not yet suspect that Laius was his father.]
Q: Why does Oedipus want to interview the lone survivor; what is his last shred of hope? [He wants to know if it was robbers or one man (line 849).]
Q:. What conflicts have emerged up to this point in the play? Which are emerging as central? [Oedipus-Tiresias, Oedipus-Creon, Oedipus-plague, Oedipus-gods/fate, Oedipus-himself (his rage, depression, haste, drive, demand to know the truth). The last 2 emerge as central; the others reflect these.]

VI. STASIMON 2 (lines 868-915). This is a significant point in the play because chorus separates itself from Oedipus for the first time.
Q: What point does the chorus make about itself in Strophe 1? [It claims to be reverent, orthodox, religious, and obedient to the laws of the gods.]
Q: What point is made about tyrants in Antistrophe 1? [Tyrants are ruled by pride of wealth and power (hubris) and often fall through impiety.]
Q: What sins are discussed in Strophe 2? [Haughtiness, pride, sacrilege, unholiness, and injustice. These are implicitly linked to Oedipus.]
Q: What does the chorus reveal about the state of religion in Antistrophe 2? [Prophecy is ignored, Apollo is abandoned, and religion slips away (915).]
Q: How is this relevant to Oedipus and Jocasta? [See below.]

VII. EPISODE 3 (lines 916-1090). The information of the first messenger (shepherd). We see Jocasta going to pray; she speaks to the chorus.
Q: How does she describe Oedipus's state of mind? [Excited, irrational]
Q: What news does the messenger from Corinth bring? Why is it good news? [Polybus is dead and Oedipus will be made king of Corinth. The news apparently frees Oedipus from the horror of the oracle delivered at Delphi.]
Q: What attitude toward prophecy and oracles do Oedipus and Jocasta express? [Both reject oracles completely. Jocasta asks, "Oracles of the gods! Where are you now?" (951-2). Oedipus asks "why should we look to Pytho's vapors?"]
Q: How is this good news about Polybus ironically reversed? [Polybus was not Oedipus's father; the baby was given to Polybus by the Messenger, who got the baby from another shepherd on Mt. Cithaeron. This shepherd worked for Laius.]
Q: What does Jocasta know at this point that Oedipus does not know? [She has put all the clues together and discovered the full horror of the truth; she knows that Oedipus, her son, murdered his father and married his mother.]
Q; Contrast Jocasta and Oedipus's attitudes toward pursuing the investigation to its end. [Jocasta wants Oedipus to stop: "pay no attention . . . give up this search . . . please don't do this thing." Oedipus is driven; he cannot give up with "clues like this within my grasp." See lines 1061-77.]
Q: What does Jocasta intend when she enters the palace? How do you know? [Suicide is indicated by her promise never to address Oedipus by any name other than man of misery and by the Choragos's reference to savage grief.]

VIII. STASIMON 3 (lines 1091-1114). The entire choral ode is highly ironic. In the first stanza, the chorus praises Mt. Cithaeron for protecting and nurturing Oedipus during his infancy. In the Antistrophe, they consider some possible explanations of Oedipus's birth; they guess that he is a child of <u>Pan</u>, <u>Apollo</u>, <u>Hermes</u>, or <u>Dionysus</u> and some nymph.

IX. EPISODE 4 (lines 1115-1190): Catastrophe, peripeteia, anagnorisis. The interview with the shepherd who gave the baby to the Corinthian and who survived the murder of Laius leads to the revelation of truth.
Q: Why won't the old herdsman look at Oedipus; what does he know about him? [He recognized Oedipus as the murderer 20 years earlier; he does not realize the full truth, however, because he did not link the man with the child.]
Q: Discuss the coincidence that this shepherd (a) saved the infant Oedipus, (b) was with Laius at the crossroads and was the lone survivor, and (c) will now be the agent of revelation? [Such coincidence suggests divine will; it also implies that a person cannot escape his or her fate.]
Q: How is Oedipus's behavior with the herdsman (threatening torture) consistent with his character? [He knows that he is about to hear <u>the dreaded thing</u>, but he is driven on by his need to bring hidden things to light.]
Q: What does Oedipus discover about himself? [See lines 1187-90; he realizes the full truth of his monstrousness in birth, marriage, and murder. This is the moment of <u>anagnorisis</u> in the play; it is also the catastrophe.]

X. STASIMON 4 (lines 1191-1232): Here, and later, the chorus draws the moral they see in Oedipus's life and provides a final reaction to Oedipus.
Q: What moral does the chorus see in Oedipus's life? [They feel that men must appraise their lives as worthless and that no mortal can be judged <u>fortunate</u> (1191-1201); in the last lines, they assert that no man can be considered happy until "he has crossed the border of his life without pain" (1543). In other words, they assert that one cannot be judged to be fortunate until he or she is dead.]
Q: How are Antistrophe 1 and Strophe 2 a summary of Oedipus's life? [The first reviews Oedipus's rise; the second reviews his wretched fall.]
Q: What are the chorus's feelings toward Oedipus now? [Pity and fear; they wish that they had never seen him.]

XI. EXODOS (lines 1233-end): Resolution, denouement, tying up loose ends.
Q: What does the second messenger report about Jocasta? About Oedipus? [Jocasta committed suicide by hanging. Oedipus blinded himself in a frenzy by stabbing his eyes with the gold pins from Jocasta's dress. The pins symbolize both the sexual crime that Oedipus has committed and Laius's goad. Oedipus blinded himself because he could no longer bear to look upon his sins.]
Q: What does the messenger say that Oedipus wants now? What does Oedipus want from the Chorus? [He wants to be exposed to the people as Thebes's pollution and then banished (1300). He wants the chorus to lead him out of Thebes.]
Q: Whom does Oedipus blame for his tragic life and fall? [Apollo, 1339-41.]
Q: What is Creon like as the new king? What acts indicate his carefulness, reverence, political wisdom, and kindness? [Creon treats Oedipus with cool compassion and calculation; he wants to consult the <u>gods</u> and have <u>sure</u> <u>knowledge</u> before he acts. He displays kindness in having Oedipus's daughters, Ismene and Antigone, brought to him and in grasping Oedipus's hand. His political acumen and careful statesmanship are evident in his assertion that "I never promise when . . . I'm ignorant."]

Discussion of Topics for Writing

1. The play follows a traditional five-stage pattern, but exposition is distributed throughout because so much of the story has already occurred when the play begins. Exposition occurs in the opening dialogue, where we learn of the plague afflicting Thebes because of the hidden murderer. Complication builds as Tiresias accuses Oedipus of the crimes and Creon delivers the message of the Oracle at Delphi. The crisis occurs when Oedipus vows to find the murderer, no matter what such an act entails. The keys to the crisis are haste and anger; these lead Oedipus down a one-way path into the tragedy machine. The peripeteia, catastrophe, and anagnorisis all occur at the same instant when Oedipus discovers the truth of his parentage. These revelations affect Jocasta and Oedipus most immediately; she commits suicide and he blinds himself. The resolution involves the passing of power to Creon and the consideration of Oedipus's future (he will be banished).

2. Oedipus was the only son of Laius, king of Thebes. Laius was warned by an oracle that his son would kill him and marry Jocasta. The baby's feet were pierced and he was given to a shepherd to expose on Mt. Cithaeron. The shepherd relented and gave the baby to another, who gave the child to Polybus & Merope, the childless king & queen of Corinth. They named him Oedipus because of his injured feet and raised him as theirs. Years later, Oedipus was taunted at a feast that Polybus and Merope were not his parents. Deeply troubled, he asked Polybus & Merope, who insisted they were his parents. But Oedipus could not rest; he consulted the Oracle at Delphi. The Oracle refused to answer his question, but told him that he would murder his father and have children by his mother. Horrified, Oedipus fled Corinth, vowing not to return until Polybus and Merope were dead. While travelling toward Thebes, Oedipus came to the junction of three roads. There, he met a nobleman (Laius) who ordered him off the road. The man struck Oedipus with a goad; Oedipus became enraged and killed the noble and all but one of the servants accompanying him.
When Oedipus arrived at Thebes, he found the city terrorized by the Sphinx; she ate Thebans who couldn't answer her riddle. At the same time, Laius's body was discovered. Creon offered the crown & hand of Jocasta to anyone who could free the city. Oedipus solved riddle (the Sphinx committed suicide), was crowned, and married Jocasta. The lone survivor of Laius's retinue returned, found Oedipus king, and asked to become a shepherd in a distant region. Oedipus ruled for 20 years and had 2 sons and 2 daughters by Jocasta. Thebes is afflicted by a plague (the play begins at this point); Oedipus sends Creon to Delphi to discover the cause. Creon learns that the murderer of Laius defiles the city by living unpunished. Oedipus begins the investigation; he swears to find and banish the murderer. Tiresias is consulted; he accuses Oedipus, who flies into a rage. The shepherd who gave the baby to Polybus is consulted. The survivor of Laius's group is consulted; he is the man who was ordered to kill the baby. Finally, the truth is revealed. Horror abounds; Jocasta commits suicide and Oedipus blinds himself (he will be exiled from Thebes). Sophocles's arrangement of the elements of the story produces a highly focused and effective theatrical moment. Pieces of the past are revealed only as they are needed to tighten the web around Oedipus. Keeping the play in the present maintains pressure on Oedipus throughout. Such an arrangement also raises the level of dramatic irony considerably. The audience knows the whole story, while the staging begins at the very end.

3. The central conflict is either Oedipus against the gods (fate) or against himself (anger, haste, irrationality). There is no right answer; a decision depends on one's view of the genesis of tragic fall in the play.

251

4. Reporting (rather than staging) violence was a convention of Greek and Roman drama. This resulted in the absence of violent spectacle, a mainstay of English and (later) American drama. There are several advantages to such a convention. The playwrights could focus on character and on the reaction to violence, rather than the violent act itself. Moreover, the spectators could (and readers can) imagine violence in more horrid detail than staging could (or can) provide (such, of course, is not the case with contemporary film and the full range of special effects available to directors).

5. Coincidence is best embodied in the single character who reappears at every crucial moment on Oedipus's life. This is the herdsman who took the infant to Mt. Cithaeron, accompanied Laius on his fatal journey, survived Oedipus's attack, and reveals all at the close of the play. Although coincidence is common in drama, this much suggests the operation of fate or the gods. Coincidence is a prime factor in arguing for a tragedy based on fate.

6. Virtually everything Oedipus says and does in the play is ironic because we know so much more than he does. His vow to hunt down the murderer, his claim that the murderer may try to kill him, his treatment of Tiresias and Creon, his joy at Polybus's death are all stunningly ironic.

7. Oedipus, like Hamlet, is a tragedy in which individual fortunes rebound on the state. Initially, Oedipus's secret guilt leads to plague and famine in Thebes. In the end, his fall leads to a shift in the kingship and possible questions about succession (where do Oedipus's two sons fit into the future of the crown?). These imply an unstable future for Thebes.

8. The Chorus and Choragos represent the Theban public; they embody calm moderation, reason, and traditional values such as reverence for the gods. The choral odes establish many of these values. They also communicate the choral reaction to the events and conflicts in the play. Stasimon 1, for example, expresses the chorus's reaction to the news about the murderer and the accusations of Tiresias. Similarly, the Choragos serves as a voice of reason and a mediator. He reminds Creon, for instance, that Oedipus often speaks in anger, without thinking. At the close of the play, the chorus draws its own moral from the fall of Oedipus; their conviction that no human can be considered happy until dead underscores the instability of power and glory.

9. The seeing-blindness contrast provides an opportunity for dramatic irony. Tiresias, although blind, can see the truth of Oedipus's parentage and guilt; Oedipus is physically sighted (until the catastrophe), but he is blind to the facts about his background, parents, and crimes. The contrast also allows Sophocles to make ironic and foreshadowing references to Oedipus's blinding of himself after he finally sees the truth.

10. Oedipus's quest for a person quickly becomes a quest for the truth of his own past. The nature of the quest changes when Oedipus realizes that he may have murdered Laius. From that point on, Oedipus is driven toward a discovery of his own past and recognition of the present horror.

11-12. These are perhaps the best (and most obvious) writing topics for this play. An essay arguing that tragedy results from character would normally point to specific instances of haste, anger, irrationality, and drive as proof. An essay advocating fate or the gods as the source of tragedy might focus on prophecy, reverence as opposed to disregard of the gods' oracles, and coincidence as the crucial factors.

The Theater of Shakespeare, pages 1173-1177.

This provides a rather detailed introduction to the physical conditions and stage conventions of the Elizabethan public theater (notably the Globe). The information is helpful and important because many aspects of Shakespeare's plays are determined by such conditions and conventions. This can be assigned in conjunction with Hamlet and/or A Midsummer Night's Dream (1384-1443). In both cases, it will help explain the less realistic aspects of the plays.

William Shakespeare, Hamlet, pages 1177-1288.

Teaching Hamlet is not an easy job, but it can be a very rewarding one. Most students approach Shakespeare's plays with a great deal of resistance and fear. You can overcome this attitude in the classroom by demonstrating that the language, although clearly different from Modern English, is comprehensible and means exactly what it says and that the play is not all that difficult to understand. The glosses and notes should help. Hamlet is a touchstone of Western civilization; your students will be enriched by reading it.

When you set out to teach the play, you should estimate what the students can reasonably hope to get out of the work and gear your presentation of the material to that level. With Hamlet and other complex plays, you will probably have to settle for less than a complete reading. Hence, you will have to establish priorities in what you hope to convey. We would suggest the following priorities: (1) What's happening--the story, the plot, the pattern of the plot. (2) Who are these people--the protagonist, his personality, his dilemma, his motives, his growth; the antagonist, his situation and motives. (3) Why should we read about a dead Danish prince, anyway--the universal ideas about human responsibility, dilemmas, choices between responsibility and desire, justice, and revenge that the play explores.

Students' appreciation and comprehension of Hamlet can be significantly enhanced by watching a production after they have read the text. Beyond the film/videotape available through Prentice-Hall, the following are available:

Videotape (1980), 222 minutes, starring Derick Jacoby. Time-Life
    Video, Box 644, Paramus, NJ 07652.
Film (1948), 152 minutes, starring Laurence Olivier. Audio-Brandon
    Films, 34 MacQuesten Parkway S, Mount Vernon, NY 10550.
Film (1969), 114 minutes, starring Nicol Williamson. Audio-Brandon.

Please note that any specific production available on film is likely also to be available on videotape in the near future. These films or tapes, and numerous other productions of Hamlet, are available from many other film distribution companies as well. The BBC-Time-Life production (1980) has obviously cut the least from the text.

The following programatic guide to Hamlet is mostly a series of questions that can be used to shape class discussion or lectures. A significant number of answers, lecture points, and points for review are also included. The guide is organized in a scene-by-scene approach to the play. Questions are indicated by the letter "Q." Answers, when provided, are enclosed in brackets. In many cases, only a line reference is given. Rosencrantz and Guildenstern are abbreviated as "R&G" throughout. The guide includes all the study questions listed at the end of the play.

ACT 1. EXPOSITION: THE ESTABLISHMENT OF CHARACTER, SITUATION, CONFLICT.

1.1: THE WATCH ON THE BATTLEMENTS, HORATIO, THE GHOST.
Q: This scene establishes that there is something wrong (rotten) in Denmark;
what aspects of the scene tell us that things are not right? [(1) The
nervousness of the watch; the first two words of the play are "Who's there,"
establishing a tense and questioning tone. (2) The appearance of the Ghost of
old Hamlet. (3) The preparations for war (lines 70-79). (4) The problem with
young Fortinbras (lines 95-107). Shakespeare thus uses minor characters here
to introduce us to a deeply troubled and chaotic Denmark.]
Q: Whom is Horatio going to tell about the Ghost? Why? [Lines 169-173.]
Q: The most important character we meet in 1.1. is Horatio; what is he like?
How is he different from Barnardo and Marcellus? [Horatio is educated and a
rationalist; at first, he thinks the watch have imagined the Ghost. He
understands the grave significance of the Ghost and his duty to Hamlet.]
NOTE: A broader approach to the scene can be achieved with three questions:
(1) What is the function of the scene? (2) What mood is established in the
scene? (3) What do we discover about Denmark in the scene?

1.2: THE COURT: CLAUDIUS, GERTRUDE, HAMLET, LAERTES, POLONIUS, &c.
This scene establishes our initial images of Claudius, Hamlet, &c. It also
works against the first scene in that it presents an image of normal activity.
Q: Which character is presented and defined first in this scene? [Claudius.]
Q: How does Claudius initially come across? [A competent administrator.]
Q: How does Shakespeare establish Claudius's competence? [The scene is
structured so that he is seen dealing well with problem after problem.]
Q: What is the problem with young Fortinbras? How does Claudius deal with it?
[Plans to invade Denmark; Claudius sends ambassadors to his uncle (17-42).]
Q: What business does Laertes raise? How does Claudius deal with it? [He
wants to return to Paris; Claudius investigates & approves (lines 43-63).]
Q: Next piece of business is Hamlet & his behavior. What is the problem with
Hamlet's behavior? [Still mourning; the clouds still hang upon him.]
Q: What sets Hamlet apart? How is his clothing different? [He is the only
one dressed in black mourning clothes; in blocking the scene, most directors
keep him well away from all the other characters.]
Q: What is Hamlet's frame of mind and attitude? [He is depressed, unsettled.]
Q: What central thematic point is introduced in Hamlet's "Seems, madam" speech
(lines 76-86)? [Appearance vs. reality, see sample essay, pages 1375-1377.]
Q: How do Claudius and Gertrude try to deal with Hamlet's sadness? [Both
assert that death is a natural and inevitable part of life (lines 87-117).
The argument is especially ironic in light of old Hamlet's unnatural death.]
Q: What does Hamlet's 1st soliloquy (129-159) tell us about him? [He is
depressed, suicidal, and bitter; he is bothered by his father's death, his
mother's remarriage, and the fact that he is not king.]
Q: What do we find out about Horatio in his conversation with Hamlet (lines
160-258)? [He is Hamlet's friend and fellow student. Hamlet wants them to be
equals (friend instead of servant); he likes and trusts Horatio.]
Q: What does Horatio tell Hamlet about? What does Hamlet decide to do? Why?

1.3: EXPOSITION OF SUBPLOT. WE MEET LAERTES, OPHELIA, POLONIUS.
The scene occurs in three conversations: Laertes-Ophelia (lines 1-51);
Polonius-Laertes (lines 51-88); Polonius-Ophelia (lines 88-136).
Q: What do we find out about the relationship between Hamlet & Ophelia? What
is Laertes's attitude toward this relationship? Why does he have this
attitude? [Hamlet is courting Ophelia. Laertes thinks Hamlet is trifling and
advises Ophelia to stay away from the prince. He is worried about her

chastity and the family's (especially his own) reputation. Ophelia's last
remark suggests that Laertes is better at giving advice than following it.]
Q: What advice does Polonius give Laertes? Is the advice good? Original? To
what extent does Polonius follow his own advice? [Students admire the advice
and Polonius. They can be led to realize that most of the advice is trite and
conventional, and that Polonius himself ignores most of it. When seen in this
context, the lines show Polonius to be pompous and a hypocrite.]
Q: What is Polonius's attitude toward Ophelia's relationship with Hamlet?
What reasons does he give for this attitude? Is he more concerned with
Ophelia or himself? What does he tell Ophelia to do regarding Hamlet? [He
holds the same (but stronger) opinion as Laertes; he thinks Hamlet is only out
for sex, and he warns Ophelia to stay away from the prince. He is clearly
more concerned with his own reputation than he is with Ophelia's feelings.]
Q: What is Ophelia like? How does she respond to Laertes & Polonius? To what
extent does she have a will of her own? To what extent is she controlled?
[Although much of this depends on how Ophelia is played, the text suggests
that she is compliant, obedient, perhaps too dutiful, and easily controlled.]

   1.4: HAMLET, HORATIO, & THE WATCH MEET THE GHOST.
Q: A key question for Hamlet is what kind of ghost he faces. What are the 2
possibilities? Why is the question important? How does the problem affect
Hamlet's subsequent action? [Spirit of health or goblin damned (lines 40-42).
The possibility of the latter produces doubt and causes Hamlet to seek proof.]

   1.5: HAMLET & THE GHOST.
Q: What does the Ghost tell Hamlet about his death and Claudius? What does
the Ghost want Hamlet to do? What special instructions does the Ghost give
Hamlet about Gertrude? [He explains that he was murdered by his brother,
Claudius, with poison poured into his ears. He wants Hamlet to revenge his
death (line 25), but to leave Gertrude's punishment to heaven (lines 84-88).]
Q: Why does Hamlet swear the watch to secrecy? [He wants to watch Claudius.]
Q: Why does Hamlet decide to pretend insanity--put on an antic disposition?
Why can't Hamlet act against Claudius at this point? [Madness will protect
him while he is trying to get the necessary proof of the Ghost's honesty.]
Q: What is Hamlet's reaction to the Ghost's demands & the problems he faces?
[At first, he swears immediate action (lines 93-112), but at the end of the
scene he complains that he was born to set the time to right (188-9).]

   ACT 1 REVIEW: Act 1 establishes the characters, conflicts, and situations. It reveals that much is wrong. The Ghost tells Hamlet about murder,
lust, and usurpation. By the end of Act 1, Hamlet knows what he must do: he
must gain confirmation of the Ghost's accusations before acting and defend
himself from Claudius while doing so. Act 1 also establishes the major
characters. Hamlet is melancholic, upset about his mother, introspective, and
traumatized by the Ghost. Claudius is smooth, politic, efficient, murderous,
lustful, and evil (if we believe the Ghost). Polonius is officious, full of
platitudes, suspicious, and wordy. Ophelia is weak, obedient, and a dutiful
daughter. Laertes is a concerned brother, and Horatio is a scholar and
rationalist who is trusted by Hamlet. The central problem here and throughout
is delay. Why doesn't Hamlet kill Claudius immediately? This is not really a
problem (see the sample essay, pages 1370-73). Since all revenge plays have
delay, the question becomes how does Shakespeare justify Hamlet's delay and
make it credible? One answer is the problem of confirming the Ghost's words.
The Ghost might be a devil; Hamlet needs more evidence. Once he gets it, he
kills--and kills the wrong man. This causes more delay. A 2nd answer: the
problem of character. Hamlet is introspective and contemplative--he thinks

255

too much. His subjective introspection accounts for the soliloquies in which
he accuses himself of delay. His sense of time is distorted.

ACT 2. COMPLICATION: THREE MAIN LINES OF DEVELOPMENT. 1. Hamlet's quest for
proof; 2. Hamlet's introspection and self-accusation in soliloquies; 3.
Claudius's defensive actions through Rosencrantz, Guildenstern, and Polonius.

2.1: FOCUS ON POLONIUS AND REYNALDO, THEN OPHELIA.
Q: What does Polonius want Reynaldo to do in Paris? What does this show us
about Polonius? [Reynaldo is to spy on Laertes and even impugn his honor to
get information. Polonius uses Reynaldo to spy just as Claudius uses R&G.]
Q: What does Ophelia report about Hamlet? [See lines 74-81, 85-97]
Q: What conclusions about Hamlet does Polonius draw? [He jumps to the conclu-
sion that Hamlet is mad for love: "The very ecstasy of love" (line 99).]
Q: What is Polonius going to do with this information? What does this tell us?
["I will go seek the king" (98): self-serving, no regard for Ophelia.]

2.2.A (lines 1-40): CLAUDIUS & GERTRUDE GREET R & G.
Q: What is the history of R&G's relationship to Hamlet? [See lines 11-13.]
Q: Why are R&G in Denmark? How does Claudius plan to use them? [See 15-18.]
Q: To what extent do R&G cooperate with Claudius? To what extent does their
cooperation justify their deaths later in the play? [Hamlet claims that they
courted power and paid the price; they clearly agree to be used for profit.]

2.2.B (lines 40-85): RESOLUTION OF THE FORTINBRAS PROBLEM.
Q: How has the threat to Denmark posed by young Fortinbras been resolved? What
does he plan to do with his army? [The king of Norway dissuaded him; he plans
to attack Poland instead, and seeks permission to cross Denmark.]

2.2.C (lines 85-170): POLONIUS'S EXPLANATION OF HAMLET'S MADNESS.
Q: Describe Polonius's language. What does it show us about him? [It is
extremely wordy; he builds himself up through artful but confusing language.]
Q: What does he report about Hamlet? How does he prove it? [He claims that
Hamlet is mad for love, and cites the letter and his behavior as proof.]
Q: How does Claudius react? [Interest & doubt: "How may we try it further?"]
Q: What plan does Polonius come up with to try it further? [To use Ophelia
and to spy on the meeting: "I'll loose my daughter to him. Be you and I behind
an arras" (162-3). Shows a complete disregard of Ophelia as a person.]

2.2.D (lines 170-220): THE CONFRONTATION OF HAMLET & POLONIUS.
Q: How does Hamlet act? On what things does Hamlet focus in his pretended
insanity? How is there method in his madness? [Hamlet pretends to be mad; he
focuses on Polonius as whoremaster, daughters, death, graves, and the
emptiness of language. All these are relevant to Hamlet's situation.]

2.2.E (lines 221-430): HAMLET MEETS R & G.
Q: What do R & G try to find out from Hamlet? How successful are they? [They
want to find out the cause of his moody melancholy & madness; they do not.]
Q: What does Hamlet want to know from R & G? Why is this important? How does
R & G's confession that they were sent for affect the way Hamlet deals with
them? [Hamlet wants to know if they were sent for (lines 265, 269, 275, 281,
284). When they admit it, Hamlet recognizes them as Claudius's tools.]
Q: What news do R & G bring Hamlet? Who is on the way to the court? [They
report the approach of the actors. Polonius brings the same news almost
immediately. In speaking with Polonius, Hamlet resumes his feigned madness.]

256

2.2.F (lines 430-end): HAMLET & THE ACTORS, THE CLOSING SOLILOQUY.
Q: Hamlet wants to hear the speech about Hecuba and the Fall of Troy. How is this relevant to this play? [Hecuba was a loyal queen; Priam was killed through treachery. There are oblique parallels to Denmark's situation.]
Q: What play does Hamlet arrange for? Why? When will it be acted? [Hamlet arranges for the actors to present "The Murder of Gonzago." The action of the play closely parallels the crimes that the Ghost has accused Claudius of committing. Hamlet will use the play "to catch the conscience of the king.]
Q: Of what does Hamlet accuse himself in the soliloquy (lines 523-62)? Are the accusations accurate? [He calls himself a dull rogue, coward, and villain for not feeling or taking action. He is, of course, now taking action, so his accusations are not literally true. Again, Hamlet's sense of delay is extremely subjective because his perception of time is so distorted.]
Q: What does Hamlet tell us about the play he wants the actors to put on? How does he plan to use this play? [The play will closely parallel Claudius's murder of old Hamlet; Hamlet hopes the king will react and reveal his guilt.]
Q: What point does Hamlet make again about the Ghost in this soliloquy? [The Ghost may be a devil trying to damn Hamlet (lines 574-79).]

ACT 2 REVIEW: Act 2 advances the conflicts of the play and focuses the action; it can be reviewed with six questions: 1. How is the characterization of Hamlet advanced? 2. What do his soliloquies show us? 3. How has Hamlet moved closer to the confirmation of the Ghost's accusations? 4. What defensive or protective actions has Claudius initiated? 5. What role does Polonius play in Act 2? 6. Does our opinion of Polonius change?

ACT 3. CRISIS AND CONFRONTATION: HAMLET'S ACT.

3.1.A (lines 1-28): CLAUDIUS AND R & G.
Q: What do R&G report to Claudius? How successful have they been as spies? [They have been unable to discover anything; Hamlet will not answer them.]

3.1.B (lines 29-55): CLAUDIUS, POLONIUS, AND OPHELIA: THE TEST OF LOVE
Q: What do Claudius & Polonius set up for Hamlet using Ophelia? [The chance encounter that will test whether Hamlet's madness is derived from love.]
Q: How is this confrontation like the play-within-the-play that Hamlet uses later in Act 3 to test Claudius's guilt? [Both are staged actions; both involve audiences; both are designed to test information through reactions.]
Q: To what extent does Ophelia's role in this test change or confirm our opinion of her? [Ever pliant and obedient, Ophelia allows herself to become a tool in the hands of Polonius and Claudius. To the extent that she is playing out their instructions, she is an actress, justifying Hamlet's references to face painting, fraud, and deceit later in the scene.]

3.1.C (lines 56-88): HAMLET'S "TO BE OR NOT TO BE" SOLILOQUY.
Q: What does Hamlet seem to be contemplating here? Is he actually suicidal? Is his contemplation personal or abstract? [Hamlet's depression leads him to contemplate death ("not to be") and suicide in an abstract and impersonal manner (cowards of us all, 83); this is really an abstract exercise.]

3.1.D (lines 89-149): HAMLET & OPHELIA IN THE LOBBY.
Q: What does Ophelia try to give to Hamlet? Why? What does Hamlet say about his feelings toward Ophelia? [She tries to return favors as part of the test; he refuses them. At this point, Hamlet is playing with Ophelia; he claims that he loved her once (115) and then denies it (118).]

Q: How does Hamlet treat Ophelia? Does his treatment (and attitude) change? If so, how and when? Why does he ask Ophelia about Polonius (130)? Does he know (or discover) that he is being watched? [Hamlet begins by toying with Ophelia and ends up in a rage. The change seems to occur at line 130 when he asks about Polonius. Since the text does not account for the shift, many directors stage the scene so that Hamlet spots movement behind the arras at this point. If staged this way, the subsequent tirade reflects Hamlet's return to feigned madness and his real disappointment with Ophelia.]
Q: What does Hamlet focus on in his tirade against Ophelia? How is this relevant? [Honesty in women, face painting, make-up, acting, seeming.]

3.1.E (lines 150-188): REACTIONS TO HAMLET'S BEHAVIOR.
Q: What is Ophelia's reaction to Hamlet? What is Claudius's? [She thinks he is mad: "O what a noble mind is here o'erthrown" (150). He is suspicious; he knows that the source of Hamlet's behavior is not love (lines 162-166).]
Q: How does Claudius plan to deal with Hamlet? [Send him to England.]
Q: What is Polonius's reaction to the confrontation? [He still thinks love caused the madness; he cannot give up his own ideas even when proven wrong.]
Q: What new plan to find Hamlet out does Polonius offer? [He proposes that Gertrude speak to Hamlet and that he eavesdrop (lines 181-187).]

3.2: THE CRISIS OF THE PLAY.
Before a close reading, ask your students what and where the crisis is. The crisis is Claudius's reaction to the play. It radically changes both Hamlet's and Claudius's behavior and sets them on a collision course; both know the truth about the other at this point.

3.2.A (lines 1-126): HAMLET'S INSTRUCTIONS AND PREPARATIONS.
Q: What points does Hamlet make to the actors about acting? About drama? [He does not want the actors to over-act or ad-lib. Drama (playing) is defined as holding "the mirror up to nature" (line 20).]
Q: How does Hamlet explain his relationship to Horatio? What does Hamlet want Horatio to do during "Gonzago"? [Hamlet likes and trusts Horatio because the latter is well-balanced, honest, and controlled. The recorder metaphor here (line 66) anticipates the same metaphor later in the scene in connection with R&G. Horatio does not fawn or flatter. Hamlet wants him to observe Claudius during the murder scene in "Gonzago" to see if his guilt will show itself.]
Q: Hamlet (line 85) says "I must be idle." What course of action does this involve? How does Hamlet sustain his antic disposition? [Idle here means foolish or insane. Hamlet sustains the illusion of madness by speaking pointed nonsense and punning suggestively.]

3.2.B (lines 126-246): THE DUMB SHOW AND "THE MURDER OF GONZAGO."
Q: What is a dumb show? What happens in this dumb show? How is it relevant? Why doesn't Claudius react to it? [It is a pantomime enactment of the entire play, including the murder. Claudius's failure to react to this enactment of his crime is inexplicable, unless we assume he isn't watching the actors. The text does not provide an answer here. In performance, however, many directors choose to have Claudius busy with Gertrude at this point.]
Q: Summarize the plot of "Gonzago." How is it relevant to Hamlet? What are the parallels between the characters in Hamlet and "Gonzago"? Why is "Gonzago" an effective test of the Ghost's accusations? ["Gonzago" includes all Claudius's major sins: murder, lust, usurpation, and an unsavory marriage. The player King represents Old Hamlet, the Player Queen Gertrude, and Lucianus Claudius. The parallels make the play an ideal test of Claudius's guilt.]
Q: How does Claudius react to the staged murder? [See lines 252-255.]
Q: Why is this the crisis of the play? What does Hamlet learn about Claudius

at this point? What does Claudius learn about Hamlet? [To this point, the play has been a careful dance in which both Hamlet and Claudius have avoided confrontation & direct action. Now, both will attempt to act: Hamlet to kill the eavesdropper in 3.4. and Claudius to send Hamlet off to execution in England. Both initial attempts at action are unsuccessful.]

3.2.C (lines 246-364): REACTIONS TO THE PLAY & EVENTS.
Q: How has Hamlet's position changed? ["I'll take the ghost's word for a thousand pound" (lines 271-2); he is convinced of Claudius's guilt.]
Q: What do R&G report to Hamlet? Whose interests do they represent? How does Hamlet treat them? Explain the metaphor of the recorder. [They represent Claudius's interests and report his rage as well as Gertrude's desire to speak with Hamlet. Hamlet treats them with scorn and anger; he accuses them of trying to play him as they would a recorder.]

3.2.D (lines 365-407): HAMLET'S SOLILOQUY.
Q: What is Hamlet's frame of mind? What is he ready to do? How does his language and imagery reflect his attitude? [He is ready to revenge (drink hot blood); images like "witching time of night" and "Hell itself breathes out contagion" suggest his commitment to bloody (and evil) deeds.]
Q: What is Hamlet's attitude toward his mother here? [This is part of Hamlet's problem; he seems more enraged with Gertrude than with Claudius.]

3.3: CLAUDIUS AT PRAYER & HAMLET'S AVOIDANCE OF REVENGE.
Q: What does Claudius have planned for Hamlet? [England, see lines 1-7.]
Q: What is Rosencrantz's vision of the state and the death of a king? Why is this vision ironic in connection with Claudius? [A king's death produces universal sadness and chaos because of the disorder in the cosmos. This is ironic because Claudius as a usurper has already produced cosmic disorder.]
Q: What does Claudius reveal in his soliloquy? How does the soliloquy affect your evaluation of him? [The soliloquy reveals that Claudius is guilty and that he <u>feels</u> guilt; it humanizes him by showing that he is not pure evil.]
Q: What reasons does Hamlet give for not killing Claudius at his prayers? Are they convincing? In character? What else is on his mind at this point? Why is Hamlet's decision here ironic? To what extent does this scene support either Hamlet's own sense that he is guilty of delay or the 19th-century argument that Hamlet's <u>tragic flaw</u> is his inability to act? [This moment is hotly debated by critics. Hamlet says that he avoids acting because he would send Claudius's soul to heaven; he wants to kill him when he will be <u>damned</u>. Some critics are struck by the uncharacteristic bloodthirstiness and bad theology here. Ironically, Claudius cannot pray (see lines 97-98). In any event, Hamlet clearly has his <u>mother</u> on his mind (line 95). Since Hamlet acts with speed in 3.4, this moment of delay should not carry too much weight.]

3.4.A (lines 1-34): THE DEATH OF POLONIUS.
Q: What is Polonius doing in Gertrude's chamber? [See lines 1-7.]
Q: How does Hamlet treat Gertrude? What frightens Polonius? How is Polonius killed? Why is he killed? Whom did Hamlet hope that he was killing? Hamlet calls Polonius a "wretched, rash, intruding fool" (line 31); is this accurate? To what extent is Polonius responsible for his own death? What does this act show us about Hamlet? [Hamlet verbally attacks Gertrude; she becomes afraid and calls for help (20-21). Polonius also calls out, and Hamlet stabs him through the arras. Hamlet hopes he has killed Claudius (26). In any event, Hamlet can act with speed. Polonius has been an intrusive plotting busybody since the play's opening. Hamlet's assessment is thus accurate; Polonius's intrusion into matters above his scope or knowledge justifies his death.]

259

3.4.B (lines 35-217): HAMLET'S LECTURE & THE GHOST'S RETURN.
Q: What two men does Hamlet compare? What points does he make about Claudius?
About Gertrude's behavior? What seems to disturb Hamlet most here? What
effect does this lecture have on Gertrude? [Hamlet compares old Hamlet to
Claudius (in production, he often holds miniature portraits of both men up to
Gertrude. He is wearing the miniature of Old Hamlet; she wears the miniature
of Claudius). He accuses Gertrude of shifting from godlike grace to a
murderer, villain, and usurper because of lust. He seems far more upset by
Gertrude's remarriage than by his father's murder here. Later, he tells
Gertrude to avoid Claudius's bed.]
Q: Why does the Ghost return? Why does Hamlet assume the Ghost has returned?
[Hamlet assumes the Ghost returns to criticize his delay (tardy son). The
Ghost says that he has come "to whet thy almost blunted purpose" (111). Many
critics take this to mean that Hamlet has become too much concerned with
Gertrude and too little with Claudius; it's a matter of focus rather than
time. Remind students of the Ghost's original orders concerning Gertrude.]
Q: What is Gertrude's opinion of Hamlet's mental state? What does He tell
her? What does she promise? [She thinks him mad. He explains that he is mad
in craft and warns her not to tell Claudius. She promises to keep silent.]
Q: What does Hamlet know about R&G and the impending trip to England? What
does he plan to do about the problem? [He knows they cannot be trusted and
are leading him to knavery. He plans to destroy them through their own
devices (see lines 200-210).]

    ACT 3 REVIEW AND INTRODUCTION TO ACT 4: Act 3 has focused on Hamlet: (1)
his efforts to confirm the Ghost's accusations; (2) his avoidance of revenge
during the praying scene; (3) his accidental killing of Polonius; (4) his
interview with his mother. Throughout Act 3, Hamlet is active. The murder of
the wrong man, however, puts Hamlet into a defensive position and gives
Claudius the upper hand. Thus, in Act 4, the focus shifts from Hamlet (who is
sent off to England) to Claudius. While Act 3 focuses on Hamlet's attempts to
gain vengeance, Act 4 focuses on Claudius's attempts to eliminate Hamlet. Act
4 begins with Claudius's first plan of attack--to have Hamlet murdered in
England. It ends with his second plan: the rigged fencing match.

ACT 4. THE TIGHTENING WEB: CLAUDIUS'S COUNTER MOVES.

    4.1: CLAUDIUS AND GERTRUDE.
Q: What does Gertrude report to Claudius? What does Claudius realize about
Hamlet's killing of Polonius? What does he plan to do with Hamlet? [She
reports Hamlet's madness and murder of Polonius. Claudius realizes it was
meant for him (13); he plans to send Hamlet to England at dawn (29-30).]

    4.2: HAMLET AND R & G.
Q: What is Hamlet's attitude toward R&G? [He scorns them as sponges who soak
up Claudius's orders, rewards, authority. They have become mere extensions.]

    4.3: CLAUDIUS AND HAMLET.
Q: How does Hamlet act with Claudius when questioned about Polonius? Why?
[He maintains the appearance of madness but drops hints to trouble Claudius.]
Q: What does Claudius have planned for Hamlet in England? [See lines 55-65.]
Q: Why does Claudius plan to have Hamlet eliminated in secret in England? Why
not simply have him killed? [2 reasons: Hamlet's popularity with the people
and Gertrude's love. Claudius wants Hamlet dead, but he wants his own hands
to appear to be completely clean. This plan is consistent with Claudius's

willingness and ability to use people to his own ends throughout the play. He
uses Polonius, Ophelia, R&G, Laertes, &c, and most of these people willingly
allow themselves to be used out of duty or the hope of advancement.]

4.4: HAMLET ON THE WAY TO THE SEACOAST & ENGLAND.
Q: Where are Fortinbras and his army going? What does Hamlet find out about
the land that will be fought over? How does this meeting influence Hamlet's
thinking as expressed in soliloquy (lines 32-66)? Of what does Hamlet accuse
himself? [They are going to fight over a barren plot of land in Poland worth
nothing but honor. Hamlet sees this instance as a rebuke of his own tardiness
and lack of passion. He argues that he has far greater cause to act than Fortinbras and yet <u>lets all</u> sleep. The charges are not an accurate reflection of
the situation; at this moment, Hamlet is powerless to act against Claudius.]

4.5.A (lines 1-70): OPHELIA'S INSANITY.
Q: What is Ophelia's condition? How does her language convey her madness?
How is her madness different from Hamlet's? [Ophelia's madness--the real
thing--is conveyed in fragmented grammar, nonsense, and oblique allusions to
Polonius's death and a lover; there is no <u>method</u> to her madness.]
Q: Why is Ophelia mad? How is madness consistent with her character? [Her
madness evolves from her father's death, Hamlet's treatment of her, and a loss
of direction. Throughout the play, she has been guided by Polonius or her
brother; now she has no one who offers direction. The madness is consistent
with her obedience, sense of duty, selflessness, and lack of will.]

4.5.B (lines 71-151): THE RETURN OF LAERTES.
Q: What is Laertes's attitude when he returns to Denmark? What does he want?
In what ways is he in a position parallel to Hamlet's? Is he more or less
justified than Hamlet? [Laertes is enraged over Polonius's death and secret
burial; he blames Claudius and wants revenge (133-4). As a son whose father
has been murdered, Laertes is an exact parallel to Hamlet; his desires are
equally just (or unjust?). This twist of the plot ironically makes Hamlet
parallel to Claudius and reveals the moral corruption inherent in vengeance.]

4.5.C (lines 152-214): LAERTES & OPHELIA, LAERTES & CLAUDIUS.
Q: How does Ophelia behave with Laertes? What is the focus of her madness?
What is Laertes's reaction? [Ophelia's madness continues; she dwells on
images that suggest Polonius's death. Laertes's desire for revenge grows.]
Q: What does Claudius offer Laertes? [See lines 197-214.]

4.6: HORATIO & THE SAILORS.
Q: What does Hamlet's letter reveal? [The method of his return to Denmark.]

4.7: CLAUDIUS AND LAERTES PLOT.
Q: What has Claudius proven to Laertes about Polonius's death? What news does
he expect from England? What news does he get? [He convinces Laertes that
Hamlet killed Polonius while trying to kill him. He expects to hear that
Hamlet has been executed; instead, he hears of Hamlet's safe return.]
Q: How do Claudius & Laertes plan to murder Hamlet? To what extent is Laertes
manipulated by Claudius? To what extent is Laertes the author of this plan?
How is Laertes's commitment to revenge different from Hamlet's? [They plan to
murder Hamlet by trickery during a fencing match. Claudius invents the plan,
but Laertes adds the detail of the poison (139-47). He manipulates Laertes to
do his dirty work, but Laertes is willing to go along. Laertes's commitment
is absolute; he is willing to <u>cut</u> Hamlet's <u>throat i'th'church.</u>]
Q: What do we find out about Ophelia in this scene? [Drowned, line 164.]

261

ACT 4 REVIEW AND INTRODUCTION TO ACT 5. Just as Act 3 was mostly
Hamlet's act, so Act 4 is mostly Claudius's. Having killed Polonius in Act 3,
Hamlet is on the defensive in Act 4; Claudius is on the offensive. The Act
contains Claudius's 2 plans for getting rid of Hamlet: the English execution
and the rigged fencing match. The re-introduction of Laertes as a secondary
revenger (and a parallel to Hamlet) complicates the neatly unfolding structure
of the play, but Laertes is quickly co-opted and absorbed by Claudius; Laertes
essentially becomes an extension of Claudius's malevolent will and a tool for
the arch-villain. By the end of Act 4, then, the two central thrusts of
motive-action are clearly established: Hamlet's desire to eliminate Claudius
and Claudius's desire to eliminate Hamlet. These two lines of force or motive
or action meet head on in Act 5, where both are resolved simultaneously.

ACT 5: VENGEANCE, CATASTROPHE, AND RESOLUTION.

5.1.A (lines 1-55): THE CLOWNS (GRAVEDIGGERS).
Q: What is the subject of the clowns' conversation? How is this subject
relevant to the play? To what extent is the conversation amusing? [The
general topic is death and decay. Death permeates Hamlet, and this scene
provides another focus on this central fact. Critics have traditionally seen
this conversation and the next (5.1.B.) as comic relief. You might want to
talk about what comic relief is. Does this conversation work as comic relief?
Why is comic relief useful at this point in the play? The interlude here
provides for a temporary relief of tension before the catastrophe.]

5.1.B (lines 56-201): HAMLET AND THE CLOWN.
Q: To what extent is this conversation also comic relief? About what do the
skulls make Hamlet think? What subject is the overall focus of this conversation? How is this subject relevant to Hamlet's earlier considerations? To
what extent does Shakespeare make his comic relief work thematically? [Again,
the focus is on death. Hamlet has spent most of the play considering death,
salvation, damnation, suicide, and the like. His abstraction in this scene
suggests a readiness to face death that is confirmed later in the act. The
comic relief is not wasted; it reflects one of the play's central concerns.
Yorick's skull makes the idea of death immediate to Hamlet. References to
Alexander the Great and Caesar suggest death's universal and levelling power.]

5.1.C (lines 201-282): OPHELIA'S FUNERAL.
Q: How does Laertes act? What point does Hamlet make about his own feelings
for Ophelia? About Laertes? [Laertes acts with exaggerated grief. Hamlet
claims that he can overmatch Laertes's act since his feelings are greater.]

5.2.A (lines 1-80): THE FATE OF R & G.
Q: What orders were R&G carrying? What did Hamlet do to R&G? To what extent
is their fate just? What is Hamlet's attitude toward their fate? [R&G had
orders for Hamlet's immediate execution (lines 18-25); Hamlet altered the
orders so that R&G would be put to instant death upon their arrival in England
(38-47). Students should be encouraged to discuss the fairness of these
deaths. Hamlet clearly thinks they deserved to die (lines 57-62).]

5.2.B (lines 81-179): HAMLET AND OSRIC.
Q: What is Osric like? Why does Hamlet call him a water-fly? What is his
language like? How is he like Polonius? How does Hamlet mock Osric? What is
Osric's business with Hamlet? [Osric is an over-dressed dandy puffed up with
his own importance. Hamlet's reference to him as a water-fly reflects his

262

dress, manners, and lack of importance. Like Polonius, Osric talks around the matter rather than to it. Hamlet mocks his manners with the bonnet business and his overly courtly double-talk by feeding it back to him (lines 109-119). Osric delivers Laertes's challenge to the fencing match. Some critics see him as a symbol of the corruption in Claudius's court.]

5.2.C (lines 179-206): HAMLET AND HORATIO.

Q: What is Hamlet's attitude toward the fencing match? [He thinks he will win (line 194) but he is very suspicious (lines 194-201).]
Q: What has Hamlet learned by this point in the play? [Patience and readiness (see lines 202-6). He accepts the providence of all things and believes that the readiness is all. Ironically, these lessons will neither help nor save him, because action is forced on him immediately.]

5.2.D (lines 207-344): THE FENCING MATCH--THE CATASTROPHE.

Q: How do Hamlet and Laertes act toward each other before the match? Which is sincere? [The men exchange pardons and love; only Hamlet is sincere.]
Q: Who wins the first 2 bouts? What is Laertes's problem? How does he solve it? [Hamlet wins both; Laertes cannot get a legitimate hit with the poisoned foil, so he stabs Hamlet between bouts. This violation of the rules of fair play underscores Laertes's corruption and his commitment to vengeance.]
Q: How is Gertrude killed? Laertes? Claudius? In what way are all 3 deaths ironic? [Gertrude is killed with the poisoned wine that Claudius prepared for Hamlet. Laertes is mortally wounded with his own unbaited and poisoned foil. Claudius is killed with both the poisoned wine and foil. The villains are killed with their own weapons: Laertes admits that "I am justly killed with mine own treachery" (290). Gertrude's death is ironic in that Claudius's weapon destroys what he was trying to preserve. Both Gertrude and Laertes name Claudius as the guilty creature before they die.]
Q; Why does Hamlet want Horatio to stay alive? What is Hamlet's final concern? [He wants Horatio alive to tell my story (lines 326-32); he is concerned about his reputation (wounded name).]

5.2.E (lines 345-386): RESOLUTION--TYING UP OF LOOSE ENDS

Q: Who will be the next king of Denmark? [Probably Fortinbras.]
Q: What does Horatio plan to explain to the unknowing world?
Q: What is Fortinbras's attitude toward Hamlet? [Fortinbras treats Hamlet with honor and respect; he calls him most royal and has the body like a soldier. Thus, Fortinbras implicitly accepts the justice of Hamlet's cause and Claudius's (as yet undisclosed) villainy.]

Discussion of Topics for Writing

1-6. All these topics focus on character. Claudius, Horatio, R&G, and Polonius are discussed at length above. Gertrude and Ophelia, the only women in the play, seem to justify Hamlet's assertion about frailty. Ophelia is the more fully developed character; we see Gertrude mostly from Hamlet's distorted perspective, and he certainly considers her morally weak. Nevertheless, Horatio confirms that the marriage followed quickly after the funeral. There is never any suspicion that Gertrude had prior knowledge or dealings with Claudius. Hence, her second marriage points toward weakness rather than evil. Ophelia, as noted above in discussions of 1.3. and 4.5, is controlled to a significant degree by the men in her life: Hamlet, Laertes, and Polonius. In her dutiful cooperation with Claudius and Polonius, she is tainted with the same sort of evil that condemns Polonius and R&G.

(TEXT PAGES) 1177-1365

Hamlet, Laertes, and Fortinbras are all parallel revengers in the broadest sense. Fortinbras wants to avenge his father's defeat and death at the hands of Old Hamlet. He seeks to do so in a straightforward manner through military action against Denmark. Although deflected from Denmark to Poland by his uncle, he ultimately claims the Danish throne and gains the dying Hamlet's approval. Hamlet's quest for vengeance is complicated by his need to prove the Ghost's accusations, his fixation on his mother's crimes, and his own feelings of guilt over what he sees as delay. These combine to postpone his killing of Claudius (but not action) until it is too late for Hamlet to escape death. Hamlet's is perhaps the most thoughtful but least effective quest. Laertes commits himself more directly to vengeance, but also allies himself with evil. He is not interested in corroborating evidence or finding truth; his is thus the most corrupt quest for revenge.

7-8. There are at least 2 ways of looking at the conflict here. If one views Hamlet as a man incapacitated by his own character and responsibilities, the conflict is internal. If one considers the play in terms of action and political dynamics, the central conflict is between Hamlet as protagonist and Claudius as antagonist. From this perspective, Hamlet's conflicts with R&G, Polonius, and Laertes are all secondary, because all these characters serve as (witting or unwitting) extensions of Claudius. In either event, resolution occurs in the catastrophe. The crisis occurs in 3.2. (see above), during the play-within-the-play. Claudius's guilty reaction fixes Hamlet's subsequent course of action and the outcome of the play.

9. In terms of immediate action, Claudius murders only one person (Old Hamlet), cooperates in the murder of another (Hamlet), and accidentally kills a third (Gertrude). The remainder of these characters are killed by Hamlet (directly or indirectly). From a broader perspective, however, Claudius is responsible for all the carnage. His original murder of an anointed king and usurpation of the throne upsets cosmic order (the Great Chain of Being) and introduces destructive chaos into the world of the play. These primal acts of destruction begin a chain reaction that finally encompasses all the deaths.

10. Appearance versus reality is a central theme and motif throughout the play. The greatest illusion masquerading as reality is the image of Claudius as a good and just king; he deceives the entire court and the population at large. This illusion makes direct action without proof very difficult for Hamlet. Other characters who are not what they seem in the play include R&G, Polonius, Laertes, and Hamlet. His antic disposition is another illusion.

11. When Hamlet begins, the state is already diseased and disordered; the first scene suggests unnatural and chaotic events. The close of the play holds the promise of order and control; Fortinbras makes a valid claim to the throne and Horatio suggests that it will be upheld. Nevertheless, Denmark has lost both a good old king and a prince with great potential. Order returns with the death of Claudius and the emergence of Fortinbras as a strong leader, but the price is monumental.

The Theater of Arthur Miller, pages 1288-1290.

This discussion provides an introduction to the modern theater and many aspects of contemporary drama and staging. It can be usefully assigned in conjunction with Death of a Salesman or with Tennessee Williams's The Glass Menagerie (pages 1564-1619).

Arthur Miller, Death of a Salesman, pages 1290-1365.

Miller's American masterpiece illustrates what tragedy has become in the modern world. The introduction to the play (pages 1290-1294) briefly surveys the stage history, the concept of the common man as tragic hero, and the critique of the American dream that parallels the fall of Willy Loman. The play, like Williams's Glass Menagerie, represents a midpoint between the total realism of Ibsen and the nonrealism of Edward Albee. And like Oedipus or A Doll's House, it embodies the end of a much longer story. Here, however, this longer story is brought into the present through dramatized fragments of memory. These scenes of past action come out of Willy's head; they are consequently subjective and distorted visions of the past rather than accurate recreations. Psychologically, they suggest (as did Freud) that the past is always in the present, shaping our thoughts, actions, fears, and dreams.

In teaching Death of a Salesman, you can focus mostly on character and theme. The chief character for discussion is Willy Loman. Students will perceive him as a good deal less heroic than Oedipus or Hamlet, but his problems are equally consuming and fatal. A key question: what makes Willy heroic? Thematically, the play explores ideas about individual dignity, the impact of a single trauma on subsequent life, and the corruption of the American dream. All these points can lead to effective discussion.

The play was originally produced on Broadway in 1949 with Lee J. Cobb as Willy Loman. Cobb was a large man; Miller had to revise parts of his original script to accommodate Cobb's enactment of Willy Loman. The present text--the one Miller published in his complete works--reflects these changes. In 1984 the play was revived on Broadway with Dustin Hoffman in the lead. This production was filmed for television and broadcast in 1985. Videotapes of this production should eventually be available for classroom use. Hoffman played Willy as a small and nervous man always on the edge of collapse. In many respects, his performance was closer to Miller's original conception than was the 1949 production with Lee J. Cobb.

Discussion of Questions

1. The first stage direction suggests that Willy's world is fragile and dream-like. We are presented with a setting that is only partly real (or realistic). Willy himself is described as exhausted; the large sample cases represent his burdens. Every move combines weariness and anxiety.

2. There are 2 clues very early in the play that Willy is losing touch with reality. One is his inability to drive (page 1296). The other is his assertion that he "opened the windshield" of the car. Later, it becomes clear that Willy could not have opened the windshield on the car he owns in 1949 (they don't open); he was remembering (reliving, dreaming about) the car he owned in 1928. Willy's confusion becomes even more evident when he slips completely into memory for the 1st time (pages 1303-11). Here, a number of events that occurred in 1928 merge together into one memory sequence.

3. Stealing is a leitmotif that runs throughout the play. In the past, Willy encouraged (or at least tolerated) the boy's thievery from construction sites (the very apartment houses that now hem him in). Biff has a long and sorry history of stealing: the football, the sporting goods, a suit, Oliver's pen. Much of his post-1928 thievery is clearly self-destructive. Happy steals in another way; he takes women from other men simply to prove to himself that he can do it. Willy himself stole illicit (extramarital) sex on his selling trips. Willy's toleration of stealing suggests a link between this sort of dishonesty and the emphasis he places on appearances (smiling, being well liked) and selling (one's product, one's self).

4. This assertion reflects the degree to which Willy can delude himself. Willy told Biff, at least by example, that dishonesty is acceptable and that

265

appearances matter more than substance. He continues to stress appearances in the present, maintaining the illusion of his pay check and insisting that Biff look and act just so (sell himself) in his interview with Oliver. In effect, this line is directly contradicted by Biff's claim (question 9) that "we never told the truth for ten minutes in this house."

5. For Willy (and for the reader or viewer), stockings become a symbol of his past infidelities and of Biff's terrible moment of discovery. Willy gave new stockings to The Woman in Boston; Linda mends her old stockings both in the past and in the present. Stockings thus emblemize Willy's guilt over his actions, Biff's discovery, and the subsequent alienation of father and son.

6. Throughout the play, Willy cannot (or will not) deal effectively with machines. He continually wrecks his car, the refrigerator is always in need of repair, and the wire recorder in Howard's office terrifies him. These machines represent the (1949) present--the world that Willy can no longer deal with adequately. The present of machines is contrasted with the past of Dave Singleman, 1928, Uncle Ben, and Willy's childhood memories of his father.

7. Willy is asking Bernard about the secret to success, achievement, dignity, and recognition--fulfillment of the American dream. He clearly understands, at least part of the time, that he and his sons have failed to measure up to society's standards for success. Charley and Bernard illustrate the truth that there is no secret beyond hard work and a concentration on substance rather than style (early in the play, Willy observes that Charley is liked, but not _well_ liked). Looked at another way, the secret might be that Willy has incorporated the wrong value system.

8. This is a very complex and disturbing moment in the play--it brings together all of Willy's desperation, confusion, and agony. On the one hand, the garden represents the past: a time before the house was hemmed in by brutal and impersonal apartment houses and before The Woman in Boston--a time when Willy was still idolized as a heroic figure by his sons. Willy's need to plant a garden reflects his desire to return to this state of grace. On the other hand, having "things in the ground" or growing can be taken to represent success, achievement, and security. Willy's desperation here reflects his knowledge that his life is mostly empty and fruitless. In addition, he understands that his sons (who are, of course, other kinds of growing things) are not thriving in the "soil" in which he has planted them.

9. Biff's line indicates his realization that the Loman men have consistently deluded themselves with half-truths and unrealistic dreams. To some extent, this continues to be true to the end of the play. Only Biff comes to a realistic assessment of his own life and abilities; he understands that he will be more content on the land. Willy remains partly self-deluded right to the end; he assumes that his funeral will be well attended and he imagines that the insurance money will make Biff a success. Happy's last lines indicate that he remains trapped in Willy's deluded visions of success.

10. Linda's final line is open to various interpretations; give students free rein with this one. It might imply that the Lomans are free of hot air and self-delusion. If so, the assertion is not true, at least for Happy. The line might also suggest that the Lomans are free from the false values and standards of Willy's American dream. Again, this is not true for Happy.

Discussion of Topics for Writing

1. The degeneration in the setting (the house, the surrounding scrim) reflects the degeneration of Willy over the years. The past (of 1928 and before) is indicated by green light, the shadow of leaves, blocking that moves characters through the wall-lines of the house, and Ben's flute music. The

present is reflected in the angry orange glow of the apartment houses and realistic blocking in which the wall-lines of the house are observed. The staging of present action is mostly realistic, while the staging of memory sequences reflects the nonrealistic nature of dreaming and memory.

2. Generally, detailed stage directions are designed to help the reader understand the play and experience it fully. In this case, however, Miller's extremely long stage directions suggest that he wrote with readers (rather than actors or viewers) in mind. Stage directions that cannot be played on the stage clearly indicate the double audience (spectators and readers) that modern playwrights address.

3. Willy's suicide is foreshadowed at the very beginning of the play when Linda asks if he smashed up the car (page 1295). Later in the first Act, Linda tells her sons that "all these accidents in the last year—weren't—weren't accidents" (1320). These comments directly anticipate Willy's vehicular suicide at the close of Act 2. Suicide is also foreshadowed and symbolized in the rubber pipe and "the new little nipple on the gas pipe" that Willy has apparently installed in the basement (1320-1321).

4. There are two crises here; both occur on stage and within Willy's mind; students will have to decide which is the primary one. The first is Biff's discovery of Willy's adultery; this single moment shapes both Willy and Biff's future (i.e., the present of the play). It also accounts for the ongoing alienation between father and son, Biff's self-destructiveness, and Willy's guilt. The second crisis is Willy's decision, while in conversation with Ben, to commit suicide; it shapes the catastrophe, which follows closely when Willy drives off to his death (page 1361), and the resolution of the play (the Requiem). Willy and Biff each experience a partial anagnorisis. Willy realizes that he has run out of lies (dreams, illusions, page 1346) and that Biff loves him (page 1360). Biff recognizes that he does not want Willy's version of the American dream (page 1359).

5. The play succeeds in various periods and cultures because the characters, conflicts, and themes remain as relevant today as they were almost 40 years ago. Willy is a universal figure, the low man instead of every man. His dreams and delusions are universal in type if not in detail. All cultures produce value systems and standards that individuals fight against (or for) in a quest for status and dignity. The details of Willy's fall may be particular to the United States, but the pattern of his struggle is transcendent.

6-7. All the characters in the present are real and realistic (the 1949 versions of the Lomans, Charley and Bernard, Howard, Jennie, and the people in the bar). These characters act and speak realistically. The hallucinatory characters that emerge from Willy's memory include the 1928 Lomans, Charley and Bernard, Uncle Ben, and The Woman. These figures are a good deal less developed or realistic; they have been flattened out and stripped of unessential characteristics through the subjective filter of memory and guilt. Their stage movement is often nonrealistic; their language is formulaic and repetitive. The 4 central symbolic characters of the play are Willy, Dave Singleman, Uncle Ben, and The Woman (Howard, Charley, and Bernard are secondary symbols). Willy, the low man, embodies failure and false values. Dave Singleman (present only by reference) symbolizes the single (or singular) man; he is Willy's personal symbol of success in the selling game. Uncle Ben represents another version of the American dream; he is the self-reliant pioneer-exploiter who opens new territories and carves wealth out of the land.

267

Willy's father is a much less well developed version of this same symbol. It is this romanticized and sentimentalized dream to which Biff is drawn at the end of the play. The Woman symbolizes guilt and trauma (as well as past pleasure) for Willy and for Biff; the sound of her laugh or a knock on the door can catapult Willy back to the horror of that moment of discovery.

8. Willy is heroic in his struggle for dignity, his willingness to go back on the road; he simply will not accept defeat. He even (mistakenly) sees his death as a heroic victory that will make people appreciate him and give Biff a new start in life. His central failing is self-delusion (lies, dreams, hot air). This blinds him to the realities of his own life and his sons' lack of ability. It can be argued that Willy's failure comes from within, from the lies and illusions he as fostered all his life. Conversely, students might argue that Willy's values reflect those imposed by a corrupt society; he measures himself against an invalid version of the American dream. From this perspective, Willy's failure is a recapitulation of society's failure.

9. Willy says to Charley, "you never told him [Bernard] what to do . . . you never took any interest in him." Charley replies, "My salvation is that I never took any interest in anything" (page 1339). The exchange epitomizes the differences between the two father-son relationships. Willy took an interest; he passed on his own values and delusions to his sons. Charley apparently let Bernard shape his own values and life, guiding only by example. To put it another way, Willy invested too much of his own life in his sons. Moreover, he willingly set himself up as a heroic ideal--an ideal that is destroyed for Biff in a single moment of revelation. Charley never fostered illusions of heroism in Bernard; there were no heroic ideals to be exposed as <u>fake</u>.

10. Linda is completely supportive of Willy; she accepts his lies and exaggerations (even when she knows they are false), and she fights for him against Biff and Happy. Linda is both an admirable and a culpable character (let the students decide which predominates); her support is both essential and destructive. It creates a reasonably strong marriage, but it also allows Willy to sustain his illusions far too long.

11. It can be argued that Biff changes--that he has the most significant and beneficial anagnorisis in the play (see question 4 above). Such knowledge suggests the potential for a more fruitful and happy life in the future. If students accept that Biff's return to the land embodies a viable alternative to Willy's dreams, then Biff's recognition implies hope. Looking at the play from this perspective, with Biff as the educated protagonist, creates a radical shift; it changes the focus from Willy's tragic fall to Biff's comedic redemption. One problem with this perspective is that Miller forces readers to be suspicious of Ben's version of the American dream and of Biff's ability.

12. Happy is an exaggerated and degenerated version of Willy. He embodies all the faults of Willy's dreams and delusions: the emphasis on externals and on being well liked, lies about achievement. He continues to pursue the same corrupt dream, "to come out number-one man" in the world of selling. His obsessive conquests of other men's women suggests a continual need to compete and prove himself to himself in the only arena in which he can still be successful. Happy is not happy, and probably never will be.

13. Willy's assertions about being "well liked" are symptomatic of his commitment to dreams, illusion, and style rather than substance. He preaches this dogma to his sons, but it has not worked for him and will not work for

them. Miller gives the explicit refutation of this philosophy to Charley (page 1340). Moreover, Charley and Bernard are living refutations of Willy's belief in style over substance.

14. Whatever else a salesman sells, he also sells himself. This is Miller's point, and it is the reason why the play never stresses the product that Willy sells. The product is incidental to the life and the dreams.

15. For Willy, 1928 was the last really good year, the year of promises, the year of "a hundred and seventy dollars a week in commissions" (page 1332). It was the year that Frank Wagner (may have) promised him a position in the home office, Biff played the championship game, and Ben last visited. It was also the the year in which Willy's adultery was discovered by Biff--the end of the boy's hero worship of Willy. For the nation, 1928 the last year of optimism and prosperity; the great depression began in 1929. These two patterns come together for Willy; 1928 was the end of hope and innocence.

16. The play attacks a specific version of the American dream that is based on style, competition, and wealth. This dream and these values are championed by Willy and Happy; Biff realizes that it is not valid for him. Howard represents success in this mode, and he comes across as self-absorbed, heartless, and petty. Charley and Bernard represent a different (and more viable) American dream--success through hard work, realism, and intelligence.

WRITING ABOUT TRAGEDY, pages 1365-1377.

This section discusses and illustrates several ways that students can plan and write essays about tragic drama. While the discussion does not focus on the elements introduced in Chapter 27, you can easily assign such an essay in connection with Oedipus, Hamlet, or Salesman. All three plays lend themselves to investigations of plot, structure, conflict, setting, character, tone, language, and theme. Oedipus and Hamlet offer excellent opportunities for writing about irony, and Salesman is especially rich in symbolism.

Because approaches to these topics are covered in Chapter 27 (refer your students to pages 1112-16 and the relevant cross references listed there), we decided to introduce two new types of essay in this chapter. The first is an essay about a problem (pages 1366-73). Here, we discuss ways of formulating and writing about a problem in literature. The sample essay (pages 1370-73) takes up the problem of delay in Hamlet. The second type is an essay on a close reading of a passage from a play (pages 1373-77). In this instance, the close reading focuses on content (rather than style) and relates the passage to a theme of the play. The sample essay (pages 1375-77) focuses on a key passage from Hamlet and links it to the theme of appearance versus reality. Both of these types of essay can be valuable and useful exercises.

CHAPTER 29

COMEDY

This chapter is designed to introduce students to the major aspects of comic drama. To that end, it begins with introductory material that discusses the nature and pattern of comedy, as well as comic characters, language, and types of comedy (pages 1378-1384). In reviewing this material in class, you might emphasize the distinction between comic and funny. Like the terms tragic and tragedy, the terms comic and comedy are used colloquially with a far broader application than is useful in understanding drama. In plays, the terms refer not only to a tone or attitude, but also to a reasonably well defined pattern of action that usually (but not always) leads to a resolution that is affirmative and regenerative. In satiric comedy, such as The Misanthrope, this regenerative impulse can be deferred (literally displaced) from the play to the audience, the readers, and the world at large.

The key points to touch on in discussing types of comedy include the distinctions between high and low as well as romantic and satiric. The chapter is designed to illustrate these distinctions with reference to two superb examples of comic drama. A Midsummer Night's Dream combines high comedy (in the overplot and the two middle plots) with low comedy (almost farce or slapstick, in the bungling misadventures of the mechanicals). The Misanthrope remains at the level of high comedy throughout. Although it contains a (very unconventional) romantic plot, it nevertheless mostly exemplifies the characteristics and impulses of satiric comedy.

As with the tragedies in Chapter 28, teaching these plays can be facilitated by using films or videotapes of performances in supplementary class meetings. Only one production of The Misanthrope is currently available in either film or videotape (52 minutes) from Films for the Humanities, Box 2053, Princeton, NJ 08540. This performance of the Wilbur translation stars Edward Petherbridge. Shakespeare's A Midsummer Night's Dream is available in numerous filmed or videotaped productions including the following:

1935 B/W Film or Videotape (117 minutes). Directed by Max Rinehardt, starring Olivia de Havilland and James Cagney. United Artists Corporation, 727 7th Avenue, New York, NY 10019.

Undated Color Film or Videotape. Directed by Joseph Papp, New York Shakespeare Festival. Films for the Humanities, Box 2053, Princeton, NJ 08540.

1968 Color Film (124 minutes). Directed by Peter Hall, RSC, starring David Warner and Diana Rigg. Audio-Brandon Films, 34 MacQuestern Parkway S., Mount Vernon, NY 10550.

1982 Color Videotape (120 minutes). Starring Helen Mirren and Peter McEnery. Time-Life Video, Box 644, Paramus, NJ 07652.

These films and/or tapes are also available from other distributors. It is a good idea to delay showing a film or tape until after the students have read the plays and begun class discussion. Too often, students come to believe that watching a film (or tape) can replace reading the play. In addition, the characterizations and interpretations created by actors and the director for a specific production will prejudice the students' own reading of the play.

William Shakespeare, A Midsummer Night's Dream, pages 1384-1443.

This is one of Shakespeare's funniest and most accessible comedies. If you teach it without (or before) doing Hamlet, it might be helpful to assign the introduction to Shakespeare's theater (pages 1173-76) and life (1177). The first of these will help students understand many of the important conventions of Elizabethan theater. The introduction to A Midsummer Night's Dream (pages 1384-86) provides a survey of plots, characters, and themes.

Teaching this play can be a delightful experience for both students and instructors alike. It provides an opportunity to deal with a number of dramatic elements at the same time. The three that can be most successfully emphasized in teaching are plot, character, and theme. Language (especially the different types of poetry) can be explored if time permits. The central plot (the 4 lovers) illustrates the New Comic pattern of blocked and then triumphant love. This plot is recapitulated (with a pathetic ending) in "Pyramus and Thisby," the play-within-the-play. The characters in the central plot are flat and conventional types that exemplify the dangers of love madness (irrational love, infatuation, dotage). In this plot and in the fairy plot, Puck serves as a jester, trouble-maker, and bizarre version of Cupid.

Thematically, the play explores at least two interconnected subjects: love and imagination. The absurdities and dangers of dotage are illustrated in the plight of the 4 lovers, the conflict produced by Titania's infatuation with her changeling child, her subsequent adoration of Bottom, and the pathetic deaths of Pyramus and Thisby. The power of imagination (and the intersection of imagination, perception, art, love, and dreams) is explored through the rehearsal process, the play-within-the-play, Theseus's commentary, and the device of love-in-idleness (the flower whose juice produces boundless infatuation by affecting perception).

Another approach to teaching structure and theme in this play is to contrast it (and "Pyramus") with Romeo and Juliet (written at about the same time). All 3 follow similar plots and offer related examinations of blind love. Romeo is commonly taught in the 10th or 11th grade; if your students are familiar with it, you can use the play as a parallel to both the comedy of Dream and the pathos of "Pyramus." In such an approach, Lysander parallels Pyramus and Romeo; Hermia parallels Thisby and Juliet. The blocking agents are similarly parallel: (1) Egeus and the old Athenian law; (2) the wall; (3) the Montague-Capulet feud. In all 3 cases, the attempt to circumvent the obstructions involves moving outside the normal constraints of law or society (into the night, woods, Ninus's Tomb, a secret marriage, away from Verona).

Discussion of Questions

1. Lines 1-19 supply exposition and characterization. Theseus and Hippolyta are to be married in 4 days; this provides the general time-frame of the play. In the past, Theseus fought a war against Hippolyta (Queen of the Amazons) and captured her (line 16-19). Their relationship, once characterized by the irrationality and passion of war, has evolved into a rational and harmonious dynastic alliance. However, they have very different attitudes toward the approaching marriage. Theseus is typically anxious and impatient; for him, time moves slowly and the moon (lines 2-6) is a blocking agent delaying the fulfillment of his desires. For Hippolyta, time is moving quickly (7-11) and the moon (a silver bow) symbolizes Diana, goddess of chastity and the hunt. Theseus and Hippolyta (along with Athens itself)

271

represent absolute order, rationality, law, and authority. Indeed, Theseus will learn in the course of the play that the rigor of the law must be relaxed in acknowledgement of the higher authority of love.

2. Hermia and Lysander are conventional and typical lovers; their problems are explained in 1.1.20-127. Egeus wants Hermia to marry Demetrius; she wants to wed Lysander. Egeus accuses Lysander of bewitching Hermia by moonlight (linking love, moonlight, magic, and irrationality). He invokes the ancient law of Athens which requires that Hermia obey Egeus, die, or become a nun at Diana's temple (since comedy is sexual and regenerative, this third choice is a comedic fate worse than death). Theseus gives Hermia four days (until his own wedding and the new moon) to choose. We also learn that Hermia and Lysander are desperately in love, that Egeus is irrationally fixated on Demetrius, that Demetrius and Lysander are identical as far as wealth and status are concerned, and that Demetrius has previously courted Helena. The ensuing conversation (lines 128-79) reveals the depths of young love (perhaps infatuation). Lysander plots an escape from Athens (156-168) by running off to a rich aunt's house (no financial sacrifice here) and Hermia agrees.

3. Helena is love-sick for Demetrius, jealous of Hermia's power to attract men, and extremely self-deprecating. Her negative self-image and low self-esteem are the result of Demetrius's scorn; although the world considers her fair, she see herself through Demetrius's eyes. Hermia and Lysander tell their plans to Helena to make her feel better. She, in turn, will tell Demetrius all to gain a moment of attention. Helena's soliloquy about love (discussed below in Topics for Writing) is a central thematic statement that provides a definition of the kind of blind and irrational love examined here.

4. They meet to assign roles for "The most lamentable comedy, and most cruel death of Pyramus and Thisby" (even the title suggests that these men do not understand much about drama). They hope to present the play at court in celebration of Theseus's marriage and thus earn a pension (see 4.2.14-15). The casting of Flute as Thisby humorously duplicates Elizabethan stage practices. Bottom's eagerness, energy, and conceit are reflected in his desire to demonstrate his acting skill and to play every role. His foolishness and limited education are established through his continual misuse of words. Here, he misuses generally (2), aggravated (69), and obscenely (91).

5. 2.1.1-145 is expository, introducing Puck, Titania, Oberon, and the conflict over the changeling. The fairy's lyric verse (2-13) is a characteristic mode of poetry for the spirits; it contrasts with Theseus's blank verse and the lovers' rhymed couplets. Puck is identified as Oberon's jester, a roguish trickster, and a trouble-maker (lines 32-58). His love of trickery and confusion becomes important later when he is trying to deal with 4 lovers.

6. The conflict between Oberon and Titania over the changeling is introduced by Puck (2.1.18-31) and explained more fully by Oberon and Titania (60-145). Titania is infatuated with the child; she spends all her time with him and ignores Oberon. Oberon is jealous, but he also has the right (as husband and king) to expect obedience and deference from Titania. Her involvement with the child is both a dotage and a disruption of her normal relationship with Oberon. This conflict is further complicated by Oberon's previous relationship with Hippolyta and Titania's with Theseus (64-80). As the ruling spirits of nature, Oberon and Titania are linked (through the Great Chain of Being) to cycles of time and season. Their discord disrupts these cycles to disastrous effect (81-117). Oberon claims that the chaos can be

fixed if Titania hands over the child. She refuses, claiming that the boy was entrusted to her by his dying mother (Why is Titania's explanation suspect?).

7. Oberon plans to humiliate and cure Titania by using love-in-idleness to put her madly in love with something monstrous. This shift of affection will make it possible for him to get the changeling. Oberon explains the source of the flower's magical power (155-72); the flower symbolizes the kind of blind and hasty love that Helena described in the 1st soliloquy. Oberon enchants Titania (2.2.1-34) by squeezing the juice from love-in-idleness on her eyes and reciting the appropriate lyric incantation; he hopes that she will wake when "some vile thing is near."

8. 2.1. and 2.2. present major complications in the lovers' plot. When Demetrius and Helena appear in the woods, he is chasing Hermia and Lysander, planning to sieze one and kill the other. She is pursuing Demetrius, seeking any attention at all (even abuse, see 2.1.202-10). He runs off, threatening Helena with injury if she follows. She pursues, claiming that she will "die upon the hand I love so well." Oberon overhears the exchange (why does he announce that he is invisible?) and decides to correct the situation by using love-in-idleness to change Demetrius's affections. Oberon's orders to Puck reveal his limitations; he does not know that there is another couple in the wood and his instructions are thus open to misinterpretation. The error occurs in 2.2. when Puck finds Hermia and Lysander, assumes they are the couple named by Oberon (why?), and anoints Lysander's eyes. When Helena awakens Lysander, he instantly falls madly in love with her (see 2.2.103-22). Helena assumes that this adoration is mockery (123-34). With the enchantment of Lysander, the love relationships among the 4 lovers move to the 2nd stage--a perfect round-robin in which no love is reciprocated.

9. In 3.1, Puck disrupts the rehearsal and transforms Bottom. He gives Bottom an ass-head for at least 3 reasons: (1) it is a good joke and consistent with Puck's love of trickery; (2) it is appropriate since Bottom (with a pun on the name) is already an ass; (3) it provides a suitably vile object of affection for Titania. When Bottom awakens Titania with his singing (3.1.115), she falls madly in love with this monster. Bottom's reaction is surprising and significant; he asserts that she has no reason to love him, but that "reason and love keep little company together now-a-days" (3.1.128-32). The speech, a key thematic statement, is ironic because Bottom (the fool) can see what none of the more noble or educated characters can understand.

10. In 3.2., Puck reports to Oberon about the transformation of Bottom, Titania's love, the harassment of the mechanicals, and the anointing of the Athenian's eyes. When Demetrius and Hermia arrive, the fairies realize that an error has occurred. Demetrius is pleading his own love; Hermia is seeking Lysander. Oberon accuses Puck of intentionally anointing the wrong man's eyes to cause trouble; he sends Puck off to get Helena and he puts the flower juice in Demetrius's eyes. While Puck did not intentionally produce this chaos, he enjoys it immensely (see 3.2.110-21); he realizes that 2 men will now woo Helena, and he finds such mortal foolishness highly amusing.

11. When Demetrius awakens under the influence of love-in-idleness (137) and spots Helena, he falls madly in love with her. This situation (stage 3 of the love relationships) exactly reverses the one that began the play; now both men love Helena and loathe Hermia. Because Helena's self-image is so badly damaged, she assumes that both men are mocking her. When Hermia joins the fray (177), Helena assumes that she is part of this confederacy of mockery.

12. Once the four lovers are together in the woods (3.2.177), things become progressively more chaotic and dangerous. The men decide to fight a duel over Helena (254-5) and the women begin to fight (at first verbally and then physically). The potential for disaster here is real (although we never believe it because Oberon and Puck remain in attendance). The men could kill each other; the women could be abandoned to wild animals (compare "Pyramus"). Oberon takes control of the situation at line 345 and orders Puck to abort the duel, mislead the lovers through the night, and use the herbal antidote to love-in-idleness (Dian's bud) on Lysander, thus restoring his love for Hermia. The play begins to reverse direction and return toward order, daylight, and Athens. Puck uses trickery to mislead the young men, prevent the duel, collect the lovers in one place, and put them to sleep. By using Dian's bud on Lysander, he moves the love relationships into the fourth stage (as realized in 4.1.): two reciprocally loving couples.

13. Resolution begins in 4.1. with the rapprochement between Oberon and Titania. Oberon uses Dian's bud (4.1.70) to release Titania from her infatuation partly because he has begun to pity her (4.1.46) and partly because she has surrendered the changeling (4.1.52-62). Oberon also orders Puck to restore Bottom to his original shape so that he can awaken and return to Athens; the events of the night will become an inexplicable dream for him. When Titania awakens, she is restored to harmony and amity with Oberon. This restoration is visually symbolized on stage by music and dancing (4.1.82-92), traditional symbols of harmony and order. This rapprochement is significant because it restores cosmic order and it suggests that order will be similarly restored at every other level of action.

14. The play reverses direction when the fairies exit and the rulers enter (4.1.101), shifting from night to day, gods to humans, and nature to society. Theseus and Hippolyta are hunting the morning of their wedding day. Theseus spots the lovers, has them awakened, and asks for an explanation of their presence together. The explanations reflect the dream-like confusion that the lovers have experienced. Lysander begins to tell how he and Hermia arrived in the wood (145-52), but Egeus interrupts, demanding legal action. Egeus has not changed; he has not gone through the long night of passion and confusion which has purged the minds and cleared the eyes of the lovers. Demetrius best expresses the changes that have occurred (159-75). He admits that fury and fancy (both irrational passions) drove him and Helena to the wood, but that his infatuation with Hermia now seems childish. Hermia and Helena do not speak. The conflict resolves into 2 reciprocally loving couples. Given this situation, Theseus overrules Egeus and abrogates the Athenian law. This reversal of Theseus's earlier position, possible because Demetrius no longer wants to marry Hermia, represents a moderation of Theseus's earlier rigidity and an acknowledgement that there are powers above the law.

15. Comedies often end in marriage, and this one has been headed toward a royal wedding since the opening. Yet this wedding and two others occur off-stage and are reported by Snug (4.2.13-15). Why didn't Shakespeare stage the weddings? One answer is found in the dynamics of the play; one line of action ("Pyramus") remains incomplete. Staging the weddings would provide premature formal closure. This, in turn, opens the question of why "Pyramus" is treated as a co-equally important line of action.

16. Pyramus and Thisby are young lovers separated by a wall because their families have a long-standing feud. They plan to overcome these obstructions by leaving the city and meeting at night at Ninus's tomb. The plan leads to

disaster because of irrational haste. Thisby arrives at the tomb first, is frightened by a lion, and drops her cape, which the lion bloodies. Pyramus, finding the bloodstained cape by moonlight, assumes that Thisby is dead and kills himself. Thisby returns to the tomb, finds Pyramus's body, and also commits suicide. The parallels between this story and _Romeo_ are numerous.

17-18. The masque combines a number of traditional symbols of harmony and order to bless the marriages (it thus replaces the wedding as the formal ritual of order and closure that ends the play). It also embodies a fusion of the 2 worlds of the play; the kingdom of night, the supernatural, magic, and dreaming flows into the world of daylight, order, and rationality. In the epilogue, Puck suggests that we should consider the play a _dream_ that we experienced while slumbering. The statement neatly puts us on a par with Bottom and the lovers. It also links fantasy and imagination (dreaming) with drama and art (illusion) and thus reinforces the connection among poets, lovers, and madmen advanced by Theseus (5.1.4-22).

Discussion of Topics for Writing

1-2. Most of the characters are flat, conventional, and representative; some are symbolic. Theseus and Hippolyta represent law, order, and rationality. Theseus changes to the extent that he learns to moderate the rigor of the law. Egeus is the conventional angry and irrational father who obstructs love. He neither learns nor changes. The four lovers are equally conventional and flat, but they are educated and purged of love madness through their long night of chaos and passion in the woods. When they awaken, their relationships and feelings have become regenerative and reciprocal love. Oberon and Titania symbolize the power and cycles of nature. In addition, they represent chaos and passion (at 1st) just as Theseus and Hippolyta represent order. They change to the extent that their relationship returns to harmony and accord. The mechanicals, also conventional, represent the lower class. Although the play is set in ancient Athens, they are quite clearly based on Elizabethan rather than Greek or mythological figures.

3. Each group of characters has a characteristic mode of language. Theseus and Hippolyta speak blank verse, as befits their status and dignity as rulers. The 4 lovers speak mostly in less dignified and more amusing rhymed couplets. When not playing roles in "Pyramus," the mechanicals speak in prose, consistent with their low status. The fairies speak in both blank verse and in rhymed couplets, but they are also the only characters to speak in lyric poetry (variously rhymed lines of iambic tetrameter and other variant meters). This kind of verse sets them apart from the rest of the characters and suggests their complete otherness from the humans.

4-5. The two-place structure, its symbolic import, and its relationship to the dramatic structure of the play are discussed in the sample essay (pages 1499-1501). Both the world of the forest and the world of the city change for the better. The woods, initially disordered (as is all of nature, see 2.1. 81-117), become ordered with the resolution of the conflict between Oberon and Titania. Similarly the city, which initially embodied overly rigid law and order, is modified by Theseus's decision to overrule Egeus and permit the marriage of Hermia and Lysander. Most of the characters who make the round-trip from city to woods to city undergo some sort of learning or altering experience which improves them. The lovers suffer the dream-like chaos of Oberon's manipulation and emerge more rational and matured. The rulers (especially Theseus) learn that law must be tempered by judgment and higher authority. The mechanicals neither learn nor change; they go to the woods to rehearse secretly and their round-trip simply heightens the confusion.

6. Midsummer Night's Dream and "Pyramus and Thisby" share with each other and with Romeo a common plot structure (up to a point) and a common thematic focus on the dangers of passion, haste, and irrational love. In all three plays, young lovers are blocked and try to overcome obstructions by going outside the law (or the city). Hermia and Lysander parallel Thisby and Pyramus and Juliet and Romeo. Egeus and the old Athenian law are parallel to the feud and wall in "Pyramus" and the feud in Romeo. The woods parallel Ninus's tomb in "Pyramus" and Friar Laurence's cell and the tomb in Romeo. The plays have parallel plots until Oberon takes charge and begins to straighten things out in Dream (3.2. and 4.1.). At the point of highest tragic potential, Dream could have turned either way—toward comedy or a tragedy of fate. Shakespeare may have included "Pyramus" simply as a parody of bad acting. This is unlikely, however, since it recapitulates the central themes of Dream from another perspective. "Pyramus" shows us and the young lovers in the internal audience in Dream that things do not always turn out well. It provides another occasion to illustrate the dangers of haste and irrationality in love.

7. The soliloquy is a key thematic statement of the characteristics of irrational love. This kind of love distorts perception and evaluation (lines 232-3); it is blind, rash, immature, changeable, and lacking in judgment (234-41). Many of the relationships in the play illustrate this type of love. Chief among these is the shift in passion produced among the four lovers by love-in-idleness. The most extreme instance of this type of love is Titania's dotage for Bottom. In some ways, the lovers are educated and transformed during their long night in the woods; they emerge into the daylight world on the day of Theseus's wedding with a stronger and more regenerative love.

8-9. Dream explores the nature of drama and the links among drama (illusion, art) and imagination (passion, madness, dreaming, and love) in three ways: (1) through the mechanicals' production of "Pyramus"; (2) through the internal audience's reaction to "Pyramus"; and (3) through thematic statements (such as Theseus's in 5.1.4-22). The mechanicals have no understanding of drama as a mimetic art. Their concerns over lion, sword, moonshine, and wall (3.1.) and the solutions they come up with indicate that they make no distinction between illusion (drama, art) and reality. In addition, they assume that their audience will make no distinction; the difference never occurs to them. Just as the mechanicals illustrate faulty understanding and horrendous acting, so the play they perform exemplifies bad writing. Here, Shakespeare ridicules the over-emotional and highly rhetorical interludes that held the stage during his youth. Notice the way Shakespeare overuses alliteration in "Pyramus" to make the lines even more humorous. The internal audience for "Pyramus"—the nobility and the 4 lovers—represent spectators more concerned with their own wittiness than with the play. For the lovers, the play-within-the-play recapitulates lessons that they have just experienced, but the connection never occurs to them. Shakespeare expects us to be a better audience, seeing both the connection between Dream and "Pyramus," and judging the lovers on their failure to see it. In opposition to all this failure, the play includes a thematic line that argues for a linkage among passion, imagination, dreaming, illusion, art, and love. This connection is articulated (negatively) by Theseus at the beginning of Act Five and underscored in Puck's epilogue.

The Theater of Moliere, pages 1443-1446

Moliere, The Misanthrope, pages 1446-1494

This is a very serious play that exemplifies the impulses of satiric comedy superbly. Moliere satirizes both his own society and unbalanced attacks against it. Students are often disturbed by Alceste and by the play's resolution. Both, however, can be understood in the context of satire. Alceste is a comic (unbalanced, excessive) character with some "heroic" characteristics. The absence of a traditional happy ending and marriage for the hero and heroine reflects the ridiculous nature of the relationship between Alceste and Celimene and their refusal to change or learn in the light of what they should learn about each other. As with most satiric comedy, however, education and change should be advanced in the world at large. The play is not unrelated to A Midsummer Night's Dream. Alceste's love affair with Celimene, the woman who represents all that he despises in society, proves that "love's irrational and blind" and that "the heart's not subject to the mind" (4.3.22-3); these are key ideas in A Midsummer Night's Dream.

A Note on Pronunciation: Although French names and accents can be off-setting to students, the characters' names in this play should pose no real problem. With the exception of Arsinoe, all the names are pronounced as though the final "e" were silent. Thus, Alceste is pronounced "Al-cest." Similarly, Celimene is pronounced "Cel-i-men." Because Arsinoe's name ends with an accent, it is pronounced "Ar-sin-o-ay." Please note that all accents have been omitted in the text of this manual.

Discussion of Questions *Alceste - unreasonable, Philinte - reasonable* ✓

1. Scene 1 introduces Alceste, Philinte, and the 3 central conflicts: Alceste versus society, law, and love. Alceste is angry, frustrated, rude, immoderate, and intolerant. He rejects all social convention and politeness as hyprocrisy; he sees all society as full of "base flattery, injustice, fraud, self-interest, treachery" (93-4). One of the central problems with Alceste is that he is equally enraged by politeness, hypocrisy, and injustice (119-20); he makes no distinctions in kind or degree. This failure makes his position amusing and unreasonable. In contrast, Philinte is calm, polite, moderate, and tolerant. He seems a reasonable alternative to Alceste, championing the customs of polite society and outward courtesies (66) to hold the social fabric (77) together. He advocates ignoring the follies of the times and adopting leniency, a pliant rectitide, and moderation (1.1.145-66). Although his position leads him into totally undiscriminating toleration--his absurd flattery of Oronte's poetic skill is a good example--his point of view is clearly the more perceptive, reasonable, and viable.

2. The 2 complications are the unexplained lawsuit (1.1.123-28, 182-200) and Alceste's courtship of Celimene (205-249). These, along with his rage against social hypocrisy, comprise the 3 major conflicts and plots in the play. Alceste's refusal to argue his lawsuit or see the judges reflects his disdain for social convention; he feels that the truth of his position should be self-evident. Later in the play, he changes position, arguing that losing the case proves that society is totally corrupt. Philinte offers Alceste solutions to all 3 conflicts in scene 1. In terms of society, he recommends pliant rectitude (149) and moderation (152). In the lawsuit, he suggests that Alceste see the judges. And in the matter of love, he advises that

277

Alceste shift from a woman who typifies the manners of our days (220) to the honest Eliante (215). Alceste rejects all 3 suggestions.

3. Alceste's claim that he recognizes Celimene's faults (1.1.227) is at least partly true; he constantly attacks Celimene's social hypocrisy. Alceste is blind, however, to the inherent foolishness of the relationship. Celimene embodies every aspect of society that Alceste detests; she is the consummate socialite and she plays the games of polite society with wit, skill, and pleasure. Alceste's attraction to her despite her faults suggests that he is both attracted and repulsed by society. It also suggests that he is not seeing Celimene clearly.

4. Oronte embodies an extreme version of the fawning social hypocrisy that Alceste detests. In 1.2.1-44, Oronte announces his vast admiration for Alceste and wants to exchange vows of friendship. Alceste politely rejects the offer (28-35). In dealing with the sonnet, Alceste is also more polite at 1st than we might expect. He clearly hates the sonnet; Philinte's 4 lines of extravagant praise (70,76, 84, and 87) elicit sotto voce condemnations from Alceste that identify the poem as frightful trash. When asked directly, however, Alceste initially couches his criticism in a thinly disguised attack on a 3rd person (92-124), giving Oronte a polite way out of the confrontation. Oronte senses that these comments are aimed at him, but insists on direct criticism. At this point, Alceste blasts away, telling Oronte that the poem is unnatural wordy play without taste, honesty, or passion (127-40). The attack nearly leads to a duel, and results in one of Alceste's many defeats. He is ultimately forced by the Court of Honor to apologize for his bluntness.

5. Alceste is a highly unconventional lover who constantly criticizes his beloved (see 2.5.141-8) and bemoans the fact that he is in love with her (see 2.1.1-8, 69-72). He objects to Celimene's enthusiastic participation in social custom and convention, calling her too melting and receptive (2.1.23). He wants her to explain her involvement with Acaste and Clitandre and to choose between him and society (2.5.3-8, 183-4). While these demands may be reasonable (the matter is open to debate), they are certainly not realistic. Celimene enjoys society too much and is far too good at witty give-and-take to abandon the world of gossip, flattery, and satirical back-biting for Alceste. Alceste's demands become more focused in Act 5, when he insists that Celimene choose him or Oronte and then demands that she abandon society completely.

6. Celimene is totally involved in the social world that Alceste detests. This is evidenced in Alceste's criticism and in her explanations of why she tolerates Clitandre (2.1.44-6) and Acaste (2.3.7-16). Her behavior represents a particular version of Philinte's tolerance, tempered with biting honesty. She is polite and charming to most when they are present, but censorious of absent friends (see 2.5). This finely developed and witty hypocrisy is tempered with honesty, especially evident in her confrontation with Arsinoe.

7-8. 2.5. is a witty tour de force for Celimene in which she displays her skill at satirical portraiture for Clitandre and Acaste by producing vicious sketches of absent gentry. The performance is quite normal (and apparently frequent) for Celimene; Eliante observes that "the conversation takes its usual turn" (25). The absent nobles are satirized as Celimene catalogues their faults. Clitandre and Acaste are satirized through their delight in such malicious gossip; they do not realize that they probably receive the same treatment when they are absent. Celimene's portrait of Alceste (2.5.111-22) is only partly accurate, and thus reflects her limited understanding of him.

Alceste does <u>love</u> <u>to</u> <u>make</u> <u>a</u> <u>fuss</u>; he enjoys his constant opposition to society and custom. He is not, however, simply an embodiment of <u>contrariness</u>. His critical position is rigidly consistent with his philosophy of rejecting any compromise with custom, convention, or even common curtesy. It is this very consistency that makes any accommodation with Celimene at the close of the play impossible.

9. Acaste adores himself. His enumeration of his own good qualities (3.1.5-28) neatly defines the ideals of the social world that Alceste hates: youth, wealth, nobility, courage, wit, taste, grace, beauty, and fine clothing. The polite conflict between the two nobles is over Celimene; both Clitandre and Acaste hope to win her. Ironically, neither has a chance; she considers both of them to be foolish and she is committed to Alceste. The nobles settle the dispute through a <u>treaty</u> (3.1.63-68) in which each agrees to abandon his hopes if the other receives any sign of favor. The pact reflects the abiding importance of polite agreement and the superficiality of the nobles' feelings for Celimene (or anything else).

10-11. Celimene describes Arsinoe accurately as a hypocrite and prude (3.3.5-23). Arsinoe's feigned moral standards grow out of jealousy and social failure; her subsequent behavior (especially in 3.5. and 3.7.) bears out this initial portrait. The confrontation between Celimene and Arsinoe (3.5.) juxtaposes the social winner with all the right moves against the pathetic loser who does everything wrong. Arsinoe hates and envies Celimene, while Celimene views Arsinoe with pity and contempt. The confrontation begins with a veneer of politeness; Arsinoe offers advise as a <u>friend</u>, obliquely accusing Celimene of immoral behavior (3.5.3-36). Celimene's reply, equally polite, is an honest assessment of Arsinoe's hypocrisy and prudishness (37-84). The 2 speeches are perfectly balanced and parallel. The tone of the exchange changes after line 85 when the women abandon polite fictions and make direct accusations. Celimene charges that Arsinoe's prudery is the result of old age, social failure, and a lack of beaux. Arsinoe charges that Celimene's social success is the result of indiscriminate sexual favors (125-148).

12. Celimene sets up her own downfall in 3.6. by leaving Alceste alone with Arsinoe and by writing the letters that prove to be her undoing in 5.4. In 3.7, Arsinoe tries to flatter Alceste and turn him against Celimene. Alceste is immune to the flattery, but stung by the hints that Celimene has been unfaithful. Arsinoe offers <u>occular</u> <u>evidence</u> (3.7.89) that Alceste has been betrayed. She is motivated by her own desire to possess Alceste.

13. Philinte's report of the meeting between Alceste and Oronte at the Court of Honor (4.1.1-30) gives Eliante an opportunity to express her opinion of Alceste; she respects (31-36) and loves (61-70) him. She considers Philinte a friend, and thinks that he is <u>teasing</u> when he politely expresses his own interest in her (71-80). Eliante is a moderate compromise between Alceste and Celimene; she is polite and tolerant, but recognizes the excesses of the age and the validity of Alceste's position. Moreover, she advocates <u>frankness</u> in matters of love (59-60), in contrast to Celimene's games.

14. Arsinoe's plan succeeds; Alceste is convinced by a letter (4.2.19-22) that Celimene has been unfaithful and has expressed her love to Oronte. He proposes to gain revenge by shifting his affection to Eliante (4.2.36-42). The plan is odd in that it uses and belittles Eliante. Celimene deals with Alceste's rage by claiming that the letter was written to a woman (4.3.69) and then turning the tables and scorning Alceste's jealousy.

15. Alceste wishes this for Celimene (4.3.147-56) ostensibly so that he might prove his love. Nevertheless, the wish reveals a great deal about Alceste's feelings for (and about) Celimene. It reveals, for example, that Alceste cannot accept Celimene as she is; he wants her without the competition of social involvement. His wish also implies that he would like her to be totally dependent on (and thus controlled by) him; such low birth and abject poverty would render Celimene powerless and insignificant, given the standards of her society. The wish thus anticipates the offer of marriage and withdrawal out of society that Alceste makes to Celimene in 5.7.

16. Alceste initially refused to argue his lawsuit; now he refuses to appeal the unjust judgment against him. Instead, he wallows in righteous indignation, claiming that the lost case proves the time's injustice and the black wickedness of the age (5.1.60-70). The substance of the lawsuit is unimportant; the lawsuit itself, however, is significant as a symbol of society's corruption and as another defeat for Alceste. It parallels Alceste's defeat in the Court of Honor (in society) and in matters of love.

17. In 5.2. and 5.3, Oronte and Alceste push Celimene toward a public choice between them. Oronte (5.2.13-16) and Alceste (5.2.17-32) each demand that she choose one and banish the other. These demands heighten the tension, but the catastrophe is produced through alternate revelations based on the indiscrete letters that Celimene has written.

18. The catastrophe occurs in 5.4. when Celimene's letters are used against her. She defeats herself by overreaching in an attempt to satirize everyone with impunity. Each person's letter attacks others. When the letters are all brought together, Celimene is revealed as having satirized virtually all her friends. All the major characters are present in 5.4; at the close of the scene, they begin to abandon Celimene. Clitandre and Acaste leave in 5.4. and Oronte leaves in 5.5. Arsinoe attempts to gloat, but she is rejected by Alceste and leaves the stage in defeat (5.6). In the resolution, Alceste and Celimene reach a final parting when she rejects his demand for married life in a wild trackless solitary place and he rejects her offer of marriage within society. This separation of lovers makes for a highly unconventional resolution, but we knew from the outset that the match was destined to fail. Eliante and Philinte provide a traditional closing union.

Discussion of Topics for Writing

1. The unities of place, time, and action provide for highly focused action and emotion. Sustaining the unity of place has the added advantage of locating all the action in Celimene's house. Her house thus becomes the hub of social activity in the play. This is consistent with her status as the consummate socialite. Wilbur's verse translation duplicates Moliere's witty and satiric effects throughout. Falling rhymes, for example, are often used to undercut characters.

2. Alceste (the protagonist) is involved in three key conflicts; he is set against society, law, and love. His ongoing war against social convention (epitomized in his conflict with Oronte) parallels his conflict against corruption (embodied by his lawsuit) and his conflict with love (in which he opposes both Celimene and his own feelings). Alceste treats all these conflicts with the same level of rage; he is comic precisely because he makes no distinction among his targets, reacting with the same moral indignation to

politeness and injustice. For Alceste, all three conflicts resolve
unsuccessfully; he loses the lawsuit, is forced to apologize to Oronte, and
must finally abandon Celimene. Given the nature of satiric comedy, however,
it is clear that the conflicts against social hypocrisy and corruption cannot
resolve within the play. The intention is to force the spectators (or the
readers) to seek resolution (reformation) in the real world.

3. These characters are flat, static, and representative. They embody
the values and ideals of society, providing a definition of the way of the
world--a way that Alceste despises and Celimene embraces. Oronte is satirized
through his fawning praise of Alceste, his abominable sonnet, and his general
behavior. Acaste and Clitandre are satirized through their monumental self-
satisfaction, their polite dispute over Celimene, and their shortsighted
enjoyment of Celimene's satirical character sketches.

4. Students' judgments of Celimene will depend on which perspective they
find most convincing. From Alceste's point of view, her worst qualities are
her politeness, hypocrisy, and enjoyment of the game. At the same time, these
represent her strengths within the context of social convention. Her attempts
to ridicule anyone not present (a weakness) are balanced against her wit.

5. Celimene and Arsinoe are polar opposites; one is an attractive and
witty winner while the other is a bitter and jealous loser who masks her envy
in prudery. Celimene, as a (mostly) skillful player of social games, accepts
social convention and public morality. Arsinoe rails against the moral values
of society to disguise her own desires and inadequacies. Even though she
flatters and back-bites, Celimene has her own kind of honesty (especially
evident in her confrontation with Arsinoe). In contrast, Arsinoe is
thoroughly hypocritical. Eliante combines sincerity, morality, honesty, and
polite tolerance; she is clearly the most reasonable, realistic, and tolerant
of the 3. At the same time, she lacks Celimene's sparkling wit and vivacity
(How can 3 such different women all be attracted to Alceste?).

6-7. The characteristics that make Alceste comic also link him to tragic
figures such as Oedipus. Eliante sees in Alceste's honesty a heroic and noble
side (4.1.35), while Philinte claims that it gives Alceste the reputation of
being a ridiculous crank (1.1.106). Alceste's most comic and tragic feature
is the inflexible consistency of his moral outrage; he reacts with the same
fury to politeness, flattery, hypocrisy, criminality, and injustice. We are
prevented from seeing him as a tragic figure by his inappropriate affair with
Celimene, the foolishness that his rigidity produces, and his failure to
achieve any self-knowledge. Alceste refuses to learn or change. He does
learn that he cannot have Celimene on his terms, but this is simply another
manifestation of his rigidity. No character changes significantly in the
play. The key moment of education (the catastrophe of the letters) changes
characters' attitudes toward Celimene, but it changes neither the society nor
the characters' attitude toward their own social behavior.

8. Moliere satirizes society by revealing the hypocrisy, egotism, and
emptiness of characters such as Oronte, Acaste, and Arsinoe. Celimene's
downfall also demonstrates the destructive sterility of double-dealing games.
Finally, Alceste's often accurate condemnations reveal society's follies and
vices. At the same time, Alceste himself is satirized as an inflexible and
overblown voice of impossible standards; he simply cannot function in the
world of the play. Which comes off worst? Let the students decide. The play
suggests that Alceste needs reforming as much as (or more than) society.

While students might sympathize with Alceste's moral fervor, they should realize that his rigidity renders him unsuitable for any real human society.

9-10. Through Philinte and Eliante, Moliere distinguishes between customary politeness and fawning hypocrisy, petty foolishness and criminal injustice. Alceste (see questions 6-7 above in this section) fails utterly to make these distinctions. The characters who embody the most balanced and rational approach to living are Philinte and Eliante. Of the two, Eliante is the more admirable; she never indulges in insincere flattery (as does Philinte with Oronte) and yet she is always polite. In addition, she champions frank- ness in matters of love. The appropriate union of Eliante and Philinte points toward a balanced and moderate compromise for society. You might consider with your students whether this is the world Moliere wants. Abstractly and theoretically the answer might be yes. It is equally clear, however, that the world would be a great deal more boring and less exciting without the rage of characters like Alceste and the wit of characters like Celimene.

WRITING ABOUT COMEDY, pages 1495-1501

Unlike the discussion of writing in the previous chapter, this material does not introduce any new types of essay. Rather, it returns to a focus on the traditional elements of drama. Students are referred to the relevant section of Chapter 27 for a general review of approaches to writing about these elements; we recommend that you encourage them to read (or reread) this material before they begin to plan and write. In these pages, we discuss specific aspects of plot, structure, character, and language that can be especially appropriate to comic drama. Keep in mind, however, that the comedies in this chapter lend themselves to almost any kind of writing assignment.

In the sample essay on A Midsummer Night's Dream (pages 1499-1501), we have chosen a paper that illustrates one way in which setting, symbolism, and comic structure may be explored at the same time. The essay thus considers and links three separate elements. In making writing assignments, you may want to consider topics that ask students to deal with one, two, or even three elements that are related and work toward a single effect. Once again, however, we suggest that you warn students about the necessity of focus, development of a few key ideas, and selectivity. As with most other writing projects, students will frequently employ the scatter method, introducing numerous observations about many elements in a disorganized manner. You should strive to encourage a selective focus.

CHAPTER 30

REALISTIC AND NONREALISTIC DRAMA

This chapter examines in some detail the differences between realism and nonrealism in drama. Unless you begin teaching drama with plays from this chapter, these should not be totally new concepts to students. Because all dramatic conventions are nonrealistic, students should be familiar with some nonrealistic devices and techniques before they read this material. The 5 short plays in Chapter 27 embody the full range of realism. The Sandbox and Everyman are the least realistic; Trifles is the most realistic. If your students have studied any of the plays in Chapter 27, you can use them as a source for specific examples in discussing realism and nonrealism.

Another way of approaching realistic and nonrealistic drama in class is to discuss the extent to which a play acknowledges or ignores its own fictiveness and the presence of an audience (or reader). Because realistic plays attempt to imitate life as closely as possible, they do not contain devices that call attention to their own fictiveness or create a direct link to the audience. The play exists in absolute isolation and we are the unacknowledged spies watching through the missing 4th wall. In contrast, nonrealistic plays usually contain devices that emphasize both the theatricality of the moment and the presence of spectators (or readers).

The 2 plays in this chapter do not represent extremes of the spectrum. Ibsen's A Doll's House is highly realistic, but the realism is at least partly undercut by the play's extensive symbolism. Williams's The Glass Menagerie, like Miller's Death of a Salesman, represents the midpoint of the spectrum, combining realistic and nonrealistic techniques.

Both plays are available for classroom screening. A Doll's House, which has been extensively produced since the 1960s, is available in two 1973 films, both in color. One (109 minutes, also available on videotape) was directed by Joseph Losey and stars Jane Fonda; the other (95 minutes) was directed by Patrick Garland and stars Claire Bloom. A 1950 filmed version of The Glass Menagerie (107 minutes, B/W, starring Jane Wyman, Gertrude Lawrence, Kirk Douglas, and Arthur Kennedy) is also available for classroom use. The films may be obtained from many distributors, including Films Inc. (1144 Wilmette Ave., Wilmette, IL 60091). If you use films to help students appreciate the plays, you might remind them that movies are very different from staged plays. In film, directors gain a much broader canvas and the ability to use cinematic effects such as close-ups and quick cuts; these are impossible on the stage. Conversely, film loses live theater's sense of the entire stage action and the intimacy that can develop between actors and the audience.

Henrik Ibsen, A Doll's House, pages 1507-1564.

Time has not dated this play or made it irrelevant. To the contrary, Ibsen seems to have anticipated our own concerns with identity crises, role playing, the rights of women, and the fulfillment of human potential. In teaching the play, there is a tendency to focus on the themes (or theses) at the expense of other elements. Ibsen's ideas are important and attractive; they inform every aspect of the play. At the same time, other elements such as character, language, structure, and symbolism are worthy of class discussion; they all work together to shape the play's impact and meaning.

The play is carefully structured to build up to the climactic confrontation between Nora and Torvald. Anxiety about money permeates the entire drama. With the appearance of Krogstad, the level of tension increases considerably, and continues to rise until the catastrophe. Nora faces a constantly expanding nest of dilemmas: Will Torvald find out about the loan and the forgery? What will happen when he finds out? What will happen to the marriage? Torvald's self-centered diatribe (1554-5) and the subsequent discussion answer these questions and comprise the catastrophe and resolution.

While contemporary trends and recent productions make it tempting to deal with A Doll's House as a feminist play, to do so would distort Ibsen's work. Nora is not the only doll in this play house of role playing and make believe; her doll-like existence is parallel to the roles imposed by society, heredity, or self on most of the other characters. The close of the play makes it clear that Torvald is as (or more) badly in need of education and self-fulfillment as is Nora; both have failed thus far to become complete human beings.

Discussion of Questions

1. The opening s.d. indicates that the Helmer family is middle class and reasonably well off. Adjectives like comfortably and tastefully as well as the specific pieces of furniture named contribute to this impression. The s.d. also indicates that it is winter; throughout the play, the warmth inside the apartment contrasts with the cold of the Norwegian winter outside.

2. Ibsen sets the tone and nature of the relationship early in the play when Nora sneaks a macaroon (1510) and then lies about sweets to Torvald (1512). The pattern of behavior is more appropriate for a parent-child relationship than for a husband and wife. Torvald often acts out the paternal role. In Act 2, he tells Nora that she can make as much noise as she pleases since he will not hear her in the study (1536). Nora partly understands the dynamics of the relationship; she tells Rank that "being with Torvald is a little like being with papa" (1539). Torvald's paternalistic and superior attitude toward Nora is reflected in the terms of endearment he uses: my little lark, my little squirrel, my little spendthrift (1510). Each of these diminishes and dehumanizes Nora. The repetition of my suggests that Torvald has objectified Nora and turned her into his possession. The repetition of little similarly indicates Torvald's perception of Nora as an object of no real significance. Nora's reference to herself as we skylarks and squirrels (1512) and her flattery of Torvald's male ego (some clever man, 1521) suggests that she is at least partly aware of the role playing and pretense.

3. Torvald's statements about borrowing (1511) indicate his tendency to moralize and to assume conventionally proper and acceptable positions that will make him appear good and responsible. Other instances of such posturing are found in his attitude toward unsavory cases (1514), money (1517), working with Krogstad (1529), and even knitting (1550). Torvald's moral posturing reflects his sexist and paternalistic attitudes, his concern with appearances, the degree to which he is trapped by background and society, and the role that he and society have successfully imposed on Nora.

4. The Helmers have spent years struggling to maintain appearances with too little money. Torvald has doled out the household funds carefully; Nora has scrimped in order to maintain a middle-class home and pay off the debt to Krogstad. Money is thus an abiding concern, especially for Nora. As the play

opens, she sees a change in their financial situation (and a release from the burden of the debt) through Torvald's new job and big salary as director of the bank. She thinks that their "hard times are over" and that "it will be splendid to have heaps of money and not need to have any anxiety" (1513).

5. Linde's arrival (1513) is the first complication of the play. Linde seems to be a striking contrast to Nora. She made an unhappy marriage for money and has had difficulty supporting herself since her husband's death. In contrast, Nora's life seems comfortable and her marriage loving. We discover, however, that Nora has her own burdens--the loan and the need to save and earn secretly to pay it back. In the course of the play, Nora moves progressively closer to Linde's initial status. Ironically, Linde moves in the other direction, toward an honest and equal union with Krogstad. At the end, the women have almost exchanged positions. Linde will find what happiness and security she can helping Krogstad, while Nora will struggle alone to become a whole person. Nora's success in getting Linde a position at the bank ironically places her in jeopardy. Torvald gives Linde Krogstad's position. Krogstad, in turn, pressures Nora with threats of exposure to get him a better position. Nora's act of kindness and self-aggrandizement (in showing off her husband's new power) thus ironically leads to her exposure and disillusionment.

6. Ibsen uses both stage directions (movement, expression, tone) and dialogue to indicate that Krogstad (the second complication) is a threat to Nora (1519). Linde starts, trembles, and turns away. Nora steps towards him and speaks in a strained, low voice. At this point in the play, Krogstad is symbolically linked with winter, sickness, and cold; when he goes into the study, Nora quickly stirs up the fire in the stove (warmth against coldness).

7. The children's scene (1522-3) is significant for 3 reasons: (1) it shows us the happy domestic world of game playing that is threatened by Nora's crime, Krogstad's knowledge, and Torvald's conventional attitudes; (2) it identifies Nora as another child as she talks and plays hide-and-seek with her children; (3) it significantly expands the image of the doll's house and stands as a metaphor for life in the Helmer household. Nora's games with her little dolly children are metaphorically parallel to the roles and games that Nora and Torvald play in their marriage.

8. Nora's secret pride is that she saved Torvald's life by borrowing the money to pay for the year in Italy. Nora tells Linde this to prove that she has known troubles (1516-18). Ibsen also hints at the crime here when Linde points out that "a wife cannot borrow without her husband's consent." The crime is forgery; Nora forged her father's co-signature on the bond with Krogstad (1526). Ironically, Nora's crime duplicates the crime that ruined Krogstad originally. Nora's motives transcend law; she forged the name in order to spare her father and save her husband (1527). Krogstad points out that "the law cares nothing about motives" (1526). At the close of Act 1, Nora is faced with the probability that Krogstad will reveal the forgery and the loan--Nora's secret joy and pride--to Torvald.

9. In Act 1, the Christmas tree is placed in the middle of the room (1527) and decorated with candles, flowers, and other ornaments. At the opening on Act 2 (the next day), the tree is stripped of its ornaments and has burnt-down candle-ends on its dishevelled branches (1530); it has also been shoved into the corner by the piano. The stripped tree and its displacement from the center of the room symbolize the erosion of Nora's happiness, the growth of anxiety, and the mounting threats to her carefully patterned life.

10. Here, as elsewhere, Nora's references to herself as your little squirrel and your skylark (1534) indicate that she is consciously playing a role for Torvald. Nora offers to play her role to the hilt ("run about and do all her tricks . . . chirp about in every room") if Torvald will let Krogstad keep his post in the bank. Nora's awareness of the role that Torvald expects her to enact leads her to attempt to manipulate him. For additional discussion of role playing, see question 2 above and questions 4 and 6 below in Topics for Writing.

11, 14. Torvald's claim that he is "man enough to take everything on himself" (1535) conforms to Nora's secret hope that a wonderful thing will happen. Nora anticipates with both dread and longing that Torvald will assume full responsibility for the loan and the forgery. She asks Linde to witness that the act was solely hers in the event that "someone . . . wanted to take all the responsibility, all the blame" (1543). At the close of Act 2, Nora is waiting for this wonderful thing (1546). This act of self-sacrifice never occurs to Torvald. Nora explains her hope for this wonderful thing in detail after Torvald's failure to measure up to her heroic ideal (1560).

12. While Torvald is Nora's husband-lover-father figure, Dr. Rank is her companion and friend. She talks to Rank about all sorts of things that she never mentions to Torvald (see 1532, 1539). The flirtation (touching Rank, showing him the stockings) is motivated partly by Nora's desire to control him and partly by her need for money; she almost asks him for the necessary cash (1538). Nora feels safe playing with Rank; she considers herself his equal (or perhaps his superior). When Rank admits his love for Nora (1538), he changes the basis of the relationship and makes it impossible for Nora to go on. She could accept Rank's love and maintain her own sense of conventional morality so long as he did not tell her about it.

13. The tarantella occurs at the close of Act 2, after Krogstad has made his threats and left the letter in the locked mailbox. The violence of the dance symbolizes Nora's mounting desperation. Torvald suggests that she is dancing as if her life depended on it and she replies, "So it does." The dance, linked to the poisonous bite of the tarantula, suggests that the poison of fear and deceit is eating away at Nora's life. Ironically Rank, who plays the piano for the dance, is also being destroyed by secret internal poisons.

15-16. Linde rejected Krogstad about 10 years earlier out of a sense of duty to her helpless mother and two little brothers (1547). Krogstad's prospects seemed hopeless, and Linde had to marry wealth. Linde suggests a union with Krogstad at this point as a kind of mutual redemption; she has faith in his real character and she needs something to work for (1548). Unlike the Helmer's marriage, this will be a union of equals based on mutual need, understanding, honesty, and self-knowledge. Linde eventually decides that this same honesty and knowledge is necessary for the Helmers. Although she had originally planned to have Krogstad recall his letter, she decides that it must be read by Torvald so that the unhappy secret will be disclosed and the Helmers can have a complete understanding between them (1549).

17. Neither is significantly moved by Rank's imminent death. Nora, who already knew about it, is preoccupied with Krogstad's letter and her hope/fear that Torvald will save her. Torvald's lack of concern reflects his consistent focus on himself and his own needs. At this moment, he is far more interested in Nora as a sexual object than he is in any news about Rank; he sees both Rank's visit and the news about the death as an intrusion.

18. Torvald reacts to Krogstad's letter with rage, indignation, and fear for his own position. He condemns Nora and accuses her of destroying his happiness and future. His concern is completely focused on himself, his own reputation, appearance, and standing in the community (notice the frequent use of first person pronouns here). Far from acting in the idealized and heroic way that Nora had imagined, Torvald immediately plans to appease Krogstad and maintain appearances (1555). Nora begins to see Torvald and her marriage clearly for the first time. The stage directions here (steadily, a growing look of coldness, coldly and quietly) indicate Nora's progressively greater understanding of Torvald and alienation from him.

19. Nora comes to understand that her marriage was without substance, communication, or meaning (1557). She realizes that she has been Torvald's doll-wife (1558) rather than a fulfilled individual. She understands that she must try to educate herself, to comprehend the world, and to fulfill her duties to herself despite the demands of social convention, religion, law, and marriage. She also sees that Torvald is an incomplete person who needs to seek his own education and self-knowledge.

Discussion of Topics for Writing

1-2. Almost all the elements are highly realistic in that they imitate reality with a high degree of verisimilitude. One of the less realistic aspects that deserves discussion is Ibsen's use of coincidence. Perhaps the least realistic element is Ibsen's symbolism. The Christmas tree and the tarantella are discussed above (questions 9 and 13). Rank symbolizes hereditary corruption and death. The macaroons become a symbol of Nora's doll-like relationship with Torvald. The children's presents (sword, doll, horse) symbolize the perpetuation of traditional and conventional sex-linked roles (1511). The locked mailbox (1543) serves as an emblem of Nora's (and women's) second-class status in society and marriage. Nora's clothing is also employed symbolically. The fisher-girl costume evokes the south, Italy, freedom, and Nora's saving of Torvald. When she wraps this costume in black (her shawl and Torvald's domino, 1554), this southern energy is transformed into a symbol of death. The final change of costume (from party clothes to severe daytime dress) and the slamming of the door make concrete Nora's emotional and conceptual shift away from Torvald, marriage, family, and convention, and toward self-fulfillment. The symbolism of Norway and Italy is discussed in the introduction (1508). You might also ask students to consider Ibsen's symbolic use of time. The play moves inexorably toward midnight. Act 1 occurs during the day; Act 2 begins in daylight, but it grows dark (1536) during Nora's conversation with Rank. Act 3 begins at night and ends at about midnight (see 1546).

3. Ibsen clearly wants us to see Nora as a victim, protagonist, and heroine, rather than a villain. He creates a situation in which Nora is trapped by convention, law, and custom. (Who is the villain or antagonist of the play? It seems to be Krogstad at first. Can we finally conclude that Torvald is the antagonist? Society?) Nora's abandonment of husband and children in the light of her duties to herself is intended to be taken as admirable. Audiences and students have not always seen it this way; traditional values can lead many to view Nora's departure as scandalous. Indeed, Ibsen was forced to write an alternative ending to forestall unauthorized tampering with the play. In this alternate, Torvald forces Nora to look upon her sleeping children and she collapses in tears, agreeing to

remain in the home as a wife and mother. Ibsen considered this ending a
disgusting travesty and advised theatrical producers not to use it. As a spur
to class discussion, you can tell students about this alternative ending and
ask them which they prefer. In order to elicit the best discussion, you
should press students to explain and defend their choice.

4, 6. Role playing is linked to the idea of the doll's house and the
doll-like existence of the characters. Nora happily plays the role as a doll-
wife that Torvald (and society) expects of her, and she is at least partly
aware that she is playing it. Her initial awareness is expressed in her
self-labelling (1512, 1534) and her comments on dancing and dressing up
(1518). At the close of the play, she comes to full consciousness of her role
playing, concluding that her home has been a playroom and she has been a doll-
wife (1558). Nora's children are also linked to dolls in the play (1522,
1558). The servants keep the doll house running smoothly; Nora contends that
they know how to run the home much better than she does. Torvald is perhaps
the most interesting doll, partly because he has no awareness of the role
imposed on him by background, heredity, and society. Unlike Nora, Torvald has
no sense that he is acting out the role he has been conditioned to play.
Nevertheless, Nora concludes that his life is as incomplete and doll-like as
hers; he unconsciously follows a set of rules and roles as constricting and
dehumanizing as those that controlled Nora's life.

5. Torvald is concerned with appearances rather than substance. This is
evident throughout the play. See, for example, his comments on his reputation
(1534), being influenced by Nora (1535), his relationship with Krogstad
(1535), and his self-centered diatribe after reading Krogstad's letter (1555).

7. Inherited or hereditary corruption (disease, evil, immorality) is an
idea that fascinated Ibsen; he explored it at length in other plays, most
notably in Ghosts. In A Doll's House, the idea is applied to Nora, Krogstad,
and Rank. Torvald asserts that Nora inherited her corruption and amorality
from her father and might pass it on to her children (see 1512, 1555). Both
Rank and Torvald contend that Krogstad's moral corruption infects his sons
(1520, 1529). Rank is the most explicit symbol of corrupted blood; he is
dying of the diseases he inherited from his morally and physically corrupted
father (see 1532, 1537).

8-9. Ibsen's ideas about marriage, growth, and self-fulfillment are
expressed partly by Mrs. Linde in conversation with Krogstad, but mostly by
Nora at the close of the play. Linde has achieved a great deal of
self-knowledge; she seeks some sort of fulfillment with Krogstad. Nora comes
to realize that her own education and development as a complete person are
more important than husband, marriage, children, law, religion, or convention.
At the same time, she begins to question the validity of forces such as
religion and law that have guided her life. Although Nora is the only
character who acts in a radically untraditional manner on the basis of these
realizations, the concepts deal more fully with human growth and fulfillment
than they do with women's liberation. Ibsen (through Nora) makes it clear
that Torvald should seek exactly the same kind of growth and fulfillment as an
individual. Nora learns, changes, grows, and acts as a result of such growth.
In terms of the play's themes, her final action represents a comedic
improvement for the better. This has not prevented generations of readers and
theater-goers from being outraged by her abandonment of marriage and children.
The question may not be resolved in class discussion, but it certainly should
provoke heated argument.

Tennessee Williams, <u>The Glass Menagerie</u>, pages 1564-1619.

This play combines realistic and nonrealistic techniques in a fairly even balance to produce a highly effective portrait of the Wingfield family. Many of the play's nonrealistic devices are discussed by Williams in the production notes (pages 1566-68). In teaching the play, you can focus some class discussion on each of these elements. All of Williams's nonrealistic devices heighten our sense of the play's fictiveness and artificiality. This, of course, is in keeping with the idea of a <u>memory play</u>. The other primary focus for class discussion is the characters. They all live in fantasy worlds or pursue dreams that are doomed to fail. Amanda seeks release in her romanticized memories of Blue Mountain; she plans marriage or a business career for a daughter who can barely speak to strangers, let alone function effectively in the world at large. Laura takes shelter in a fantasy world built on old phonograph records and a collection of glass figurines. Tom, the would-be poet, dreams of a life of adventure based on the movies--his mode of escape from the apartment and the warehouse. Even Jim, "the most realistic character in the play," embodies failure. He has not fulfilled the promise he seemed to have in high school and his dream of jumping from the warehouse to an executive position by way of night courses in public speaking and radio engineering is overly optimistic.

Discussion of Questions

1. The setting defines a world of poverty, deprivation, and desperation. Key adjectives include <u>warty</u>, <u>overcrowded</u>, <u>lower</u> <u>middle-class</u>, <u>dark</u>, <u>grim</u>, <u>narrow</u>, and <u>sinister</u>. The alleys symbolize dead ends, confusion, and entrapment--the world that Tom wants to escape. The fire escape represents both the squalor of the Wingfield's world and a way out.

2. The 5th character--the missing father--is present in his often illuminated photograph (see pages 1568-9, 1581, 1599). The image of the father in his World War I uniform parallels Tom's appearance on stage in the uniform of a merchant sailor. The father and son both attempt to escape by abandoning the family. Amanda remarks that Tom's attitudes and behavior are similar to those of his father (1584-5). Tom also compares himself to his father, claiming that he followed in his father's footsteps (1617).

3. Amanda describes her (probably half-imagined) genteel past in Blue Mountain and her success with Gentlemen Callers in scene 1 (pages 1571-2). These memories come up several times in the play (1591, 1595), contrasting with the decay and poverty of life in Saint Louis. Amanda's habitual retreat to the past and her repetition of these memories is indicated by the way Tom and Laura react to the story; they have heard it all many times before, but Laura insists that Tom "let her tell it" because "she loves to tell it."

4-5. Laura was unable to deal with her own fear, shyness, and insecurity at Rubicam's; she became ill during the 1st typing test and stopped going to class thereafter (1573-77). Laura's failure provokes a crisis for Amanda and leads to the central crisis of the play. Amanda refuses to face the reality of Laura's incapacities; she sees 2 possible futures for Laura--business or marriage. Either would make Laura secure and save her from becoming the barely tolerated maiden lady that burdens many families. Because Laura fails at business, Amanda turns her attention and energy to getting a Gentlemen Caller. This evokes the image of Jim, the one boy that Laura admired (from

afar) in high school. This image and memory of Jim foreshadows his visit in
the last scene. Amanda's plan to marry off Laura is impracticable because of
Laura's insecurity, withdrawal, and inability to deal with social situations.

6. The argument highlights the central concerns of the two characters.
Amanda is worried about survival of the family and, more particularly, Laura's
future; she accuses Tom of being self-centered and trying to run away from his
responsibilities. Tom considers himself self-sacrificing. He is disgusted
with his life at home and at the warehouse and he wants to escape from the
apartment and the Continental Shoemakers to adventure. He claims that he has
given up all his dreams to support the family. Laura is spotlighted
throughout the argument (see 1567) because Williams wants to emphasize the
impact of this conflict on her feelings and future. Amanda's concerns and
Tom's ultimate decision to leave both have a profound effect on Laura's life.

7. Amanda wants Tom to accept responsibility for Laura. She asserts that
Tom can go "wherever you please, on land, on sea" as "soon as Laura has got
somebody to take care of her, married, a home of her own" (1585). While
Amanda irrationally sees this as a real possibility, Tom recognizes the
improbability of Amanda's vision of the future. Tom ultimately rejects
responsibility for Laura, but the end of the play reveals that he cannot
escape from either the memory of Laura or his own guilt over leaving.

8. Tom describes Europe in scene 5 as being in turmoil, on the edge of
war and destruction. This is suggested by references to the Spanish Civil
War, Hitler, and British appeasement of Nazi Germany. In contrast, the United
States is described as being blind, unaware, asleep, and self-indulgent: "here
there was only hot swing music and liquor, dance halls, bars, and movies, and
sex" (1588). The song, "The World is Waiting for the Sunrise," is ironic in
the light of events in Europe and the approach of World War II.

9-10. Scene 5 contains the announcement (annunciation) of the impending
visit of Jim, the Gentleman Caller. Amanda sees Jim as a potential husband
for Laura; she goes to extraordinary lengths to present Laura and the family
in the best light. Her expectations are unreasonable and unrealistic; she
cannot or will not see Laura's limitatons. Tom is a good deal more realistic;
he observes that "lots of fellows meet girls whom they don't marry" (1590) and
he is aware that Laura is crippled, different, and peculiar: "She lives in a
world of her own--a world of little glass ornaments" (1592). Laura is
terrified by the idea of a Gentleman Caller (1594). She becomes almost
totally incapacitated, however, when she discovers that it is Jim O'Connor;
she refuses to answer the door or sit at the table, and she seeks refuge in
her old phonograph records (1596-7). She behaves this way partly because of
her shyness and inability to function with people and partly because Jim has
embodied her secret fantasy of having a boy friend since high school.

11. Laura begins to relax and blossom during her conversation and dancing
with Jim. Williams describes the moment as the climax of Laura's secret life
(1603). Jim's upbeat manner, his encouragement, and his facile diagnosis of
Laura's inferiority complex begins to put Laura at her ease. She converses
normally and even manages to dance. Her use of Jim's old high-school nickname
--Freckles (1611)--indicates the degree to which she has warmed toward Jim.
The kiss (1612) is the climax of Laura's fantasy and her brush with life. Jim
likes and pities Laura, but she has never been part of his consciousness. He
finds her different from other girls and he encourages her to think more
highly of herself. He is clearly attracted to her, but he cannot explain or

understand his feelings (1612). After the kiss, however, Jim realizes that he has gone too far and misrepresented himself. He withdraws emotionally, tells about his engagement to Betty, and leaves almost immediately. His faith in the power of his and Betty's love to create a good life is as unrealistic as Tom's dreams of adventure or Amanda's plan to marry off Laura.

12. The unicorn symbolizes Laura (as does the whole glass menagerie). Like Laura, the unicorn is unique, isolated, peculiar, different, fragile. The broken unicorn (missing its horn) is ironically more normal; Laura observes that the "horn was removed to make him feel less--freakish. Now he will feel more at home with the other horses" (1611-12). This may symbolize Laura's momentary emergence from fantasy to reality and her normal interaction with Jim. Laura's giving Jim the broken unicorn as a souvenir represents the end of Laura's hopes to be less freakish and her rejection of normal life. In a sense, Jim carries Laura's potential for a normal life away with him; after she gives him the souvenir, she crouches beside the victrola to wind it up.

13-14. Tom, as narrator in the present, indicates that he escaped from the apartment and the warehouse, and "travelled around a great deal" (1617). He has not, however, escaped from memory, guilt, or Laura. Laura and Amanda face a bleak existence in Saint Louis. Although Amanda ends the play comforting Laura, the extinguished candles suggest the end of hope.

Discussion of Topics for Writing

1-2. The nonrealistic aspects of this play include the setting, lighting, music, screen devices, use of a narrator, direct address to the audience, and the idea of the play as memory. Each of these will lend itself well to class discussion and/or writing assignments. There is, of course, no "right" answer to which is the most effective; all contribute to the total impact and meaning of the play. Williams probably incorporated the screen device to provide thematic focus for scenes or parts of scenes; it focuses our attention on the idea or event that Williams felt was most significant at any given moment. This may be an advantage to readers or viewers, but it also suggests that Williams did not have enough confidence in his writing; the play communicates its ideas and meaning quite effectively without the projected images. In production, the device has been judged to be distracting and unnecessary. At the same time, however, it would contribute to our sense of watching a play that makes no effort to imitate reality.

3. Amanda escapes into her memories of an idealized Southern past of plantations and genteel society (see 1571-72, 1595). Laura seeks refuge in a fantasy world defined by the glass menagerie and the phonograph records left behind by her father (see 1573, 1592, 1597). Tom escapes by going to the movies where he can experience adventure vicariously (see 1579, 1598-99).

4. A case may be made for each (paper assignments might ask students to choose one and make the case). Amanda, as protagonist, battles against poverty and abandonment in a vain (and heroic?) attempt to sustain genteel values, hold the family together, and provide for Laura's future. Tom, as protagonist, struggles for artistic expression and escape from his tedious and troubled life in the apartment and the warehouse. Laura, as the most passive character, is also the most difficult to cast as protagonist. One might argue, however, that her scene with Jim, the climax of the play, embodies her struggle to gain a normal life.

5. This distinction is discussed in the sample essay (1623-25). Tom as character strives for escape, adventure, and self-expression. Tom as narrator understands that one can never escape from the past, memories, or guilt.

6. Laura's crippled foot is a visual representation of her crippled spirit or soul. This, in turn, accounts for her shyness, withdrawal, and inability to cope with the world at large. Williams uses Laura's high-school memories, the episode at Rubicam's, and her initial reaction to Jim's arrival to illustrate Laura's limitations. The glass menagerie is part of Laura's fantasy world; she constantly retreats to this world of old records and glass figurines. The menagerie also symbolizes Laura in its fragility.

7. In using this as a writing assignment, you might ask students to focus on either Amanda's laughable or her admirable qualities. For a longer essay, have students deal with both. Amanda's pretensions toward gentility, her idealization of her past, and her unrealistic assessment of Laura are both pitiable and laughable. Her fierce attempts to provide for Laura's future, however, are heroic and admirable. Williams seems to want to leave us with the latter image at the close of the play. When Amanda silently comforts Laura, her silliness is gone and she has dignity and tragic beauty (1617).

8. Jim is realistic in the sense that he is the most nearly normal person in the play, "an emissary from the world of reality." He is an optimistic and energetic would-be achiever who is concerned mostly with himself and his own dreams. Jim's goals (an executive position, a perfect marriage) reflect the American dream of self-improvement and upward mobility; they are more normal (acceptable) than Tom's dreams of artistic expression and escape. Even so, they are almost as unreachable as Tom's. Jim's momentary interest in Laura probably grows out of the fact that she remembers his high-school glory days. His realism is qualified by the fact that Tom (and Williams) use him as a symbol of "the long-delayed but always expected something that we live for."

9. Any one of these topics would make an adequate writing assignment. Family in the play is presented as a network of contradictory desires and hopes; this is embodied in the ongoing conflict between Tom and Amanda. From Tom's perspective, family is also a trap. Poverty complicates the dynamics of the family considerably; it motivates Amanda's desperate efforts to secure Laura's future and it keeps Tom trapped in the warehouse. Personality is shaped by the past (Amanda's memories, Jim's high-school achievements, Tom's memories), dreams, and physical form (Laura's crippled foot). The close of the play suggests that one cannot escape from the past.

10. Tom focuses on the geopolitical and economic social background of the dramatized events twice (see 1569, 1587-88, and question 8 above). In each instance, the relative calm and ignorance of the United States is contrasted with the growing chaos in Europe. The contrast--and Tom's retrospective awareness of it--might suggest a number of considerations for discussion or writing: (1) the self-absorption of the Wingfields parallels national blindness; (2) Laura's fantasy world parallels the national fantasy of approaching peace and prosperity; (3) Tom's memories of Saint Louis represent a mid-point between Amanda's idealized Southern past and the national future of war.

11-12. Like A Doll's House, this play contains a wealth of symbolism. Writing assignments can be geared to a specific type or specific line of symbolism. The 2 symbolic characters are Jim and Malvolio the Magician (1581). Symbolic places include the alley, fire escape, Guernica, Blue Mountain, the

Paradise Dance Hall, and the warehouse. Symbolic actions include Laura's polishing the glass figures, playing the victrola, and the 2 instances in which glass figures are broken (1580, 1611). Symbolic objects and images include the photograph, blue roses, the unicorn and the glass menagerie, movies, and the coffin. The diffuse line of religious imagery and symbolism relates to all 3 central characters. Malvolio's escape from the coffin suggests resurrection or an escape from death (Lazarus); both are linked to Tom's desire to escape. The Ave Maria ironically celebrates Amanda as a mother. Paradise Dance Hall--across the alley from the apartment--embodies a false heaven (reflecting the national blindness) contrasting to the hellish life of the Wingfields. The annunciation and the candles give Laura a religious aura that heightens her pathos and isolation.

13. Although students should be encouraged to develop their own responses to the play, it seems to us to be more tragic than comic. All the central characters fail. Amanda and Laura are abandoned by Tom and Jim; Tom finds that he cannot escape the past. Tom is the only character who learns or gains self-knowledge in the play. In a larger context, both religion and the American dream of adventure (Tom) or upward mobility (Jim) fail. Tom travels, but he achieves neither the artistic fulfillment nor the Hollywood-inspired adventure that he craves. Jim's failure to live up to his high-school potential suggests that he, too, is destined to remain trapped (in the warehouse, the past, marriage, unfulfilled dreams). The religious imagery that runs through the play ironically highlights a series of failures: Tom is not reborn; Amanda fails as a mother; the annunciation leads to a disaster instead of a miracle; Laura blows the candles out.

WRITING ABOUT REALISTIC AND NONREALISTIC DRAMA, pages 1619-1626.

This material surveys approaches to planning and writing essays about realistic and/or nonrealistic aspects of plays. Again, the primary focus is on the traditional elements of drama. Here, however, the approach emphasizes the relative realism or nonrealism of the element and the degree to which this, in turn, affects the impact and meaning of the play.

In developing (or having students develop) a writing project that engages the issue of realism or nonrealism, you have the option of calling for a relatively simple or a somewhat more complex essay. At the simple level, you might simply ask students to select an aspect or element of a play and prove that it is realistic (or nonrealistic). Such an essay might demonstrate the realism of one of Ibsen's characters or the nonrealism of the lighting in The Glass Menagerie. At a more complex level, you can ask students to discuss both the realism (or nonrealism) of a specific element and the effect thus produced. This is the more difficult but more rewarding assignment; it will help students learn a good deal more about the play at hand.

THEMATIC TABLE OF CONTENTS

The selections in <u>Literature</u>: <u>An Introduction to Reading and Writing</u> are arranged on the basis of literary elements (rather than historical period or thematic focus) in each of the chapters except "Additional Stories" and "Additional Poems." The front end-papers of the text provide a chronological listing of the authors included. On occasion, however, you may find it useful in teaching to group works together according to their subject or theme. To that end, we provide here an alternate table of contents that regroups the the selections into 18 separate thematic categories. Because most good literature opens doorways of the mind to many different kinds of ideas and realizations, it often defies this kind of classification. As a result, such a table of contents can only begin to suggest one or two thematic approaches to any given work. The following classifications are advisory at best; they are not meant to dictate approaches or interpretations. Works that are included in more than one thematic category are marked with an asterisk.

ART, LANGUAGE, IMAGINATION, AND INSPIRATION

NATURE AND HUMANITY

SHORT STORIES

POETRY

FAITH AND DOUBT

SHORT STORIES

POETRY

THEMATIC TABLE OF CONTENTS

LOVE, COURTSHIP, AND SEDUCTION

THEMATIC TABLE OF CONTENTS

DRAMA

WOMEN AND MEN

In addition to the titles listed below, this category includes all works noted under "Love, Courtship, and Seduction" and under "Husbands and Wives."

SHORT STORIES

POETRY

LIFE'S VALUES, CONDUCT, AND MEANING

SHORT STORIES

POETRY

THEMATIC TABLE OF CONTENTS

306

THEMATIC TABLE OF CONTENTS

VISIONS OF DEATH

SHORT STORIES

POETRY

THEMATIC TABLE OF CONTENTS